**Black Performance and Cultural Criticism**
Valerie Lee and E. Patrick Johnson, Series Editors

# Prisons, Race, and Masculinity in Twentieth-Century U.S. Literature and Film

## PETER CASTER

 THE OHIO STATE UNIVERSITY PRESS • COLUMBUS

*F 167500676*

*Rcu*

Library of Congress Cataloging-in-Publication Data
Caster, Peter, 1972–
Prisons, race, and masculinity in twentieth-century U.S. literature and film / Peter Caster.
    p. cm.—(Black performance and cultural criticism)
Includes bibliographical references and index.
ISBN 978–0–8142–1073–4 (alk. paper)
1. Imprisonment in literature. 2. American literature—20th century—History and criticism. 3. Imprisonment in motion pictures. 4. Masculinity in literature. 5. Masculinity in motion pictures. 6. African Americans—Race identity. 7. Motion pictures and literature—United States. 8. American literature—Film and video adaptations. 9. Executions and executioners in literature. I. Title.
PS228.I66C37 2008
810.9'3556—dc22
                    2007034428


This book is available in the following editions:
Cloth (ISBN 978–0–8142–1073–4)
CD-ROM (ISBN 978–0–8142–9150–4)


Cover design by Dan O'Dair
Text design by Juliet Williams
Type set in Adobe Bembo
Printed by Thomson-Shore, Inc.


The paper used in this publication meets the minimum requirements of the American National Standard for Information Sciences—Permanence of Paper for Printed Library Materials. ANSI Z39.48–1992.
9  8  7  6  5  4  3  2  1

# Contents

# Illustrations

# Preface

AT THE 1886 meeting of the National Prison Association,[1] Hamilton Mabie, who would later become an eminent literary scholar and editor of the turn-of-the-century United States, gave a lecture titled "The Press and Crime," describing how newspapers and fiction shape the public perception of imprisonment. Four decades later, in 1929, the president of that organization, George C. Erksine, declared in his keynote address, "Probably never in recent times has the attention of the public been centered on crime and criminals as it is to-day. The head-lines of the morning paper, the table of contents of the current magazines, a casual glance at the shelves of any book store, the growing list of federal, state and municipal crime commissions, all bear witness to this modern trend."[2] The literary scholar and prison administrator both address the need for acknowledging the record of crime and punishment as it has been described in popular representations, whether fictional or not. Slowly, the NPA, which became the American Prison Association in 1908 and the American Correction Association in 1955, began to do so. In 1974 two of the nine papers presented on the psychological treatment of prisoners responded directly to Stanley Kubrick's representation of prison "rehabilitation" in *A Clockwork Orange* (1971).

Over the next two decades, prison administrators continued to lament that imagined prisons shape public understanding of incarceration. In 1998 ACA President Reginald A. Wilkinson offered this anecdote: "I wrote a letter to the HBO producers of the dramatic series entitled: 'Oz.' I explained that the stereotyping and misrepresentations of the corrections profession in their drama is unacceptable. Of course, the response that I received was that the show was designed to 'entertain' and was not meant to depict reality."[3] Wilkinson's criticism points to the permeability of imagination and actuality, particularly for audiences regularly fascinated by reality entertainment, and the complaint was echoed the next year by Angela Davis's critique of skewed public perception due to the "grossly sensationalized genre of Hollywood prison films."[4] The evidence is on their side, as indicated in recent studies of actual police practices and representations of minorities in fictional crime series on television; one such study concludes that "the viewing of fictional programming may lead to associations of minorities with crime, victimization, and criminal justice themes."[5]

The vexed relationship of "fictional programming" and actuality in the representation of prisons gained clarity for me the summer of 2001, when a particular incident illustrated how the imagination of incarceration can overwrite its actuality. One Sunday afternoon Turner Network Television (TNT) featured Frank Darabont's *The Shawshank Redemption* (1994),[6] a well-known Academy Award Best Picture nominee in which Tim Robbins and Morgan Freeman play long-term convicts whose friendship redeems each of them. At the same time, the Discovery Channel screened the documentary *Maximum Security Prisons*—or rather it was scheduled, but there was a problem with the cable signal, and Discovery displayed only a blank monitor. That blankness contrasted sharply with *The Shawshank Redemption,* where actors play convicts on-screen, the characters sitting in a theater watching a Rita Hayworth film. When Andy Dufresne (Robbins) leaves the theater, he is attacked, brutally beaten, and presumably raped by a group referred to as "the Sisters." On the Discovery Channel, *Maximum Security Prisons* ended and *Supermax* began its account of a high-security facility, but the signal remained blocked and the screen dark. Back on TNT, in *The Shawshank Redemption,* Andy tries to get funding from the warden to buy new books for the prison library.

Too much could be made of whatever technological glitch left *Maximum Security Prisons* unwatchable that afternoon—though Martin

Luther King III cites a similar experience he had the same year, one he recounts in his keynote address at the 2001 ACA conference.[7] There is a crucial lesson in the blank screen of *Maximum Security Prisons* as a documentary contrasted with the glossy and familiar look and characters of Frank Darabont's film, with its coherent, humanist narrative, in which a white man imprisoned for a crime for which he is innocent learns about compassion from a black man who is guilty. The documentary would not have provided access to some unmediated "real," given that it, like *The Shawshank Redemption,* would feature the efforts of producers funding the venture, a director choosing and structuring scenes, editors building narrative continuity, and the rest of the production crew that make film and video such collaborative work. However, there are critical differences between depictions by actors and by prisoners, fictional narratives and documentaries, the realistic and the "real." Certainly there are challenges to authenticity and the problems of the real, but an important separation remains between Freeman (playing Red) and *Supermax* prison inmate Kenny Collins, who speaks in the prison protest "Live from Death Row,"[8] described in chapter 8. The difference between the popular Hollywood film and the unseeable Discovery documentary illustrates one of the central tenets of this book: that actual prisons contrast sharply with their many representations in books, films, television, and other media. These screens of the imagination offer the projections of what is both hoped and feared to be true of prisons, places that are by definition difficult to access—except by black men, who enter far too easily.

There is a simultaneous causality and disjuncture between the historical record and popular fictions, a difference that is particularly stark for imprisonment as it is endured by those within and imagined by those without. A largely unremarked tension exists between the set of social and institution practices of incarceration and its many descriptions varying in media, genre, popularity, and stakes in the real. Prisons are a ubiquitous part of how contemporary U.S. culture imagines itself, as suggested by the more than 250 U.S. films featuring men in prison and almost 100 focusing on women in prison.[9] However, aside from the incarcerated population and those who work and visit there, actual prisons are closed off from visibility, thus creating a space for imagined interiors, whether projected on-screen or cast on the page to reveal the mystery. Nevertheless, that unveiling often merely capitulates to the contradictory fantasies of audiences who conceive of prisons in varied ways: as forces of order; places of rehabilitation; torture chambers of psychic, physical, and sexual violence; consolidations of uniformly violent, dangerous, and, most often, black criminals; medieval dungeons or high-tech facilities; or all of these at once. These fantasies, particularly in the absence of lived experience, prove formative for widely held assumptions regarding actual incarceration. Various critics of popular culture such as Henry A. Giroux, Ed Guerrero, and bell hooks argue that fictions shape public perception,[10] but producers and audiences also speak to that matter themselves. For example, a 2002 advertisement in *Premiere* magazine for the Suncoast film retail company features a store manager's pitch for the company's products with this endorsement of *The Shawshank Redemption:* "They do a great job of capturing how it must feel to be behind bars and then be free again."[11]

Those not themselves incarcerated look to popular and provocative projections, and this book explores that *must,* that subjunctive, that imagined actuality. As inmate Simon "Sam" Guitierrez of Statesville Prison, Illinois, writes, "Prison life is really nothing like what the press, television, and movies suggest."[12] The fascination with imprisonment emerges in the gap between historical actuality and its imagining. While I am not claiming an unmediated real, this book does focus on texts that traverse that gulf, works that make some claim to the real even as they are held in tension between imagination and actuality. That impulse guides the selection of three novels, William Faulkner's *Sanctuary* (1931), *Light in August* (1932), and *Go Down, Moses* (1942); two books situated between cultural biography and fiction, Eldridge Cleaver's *Soul on Ice* (1968) and Norman Mailer's *The Executioner's Song* (1979); three films, Tony Kaye's *American History X* (1998), Norman Jewison's *The Hurricane* (1999), and Liz Garbus, Wilbert Rideau, and John Stack's *The Farm: Life Inside Angola Prison* (1998); and two performances, Ken Webster's *Jury Duty* (1999) and a 1999 protest, "Live from Death Row,"[13] where actual prisoners communicate via speakerphone with an assembled audience.

The movement back and forth between history and imagination is of course not restricted to books, films, and performances, as it also shapes national politics in significant ways. George H. W. Bush's 1988 presidential campaign famously deployed the image of Willie Horton and thereby drew on the long-standing mythic fear of black men as rapists in order to attack Democratic candidate Michael Dukakis's record on crime. For many, the single repeat offender of the ad campaign that prominently featured Horton's police file photo represented black masculinity in general. Five years later, with an increasing number of black men behind bars, the commissioner of Pennsylvania's Department of Corrections claimed, "The Willie Horton phenomenon has affected just about every correctional system in this country."[14] Prison administrators suggest that imagined fears contribute to actual incarceration. However, imprisonment is not fantasy but daily lived experience for more than two million people. Corrections cost U.S. taxpayers over $60 billion in 2001, with half of that spent on prisons, which contain a population overwhelmingly male and more than 40 percent black. Another 4.7 million people are on parole or probation, or are held in an alternate facility. Those numbers reflect a fourfold increase in the rates of imprisonment since 1980. Furthermore, among those in federal and state prisons and county jails, black men are overrepresented by a factor of more than seven in comparison to white men, and a factor of almost three in comparison to Hispanic men.[15] That overrepresentation of black men in prison presents a reversal of their historical *under*representation in many public forums, from involvement in political leadership to inclusion in national literature. There are of course numerous structural (i.e., economic) factors shaping race and possibility in the United States, but the sheer number of imprisoned black men is both a cause and a consequence of an expectation of criminality.

The stakes are high in the critique of the representations of imprisonment—the connections between imagination and actuality and those in and out of prisons—especially because of the dangerous temptation to equate black masculinity with criminality. There is jurisprudential law, easily understood as historically contingent: the contradictions and revisions between the separate but equal of *Plessy v. Ferguson* (1896) and its overturning in *Brown v. Board of Education* (1954), for example. Then there is natural law, seemingly axiomatic and universal. The problem is that centuries of racism shape the cultural landscape of both fiction and social expectation. Repeatedly and uncritically participating in fictions governed by the inexorable logic of "realism" maintains long-held stereotypes. Twentieth-century representations of black men too often capitulate to the black supermasculine menial, who becomes the criminal and thus the prisoner.

That overrepresentation of black men in prison equally serves opposite arguments. First, inequalities in education, employment, and social services have perpetuated the disenfranchisement of black men even as the criminal justice system inequitably punishes them; second—its opposite—black men are "naturally" more likely to commit crimes. Of course, endorsing the latter of these is unequivocally racist and ignores the racial injustice throughout U.S. history. It is claimed only by those as unafraid of their own racism as *American History X's* white supremacist Derek Vineyard (Edward Norton): "One in every three black males is in some phase of the correctional system. Is that a coincidence or do these people have, you know, like a racial commitment to crime?" However, the repeated projections on page and screen cast shadows that color criminality and create cultural expectation, the relentless process by which an imagined symbolic of realism overwrites the real. While the terms *imaginary, symbolic,* and *real* carry with them Lacanian associations, their meanings are not bound there. It is only an accident of history that Lionel Trilling's essay "Reality in America" appeared in *The Liberal Imagination* (1950),[16] but the *Imagination's* containment of "Reality" at least suggests that imagining the real takes place beyond psychoanalysis. Antonio Gramsci makes this point in his description of utopian "concrete fantasy," a counterhegemonic strategy of alienated groups.[17] However, imagination can participate in repression as well as in resistance.

My personal hope, and scholarly dedication, is that constructing a clearer sense of popular conceptions of imprisonment and their tension with the historical record can create the possibility for those expectations to be recognized, reappraised, and reorganized. Gaining a clearer sense of the historical processes of representation and expectation may help unbalance the tacit equation of criminality with black masculinity—because the black man accused of murder, sex crime, or assault still maintains a mythic force in the United States. Euphemistic courts of public opinion try cases in ways similar to conventional jurisprudence. They share the characteristic of situations of undecidability that nonetheless demand decisions. Courts both literal and figurative reach conclusions that in effect simultaneously record and invent history, retroactively determining what has happened already. Legal courts do so with the attendant material consequences of exoneration, fine, or imprisonment. However, such actual trials mandate the presence of the accused; there is no comparable imperative of habeas corpus in courts of public opinion. Popular conceptions of blackness and crime can take place in the absence of either one. Decades of representation have effects less immediately tangible but nonetheless pervasive, as the equation of black masculinity with criminality is balanced through the fulfillment of the desire to see black men in prison.

There has been insufficient critical attention paid to the relationship between actual imprisonment and the ways in which it is imagined and represented, particularly with regard to race. Still, popular music, especially the predominantly black cultural production of hip-hop, has given its voice to incarceration with a mix of glorification and harsh criticism. Rap artists like Snoop Dogg, Ja Rule, the Geto Boyz, and DMX offer prison as a setting in their lyrics, album covers, liner notes, and videos, attesting to the degree to which incarceration in the experience of black men and their communities has been naturalized both actually and in representation. Ja Rule goes so far as to title his 2003 album *Blood in My Eye*—album cover replete with background prison—a nod to George Jackson's prison-writing treatise.[18] In addition, hood films of the past two decades feature rap stars such as Ice Cube, DMX, Snoop Dogg, Nas, and Tupac Shakur[19] and represent young black men trapped in a nihilistic world of criminality, bound for prison or violent death, and often do so uncritically, without attention to other possibilities. Nevertheless, there are musicians in rap and other genres who testify to the social forces shaping imprisonment. In 1988 Public Enemy linked black masculinity to political imprisonment in "Black Steel in the Hour of Chaos," and NWA derided racial profiling in "Fuck the Police."[20] The problems of the African-American community feature prominently in the art form that rapidly became its voice, and Public Enemy front man Chuck D has frequently called rap the "black CNN."

At the close of the twentieth century, as rates of incarceration and the overall prison population reached unprecedented levels, Public Enemy continued to describe racial imprisonment practices, acknowledging in their song "I" (1999) that "prison for me is an industry," and suggesting, "Maybe prison is the skin I'm within"[21]—insinuating both the racial bias of criminalization and the boundaries of the self. That year saw similar critiques from others, as political rockers Rage Against the Machine describe in "Calm Like a Bomb": "There's a mass without roofs / a prison to fill."[22] In a similar vein, but much more specifically, Mos Def's "Mathematics" (1999) clarifies the scope of the problem, intimating that black unemployment causes the crime contributing to the "global jail economy," and explaining that expanding sentencing only increases the racial aspect of prison populations:

stiffer stipulations attached to each sentence
budget cutbacks but increased police presence
and even if you get out of prison still livin'
join the other five million under state supervision
this is business, no faces just lines and statistics
from your phone, your zip code, to SSI digits
the system break man, child, and women into figures
two columns for who is, and who ain't niggaz.[23]

Mos Def's accurate mention of longer sentences as a major cause for prison expansion is joined by increased penalties for drug crimes in the "Prison Song" (2001) of System of a Down, an Armenian metal group. They declare, "Minor drug offenders fill your prisons," then continue:

all research and successful drug policy show
that treatment should be increased
and law enforcement decreased
while abolishing mandatory minimum sentences
they're trying to build a prison
(for you and me to live in).[24]

These popular artists offer an analysis of incarceration at the turn of the twenty-first century that resembles the work of critics such as Derrick Bell, Bell Gale Chevigny, David Cole, Angela Davis, Steven Donziger, Auli Ek, H. Bruce Franklin, Ruth Wilson Gilmore, Tara Herivel, Marc Mauer, Quentin Miller, and Paul Wright, all of whom point to racial inequities in increased incarceration and longer sentences.[25] In his 2000 MLA presentation, Franklin declares: "Just as we now assume that one cannot intelligently teach nineteenth-century American literature without recognizing slavery as context, one cannot responsibly teach contemporary American literature without recognizing the American prison system as context." Franklin's call here echoes the emphasis on incarceration patterns made in Mary Helen Washington's presidential address at the 1996 American Studies Association meeting and Davis's jeremiad there two years later.[26] Since then, imprisonment has grown as an organizing topic for panels at academic conferences and collections of essays, but it remains insufficiently addressed as a central issue in U.S. history and literary studies. In drawing attention to the historical context of imprisonment, Franklin relies on the tacit relationship of historical and literary study to assert the significance of incarceration in the contemporary United States, as well as in its literary history. In pairing slavery and imprisonment, he claims both their related practice and their equal importance in constructions and revisions of the nation and its literature. The rhetorical gambit is powerful—my interest lies in joining these critics and historians in demonstrating the degree to which that assessment is accurate.

# Acknowledgments

WRITING THIS BOOK has been one of the few constants in my life from 1998 to 2006, though sustained through those tumultuous years also has been the support of a scholarly community, friends, and family in whose work and words I have found a place like home. Most of all I thank Evan Carton, whose mentorship meant equal parts encouragement, challenge, and faith. The scholarship and personal guidance of Phil Barrish, Timothy R. Buckner, Jill Dolan, Barbara Harlow, David Oshinsky, and Warwick Wadlington contributed directly to the writing of this book, and I thank them for their tireless reading and discussion. Many others have provided useful feedback on early drafts, and I thank Zachary Dobbins, Veronica House, Martin Kevorkian, Richard Schechner, Julie Sievers, Douglas Taylor, and the staff and reviewers of *The Drama Review* for their editorial effort and permission to reprint parts of chapter 8. The Austin, Texas, playwright Ken Webster provided extensive personal background for the origin of his excellent play *Jury Duty*.

Various institutions also shaped this manuscript. Generous financial support came from the Livingston Fellowship through the University of Texas at Austin, as well as their Presidential Graduate Fellowship. The University of South Carolina Upstate has provided a vibrant scholarly community from which this book and I both have gained much, and the university also made significant contributions to this project in release from teaching duties. Conversations with students in literature, film, and criminal justice courses at the University of Texas at Austin, Huston-Tillotson University in Austin, and the University of South Carolina Upstate in Spartanburg helped shape my thinking in valuable ways. Early versions of chapter drafts were presented at numerous conferences, including those of the Modern Language Association, American Studies Association, and American Comparative Literature Association. Sandy Crooms, Maggie Diehl, and other staff members of The Ohio State University Press provided excellent support in the completion of the book, and two outside reviewers made excellent suggestions to focus its argument.

Friends in Austin, Texas; Corvallis, Oregon; and Sacramento, Oakland, San Francisco, and Bishop, California, proved generous in the allotment of time for conversation regarding this project and the homes in which to write it. I offer special thanks to Kristy and Steve Edwards, Greg Gambetta and Janine Marello, Craig Malik and Beth Marszewski, Jesse and Tina Moore, Janice Pfeiff, Deanna and Erich Simon, and Kristen Tan, without whom I could not have completed this project. Most of all, I thank my parents, John and Angi Caster, who provided intellectual, emotional, and financial support throughout my education and proved the best models for joining personal and professional commitments.

Finally, I acknowledge the debt this book owes to more than two million people imprisoned, so many and too often for so little. I thank the activists, researchers, scholars, and teachers in many disciplines who work to improve prison practices, policies, and living conditions. The American Correctional Association through its 137-year history has demonstrated dedicated professionalism and leadership that merit greater acknowledgment. I would also like to recognize the state and federal governments, prison administration and staff, private companies building and managing prisons, and voters and those who fail to vote. It is due to the combination of our efforts that the prison system has become what it is.

# 1

# Imprisonment in U.S. History and the Cultural Imagination

> Not courthouses nor even churches but jails were the true records of a county's, a community's history, since not only the cryptic forgotten initials and words and even phrases cries of defiance and indictment scratched into the walls but the very walls themselves held [ ... ] the agonies and shames and griefs.
>
> —William Faulkner, *Intruder in the Dust*[1]

THIS BOOK organizes its study of the representation of criminality and imprisonment from 1931 to 1999 through a set of texts that emphasize the tensions between imagination and history. Faulkner's *Go Down, Moses* focuses on crime and punishment in reconstructing the racial past of the Old and New South. The novel begins with the chase for an escaped slave and ends four generations later with a black man imprisoned and executed in Chicago, his body returned to his native Jefferson, Mississippi—a narrative trajectory scarcely noted by Faulkner's many admirers, but a dominant structural pattern in a novel often suggested to lack one. Faulkner suggests that the character's criminality is part of a pattern of racial inequity perpetuated through a genealogical span, beginning with Southern slavery and progressing through jim crow to 1940.

In *Soul on Ice,* Cleaver operates in various registers, sometimes, like Mailer, observing himself watching the time of his time, commenting on contemporary events and popular culture, though in his case with a prison-cell view. Cleaver's account of a black man's "becoming" in prison at times resembles social criticism and, at other times, mythmaking, with his description of crime, imprisonment, race, and gender. A decade later, Mailer's *The Executioner's Song* claims to be a "true life novel" in its subtitle and narrates the history of its present, excerpting news clippings, interviews, and other materials that provide a texture of historical documentation to the narrative of Gary Gilmore's crimes, trial, and execution. Mailer demonstrates the role narration plays in telling history as he documents the media circus surrounding Gilmore's case, which involves lawyers playing the part of reporters, reporters shaping popular opinion, and movie producers contributing to the outcome of events.

Similarly, the three films and two performances surveyed in this book all variously situate themselves in actuality. *American History X* offers a code of realism, its characters spouting incarceration statistics to substantiate its truth-value. *The Hurricane* draws from past events and incorporates a cinema verité style and even occasional news footage, while *The Farm* is a full-fledged documentary. The play *Jury Duty* is based on a true story, and the activist demonstration "Live from Death Row" protests the death penalty and is thus a historical event only addressed here as a performance.

Despite their differences of genre and media, these are all representations of crime and punishment shaped by imagination, but invested in operating in historical terms, drawing relationships between fiction and actuality. This first chapter establishes the book's methodology of textual analysis, incorporating tactics of psychoanalysis with the larger strategy of historically accounting for the production and reception of these books, films, and performances. It next offers a brief history of U.S. imprisonment, describes the cultural imagination as popular representations of varying truth-value, and proposes the category "prisoner" as an index of identity, an important matter given the prevalence of incarceration and the relative scarcity of literary and cultural criticism of prison representation.

These books, films, and performances are addressed foremost as a part of a historical record, telling a type of truth in their various adherences to frameworks of fiction and nonfiction. I situate their representations of imprisonment with respect to two other means of knowing actual past prison practice and policy: first, in the anonymous exactitude of statistics as accounted by historians, sociologists, and the U.S. Department of Justice; and second, in registers ranging from praise to polemic to declarations of policy and academic research as offered in the annual proceedings of the nation's foremost organization of prison administrators, by turns the National Prison Association, the American Prison Association, and the American Correctional Association. These representations receive greater texture by drawing upon U.S. historiography to demonstrate that prison history is central to national history.[2] The effort in each chapter is to offer theoretically inflected explorations of the mutually informative relationships of actual imprisonment and its representation, wherein the depictions of prisons and prisoners are held in tension between imagination and history.

The historical expanse of the study and the many genres and media show the degree to which incarceration, a concealed practice, proliferates in the language and images of the twentieth-century United States. The descriptive analysis at times is offered in broad strokes because the picture is large, but it is drawn in finer detail to describe the prison history shaping these books, films, and performances. That variety demands a range of critical approaches sensitive to the ways in which different works operate while attendant to the historical contexts from which they are inseparable. Texts that are literary, bureaucratic, theoretical, documentary, and ephemeral function differently, but bringing them together is necessary both to demonstrate and to interrogate the unacknowledged pervasiveness of imprisonment in the popular imagination and in historical actuality—and to show how each has affected the other. That approach involves multiple strategies of investigation, including close analysis of the works themselves that is sensitive to their various media, to the historical and cultural moments of their production and original reception, and to the texts' implication in individual and collective psychoanalytic models.

That combination of efforts conducts this book's proposition that the history, literary and otherwise, of the United States is indivisible from that of its prisons. First, imprisonment is a condition of human experience that shapes the identity of those incarcerated and the national identity of the state that imprisons. Second, the history of racial incarceration in the nation tacitly criminalizes black masculinity in the cultural imagination, in effect if not in intent a strategy of racial containment, which many of these texts render visible and often contest. Third, the texts under discussion generally offer a tactic of resistance in an expanded model of personal identity, a social subjectivity emphasizing an engagement with history and a collective sense of the self in that history at odds with the American ideal of autonomous individualism. Historically, incarceration has been a place of struggle between forces that would isolate the prisoner and the efforts to demonstrate the social and historical contingencies of imprisonment.

The degree to which these books, films, and performances implicate themselves in their respective histories complicates the approach of historical contextualization that has been the dominant trend in U.S. literary criticism since the 1980s. Such historicism incorporates fiction, documentary evidence, and historiography as a way of making sense of history, literary and otherwise. The presumption of that methodology is that history can be understood as a social unconscious, its direct access unavailable after the fact, and therefore mediated through its textualization and subsequent interpretation.[3] John Sloop makes such a point in his study of the representation of prisoners in nonfiction periodicals: "[T]he weight of past narratives and characterizations of the prisoner work as social forces in shaping the depiction and motives of the prisoner of the present and hence force the issues of race and gender. Because the public has a memory of the discourses concerning prisoners, however ephemeral, all new constructions of the prisoner begin with past characterizations as a base."[4] Representations with claims to the real play an important part in defining the shape of what might be understood as the *cultural imagination,* the pages and screens of thought and belief in which people recognize themselves and others.[5]

The "real" of history is fleetingly experienced, lastingly available only in its textual narration, and the stories which tell that history are inflected by the circumstances of their own making. These descriptions of cultural production and historical process are not solely the domain of theorists and critics, but are part of popular culture itself. As Rage Against the Machine front man Zack de la Rocha describes such historical narrativization in the song "Testify," opening the band's 1999 album: "Who controls the past now / Controls the future / Who controls the present now / Controls the past / . . . Now testify!"[6] This book, then, renders a history of imprisonment in order to contribute to the imagination of a different future.

The confluence of the personal, the cultural, and the historical in the constructions of character in books, films, and performances invites historically and, at times, psychoanalytically nuanced approaches. The texts that are widely or highly regarded (or both) at particular historical moments can be understood as meeting some need, fulfilling some lack or expectation in their representations. This book therefore makes occasional use of psychoanalytic terms to describe how these books, films, and performances function, the ways they operate in helping shape the cultural imagination. Incorporating such an interpretative framework does not fulfill an ahistorical theoretical imperative. Instead, doing so responds to the degree to which the texts surveyed regularly implicate both individual and social accounts, and challenge the distinctions between the personal and cultural past and between imagination and history—what might be remembered, known, believed, and recorded to be true. The works surveyed traffic back and forth between historical and imaginative fields of discourse, and each is shaped by and contends with social expectations informed, in part, by the layered representations of the cultural imagination. The analysis conducted, then, tracks among various discursive registers of theoretically inflected and historicized readings to demonstrate how works making a claim to the real tell their own sort of truth.

Such study unites various theoretical approaches, whether historicizing, psychoanalyzing, or emphasizing differences in the performances of and limits to cultural identity. This book makes use of various vocabularies and methods (most explicitly those of Freud, Lacan, and Deleuze and Guattari, and, more implicitly, Foucault, Jameson, and de Certeau) in order to clarify aspects of texts that might otherwise escape notice. These matters are many, but related: the social unconscious of Faulkner's imagined Jefferson, Mississippi; the misrecognition of blackness as criminality; the "Negro" crimes and sentences of *Light in August, Soul on Ice, The Hurricane, The Farm,* and "Live from Death Row"; the community accountability for crime and punishment in *Go Down, Moses, Soul on Ice, The Executioner's Song,* and virtually all of the films and performances; schizophrenia as described in *Soul on Ice, The Executioner's Song,* and *The Hurricane;* and the resistance to individual autonomy and support for social identity in many of the texts. Psychoanalytic terminology describes the representation of character and agency in narrative, because such depictions offer a literary mirror of subjectivity. Lacan's theorization of identification provides a powerful tool for understanding how characters in books, films, and performances are situated within symbolic orders, as well as how audiences and producers of texts misrecognize themselves in them. However, Deleuze and Guattari also prove useful in their rejection of the primacy of that "I" and of the investments in personal history that psychoanalysis makes. They instead emphasize social context and place, nicely encapsulated in their claim, "A schizophrenic out for a walk is a better model than a neurotic lying on the analyst's couch."[7]

However, this study works to guard against the seduction of those theoretical discourses. In the effort to better illuminate cultural functions of prisons as they are projected on page, screen, and stage, such application can shine so brightly as to obscure the representations themselves. At one extreme, criticism wholly in one vein or another can inadvertently treat the theoretical discourse as a closed symbolic order, the self-substantiating name-of-the-father. At the other, working with a variety of models can lead to muddied or specious application or appropriation, poaching and name checking. To avoid these pitfalls, I have foregrounded accounts of the texts themselves, incorporating terms and approaches and thereby hoping to clarify rather than cloud how imprisonment and the identity of the prisoner function in different ways over time. I balance theoretical reading with an account of the diverse interests producing and receiving books, films, and performances—writers, directors, producers, and audiences demonstrating varying levels of disinterest, dismay, and desire regarding black men in prison—to bring together the mechanics of production with the various responses of theorists, critics, and general readers and viewers.

The effort here is to apply various theoretical vocabularies bridged by shared participation not only in the topic of imprisonment, but also through the historicist imperative to relate these texts to the contexts from which they are inseparable. Indeed, I hope to demonstrate that any particular lens of this or that theory attentive to what these texts do, what they produce, always is implicated in history and its narration. "The history of now"—my phrase to suggest the effort to think critically about the present as both a set of consequences and a site of struggle—is at once the product of what has already happened, and the process of a cultural imagination recreating that past in its own terms, thereby laying a blueprint for future images and imaginings. The historical and material overwriting of prisoners in the United States has limited dramatically their ability to participate in that process. The right of habeas corpus in the court of public opinion is not one constitutionally upheld, and the reiterative projections of imprisonment shape documentary and other aspects of the historical record that then reinforce mainstream imaginations of imprisonment. Scholars, therefore, must make a greater effort to return prisoners to history, to recognize the changes through time in what it means to be imprisoned, a demarcation of human experience that carries tremendous cultural force.

In the opening epigraph of this chapter, a provocative passage from *Intruder in the Dust* (1948), Faulkner imagines the history of Yoknapatawpha County scratched into the walls of its jail in a nearly illegible graffiti of identities and indictments—a linguistic reversal, as the accusations are offered by those themselves convicted and imprisoned. The novel itself is not among the author's most heralded, and even his avid readers may be unfamiliar with its narrative. However, one of its characters is very familiar, Lucas Beauchamp, a name recognized from *Go Down, Moses,* where he plays alternately trickster and tragic hero, a black sharecropper who repudiates the wealth but not the pride of his white McCaslin grandfather. In *Intruder in the Dust,* Beauchamp spends almost the entire novel in jail, anticipating his lynching by the family of a white man he is said to have killed, until he convinces the nephew of the county attorney to undertake the role of detective, exhuming the corpse of the murdered man to prove his innocence. Readers see in Lucas a black man awaiting execution by mob or jury, a figure with a lineage extending back in history and in fiction to Nat Turner and William Wells Brown's George Green of *Clotel* (1853).[8] (Coincidentally, Nat and George are also the names of Lucas's daughter and her husband in *Go Down, Moses.*) Turner's actual death sentence and Green's fictional one are both pronounced in response to slave rebellion, while the threat of lynching for a murder he did not commit hangs over Beauchamp. Various characters remark that he is actually punished for his pride—conveyed from his white ancestor—and his repeated refusal to "*be a nigger.*"[9] In the eyes of the townspeople of Jefferson, sitting behind bars is the first time Lucas looks like a black man.

The past imagined in the walls of the jail in *Intruder in the Dust* is not written in the novel, and readers must turn to *Go Down, Moses* for a richer sense of how crime and punishment shape cultural history—to read, in effect, the "agonies and shames and griefs" in the prison walls. That writing on the wall toward which Faulkner gestures in *Intruder in the Dust* is actually recorded in the well-known ledger section of "The Bear" in the earlier novel, though the "cryptic forgotten initials and words and even phrases" there conduct a record of slavery rather than imprisonment. In Faulkner's fictional nineteenth- and twentieth-century South, there is not necessarily much change among various practices of racial social control. The opening episode of *Go Down, Moses,* for instance, is a vignette featuring Beauchamp's father, a slave, whereas the next section depicts the jim crow Mississippi of an elderly Lucas, who asks if he will be plowing the crops of Parchman Farm, a prison, instead of his tenant farm. The sense is that there would be little difference.[10]

Unlike other Yoknapatawpha landmarks, Parchman Farm is a matter of historical fact, and David Oshinsky, in his book *"Worse Than Slavery": Parchman Farm and the Ordeal of Jim Crow Justice* (1997), demonstrates that antebellum strategies of racial containment were perpetuated in such prisons. The degree to which Southern racism informed incarceration in the years following Reconstruction appears in the claims of prison officials of the time. A South Carolina chair of a prison's board of directors in 1888 declared that prisons in the state existed to house freed slaves: "After the emancipation of the colored people, whose idea of freedom from bondage was freedom from work and license to pillage, we had to establish means for their control. Hence came the penitentiary."[11] The same year, an Alabama prison administrator blamed a 250 percent greater mortality rate among black prisoners on their weak constitutions.[12] However, prison history in the United States cannot be collapsed to the racism of jim crow—when black men were imprisoned for hazily defined and variously enforced crimes such as mischief and vagrancy, prison administrations stood to make small fortunes leasing black and white convicts as contract labor, and conditions proved so inhumane that five to ten years effectively mandated a life sentence. The history of incarceration extends both before and after jim crow.

Walnut Street Jail was established in Philadelphia in 1776 and became the nation's first prison in 1790. Walnut Street represented a fundamental change in punishment, a shift from the bodily abuse of stocks, whipping, and execution to confinement and discipline. The most prominent proponent of such a system was an ardent abolitionist and the nation's preeminent medical doctor, Benjamin Rush, who signed the Declaration of Independence alongside Benjamin Franklin and presented a proposal for a penitentiary model in the latter's living room in 1787. That plan emphasized reform, prevention, and deterrence through "bodily pain, labour, watchfulness, solitude, and silence."[13] Rush's description, informed by Enlightenment ideals of justice and Protestant imperatives of discipline and work, was endorsed by Thomas Jefferson, who made further revisions, including offering changes to the criminal code as well as to architectural drawings. The *jail,* which held prisoners until their sentencing or for very brief durations, became the *prison,* where confinement was the punishment. Many of those confined at Walnut Street were African-Americans, overrepresented by a factor of more than seven when compared to whites, primarily serving sentences for property crimes such as theft.[14] The rapid expansion of incarceration led to overcrowding at the downtown Philadelphia facility, and Pennsylvania's Eastern State Penitentiary at Cherry Hill was built to replace it in 1829. It was the largest building in the United States at the time. Prisoners in the Pennsylvania model of isolation almost never left their cells, laboring, sleeping, and eating in close to absolute isolation for the duration of their sentences.

An alternate model of congregate imprisonment developed at Auburn Penitentiary in New York, built in 1819, where prisoners slept in separate cells but worked together in silence enforced by frequent whipping. Out of favor as a punishment per se, whipping remained accepted as a means of discipline within prisons. The Auburn model typically proved more profitable than the Pennsylvania system, and debates over the relative merits of the two resulted in a battle of pamphlets whose rhetorical volume approached that of contemporary arguments for and against slavery.[15]

Both models maintained at least the idea of rehabilitation of the individual as a component of Jacksonian democracy, and their construction and practices proliferated throughout the United States, attracting international attention and emulation. Alexis de Tocqueville's journey through the nation in 1831, which led to his *Democracy in America* (1835),[16] was originally intended, in part, to inspect the prison system in order to provide a model for the French government. The system lost esteem, however, as attention shifted away from reform in the 1850s, and prisons increasingly holding African-Americans and new immigrants received less money for construction and maintenance. Ballooning numbers made the isolation and silence of the Pennsylvania and Auburn models no longer tenable due to overcrowding and insufficient staffs, negative factors compounded by the lack of sanitation and health services, as well as by harsh labor conditions.[17] Even any intention of reform faded in the subsequent decades, until the deplorable conditions surveyed by an examining committee and the urgency to organize and professionalize correctional policy led to the formation of the National Prison Association in 1870. Rutherford B. Hayes, the U.S. president from 1877 to 1881, was the organization's first president, in 1870, and thereafter from 1883 until 1892, a tenure twice as long as any other head of the association. Aspects of a proto-Progressive platform appear in his keynote address at the NPA congress in 1888, which links criminality and its attendant imprisonment not to deficient character but to socioeconomic factors such as unemployment.[18] A reverend speaking after Hayes cites a warden's view that one-third of prisoners do not belong in prison, one-third should be there forever, and one-third should have in-and-out privileges.[19]

However, all the prisoners *were* there, and the renamed American Prison Association renewed its commitment to reforming prisoners on its sixtieth anniversary, in 1930, without more substantively addressing the consistently deleterious conditions of the nation's prisons. What approaches might prove rehabilitative and reduce recidivism remained up for debate, and experiments in education conducted by Zebulon Brockway at Elmira Reformatory and elsewhere in the 1880s and 1890s gave way to a medical model of treatment. Doctors and administrators advocated psychological classification and individualized remedies, but budgets did not provide the resources for the implementation of those practices. There were also growing challenges to the labor that typically accompanied imprisonment. Abuses of convict leasing had decreased, but even the possibility of humane work came under legal attack by organized labor and industrial interests concerned about marketplace competition, culminating with the Hayes-Cooper Act (1935) and the Ashurst-Sumner Act (1940), which sharply prohibited productive inmate work, making occupation for prisoners increasingly rare.

Even as the APA again changed its name in 1955 to the American *Correctional* Association to emphasize the imperative to reform, it was a gesture more conciliatory to aspiration than actuality. However, the *Brown v. Board of Education* decision the year earlier had laid the basis for subsequent improvements in prison conditions in the 1960s. National movements organized around the struggle for racial equality led to the Civil Rights Act in 1964, which drew from laws that were written in the years after 1865 to protect the rights of former slaves and then served as a constitutional basis against discrimination a century later. By extension, the Civil Rights Act also provided for prison reform, as did the expansion of the writ of habeas corpus, the guarantee of appearance in court, one of the rights suspended by the British government, thus precipitating the Declaration of Independence, which Rush signed. These expanded applications of federal law reversed the "hands off" policy that had previously relegated prison oversight entirely to states. In 1970 many jails and prisons—largely in the South—were declared practices of cruel and unusual punishment for operating little better than slavery.[20] Derrick Bell and other legal scholars and historians of critical race theory link such disregard sustained over the subsequent decades directly to the overrepresentation of people of color in prison, thus deeming it a consequence of racism.[21] In 2005, thirty-five years later, lethally inadequate medical treatment for prisoners in California, the nation's largest system, sent prison health care into receivership after a lengthy legal battle. U.S. prisons have shifted from international admiration in the early nineteenth century to global condemnation at the beginning of the twenty-first. In many ways, then, U.S. prison history *is* national history.

There is more of the story to tell, but an obvious question remains: what does prison history have to do with U.S. literature? Certainly there is Beauchamp in the Jefferson jail throughout most of *Intruder in the Dust,* and careful historical study of Mississippi imprisonment practices through the first half of the twentieth century might demonstrate the degree to which the narrative account does or does not match actual incarceration practices of the place and time. However, I am less interested in Lucas Beauchamp than I am in the people of Jefferson who want, who *need* to see him behind bars. That history of desire and fear is much longer and more complex. It is a matter of cultural expectation constituted in the tension between imagination and historical actuality; the real of the latter is mediated, accessed through representations and narrations of all shapes and sorts. Books, films, performances, and other forms of discourse emerge from, are inflected by, and transform the diverse sets of social practices and participatory spectatorship that make up culture. Their historically specific analysis provides a valuable instrument by which to gain a sense of the tenor of time and chart its change. Furthermore, the texts of this book cue themselves to be read as telling a sort of truth, as they traffic back and forth between actual and imagined histories of what audiences want, need, and fear to be true of incarceration.

The books, films, and performances studied in this book either foreground or vividly repress how race shapes practices and patterns of imprisonment. W. E. B. DuBois declared in 1903 that the "problem of the twentieth-century is the problem of the color line,"[22] and Martin Luther King III quotes this line as well before the American Correctional Association in 2001: "I submit to you that our problem is still the color line."[23] The racial division sees its starkest enactment in U.S. prisons, where, a century after DuBois, rates of imprisonment for black men drastically outpace those for white. That overrepresentation in actual numbers both emerges from and contributes to the phenomenon of conflating black masculinity and criminality. In *Thirteen Ways of Looking at a Black Man* (1997), Henry Louis Gates Jr. offers an anecdote of a black male professor mistaken for a criminal and writes, "I don't know a black man who doesn't have at least one [of these stories] to tell."[24] The novels, memoirs, feature films, documentaries, and performances surveyed in this book tell more of these stories. In *Light in August* the murder of Joanna Burden prompts the townspeople of Jefferson to hope, to know a black man did it.[25] Dale Pierre is a background character in *The Executioner's Song,* but he is a black man whose defense costs a district attorney hopeful's chance at election, because that defense lawyer has come to believe the man was innocent, "convicted by the Jury because he was black."[26] The arrest of Rubin Carter and John Artis initiating their imprisonment in *The Hurricane* begins with their being pulled over; when an officer tells them that the police are looking for two black men, Carter responds, "Any two will do?" In "Live from Death Row," Jody Lee Miles, a white man, testifies on the raced nature of the death penalty from the vantage point of death row. This misrecognition of blackness as criminality serves as the focal point of analysis.

The structural design of this project draws attention to the pervasiveness of imprisonment in a variety of twentieth-century U.S. texts. To focus on a single medium or genre, or to read synchronically and survey a set of contemporaneous texts, or to scan diachronically and track through time the writing of a single author such as Faulkner would localize the degree to which the imagined prisons have saturated U.S. cultural production. This book thus broadens its scope and reads at a slant in cutting across culture and through history to demonstrate the proliferation of images of incarceration. The three periods bracketed by the texts surveyed offer rates of change from 1929 to 1942, 1968 to 1979, and 1980 to 1999. The first period demonstrates how Faulkner's view of raced crime and punishment and the social responsibility for it evolved, when both his fiction and the historical record suggest an equation of lynching and execution in the South. The second charts the possibilities of understanding imprisonment as a historical and political phenomenon in 1968, and the disappearance of that definitional context by 1979; between Cleaver and Mailer there are diminishing possibilities for situating prisoners in history. The third period involves an unprecedented increase in imprisonment. The films and performances of 1998 and 1999 show how the fascination with imaginary prisons at the brink of the twenty-first century obscures their concrete actuality, a tendency resisted in more-marginal productions, such as *The Farm,* discussed in chapter 7, and the drama and demonstration described in chapter 8.

All of these representations foreground incarceration in a manner that literary and cultural critics largely have missed. Humanities and social sciences scholarship of the past quarter century increasingly has organized its inquiry through matters of identity, of gender, race, class, ethnicity, and sexuality—differences constituted in, and themselves shaping, history. Increasingly, identity has been addressed not as a stable ontological categorization, but as a culturally situated struggle among competing groups, enacted by individuals through socially coded performances. A definitional statement made by the American Prison Association provides a point of entry into the performative character of criminalization and its attendant incarceration. The first of the NPA's Declaration of Principles, established in 1870 with the organization's founding and revised and reaffirmed sixty years later in 1930, lists a set of definitions: "Crime is a violation of duties imposed by law, which inflicts an injury upon others. Criminals are persons convicted of crime by competent courts. Punishment is suffering inflicted upon the criminal for the wrong done by him, with a special view to secure his reformation."[27] The organization renewed those principles yet again, sixty years later, in 1990.[28] Crime, then, is an act against written law with its own effect: injury. A person becomes a criminal, however, not in committing the act of a crime, but through declaration by the court; criminality is a determination by a judge or jury. Criminalization is thus a jurisprudential process, not coincident with the commission of the crime but, rather, an effect of conviction.

That can seem a matter of linguistic hairsplitting until one considers the number of laws broken regularly in virtually all social segments of the United States: stock market insider trading, exceeding the speed limit, the at times lethal negligence of pharmaceutical companies and other corporate failures, the battery and aggravated assault of spousal and child abuse and acquaintance rape, driving while intoxicated, illegal drug use (and the attendant sale)—whether by professional athletes, right-wing polemicists such as Rush Limbaugh, or the inner-city populations he regularly demonizes—or any number of infractions that are part of the texture of everyday life as it is practiced and imagined in culture. According to the APA Declaration, the cynical maxim "It's not a crime if you don't get caught" is framed more accurately in terms of the process of criminalization rather than the commission of crime. A person is not born a criminal and does not become one in breaking the law, but only through a court's conviction.

That determination has consequences, such as in the 2000 U.S. national election, when the definition and deployment of the categories of "prisoner" and "probable felon" as well as the interpretation of those identities helped shift the outcome of the presidency. The purging of voter rolls during the highly contested 2000 U.S. presidential election in the state of Florida illustrates the tense interplay of blackness and the identity of prisoner. Florida was one of thirteen states that at the time prohibited former offenders from voting unless granted particular clemency, even after their sentences were completed. The names of thousands of men and women were on waiting lists to have their rights reinstated, and the delay at the office of Governor Jeb Bush, George W. Bush's brother, was two to three years. At the time, black men and women outnumbered white by 3.3 in Florida prisons. More than 30 percent of the black men in Florida could not vote because of previous convictions, and black voters in the state voted for Democratic candidates typically by a margin of nine to one. Therefore, a tremendous number of potential voters, many of them black men, already were removed from the democratic process due to state law and bureaucracy.

In addition to the people already on record as ineligible to vote due to a prior conviction, a list of more than fifty-seven thousand names of "probable felons" was assembled and distributed to the county voter-registration boards in order to facilitate their removal from the catalog of eligible voters. The list featured ten times the number of names generated for previous elections, an increase the U.S. Commission on Civil Rights attributed to gross extrapolation of the data, such as close but not precise matches of names and dates, and outright mistakes, such as a woman being mistaken for her sister, an ex-offender, and a man barred from voting in 2000 for a conviction alleged to have occurred seven years in the future.[29]

Such disenfranchisement illustrates how criminality is an identity historically subject to categorization, description, and definition to the extent that it transforms "persons" to "felons" whose very delinquency follows and defines them even after serving their sentences or in the absence of any offense at all. The practice of surveillance and strategic reading of the voter rolls in this case effectively produced criminals in the absence of any actual crime or injured party before the assignment of the "probable felon" status, which itself constituted its own injury in the loss of voting rights. The list and its use illustrate Michel Foucault's claim that "prison, and no doubt punishment in general, is not intended to eliminate offences, but rather distinguish them, to distribute them, to use them; that it is not so much that they render docile those who are liable to transgress the law, but that they tend to assimilate the transgression of the laws in a general tactics of subjection."[30] The "probable felon" list produced criminality where there often was none, and to profound political effect.

A common criticism leveled against Foucault, that he mistakenly equates intent with effect, seems similarly applicable in this situation with regard to whether Florida's effort in this instance was intentionally racist. However, the Voter Rights Act (1965) is explicit on the matter that intent and effect need not be coincident to determine that voters have lost their constitutional right to vote. In the executive summary of the findings of the U.S. Commission on Civil Rights' investigation of the 2000 election in Florida, the Commission determined, "The VRA does not require intent to discriminate. Neither does it require proof of a conspiracy. Violations of the VRA can be established by evidence that the action or inaction of responsible officials and other evidence constitute a 'totality of the circumstances' that denied citizens their right to vote." That "totality" includes "voting procedures and voting technologies and [ . . . ] the laws, the procedures, and the decisions that produced those results, viewed in the context of social and historical factors."[31] The Voter Rights Act provides powerful leverage to the analysis of the historical practices of incarceration identified in this book: the question of racist intent, in other words, is not the point in the overrepresentation of black men in prison. The *effect* is the key, as becomes clear in the American Correctional Association's official endorsement in 2001 of the "restoration of voting rights" to former felons after the completion of a sentence: "Disenfranchisement," the ACA argues, "disproportionately affects segments of the population," and fulfills no corrective purpose.[32] Nevertheless, states continue to disenfranchise, demonstrating that imprisonment produces a particular identity, the prisoner and former prisoner—and the possibility of being misrecognized as a "probable felon."

Criminalization is thus a matter of interpellation, of being named. The term invokes Louis Althusser and his claim of subjects as hailed into being.[33] He offers the example of a policeman's call, "you there!," which implies both the threat and the psychoanalytic guilt presumed in such a naming, and he describes that hailing as the entry of the subject into history.[34] That singular interpellation as identity formation is nicely exemplified with regard to race and gender in such noted examples as Frantz Fanon's "Look, a Negro!" and Judith Butler's "It's a girl!"[35] Like those interpellations, the identity of the criminal, and subsequently the prisoner, has its presumably straightforward cause, originary and singularly definitive: the person is black and not white; the newborn child has these sexual parts and not those; the accused is guilty rather than innocent. However, as with other indices, the facticity of criminalization and the incarceration with which it has become increasing equivalent are not always so straightforward. The black and white of race is particularly vexed, at times denoting a *perception* of skin color and thus far more a psychological and cultural matter than one of biology, in other instances signifying ethnicity or ideology.

The identity of *prisoner* differs from race, ethnicity, gender, sexuality, and other matters of human difference in that it is not determined through one's genealogy or culturally encoded behaviors, not necessarily written on the body or its willful performances. Imprisonment occurs through processes in which a subject's agency varies, from extensive, as in the conscious decision to commit a serious felony, to none at all, as in innocence or accident. It can occur at virtually any point in one's life, a seemingly sudden ontological transformation wherein a person becomes an alleged criminal, then a convict and felon, accompanied by a set of legal ramifications ranging from registration to incarceration to execution. Given that anyone can become a prisoner—though, of course, some are far more likely than others to do so—incarceration in part resembles the category of disability. Disability studies has emerged as a crucial category of human experience in the humanities and social sciences since the Americans with Disabilities Act (1990). The comparison between imprisonment and disability perhaps invokes immediate responses of a naïve ethical equivalency, but even a glance at history, literary or otherwise, demonstrates how each has been treated as a sign of moral failure. The clearest example of this phenomenon in U.S. letters is Nathaniel Hawthorne's *The Scarlet Letter* (1850) and the titular mark Hester Prynne bears in her community after completing her sentence. The narrative indicts the culture that punishes her, even as it signifies Roger Chillingworth's moral decrepitude through his increasing physical deformity, a bodily disfigurement and disability equated in the novel with evil. Those associations of disability have faded as our culture has grown more knowledgeable regarding the many sorts of physical and mental difference and their many causes; it is past time for us to gain a clearer sense of the many variations of criminalization and their own multiple causes.

I describe the category of prisoner as a matter of identity, because identity serves as the hinge between *I* and *we,* the axis between psychoanalytic and historicizing approaches so attuned to single and plural, the individual subject and the social body. The books, films, and performances addressed in this book all are invested deeply in matters of human agency and the sense of its possibility with regard to criminality and imprisonment. Those investments invite different ways of reading, particularly psychoanalytic and historicizing, two approaches often understood as occupying opposite poles.[36] The difference can be understood as one of scope. Psychoanalytic approaches offer a microphysics of authority focused on the individual subject, wherein the origins of character can be traced to an uneasy combination of difference and universality: idiosyncratic personal history organized through the cross-cultural and transhistorical terms of psychoanalysis that describe human experience.

In contrast, historically nuanced study offers a macrophysics of power and its operation over time in cultural terrain split along fault lines of human difference: race, gender, ethnicity, sexuality, class, and other engines of history. This is part of the reason that most attempts to bridge the perceived gap between the two approaches have located themselves in the study of race[37]—psychoanalysis largely defined by

Freud and Lacan, after all, already was organized by gender and sexu-ality. Some critics and theorists bridge this gap, though given the prevalence of historical study, such efforts can sometimes seem an offering by apologists, or an attempt to leverage the cachet of his-tory. Cultural critics and theorists working in the register of psycho-analysis might object to this description,[38] but even the most fully developed dual approaches often open with an apology regarding psychoanalysis's traditional emphasis on individual and family dramas. The question so famously posed by Carolyn Porter, "are we being historical yet?,"[39] continues to ring among critics bridging theoreti-cal vocabularies. Rather than pretending to offer any unifying theory, this book traffics between the micro- and macro- approaches, as these texts themselves do in their accounts of the individual and social forces that shape criminalization and its attendant imprisonment.

While *prison, race,* and *masculinity* are the key terms of this book, I sometimes employ a fairly uncomplicated treatment of the latter two, foregrounding incarceration. As prison studies becomes more central to historical, literary, and cultural studies, then analyses that are more specifically inflected will continue to appear to emphasize how imprisonment shapes gender and sexuality. For example, patriarchy as man-is-dominant engages prisoners in a subordinate role to "the man" who keeps them down; within that hierarchy, male prisoners subordinate one another, sometimes in violent rituals of male prison rape wherein the victim consequently may be perceived as homo-sexual while the perpetrator is not.[40] Nevertheless, this study largely treats incarceration as the primary variable in the cultural function of imprisonment, and while its purpose and practice change historically, it remains linked to race.

The development of *The Heath Anthology of American Literature* offers a means to trace how, since the 1970s, identity and the politics of identity have grown to be understood as the fault lines of cul-tural history and the fundamental organizing principles for humanities and social sciences. As the most prominent of the collections orga-nized to emphasize the multicultural nature of U.S. literary history, the anthology offers one commonplace to address the attention to cultural difference as well as the relative scarcity of the discussion of incarceration. The self-professed genealogy offered in the collection's preface traces its origins to discussions challenging the national canon in 1968 and then the 1979 project titled "Reconstructing Ameri-can Literature," which led to the so-titled 1982 conference at Yale and to a text of the same name providing pedagogical strategies for reformulating national literature courses.[41] Early participant Richard Yarborough later became the associate general editor of the anthology, which in its 2005 edition includes a section on prison literature. In a 2003 lecture Yarborough addresses representation of black masculinity in "recent U.S. historical cinema."[42] He calls attention to the trend of the Europeanization of black masculinity in these films, each of which is a historical drama leveraging the cachet of being "based on a true story." However, he does not point out that his selection of *Amistad* (1997), *Rosewood* (1997), and *The Hurricane* includes representations of the early-nineteenth-century revolt, a massacre, and an unjust imprisonment, an arc that follows the historical telos of slavery, jim crow lynching, and the raced incarceration of black men—the history that underwrites this book. Yarborough's oversight is no pernicious disavowal of a nation's raced corrections history. Instead, he overlooks imprisonment, quite literally "sees over"[43] the phenomenon I describe: pervasive imagination's concealment of the history of imprisonment, where almost one of every three black men and one out of every twenty-three white men are likely to be imprisoned at some point during their lives.

Given that human cost and the proliferative representations of imprisonment, it is curious that there has not been more of a corresponding discourse in film or literary studies. Bruce Crowther's *Captured on Film: The Prison Movie* (1989)[44] is an encyclopedia rather than an analysis of movies set in prison; Nicole Rafter's *Shots in the Mirror: Crime Films and Society* (2000)[45] includes a provocative chapter focusing on prison films, but it also emphasizes breadth rather than depth. Though many books make prisons both marginal and central to their narratives and settings,[46] there is insufficient analysis focusing specifically on representations of imprisonment in U.S. literature. H. Bruce Franklin's *Prison Literature in America* and Dennis Massey's *Doing Time in American Prisons: A Study of Modern Novels* (1989) are critical entries in the field, as is Auli Ek's *Race and Masculinity in Contemporary American Prison Narratives* (2005). While Ek and I engage some of the same imaginative works and some of the same critics and theorists, we differ in scope and method. The scope of her book is largely a present not specifically linked to past practices. The basis for that presentism is probably indicated when she suggests that the prison films she critiques "resist the postmodernist mode of examining the complexity of concept and values."[47] I am skeptical that only postmodernism studies such matters, which simply could be called careful analysis. Furthermore, that "mode" is generally suspicious of historical periodization in particular and continuity in general, but archival work and other historical evidence demonstrates constancies of racial control within corrections. Nevertheless, Ek rightly demonstrates that "the image of the criminal serves symbolic social and cultural needs" inextricably linked with racial difference.[48]

Such study has proven marginal to the more developed area of law and literature, in which prisons appear scarcely, if at all.[49] These works sort the differences and dependencies between the two discourses of law and literature, twin fields focusing on the uses and effects of language. Their paired study addresses the literary representation of law as agonistic inquiry, the courtroom as stage and place of contest, the function of the tropes of jurisprudence in literature, and the application of literary examples and methodologies to law. In addition to such texts that focus primarily on the depictions of trials, David Guest offers a critique of U.S. fiction representing the death penalty in *Sentenced to Death: The American Novel and Capital Punishment* (1997).[50] However, much lies unexamined in the space between trial and execution, and death is not the only sentence. The limited critical enterprise drawing attention to the narratives of imprisonment offered in U.S. literature reproduces the larger invisibility of imprisonment for those not themselves in prison.

That absence of more-critical comment on representations of imprisonment occurs, in part, because of the evolution of the term *prison*. The semantic shift from a condition of captivity to a place of punishment reflects the crux of Foucault's argument in *Discipline and Punish,* in which he charts the shift of punishment of the body to discipline and individuation. The legitimacy of the historiographical method of Foucault's *Discipline and Punish* has received significant criticism.[51] Though it is written as critical theory and a "history of the present,"[52] it still does draw primarily from eighteenth- and nineteenth-century prison history—if to illustrate its points rather than serve as their basis. In addition, some subaltern studies, the analyses of power's sedimentation of culture, have been informed by prison practice. For example, it is difficult to conceive of Gramsci's rich description of hegemony not inflected by his situation of writing within prison walls. Dick Hebdige draws heavily from Gramsci in his definitive *Subculture* (1979),[53] and he frames his argument with the prison writing of Jean Genet. Therefore, some of the critical theory formative of historically nuanced cultural study has been shaped by actual and imagined incarceration. However, theoretically informed analyses of literature typically employ *prison* to mean a general sense of confinement, rather than a specific material condition.[54]

Such figurative use likely has been informed both by Foucault's emphasis on the organization of power (for which imprisonment is largely a metaphor) and by Jameson's use of the term in his critique of formalism in *The Prison-House of Language* (1972).[55] Jameson and Foucault drew titular attention to prisons even as the first, in his argument, and the second, in his employment by subsequent critics, made imprisonment figurative, a metaphor for the limits of formalism and the operation of power, respectively. Jameson's and Foucault's work proved valuable for analyses of cultural production attendant to historical conditions, but the shift to prison as an abstraction overwrites what is itself a material circumstance, a bait and switch of the literal and the figurative that reproduces the gap between actual and imagined prisons.

This book certainly relies on Foucault's work on prisons in addition to his formulation of history as a genealogy of discourse, power, and discursive authority, as well as on Jameson's emphasis on historicity and the embedded politics of texts. However, prison as a metaphor causes a slippage, since academics writing about images of imprisonment as punishment end up writing about an existential state. For example, Martha Duncan's *Romantic Outlaws, Beloved Prisons* (1996),[56] in examining fiction from Aeschylean tragedy to twentieth-century fiction through the lenses of political science and law, flattens or effaces the cultural and historical contingencies of the texts she reads, and writes a sense of the popular at the expense of the complexity of historical actuality as it might be understood through various records and textualities. In analyses such as these, prison becomes a trope.

That trope making is not unexpected, as "prison" provides a powerful and polymorphous sign. For Frederick Douglass, there is the "prison-house of slavery," while race itself is such a state in DuBois's description of whiteness as a "prison-house closed round about us all." Richard Wright describes America as "a black sprawling prison full of tiny black cells," and for James Baldwin there is the "sunlit prison of the American dream." To Malcolm X, whose own experience made prison more than a metaphor, "our color became to us like a prison."[57] Given the power of the image, it should not come entirely as a surprise that imprisonment becomes a metaphor for the racial operation of power. Nevertheless, the focus in this book remains on prison not as a metaphorical state or a feeling of being confined, but as a real and imagined place of bodily confinement within wire and concrete.

The distinction is important. For instance, at his best Ioan Davies in *Writers in Prison* (1990) makes salient points regarding how prison writers counter strategies of domination; at his worst, Davies commits solipsistic excesses in claims such as "the metaphoric prison and the real prison are ultimately one and the same," and "Death Row becomes the land that we all inhabit."[58] Something is lost when imprisonment becomes primarily a metaphor, either for the circuitry of force in societies or for a bleak perception of a psychological or philosophical condition. There are rhetorically powerful reasons for challenging the distinctions between those in and out of prison. Indeed, the lack of widespread concern regarding imprisonment practices can be attributed, in part, to the lack of identification, of mutual recognition between those imprisoned and those not. However, any such challenge to definitions of criminality and practices of imprisonment must be grounded in the specificity of material, cultural, and historical conditions.

There is attention to such experience in examinations and collections of prison writing, the discursive work of prisoners themselves. Bell Gale Chevigny and Franklin, in particular, have addressed the constructed invisibility of prisons by focusing on prisoners' texts. Franklin argues that the main lines of American literature can be traced from the "plantation to the penitentiary."[59] His *Prison Literature in America* offers extended readings of the writing of captives, from slave narratives to writing of the mid-1970s. He shifts from reading these works to offering more of the writing itself in his collection *Prison Writing in 20th-Century America* (1998). That anthology and Chevigny's *Doing Time: 25 Years of Prison Writing* (1999) both underscore that the wording of the Thirteenth Amendment effectively made racial incarceration a de facto extension of slavery.[60] They primarily emphasize the self-representations of prisoners themselves. Similarly, prison teachers and activists such as Robert Ellis Gordon and Kathleen O'Shea juxtapose prisoners' stories with their own, writing themselves in the spaces between the prison writing they include in, respectively, *The Funhouse Mirror: Reflections on Prison* (2000) and *Women on the Row: Revelations from Both Sides of the Bars* (2000).[61]

Such prison writing and its study—the prisoners, teachers, scholars, and activists producing and drawing attention to the writing describing prison from the inside, largely in an effort for social justice—are excellent and necessary in their own right. This book has a different though related strategy and draws attention to the sheer pervasiveness of prisoners both real and imagined, written and screened from both sides of prison walls. The views from inside and out create dual vantage points from which to examine the degree to which those in prison and the nation that imprisons mirror one another, as such reflection proves a key trope for the growing body of prison writing. A poem printed in the prison magazine the *Angolite* in 1985 poses the matter this way:

Go ahead
Lock us up
Lock us all up
Lock away the ones you see
In the mirror while you're shaving
Because we're all just reflections
Of your world
Of the world you think we've left behind.[62]

Like this poet, Chevigny claims that "prison *reflects* the state of society," and Attica historian Tom Wicker argues that what happens inside the walls "inevitably *reflects* the society outside."[63] However, as Gordon's titular "funhouse mirror" suggests, the reflection can distort and prove grotesque.

Such mirroring and the (mis)identification it implies require a closer look. While generally the imagination of prisons overwrites their actuality, this book also demonstrates that prisoners and the culture that incarcerates sometimes mirror one another, sometimes reflect *on* one another, and fundamentally alter one another. For example, Faulkner's description of the cause of criminality in the early 1930s is the same as that offered by prison officials of the time. Cleaver writes a prison-cell view of domestic and international policy of the mid-1960s, and he and Mailer train their critical gazes on the absurdities on both sides of prison walls. However, the depictions back and forth not only represent history, but play a role in its development. Representation offering itself as "real" participates in the texture of that reality, changes the course of human events. Cleaver's writing in 1968 made him a key figure in ACA discussions of the early 1970s. Mailer's "true life novel" scrupulously (and sometimes less so) documents the events surrounding Gary Gilmore's incarceration and execution in

1976 and 1977, including how television producers, reporters, lawyers, and writers shaped the events they recorded. The documentary *The Farm* is at once part of the historical record and itself critically informed by prior imaginings of prison. The literature and film of the cultural imagination less reflect historical actuality than they play a dynamic role in it. What Richard Poirier writes of Mailer is true of many of writers and directors surveyed: "I would take his engagements with language as political rather than simply literary ones: they are a way of discovering how to hold together elements that perhaps by nature would tend to destroy one another, both in a political and in a literary structure."[64] Sorting the political, historical, and literary structures of these books, films, and performances makes their categorization difficult, as they all blur boundaries of fiction, history, and myth in their imperative to tell the "truth."

The truth they tell, particularly with regard to racial oppression, often demonstrates undermined ideals of equality, at times imbuing these books, films, and performances with a rhetoric of dissent familiar in U.S. literary history.[65] Such dissent has become associated not only with the self-representation of black men, but also with their representation by others, a rhetorical strategy often relating twentieth-century imprisonment to nineteenth-century slavery. For example, the films set in prisons in chapters 5, 6, and 7 all cite that racial history. Vexed as its depiction of black masculinity is, Kaye's *American History X* closes its narrative of imprisonment and racist violence in the 1990s with an epigraph from Abraham Lincoln calling for racial harmony. *The Hurricane* draws verbatim from the autobiography of Rubin Carter written in prison, where he identifies "Carter" as the "slave name" from ancestors working fields in the South.[66] The documentary *The Farm* chronicles the lives of six inmates, four of whom are black, in the slave plantation turned penitentiary. Furthermore, Faulkner's *Go Down, Moses,* with its central conflict beginning in slavery in the antebellum South, ends more than a hundred years later in a chapter that shares the title of the book, drawn from a nineteenth-century spiritual. Not only Franklin and other critics, activists, and historians, but also directors and writers draw the comparison between slavery and incarceration, the latter as the extension of the former.

Nevertheless, Faulkner's position in writing *Go Down, Moses* is not the same as that of Cleaver, in *Soul on Ice,* or Carter, in *The Sixteenth Round,* each telling his own history; there is no ethical equivalency or naive postmodern collapse of all distinction between novel and autobiography. While meaningfully related, there remains a difference between the imprisoned character of Butch Beauchamp in a fictional 1940s and those actually in prison then. Mailer's articulation of masculinity in the characterization of the "white negro,"[67] though endorsed by Cleaver, does not equate to the blackness of Cleaver himself. I am not interested in discussions of authenticity as such, untethered from historical and cultural contingencies. However, critics such as Chevigny, Franklin, and Barbara Harlow usefully describe the literature of prisoners as *prison writing,* as opposed to prisons *in* writing, the representation of prisoners by those not themselves incarcerated.[68] The selection for this book balances views from within and without prison walls. Faulkner writes and Kaye films from outside, but Cleaver is behind bars. *The Executioner's Song* and *The Hurricane* both draw from prison writing, and the latter at times filmed on location inside Ralway Prison. *The Farm* is shot almost entirely within Angola State Prison, with one inmate, Wilbert Rideau, receiving directorial credit. "Live from Death Row" allows prisoners to speak for themselves, an effort Webster's *Jury Duty* takes pains to re-create.

Prisoners' self-representations and their depictions by others are joined in order to offer views from both the margin and the center, with an eye toward clarifying how the prisoners are defined from within and without. At the turn of the twentieth-first century, prisons are split between lived experience for an unprecedented number of U.S. citizens and a polymorphous sign in the cultural imagination. Describing the relationship between the history and the representation of incarceration requires historiographical approaches joined with ways of reading that illuminate and clarify evolving notions of criminalization, imprisonment, and the social responsibility for prisons and prisoners.

Chapters 2, 3, and 4 are organized around the five literary texts surveyed in this book, representations of imprisonment written from both sides of prison walls: Faulkner's three novels from without, Cleaver's account from within, and Mailer's crossing back and forth. Chapter 2, "Literary Execution: Race, Crime, and Punishment in Three Faulkner Novels," examines criminality in *Sanctuary* and *Light in August,* and more extensively in *Go Down, Moses.* All close with the deaths of characters condemned for murder; in the latter two, the characters are of mixed race. The earlier novels treat criminality in psychoanalytic terms of family history and early childhood. It is a model that these early novels do not seem to trust but for which no other option seems available. The views of criminal cause correspond to those of prison officials of the time, who relied on records of personal history and psychological classification. In contrast, *Go Down, Moses* offers a social rather than personal history producing the criminal. Its narrative trajectory implies that twentieth-century incarceration is the inexorable conclusion of slavery and jim crow, a radical claim at the time. In the final pages of the novel, responsibility not for the crimes but for the condemned falls to the white male business community. The representation of incarceration and execution at times capitulates to assumptions of blackness, masculinity, and criminality, but in the end *Go Down, Moses* challenges its contemporary views of wardens and other prison officials as recorded in the transcripts of the American Prison Association.

Chapter 3, "*Soul on Ice,* Schizoanalysis, and the Subject of the Prisoner," focuses on Cleaver's engagement with autobiography and cultural critique. His description of imprisonment regularly shifts from personal experience to contemporary historical events. Cleaver disdains the emphasis on the individual in psychoanalysis, instead beginning a social analysis to sort the divisions of criminality, race, and gender. In 1968 he participated through direct involvement and writing in efforts of cultural change at a time when radical transformation seemed possible, not only to activists but also to American Correctional Association administrators of the time. Indeed, following the release and widespread acclaim for *Soul on Ice*—it sold two million copies and was the New York Times Book of the Year—prison officials responded to its critique in contradictory ways, from disdain to positive recommendation. Cleaver and ACA presidents viewed their historical moment as one at the cusp of revolution, facing a transformation in what counted as crime and punishment at a time when the nation was divided deeply with regard to the possibilities of youth movements and racial unity. Cleaver's social analysis, while preparatory, self-serving, and contradictory, offers a powerful approach to accounting for what he considered a cultural hysteria.

Chapter 4, "*The Executioner's Song* and the Narration of History," tells a different story of a prisoner, and while similarly situated between personal and social, it appears after the revolt at Attica, after the dismantling of rehabilitation programs, after the Rockefeller drug laws, and at the beginning of the precipitous rise in incarceration rates. The "true life novel" departs from social and cultural implications of raced criminality, offering instead a bleak account of seemingly inevitable, unexplainable, and race-neutral violence. Gilmore's crimes as Mailer describes them are violent and intentionless phenomena, the individual action of a sociopath acting without cause or direction. Mailer offers his bleak account of Gilmore as a prisoner and Gilmore's effort to maintain autonomy through ruthlessly pursuing his own death. However, Mailer maintains a narrative method sensitive to social interdependency and the unavailability of that very individual autonomy. In the effort to tell the truth—and leaving himself out of it—Mailer unravels Gilmore's effort to opt out of history, even as he demonstrates how storytelling shapes the history it tries to tell.

Films are the focus of the three chapters thereafter. Chapter 5, "The Contradictions of 'Documentary Realism' in *American History X*," demonstrates how the film's many "authors" claim the real and the effects of that effort. Screenwriter David McKenna draws from his own experiences in Southern California to tell a story that Tony Kaye films in cinema verité style, and actor Norton cribs statistics from the governor's office to add lines for verisimilitude. Critics have praised the film's realism, and some teen audiences have questioned whether it is based on a true story. The film describes the incarceration of a white supremacist gang leader (Norton) and his subsequent repudiation of racism, a lesson that led to the film's recommendation by Amnesty International and to broad screening in schools. However, the film's editing in postproduction so emphasized the believability of the charismatic leader's racism and disregarded the humanity of its black male characters that it leaves available an entirely different message: all black men are criminals, and prison redeems both black and white men to become the "better angels of our nature." *American History X* overwrites its own anti–white supremacist tag line, "Some legacies must end"—accompanied by a skinhead's swastika tattoo—in its whitewashing of racism's causes and costs.

Chapter 6, "'Based upon a true story': *The Hurricane* and the Problem of Prison Redemption," critiques another representation of racial tension and men in prison. Norman Jewison's *The Hurricane* combines biographical and fictional elements, incorporating documentary footage in the feature film based on the imprisonment of professional boxer Rubin "Hurricane" Carter. The film demonstrates the risks of the "apprehension" of history, both the claim to the real and the anxiety over its misrepresentation. Like *American History X, The Hurricane* offers racism not distributed through social structures but consolidated in particular individuals, as Yarborough and others have noted. More significant, the film's condemnation of racial incarceration is undermined by its feel-good narrative, its "triumph of the human spirit" genre.

Chapter 7 is *"The Farm:* 'This is no dream or nothing made up, this is for real.'" Realistic films become part of a mediascape helping to define the shape of a given reality. Fictional films set in prison thereby foster the expectations viewers have of what prison really must be like, shaping the production of a documentary set in prison and featuring actual prisoners. *The Farm,* more than *American History X* and *The Hurricane,* successfully represents contemporary raced imprisonment as a consequence of a history of racism. The filmmakers draw attention to the fact that the Louisiana State Prison is on the grounds of a former slave plantation and that the prison perpetuates some of the plantation's practices. Nevertheless, at times it also fills a shape established by prior fictions, demonstrating how documentary can capitulate to the same popular expectations as would-be blockbusters. Narrative conceits of earlier fictional films set in prison shape the production of documentary.

Chapter 8, "Staging Prisons and the Performance of History," turns from books and films to two performances from the fall of 1999, an activist demonstration and a play that both directly concern imprisonment. A staging of "Live from Death Row" offers a chance for dialogue between a community audience and prisoners. To hear them speak is an invitation to take a stand against the death penalty, as well as against raced incarceration practices. *Jury Duty* is a play based on a true story that was performed in one instance as a fundraiser for a social work program. Ken Webster's drama draws from his experience on a criminal trial jury to recount, in a series of retrospective monologues, a white female character's crime and trial, as well as the deliberations of members of the jury. The former demonstration emphasizes how race and class create the expectation of the criminality of black men and their consequent imprisonment, while the latter departs from the racial focus to point out how gender and sexuality inform cultural expectations of crime and punishment as well. They provide a sense of the immediacy and actuality of incarceration in their claims for a broader social responsibility for prisons and prisoners.

Critics, teachers, readers, and citizens must interpret the history of imprisonment as it has been represented in order to better understand how and why incarceration currently operates as it does, locking up two million people, many for nonviolent offenses, a tremendous proportion of them black, most of them from poverty. What counts as a crime varies culturally and historically, and the United States is likely to maintain prisons to separate some individuals from the rest. Sigmund Freud argues in *Civilization and Its Discontents* (1930) that organizations of humanity such as nation-states quell internal discord through marking some group as "other" and reacting to that difference through violence and oppression,[69] and we can view transhistorical, cross-cultural, and international examples of such phenomena. The United States of America is known popularly as the land of the free, and that definition may well depend on some of its citizens *not* being free, losing access to life, liberty, and their pursuits. However, massive increases in U.S. imprisonment in the past quarter century have not fostered peace, and while our society may well think that some people belong in prison, we cannot strive for a perfect union of "we the people," and certainly cannot attain it, when so many are in prison in large part because they are black or Hispanic and often poor.

# 2

# Literary Execution

## Race, Crime, and Punishment in Three Faulkner Novels

> If I'm going to finish my crop in this county or finish somebody else's crop in Parchman county, I would like to know it soon as I can.
>
> —Lucas Beauchamp in *Go Down, Moses*[1]

> Most whites thought of Parchman as a model prison, and the press carried endless stories of its profitable ways [ . . . ]. William Faulkner lived in Oxford, only eighty miles east of the farm.
>
> —David M. Oshinsky, *"Worse Than Slavery":*
> *Parchman Farm and the Ordeal of Jim Crow Justice*[2]

AS IMAGINED by William Faulkner, Yoknapatawpha County was not far from Parchman, with its actual prison well-known for harsh conditions and contracted convict labor, making it bear harsh resemblance to plantation slavery. Along with early-twentieth-century Mississippi judicial practices almost indistinguishable from lynching, race colored criminality as it was both practiced and imagined in the American South. This chapter demonstrates that *Sanctuary, Light in August,* and *Go Down, Moses* chart a shift in Faulkner's sense of the causes of crime and the justice of punishment. All three novels implicate race with violence in a fashion that mirrors the historical record of Southern practice in the first half of the twentieth century. The earlier novels trace crime to individual history and equate judicial decision with lynching; in contrast, *Go Down, Moses* abandons the emphasis on personal biography, turning instead to a broader social context, community accountability for the criminal, and sharp distinction between lynching and execution.

My claim of an evolved sense of crime in Faulkner's writing, then, involves matters of human agency and the sense of its possibility at particular times and places, and thus incorporates psychoanalysis's emphases on both the individual consciousness and the plural sense of social history. Faulkner himself shifted from emphasizing the former to the latter in his account of forces that shape criminality between his writing of *Sanctuary* and *Light in August* and then *Go Down, Moses* a decade later. While I make some use of the psychoanalytic terminology prevalent during these novels' writing and reception, I am less interested in interpreting them wholly within a Freudian or Lacanian framework than I am in reading them comparatively as bracketing a change in the writer's sense of individual autonomy, the retribution for crime, and the social responsibility for punishment. Their respective accounts here are situated with regard to other texts as well, particularly the historical record of lynching and the credence prison officials gave to psychological classification and the individuation of prisoners from 1929 to 1942. The causes of criminality, the sorts of punishment, and the relation between the criminal and society described in those transcripts provide a historical record in tension with the history Faulkner imagines.

Faulkner's "own little postage stamp of native soil"[3] offers a mythic South at once old and new, fictional and immediately recognizable, a product of the author's imagination and his history—both his personal experiences and the tensions of cultural difference deeply marking the United States from the 1920s to the 1950s. Nineteen novels and many shorter works in their aggregate produce the fictional county and survey a common landscape over a hundred years. Antediluvian characters with extended and entwined genealogies cultivate relationships among the twelve hundred lively fictions populating the twenty-four hundred square miles of wilderness, farmland, hamlets, and towns.[4] To see what stays the same in Yoknapatawpha and what changes is to mark how Faulkner, his world, and his view of it alter as well. In the passing of time, the writer's representation of the set of human relations alters, human agency and possibility changing in the steepening shadow of history. It is the work of 1929 to 1942, particularly *The Sound and the Fury, Light in August, Absalom, Absalom!,* and *Go Down, Moses,* that most critics suggest includes Faulkner's most significant writing,[5] a historical period most recognizable as the Great Depression yielding to World War II, when harsh economic and cultural effects were suffered sharply in rural communities. Yoknapatawpha illustrates the poverty, class and race conflicts, transient populations, and rural to urban shifts experienced in the actual South and elsewhere in the country.

Less well-known regarding this time is that it was the period of the greatest number of executions in recent U.S. history. From 1930 to 1942, between 123 and 199 state executions took place each year, the most during any such period. During that time, black men disproportionately received the death penalty in comparison with white men. While the frequency of lynching reached new lows by the 1930s, some historians suggest a correlation of that racial violence to execution practices.[6] Furthermore, a statistical correlation between lynching and execution has received insufficient notice. Arthur F. Raper's groundbreaking study of lynching in 1933 demonstrates that while the terrorism of lynching rested upon the myth of a black man's rape of a white woman, less than one-sixth of the documented lynchings between 1880 and 1930 involved such accusations.[7] Exactly the same proportion of state executions of black men between 1930 and 1942 was for the crime of rape, more than eight times the frequency of white men, hinting at a substitution effect between lynching and racial execution; arguably, the latter practice replaced, at least in part, the former.[8]

It was against this historical backdrop of race-based lynching giving way to the relatively frequent state-sanctioned hangings, shootings, and electrocutions that the initial readers of *Sanctuary, Light in August,* and *Go Down, Moses* encountered the death sentences of Lee Goodwin, Popeye, Joe Christmas, Rider, and Samuel "Butch" Beauchamp. These five characters split the difference between lynching and execution, but where the practices are separated only hazily in the earlier works (Christmas's death is both), they are distinguished sharply and are explicitly racial in *Go Down, Moses.* That transformation culminates in a repudiation of racist lynching, even as Faulkner acknowledges that the turn from mob to jury does not release the society that executes from the responsibility for the condemned.

Noel Polk points out that in Yoknapatawpha's county seat "the two chief features of Jefferson, Mississippi's architectural landscape are the courthouse and the jail."[9] It is surprising, then, that crime and punishment in Faulkner's fiction have received so little notice. Just as

Faulkner's critics have not sufficiently addressed the matter of incarceration and execution, David Guest's survey of the representation of the death penalty in twentieth-century U.S. literature, *Sentenced to Death,* does not touch on Faulkner. However, *Sanctuary, Light in August,* and *Go Down, Moses* all center on the origins of criminality and its punishment, most particularly when Popeye's and Christmas's executions are contrasted with Butch Beauchamp's at the conclusion of their respective narratives. Those closures differ as personal psychoanalytic history gives way to larger social and genealogical history in creating the criminal. *Sanctuary* and *Light in August* end with the romantic tragedy for which Faulkner is so well-known, where the aesthetic of the language offers the saving grace. In contrast, *Go Down, Moses* closes with a starker vision that stages how criminality is the responsibility of a society defined in the cultural differences of an explicitly democratic Jefferson, the county seat of Yoknapatawpha.

The three novels offer a changed sense of crime, criminals, causes of criminality, and punishment. The definition of crime and the purposes of punishment have been and remain culturally and historically contingent. Relevant definitions are offered by the American Prison Association, which reaffirmed in 1930 the first of the principles included in its Declaration: that crime "inflicts an injury upon others," that criminality is determined by "competent courts," and that punishment is "suffering" designed for the purpose of "reformation."[10] The condition of criminality is treated through punishment intended to reform, to remake the criminal. However, which acts are considered criminal and the strategies of improvement vary in place and time. For instance, a variety of policy changes in the New Deal era of the 1930s was a culmination of Progressive efforts and addressed the matter of reformation, including education, paid labor, psychological classification and treatment, and parole programs. Such strategies of rehabilitation came under sharp scorn in Faulkner's own Mississippi, and one newspaper, the *Daily Clarion-Ledger,* claimed in a 1934 editorial that it was "dangerous for society to fall into the error that science can, through a little remodeling, make model citizens of all hardened criminals."[11] None of these five of Faulkner's criminals is remodeled; rather than reformed, made anew, they are destroyed in their death sentences. However, their deaths and the paths to those ends are not the same; the changes are criminality's causes and punishments, and the social responsibility for them.

The narratives of all three novels are determined largely by violent crime, and the commission, discovery, and punishment of those crimes serve as the points of gravity around which Faulkner's trademark style of narrative loops in whorls until it circles back to tell and retell events that, chronologically, occur before. *Sanctuary* builds in tension until Popeye murders Tommy and rapes Temple Drake, for which Goodwin is accused; Horace Benbow, in defending Goodwin, tracks Temple to a Memphis whorehouse, where Popeye has confined her. Temple falsely accuses Goodwin, who thereafter is lynched, while Popeye vanishes only to reappear and be tried, convicted, and executed because of his tacit admission to a murder he did not actually commit. In *Light in August,* Joe Christmas's childhood memory of a sexual scene is linked through the racial epithet *nigger* to his ambiguous race. Those associations bind sexuality and racial violence for him until he finally kills Joanna Burden—who has run the gamut from rape victim to lover—and is later indicted and escapes, before finally being shot and castrated by a deputy of the posse.

Chronologically speaking, *Go Down, Moses* begins with Carothers McCaslin's rape of the slave Eunice and then their daughter, Tomasina, a genealogy extending through that patriarch's white sons' pursuit and capture of the escaped slave who is their half brother, which leads to the marriages that perpetuate black and white McCaslins both. Those raced and entwined genealogies provide much of the shape possessed by the baggy monster of a novel. The narrative outline of *Go Down, Moses* is cast in sharper relief in noting its two ends. First, in the penultimate section of "Delta Autumn," the sins of the father, incest and miscegenation, are renewed in Roth Edmonds's son borne by his distant relation, she by four generations and he by five removed from Carothers McCaslin, the all-father. The second finish is the execution, in the titular chapter, of Butch, a son four generations after McCaslin, though his is a genealogical dead end. It is also an official death in counterpoint to Rider's lynching at the midpoint of the novel. The narrative ends of Goodwin, Popeye, Christmas, Rider, and Butch are deaths brought about by combinations of criminality, blackness, and sexual violence. Goodwin offers the exception proving the rule, a rare to the point of unique representation of the lynching of a white man in the twentieth century. The crimes and punishments of Christmas, Rider, and Butch Beauchamp link directly to their race, and Goodwin and Christmas are accused of rape, resulting in their sexual mutilation. Lynch mobs kill Goodwin and Rider, in contrast with the judicially sanctioned deaths of Popeye and

Beauchamp. Christmas's castration and death at the hands of ad hoc deputy Percy Grimm falls between lynching and execution.

Juries sentence Goodwin, Popeye, Christmas, Rider, and Butch, or Faulkner describes such verdicts as foregone conclusions. Goodwin's and Popeye's respective juries each deliberate just eight minutes before returning with convictions. For Christmas, the "Grand Jury was preparing behind locked doors to take the life of a man whom few of them had ever seen to know."[12] Rider's lynching is a given to the deputy sheriff (and deputy narrator) of the second half of "Pantaloon in Black," even before the jailbreak, and news of Butch's impending execution is carried on the newswire. Indeed, incarceration in Faulkner's fiction at first seems anachronistic, as cells, in all of these cases, serve only to hold prisoners until their punishment, rather than the confinement serving as the punishment itself.

That is, pre-Revolutionary practices housed prisoners in jails to await their public and bodily punishment. Enlightenment arguments offered in Europe by Cesare Becarria and in the United States by Benjamin Rush shifted bodily punishment at the end of the eighteenth century to the containment, concealment, and control of imprisonment, a shift Foucault famously describes as the shift from punishment to discipline. But the incarceration in the cases of all five of these characters is only a brief period before their deaths by execution or lynching. Regarding these two practices, Faulkner, in his letters—belles and otherwise—does not always significantly differentiate between the acts of mobs and juries. In a 1931 letter to the Memphis *Commercial-Appeal,* for instance, he suggests that "both had a way of being right."[13] The mutual legitimacy Faulkner offers in that letter is at odds with the negative view of lynching in his short story "Dry September," written the same year, or with *Light in August* a year later. The attributed rightness of mob and jury is one that should trouble readers of Faulkner, but their relation in the South is a matter of historical record.

The seeming anachronism of punishment in these Faulkner novels as well as Faulkner's dangerous equation of mob and jury reflect related matters of criminality and race in early-twentieth-century punishment in the South in general and Mississippi in particular. First, the public spectacle of lynching perpetuated the visibility of officially conducted bodily mutilation and execution that were more common of eighteenth-century punishment practices continuing until the Civil War. In addition, branding and other maiming for both white and black criminals, even for minor crimes, continued in Mississippi decades past the national norm.[14] The overdue revisions to Mississippi's criminal code in 1835 did not protect slaves, and postbellum racial tensions perpetuated violence against black men and women, particularly with the end of Reconstruction. Lynching decreased by the 1930s, during which time executions ceased being public, and states assumed the responsibility for executions from cities and counties. However, given the identical statistics of lynching and the execution of black men in the case of rape, the latter practice may have perpetuated the practices of the former, contributing to the high rates of execution in Southern states.

The statistical parallel between lynching and official execution is not the only correlation between the two. Law enforcement officials in the South regularly abetted lynch mobs, whether directly, by handing over victims, or indirectly, by providing insufficient protection for prisoners. Such complicity drew national scrutiny after the 1906 lynching of Ed Johnson in Chattanooga, Tennessee. Three years later, the U.S. Supreme Court determined that law enforcement officers had insufficiently protected Johnson. The court initiated the only criminal trial in its history to find the sheriff and two deputies guilty of contempt of court in *United States v. Shipp* (1909). Still, Congress's failure to pass the Costigan-Wagner Act in 1935, which would have made such complicity a federal crime, resulted from the opposition of Southern states. The blocking of Costigan-Wagner demonstrates the embedment of lynching in Southern culture in the 1930s, thus establishing the basis for it to inform official execution practices as conducted by state governments. For example, a Mississippi sheriff initially appointed a rape victim's father as hangman in a 1934 case, a trial where the jury debated all of seven minutes.[15] The eight-minute juries of both Goodwin and Popeye in *Sanctuary* seem eerily prescient of that incident. The supervisor of the U.S. Probation System in 1930 could address the American Prison Association and "rejoice that their day of activity is 1930, rather than 1830, that vengeance of the state, of retribution, has largely given way to correctional ideals."[16] However, the APA from 1870 to 1930 largely featured Northeast membership, and those ideals did not necessarily extend to the South, to Faulkner's Mississippi.

What this means for Faulkner's fiction is a reappraisal of distinctions between lynching and execution, and a treatment of the sensational and violently retributive cases of Goodwin, Popeye, and

Christmas as less exceptional than representative. Goodwin's conviction in *Sanctuary* includes District Attorney Eustace Graham's closing argument in court in favor of lynching, to which Goodwin's defender, Horace Benbow, objects and which the judge sustains; in the end, the townspeople have their will done. In like fashion, Percy Grimm is at once deputy and knife-wielding mob member. The blurring between the punishments, coupled with Faulkner's 1931 letter to the Memphis paper equating juries and mobs, offers them a mutual legitimacy in his writing of the early 1930s, an equation that Faulkner no longer found tenable a decade later. In place of a lawyer's argument for lynching in court or a deputy castrating a criminal, there is a sharp divorce between mob violence and jurisprudential decision in *Go Down, Moses,* between the tragedy of Rider's lynching in "Pantaloon in Black," offered in an ironic register at the novel's center, and Butch's execution at the end.

The shared narrative closures of jurisprudential decision and consequent violent deaths among these novels suggest their comparison, but the most interest lies in the differences among their criminals, their origins and executions, and the difference those differences make. Also, with regard to race, the virtual equation of black masculinity with criminality—an equation by no means Faulkner's alone and one of the most pernicious in U.S. history—is not effaced in the later work, but their relationship is more complicated than in the earlier novels. Indeed, with its setting, which spans from 1840 to 1940, *Go Down, Moses* implies in its narrative trajectory that twentieth-century incarceration is the inexorable conclusion of slavery and of jim crow thereafter, and that it is thus an explicitly racial practice. While more of *Sanctuary* likely takes place in jail than any other of Faulkner's novels, possibly surpassed only by *Intruder in the Dust,* imprisonment in *Sanctuary* serves more as a gothic set piece rather than a culminating thematic force, as it does in *Go Down, Moses.* The latter novel, with its sprawling historical setting and at times only tenuously linked characters, has as one of its most central narrative drives the critical representation of the enslavement and imprisonment of its black characters. Tomey's Turl as a slave in "Was" gives way to Lucas Beauchamp, who twice considers reaping cotton not on the Edmondses' plantation but in the prison fields of Parchman Farm,[17] followed by Rider and his incarceration and lynching; the novel concludes with Butch Beauchamp and his seemingly inevitable execution. Faulkner breaks from the bleak certainty of that narrative trajectory in the final coda, when the white male business community takes financial responsibility for Butch's funeral and the entire town of Jefferson assembles to witness his return.

## "This Modern Trend" of Crime—
## and Psychoanalysis

To return to *Sanctuary,* the first of the novels for which crime and punishment are so crucial: Faulkner's depiction of Popeye's impotence and the symbolic substitution of his sexuality take on explicitly Freudian implications numerous times, not the least of which is Temple stealing his pistol or repeatedly calling him "daddy."[18] Indeed, their sexual relationship, such as it is, mediated by Red though orchestrated by Popeye, at times seems not only derivative from but also a parody of Freudian myths of erotic neuroses. With Popeye's whinnying like a horse in his voyeurism, he is a gelding to go alongside the Rat Man, the Wolf Man, and the rest of the mythological zoo of sexual disorders. Psychoanalytic readings are pervasive in the criticism of *Sanctuary* and in accounts of Popeye, Temple, and Horace and Narcissa Benbow. Given the name of the last, Freud's accounts of narcissism, the repeated motif of mirrors throughout the novel, and Lacan's claim of mirroring in identity formation,[19] it is not difficult to see why psychoanalysis has proven so pervasive.

However, most relevant to the matter of criminality and causality at hand is the coda that takes place in the final chapter, the trial, after Goodwin's lynching. Popeye's arrest for killing a policeman, when he was instead shooting Red, immediately gives way to his unremembered infancy: his mother's courtship, marriage, abandonment, and disease; Popeye's own near murder as an infant; his sickness, curtailed sexual development, and homicidal tendencies even as a child.[20] Framed as it is between his arrest and trial seven pages later, it is difficult not to read that curt life story as an explanatory cause, what Guest describes as a diagnostic biography and what prison officials at the time sought in a case record, retroactively tracing crime to early biography: "A case record should reveal a man's very soul," the criminal type determined in "the individual's life history."[21] In the case of Popeye, the coda offers a causal narrative for the crime he actually committed (the murder of Red) to balance his execution for the crime of which he is innocent (the murder of the policeman).

Faulkner claims in the introduction to the 1932 Modern Library edition of *Sanctuary* that his mercenary writing process for the novel deliberately catered to his imagined audience, "what a person in Mississippi would believe to be current trends."[22] Among those "current trends" Faulkner sought to exploit are criminality and its psychological cause. The pulp detective fiction of the 1920s as well as films such as Alfred Hitchcock's *Blackmail* (1929) and *Murder!* (1930) may have been some of the crime fiction Faulkner surveyed, and he was not the only one viewing that cultural landscape. APA President George C. Erksine began his presidential address of the 1929 annual congress by pointing out the centrality of crime in the cultural imagination: "The morning paper, the table of contents of the current magazines, a casual glance at the shelves of any book store [ . . . ] all bear witness to this modern trend."[23] Erksine's "modern trend" of the pervasiveness of criminality's representation was likely one of the several "current trends" to which Faulkner refers; psychological analysis is another. Erksine closes his address with an emphasis on the necessity of psychologically profiling criminals,[24] and five of the forty-two papers presented during the general session of the 1929 conference focus specifically on psychological approaches to criminology with an emphasis on childhood experience.

The approaches endorsed by the APA less resemble Freudian emphases on the unconscious and sexuality than they do the individual personality development described by Alfred Adler, who split from Freud and his approach in 1907. One indicator of that association appears in the discussion following a paper, given at the 1930 APA congress, that treats criminality largely as a psychological disorder, prompting an anxious questioner to suggest that the profiling described in that presentation might give a prisoner "a real inferiority complex."[25] That complex is a misreading of Adler's theory of self-assertion, though that slip, as well as the confusion between Adler's and Freud's approaches, was common at the time. A 1925 *New York Times* article archly suggests that the psychological disorders "Freudians attribute to repressed sex impulse, Adler attributes to a deficiency in the mechanism of self-assertion to the 'inferiority complex,' which today is on the tongue of thousands who have no idea of what they are talking about."[26]

So "a person in Mississippi," or the larger audience that Faulkner knew, believed, and hoped to gain, might have difficulty sorting between schools of psychoanalysis that developed through the late

1920s, notably with the publication of Freud's *Civilization and Its Discontents* and Adler's *The Case of Miss R: The Interpretation of a Life Story* (1929)[27] in the years immediately preceding the release of *Sanctuary*. Psychoanalysis as part of the texture of culture at the time thus informs the diagnostic narrative Faulkner offers, and Popeye's seems particularly Freudian. The character's infancy and impotence are a sum of the primacy of preconscious sexual development and anatomy as destiny, the two Freudian maxims of psychoanalytic subject formation. The explanation of Popeye's criminality narratively follows the crime, much as psychoanalysis retroactively locates original cause as secreted in unconscious memory. Still, given the almost tacked-on nature of Popeye's biographical vignette, it seems possible to read it as Faulkner's capitulation to a model of behavior he did not believe, but for which he did not have an alternative. Not until *Go Down, Moses* would he develop a social and cultural genealogy for subject formation as an alternative to a repressed personal history based largely on sexuality.

Though Faulkner expands the sophistication of character in *Light in August* compared to *Sanctuary,* Christmas's crime and thus his subsequent execution, like Popeye's, has an explanatory narrative, an original cause in the primal scene. Whereas Popeye's arrest triggers his Freudian coda, the return to Christmas's childhood occurs immediately after he begins walking to the house of Joanna Burden, where he will kill her. The recollection of the primal scene, written through with the obligatory guilt, even opens with a fair description of the operation of a Freudian unconscious: "Memory believes before knowing remembers. Believes longer than recollects, longer than knowing even wonders. Knows remembers believes."[28] That introduction gives way directly to the description of the orphanage, the setting of both his theft of toothpaste and his observation of the dietitian and Charlie's sexual encounter, the origin of Christmas's guilt, guilt which is subsequently tied to Christmas's race when the dietitian names him "nigger bastard" to end the scene.[29] That moment is easily read as simultaneously one of birth and one of entry into the social (symbolic) order, albeit an order of violence, sexuality, and racism. Upon Christmas's declaration, "here I am"—his first speech offered as a child—to interrupt their intercourse, the dietitian drags him "violently out of his vomit" to name him.

That moment lays the basis for the subsequent hundred-plus pages accounting for Christmas's battles with that misplaced guilt, not the shorthand diagnostic biography of Popeye, but one still chronicling both his youth and his crucial violent acts: first, beating the black prostitute in the shed, and second, felling his father. The first stages again the primal scene, and in case readers miss the association of sexual maneuvers in the dark, Faulkner provides Christmas's recollection in that shed upon seeing the woman—"There was something in him trying to get out, like when he had used to think of toothpaste."[30] Whatever Christmas knows, remembers, or believes of sex is bound with that originary moment, his entry to a raced and gendered symbolic that names him "nigger bastard," and links sex with blackness and violence. That first criminal violence against women rises with Bobbie, escalates further with another prostitute beaten nearly to death, and culminates in the murder of Joanna Burden.

Like the personal history that scripts the beginning of Popeye's criminality and narratively appears as the basis for his end, Christmas's origins direct him to his death, though the strictly Freudian structure of the former gives way in the latter to one best understood through a combination of Freud and Lacan. His witness of the primal scene enters him into the symbolic order, the "here I am" of linguistic participation in a world beyond himself. Those Lacanian associations increase when he strikes the adopted parent McEachern at the dance hall. The oedipal violence of vanquishing the father ceases to be entirely literal and shifts to the symbolic. In assailing the elder McEachern with the chair, Christmas commits the "Shalt Not,"[31] striking down the literal father, a scene Faulkner casts in the terms of the name-of-the-father in gesturing to the Ten Commandments. *Light in August* later repeats the scene of railing against the Father, down to the detail of wielding furniture, when Christmas suspends his own ambiguous escape to interrupt a revival hymnal to preach blasphemy from the pulpit, brandishing a bench leg.[32] Whereas Popeye's criminal psyche seems not entirely satisfactory—but either the best Faulkner could offer or what he considered his audience to expect—Christmas offers a much more complex figure in terms of his violence and its constituent causes. Still, a symbolic narrative larger than the self collapses back to the individual, the personal guilt of witnessing the primal scene. Faulkner returns to that admission for the adult Christmas, when he stops running and says to himself, "Here I am."[33] The recognition of self surrenders to consequence, and its verbatim repetition links the two moments, tracing his punishment back through his personal history to his emergent consciousness.

Christmas's history is personal, its deployment determined, a chain of events tracking back through dysfunctional and racial sexual relationships, to an abusive father, to an unpunished theft of toothpaste. In that originary moment Faulkner seems again to almost parody a psychoanalytic subject, a psyche unable to abandon the burden of unconscious guilt. That sense of self is entirely singular, determined by the circumstances shaping Christmas's character, the rich description taking place largely between the definition of the unconscious— "Memory believes before knowing remembers"—and Bobbie's "*that will do,*" which halts Christmas's beating, a command half-heard as he fades into unconsciousness.[34] I am not suggesting that the development of Christmas's character takes place outside of history, for the racing and gendering of the sexual violence that are the beginning and the end of his criminality are matters of social difference and its powerful inscription. Instead, it is a matter of emphasis on the relationship between subject and history—in effect, the location of agency. One of *Light in August*'s many narrators, Gavin Stevens, describes one of its other storytellers, Christmas's grandmother Mrs. Hines, as narrating in terms that "had already been written and worded for her."[35] Stevens describes Christmas's criminality in a similarly determined manner, criminality defined by his incarceration, itself built from "whatever crimes had molded him and shaped him and left him at last high and dry in a barred cell."[36] According to Stevens, the criminal is what events have made him.

These are two different sorts of determination, one of scripted events as foregone conclusions, the other as the sort of naturalism Richard Wright would employ eight years later in *Native Son,* a comparison Eric J. Sundquist makes as well in *Faulkner: The House Divided.* That sort of naturalist determination of criminality is also expressed by Howard A. McDonnell a year after the publication of Wright's novel. McDonnell, a state representative in 1941, suggested in a speech in the Mississippi House of Representatives that "crime and criminals are the natural results of a given cause."[37] Still, regardless of whether narrative events are treated as scripted ("written and worded") or as determined by environmental conditions, both sharply curtail agency. Such agency, or personal choice in a given circumstance, regularly serves as the axis between the determining forces of heredity and environment at the 1929 and 1930 APA conferences.[38] However, what those forces of heredity and environment might be, specifically, remains unspoken in the discussions, and the question of race is not raised. Indeed, the proceedings of the annual congress from 1929 to 1932 never substantively mention race, and a census of prisoners provided in the 1929 report makes no mention of it either.[39]

The history not recorded there is imagined in Faulkner's writing. For Christmas, the fundamental indeterminate determination is racial difference, and blackness in the novel is regularly associated with criminality. At one point in *Light in August,* the accusation of blackness is worse than that of murder. When Lucas Burch/Brown tells the marshal that Christmas is "a nigger," the officer responds, "You had better be careful what you are saying if it is a white man you are talking about [ . . . ] I dont care if he is a murderer or not."[40] To the sheriff, being called a "nigger" is imagined as worse than being a murderer. Such logic reads in reverse as well, that to be black is to be automatically a criminal, the ruthless irrational logic of racism in early-twentieth-century Mississippi. One white local told a visitor in 1908, "When there is a row, we feel like killing a nigger whether he has done anything or not."[41] Punishment does not actually require a crime when blackness and criminality are not separable in the cultural imagination of the early-twentieth-century South. To the townspeople of Jefferson, the two compound one another. Hearing of Burden's death, they "believed aloud that it was an anonymous negro crime committed not by a negro but by Negro and who *knew, believed, and hoped* that she had been ravished too" (emphasis added).[42] Like the description of Christmas's unconscious, which "knows remembers believes" half-truths of Christmas's race and original sin, the town is of one mind and "knew, believed, and hoped" murder to be explicitly racial and sexualized.

Crucial to the town's unconscious, then, is the fantasy of a black man's rape of a white woman, an imagined event that inextricably binds lynching and execution even as it conceals the historical actuality of white male slave owners raping black women. *Light in August* reveals the former while leaving the latter unspoken, and so it largely remains in Faulkner's writing until *Absalom, Absalom!* and to a far greater extent in *Go Down, Moses. Light in August* sees the imagined unity in blood vengeance fulfilled in Christmas's execution on Grimm's terms, directly hailing that fantasy: "Now you'll let white women alone, even in hell." It is toward this end that Christmas walks with an inevitability pervasive in the novel.[43]

He leaves the scene of Burden's murder, "moving from his feet upward as death moves," and thereafter sees, according to Stevens, "an incipient executioner everywhere he look[s]."[44] Given how any passersby might join a lynch mob, Christmas very well might see in any face a potential executioner. He perceives his position as held in tension between acted upon and acting (*"Something is going to happen to me. I am going to do something"*) before Burden's death, and walks as if surrounded by executioners thereafter, but the killing is not the crux. Directly before the death drive of walking toward execution, he thinks, "'I have never got outside that circle. I have never broken out of the ring of what I have already done and cannot ever undo.'"[45] In fine modernist fashion, he is a circle enclosed on the outside. By race, deed, and name, he is the simultaneous capitulation and resistance to what other people have called him: "nigger," Christian, McEachern. He repudiates the name of the father even as he assumes the implacable ruthless violence that defines his adopted parent, the aggression that colors his sexual behavior. In the last instance, he returns to the beginning, as circles do, in the repetition of "here I am" that binds the commission of murder with the originary moment, in which the perceived crime of toothpaste theft remains inextricable from the observation of the primal scene.

Like the issue of his race, Christmas's death as lynching or execution maintains the ambiguity, the resolute tension of *both-and*. Rather than strictly the fulfillment of either the death wish of the condemned or the capricious cruelty of an omnipotent opponent, Christmas's execution ends for him—if not for the community—the play of tensions, of ambiguities of character and action. The uncertainty of his blackness and parenthood occupy the central ambiguity of a character encased in nonabsolutes. Is he black or white? Was Joanna's death murder or self-defense? Is his death an execution or a lynching? For Faulkner too there is that unknowability, the complex and contradictory senses of race, crime, and justice. Nowhere is that "is–is not" of the riven self made more clear than in the writer's equation of lynch mobs with juries in his belief that both "have a way of being right" from the letter cited earlier and printed a year before *Light in August*.

There is no such rightness in Christmas's death and mutilation, committed with sufficient savagery to see one would-be executioner vomit, another circular return at the character's death to the vomit of his primal scene. Faulkner offers the violence as tragic, then transcendent, in the dying Christmas, a romantic assumption wherein the character ascends bodily into the community's memory:

[Christmas] seemed to rise soaring into their memories forever and ever. They are not to lose it, in whatever peaceful valleys, beside whatever placid and reassuring streams of old age, in the mirroring faces of whatever children they will contemplate old disasters and newer hopes. It will be there, musing, quiet, steadfast, not fading and not particularly threatful, but of itself alone serene, of itself alone triumphant. Again from the town, deadened a little by its walls, the scream of the siren mounted toward its unbelievable crescendo, passing out of the realm of hearing.[46]

Christmas's end in *Light in August* is the first of its three closures, the other two being those of the Reverend Hightower and Lena Grove. The ironic romanticism of contest with a sportive God of Christmas's last pages turns to the linguistic redemption of romantic style. The nameless, omniscient narrator foretells the future, knows the townspeople's memories, present and future, "for ever and ever." Christmas's ghost somehow looms in Jefferson's shared memory, forever harmless, calm, and somehow victorious. My repeated "somehow" draws attention to the indefinite quality of this description, the "seemed," the three-times-repeated "whatever" of valleys, streams, and children in a town whose courthouses, churches, and jails disappear in this imagined future of natural and transcendental imagery: "streams of old age" where time is a river in which one might fish. The indefinite description makes that future history as inevitable, impotent, and all too late as the siren's scream, which is "unbelievable" and fades to silence. The possibility for romantic redemption is worn-out, but it lacks a substitute. Similarly exhausted but without alternative is a psychoanalytic model of character, the cause of criminality and its attendant incarceration and execution in *Sanctuary* and *Light in August.*

## Invoking Jefferson's "Corporate Limit"

Ten years later, in *Go Down, Moses,* Faulkner repudiated that model of criminality and, by extension, subject formation. There are similarities across the characterizations of Popeye, Christmas, and Beauchamp, who as criminals all play the role of the stereotypical gangster, the hardman. In *Sentenced to Death,* Guest describes the characterization of the "hardened convict, or criminal 'hardman' [ . . . ] a cold-blooded, unpredictable, and violent persona."[47] These are the definitive masculine traits of invulnerability, mastery, and activity. Christmas reproduces Popeye's gangster caricature nearly to the last detail, with his sloping hat and drooping cigarette, his casual violence and more casual crime of selling liquor, and the rumors of business with a gun in Memphis. In *Go Down, Moses,* Butch is literally hard, his face "impenetrable," his hair "lacquered" and head "bronze," his name "Butch" a parody of masculinity, and he answers the census-taker question about what will happen to his corpse with the words of the hardman: "What will that matter to me?"[48] The hardman does not resist his death sentence but, according to Guest, "accepts it and seems to welcome death."[49] Like Christmas, Butch plays the hardman.

However, their means of each becoming that way differs dramatically between the novels. Instead of personal history as the first cause of criminality—the sum of determining forces embodied in a single life but nevertheless traceable to an originating moment—Faulkner creates a larger social frame, history as the tracing backward of genealogy. Whereas Quentin Compson cuts his psychology class in *The Sound and the Fury* in order to play his own analysand in the talking cure of stream of consciousness narrative, the schooling offered by Cass and Ike at the heart of "The Bear" is history. They read the records of the ledgers to envision and revise a narrative of their family and, by extension, the South. *Go Down, Moses* ends as the original text of *Sanctuary* opens; in the drafts prior to its final publication, *Sanctuary* began with a black man accused of murder awaiting his execution. Butch, like Popeye, is condemned for the murder of a policeman. Popeye offers no defense, and Butch does not offer much of one either, though what he says of himself is at least true of Popeye: "It was another guy killed the cop."[50] The substitution of accusation for actuality in the case of Popeye is a sheer unknown for Butch, for readers are never sure whether Butch did in fact kill anyone. That ambiguity features in Christmas's crime as well, as his murder of Burden is at least partly self-defense. Nevertheless, while their respective narratives leave undecided, or at least problematic, the question of agency in the commission of crime, all three characters are named as criminals in courts, which the APA's first principle defines as separate from the commission of crime.

The novels themselves cannot fully resolve that uncertainty, as the moments of the crimes do not appear in the narrative; with regard to punishment, only Christmas's death takes place in the story. The narration of Popeye's execution stops just short of his actual death, as the sheriff opens the trapdoor of the hanging scaffold, and the description does not as closely approach Butch's end. Readers encounter him in his cell the day before his execution and then afterward, as his casket arrives in Jefferson. Most important, though, is the lack of an explanatory personal history for Butch's criminality. The explanation of biography offered for Popeye and Christmas lacks a parallel in the case of Butch, one end of the McCaslin genealogy. Like Edgar Allan Poe's Fortunato, Beauchamp arrives only to be sealed away behind walls, to his death, for reasons obscure and unavailable. The little that readers do know of Beauchamp's past they know through District Attorney Stevens's remembered reading of the "papers of that business," the authoritative discourse that scripts the condemned man as "some seed not only violent but dangerous and bad."[51] However, that narrative explanation is not the only one available, and the reader possesses the preceding episodes of the novel, also "papers of that business," which offer a competing narrative, an entire other discourse. That narrative, with its chronicle of miscegenation and sexual violence, of tangled or misplaced desires, writes a history of character thematically similar to Christmas's: raced and gendered violence shaping the acts that make the criminal, the prisoner. However, Butch's story is different in terms of scope, and he is claimed by a social body extending beyond his own skin.

I am highlighting distinctions of individual and social subjects and their histories as well as distinctions between atomistic and social senses of selfhood, because the process of individuation is one means by which institutional forces such as incarceration function. Discussions at the annual APA meetings were rife with the aim of individualization: "We must learn to individualize"; "Throughout our prisons we need individualization."[52] That repeated imperative seems most often to refer to treating prisoners either, in humanist fashion, as unique individuals, or, in line with Adler, as the products of their respective personal histories. However, there is a less-favorable reading available that more closely resembles the Foucauldian prisoner, the disciplined subject. Individuals and the means of their production are framed in two specific claims made at the APA conference at moments contemporaneous to the publications of *Light in August* and *Go Down, Moses*. One member, Maud Ballington Booth, was in 1932 a sufficiently prominent Volunteer of America and member of the APA to the extent that she received a standing ovation in introducing another speaker later in the conference,[53] and years later had a service award named in her honor. In her presentation, "Individualization in Prisons," she describes the means of making prisoners into individuals in terms of work and emotion. They should perform hard labor, she argues, to earn personal, congratulatory attention from wardens and officers. She suggests that the discipline of such work and its rote affective response will transform convicts into soldiers, prepared so that upon leaving prison, "they go out into the world and they take up that burden and they fight that battle."[54] Recognition as reward purposed to further good works sutures the rhetoric of hailed individuality—Althusser's "hey, you there!"—to the Victorian hymn "Onward Christian Soldiers," made popular as a marching tune in the early twentieth century.

Ten years after Booth's speech, the rhetoric of war became tenuous in the context of actual overseas battles, and required revision. The 1942 APA conference proceedings include much commentary on the role of the prison system in wartime. One lecture in particular focuses on military service and the psychopathology of criminality and determines that some released, paroled, or even current prisoners may be drafted for military service—such as is the case of Lee Goodwin's service in World War I in *Sanctuary*. However, the contention is that those with long records of even minor criminality must not serve. Even if such a person has only a single and minor conviction, a long arrest record (even without conviction) demonstrates "a wholly undesirable fellow," a psychopath, discipline problem, or gangster.[55] Given that a record of arrest rather than conviction determines the nature of such a prisoner, the truth of guilt is legislated not by the judicial system but, rather, by the police, the prison board, and the Selective Service. Such a practice is the sort Foucault critiques in his analysis of a prison system that continues surveillance of released prisoners and "pursues as a 'delinquent' someone who has acquitted himself as an offender."[56] The surveillance of records thus produces the psychopath and gangster through the selective reading of criminal history. The armed forces cannot draft such a man, because he already is a soldier, one at war with the United States.

For governing bodies to interpret criminals as being at war with the United States effectively legitimizes violence against them. One defining principle of a nation-state is its right to the enactment of violence; such is the legality of war. Imprisonment—the forcible incarceration of a citizen or a population—demonstrates one means by which a nation-state wages war on its own people, and execution demonstrates the most severe expression of that war. Isolating inmates demonstrates the military strategy of *defeat in detail,* where an army beset by a superior number isolates one component of that force to develop localized superiority. There is a race-based precedent for this dating back to the eighteenth century, when Boston Selectmen proclaimed, "If more than two Indians, Negroes or Mulatto servants or slaves were to be found in the streets or highways [ . . . ] every one so found shall be punished at the House of Correction."[57] The eighteenth-century ruling is one of white racist hysteria manifesting itself in the refusal to allow (even to the extent of criminalizing) any social body distinct from its own whiteness.

The military metaphor of divide and conquer seems particularly apt in the case of incarceration, given the understanding that defeat in detail, when applied to prisons, presumes at some level the superior numbers of criminals—which is true inside prisons, where there are proportionally fewer correctional officers and administration. In the South of the early twentieth century, those numbers were similarly disproportionate, and Faulkner's account of Yoknapatawpha County's population as "Whites, 6298; Negroes, 9313," in the map included in the first edition of *Absalom, Absalom!,* speaks to actual population disparities in Mississippi. Jim crow–era laws, through such ill-defined "crimes" as mischief and loitering, effectively criminalized blackness. Criminalization and incarceration therefore function as a strategy of racial containment; individuation demonstrates the fullest extent of that detail,[58] and execution is the grimmest defeat. Prisons defeat in detail through isolation, producing individuals in order to overcome them, and the death penalty does so absolutely. Such individuation, then, favors biographical first causes and the personal histories of Popeye and Christmas.

*Go Down, Moses,* however, presents a different case. Instead of a personal story as diagnostic biography, a social and genealogical history is the only explanation readers have for Butch's criminality and execution. At one point in *Light in August,* Gavin Stevens suggests that Christmas literally embodies the conflict of black blood and white blood. The conflict between black and white blood ending in Butch is staged not in his singular body, but in the sequence of battles perpetuated through the book—the incest and miscegenation that make the book and Butch (the text and the character both) end in death row and the return to Jefferson. The contests of black and white blood begin with Carothers McCaslin's presumed rape of Eunice and their daughter, Tomasina, and continue in her son, Tomey's Turl, fleeing from his half brothers and dealing the cards to Hubert Beauchamp. The blood feud carries on in Lucas's violent physical contest with Zack and battle of wits with Roth thereafter, the same Roth who sees Butch leave Jefferson. Butch lacks a personal diagnostic biography, but his genealogy locates him as having emerged from a history of racial violence.

At first glance, Christmas and Butch, their deaths, and the histories that precede them all seem quite different. Readers have substantial access to Christmas's thoughts, actions, and perceptions leading up to his crime and following it, and we have a fairly clear sense of Joanna Burden's death. Beauchamp remains a cipher, his story brief, the murdered policeman unknown, and Butch's own culpability for the crime far less known than Christmas's. Also, Faulkner renders Christmas's execution at the hands of a single rogue deputy in horrific detail, while the scene of Beauchamp's death by anonymous penitentiary officials is textually absent. Christmas's personal history, which much of the novel comprises, offers the forces of race, childhood experience, and circumstance to shape the hand that holds the razor. Since we know virtually nothing of Samuel Worsham Beauchamp's narrative, it is neither *Sanctuary*'s brief interlude of Freudian coda nor *Light in August*'s lengthier description of Christmas's upbringing, but the acts of generations scripting his end. However, despite the differences between the streams of action that lead to the executions, and to the wake that follows each, Faulkner includes textual cues that suggest and even demand a paired reading, particularly in the dual appearances of District Attorney Gavin Stevens.

Stevens appears at the close of each novel as a sort of psychopomp, shepherd of the dead and arranger of funerals. In each case, he negotiates with the condemned men's grandmothers to make sense of the raced deaths of their grandsons. In *Light in August,* Stevens is the "District Attorney, a Harvard graduate, a Phi Beta Kappa: a tall, loosejointed man with a constant cob pipe, with an untidy mop of irongray hair, wearing always loose and unpressed dark gray clothes."[59] Clearly Faulkner has his mind on that description when he writes the attorney ten years later in *Go Down, Moses* as having "a wild shock of prematurely white hair," "a thin, intelligent, unstable face, a rumpled linen suit [ . . . ] Phi Beta Kappa, Harvard, Ph.D."[60] In the earlier novel, the lawyer imagines Christmas's end for his friend the professor, a proxy for readers of the novel. He plays the role Shreve makes axiomatic for Faulkner's most acclaimed work, the "let me play a while now,"[61] toward which so many scholars have gestured as the crux of Faulkner's most involved narratives, the hinge of meaning making where various audiences, including readers, share in narration.

Part of Stevens's play in the narrative is a lengthy account of Christmas's vexed escape attempt, which the attorney describes in terms of competing black and white blood. Faulkner critic Jay Watson indicts that racializing as "at best shaky, at worst racist and absurd."[62] However, Stevens undercuts his narrative authority with regard to what the grandmother, Mrs. Hines, might have told Christmas before his doomed escape, when he admits, "But of course I dont know what she told him. I dont believe that any man could reconstruct that scene."[63] Not any single narrator in *Light in August* can tell the story, but a decade later, several might. Narrative reconstruction is method and topic of that central section of "The Bear," where Cass and Ike mirror Shreve and Quentin, retelling not only much of the narrative to that point, but also the Civil War and Reconstruction.

The Gavin Stevens at the end of *Go Down, Moses* does not tell the story of Butch, whom he knows, remembers, and believes to be a "bad seed"; he does not because he cannot. Instead of assuming the role of narrator for a story not his own, as does the deputy who tells Rider's story but remains unmoved by it, Stevens is less narrator than actor at the end, less unmoved than constantly in motion through Jefferson's square, from his office to that of the newspaper editor, back to his office, back to the newspaper, then from "store to store and office to office about the square," then to Miss Worsham's. Stevens is no analysand on a couch, but a man of two minds out in the city, believing Butch a "bad seed" but offering time and money for his return.[64] Stevens has added to Worsham's twenty-five dollars what change he collects from the businesses in the square and nearly two hundred dollars out of his and the editor's pockets to buy Butch's passage back to Jefferson.

That return figures differently to those who bring him back, and not only in terms of money. To his grandmother, Molly Worsham Beauchamp,[65] Butch operates in symbolic, biblical terms—Benjamin sold by pharaoh; to Stevens, Butch is the responsibility of a white, middle-class community. While first convinced that the death that has not happened yet can be ignored or concealed, Stevens, at the unmade bequest of a woman he barely knows, ends up footing much of the bill—in labor, time, and money—for bringing the body back to Jefferson. His act is an acknowledgment of half-understood responsibility. In *Light in August,* Christmas bears a personal guilt, which sets him to self-destructive behavior such as taking the braggart Lucas as his partner in the moonshine operation or confronting the black parishioners. *Go Down, Moses,* in contrast, features a social responsibility in Stevens's work to have the town bring home its own, funds gathered as coins in a door-to-door mission to retrieve a man described in Stevens's own words as "a dead nigger" but acknowledged in his effort as a native son of Jefferson.[66]

Stevens's concluding actions and their result demonstrate a far-richer model of community than the singular town whose memory Christmas is to haunt. Beauchamp does not vanish into memory but returns to become materially present in town, as the funeral procession circles the twin bastions of the New South, the "Confederate monument and the courthouse,"[67] to bury him just outside it. The sign passed—"Jefferson. Corporate Limit"—marks Butch's return to the social body, his life and death to be recorded in the public voice of the local newspaper at Molly's demand. Butch's relationship with the social sphere, then, represents a different sort from that of Christmas, the mixed-race criminal of a decade before. Faulkner offers Christmas's isolated individuality in terms of an atomistic self, and the location of that self—"Here I am"—is an acceptance of punishment. Elsewhere in *Light in August,* Byron Bunch describes that self-declaration as "I-Am," "the relinquishment of which is usually death."[68] Ten years later, in *Go Down, Moses,* Faulkner's Beauchamp is claimed by a wider social system that acknowledges his body as part of a "We-Are" when he returns to the town's corporate body, the simultaneity of collective and singular that is Jefferson. In *Light in August,* Jefferson as a town often has a single and typically white point of view. Of Bunch's Saturday work, "the town itself or that part of it which remembers or thinks about him, believe that he does it for the overtime."[69] That unified point of view appears again at Christmas's death and assumption to memory, when Jefferson knows, remembers, and believes as one mind.

The differences between this conclusion and the one of *Go Down, Moses* are tremendous. Jefferson's town square in the latter novel is not that a priori monolith, but is divided far more deeply. Stevens must call on the town's members individually in his breathless request for funeral funds: "It's to bring a dead nigger home. It's for Miss Worsham. Never mind about a paper to sign: just give me a dollar. Or a half a dollar then. Or a quarter then."[70] Like Lucas facing Zack in the novel's episode "The Fire and the Hearth," Gavin is going to do something, then other people are going to do something, and then it will all end, and be all right.

Of course, it will not be all right. History is not corrected so easily; accounts are not so simply set in balance. However, Stevens succeeds in some regard when he hails townspeople, calling on them with his rote speech for donation without writ petition or receipt, a sort of Progressive activist. What he gains offsets his and the editor's personal expenditure, but the change largely gathers the crowd itself, the body of people to receive the casket, a reception narrated not as one unified memory or a single opinion, but as a crowd described in the differences of those who come to watch. They are "the number of people, Negroes and whites both." They are the "idle white men and youths and small boys and probably half a hundred Negroes, men and women too." They are those "who had given Stevens the dollars and half-dollars and quarters and the ones who had not."[71] No longer a monolith, Jefferson is now black and white, young and old, men and women, jobless and workers and businessmen, an audience made of their differences of race, age, gender, and class that nevertheless, however briefly, becomes one crowd of watchers to witness the history that Molly demands be recorded. It is no request she makes of the editor, but a command: "You put hit in de paper. All of hit."[72] Where Christmas somehow enters an imaginary, unconscious memory of a singular town, Butch's staged return before an audience and entry into the records of history are conceived and midwifed, bought and paid for by four people working and paying together, the four who ride behind the body: Molly Beauchamp, Miss Worsham, the newspaper editor, and Stevens.

I do not mean to suggest that Butch's funeral and the audience for that return are the saving grace of *Go Down, Moses,* its relief, a reparation or absolution of racial injustice, letting anyone off the hook. Faulkner describes the editor and the attorney in an ironic register, as "the designated paladin of justice and truth and right" and "the Heidelberg Ph.D.," respectively.[73] Their acceptance of responsibility is constantly forced upon them, directed by others—"other" in terms of race and gender—such as Molly Beauchamp and Miss Worsham. Stevens agrees to account for Butch's death, to become responsible in a manner that does not level the balance but acknowledges the existence of a racial debt.

Many critics have missed this. Erik Dussere compares the ledgers in the fourth section of "The Bear" in *Go Down, Moses* with Toni Morrison's *Beloved* (1987) and *Sula* (1982) to draw excellent points regarding the challenge to and impossibility of balancing the historical debt of slavery.[74] However, by restricting his reading of *Go Down, Moses* entirely to "The Bear"—a common misreading of the novel—he misses the role Butch's return plays. Phillip Weinstein, rather than ignoring him entirely, reads Butch as "not there" and at some level Faulkner's failure.[75] Similarly, Eric Sundquist suggests *Go Down, Moses* would be better off without Butch, a consequence of the aforementioned common misreading of the text as primarily or only Isaac McCaslin's story. In Sundquist's survey of Faulkner's writing from 1929 to 1942 and in a landmark critique, an early component of the more historically and culturally nuanced approaches developed in Americanist study through the 1980s and 1990s, he suggests that *Go Down, Moses* would be improved if it ended with "Delta Autumn."[76]

I am not suggesting that Butch is the novel's focal point, a move akin to Thadious M. Davis's gambit in *Games of Property: Law, Race, Gender, and Faulkner's* Go Down, Moses *(2003)*[77] of treating Tomey's Turl as the main character of the novel. However, reading him as "not there" or wishing him gone misreads what I am suggesting is one of the dominant narrative trajectories that structure the novel, which is not a novel of Aristotelian accord of time and place, or one of organic unity and fulfilling the modernist emphasis on the external world interpreted by any particular consciousness. Instead, the framework for the novel is a patchwork history, disjointed and barely held together by the struggle for its making and telling, its span over a century, narratively suturing slavery to jim crow and lynching, to racial incarceration and execution. The fictional Northern court convicts Butch and sends him to death; however, the townspeople of Jefferson assemble as a court of public opinion present for his (and their) judgment. Lynching demonstrates the complete equation of courts of public opinion with judicial process in the execution of mob "justice"—such is the case in these novels for Goodwin, Christmas, and Rider. *Go Down, Moses,* in its final pages, presents a different resolution, in which Faulkner, through his proxy Stevens, painstakingly recalls the body of Butch and brings together a public to witness the return.

The analysis of Faulkner's *Go Down, Moses,* in particular, occupies a chapter of this book precisely because of that previously unremarked but crucial strand of narrative coherence. The cultural history the novel charts and its link of slavery to jim crow–era lynching and to incarceration provide an organizing principle, as they suggest a decisive response to the question critics have raised since the book's publication as to whether it even has a discernible structure. Furthermore, to expect from the novel a conventional narrative gravitating around a main character has led many to misread Isaac McCaslin as the novel's protagonist, irrespective of his absence from many of its episodes and conflicts. Doing so mistakenly places white masculinity at the center of history, even though much of the novel's power develops through a black family's resistance to both marginalization and various practices of racial control.

*Go Down, Moses* offers, in that last instance, a thick description of how history is staged in a community made up of the tension between singular and plural, a collective of individuals called together, however briefly. *Light in August* relies on an exhausted rhetoric of redemption to imagine social unity at Christmas's death in the first of its three closures. *Sanctuary* does not even offer that much in its two endings, the first of which is the nearly parodic account of Popeye's execution, when Popeye's curt scaffold request for the sheriff to fix his hair receives the reply, "I'll fix it for you," as the trapdoor opens.[78] That death sentence also precedes flights of language, though the turn to Temple seems not redemption but indictment. She departs with her father from a "gray day, a gray summer, a gray year" into dissolution, and in the final line into "the embrace of the season of rain and death."[79] *Go Down, Moses* does not rely on either strategy: the exhausted and unbelievable siren over Christmas's assumption to collective memory, or the ironic dissonance of execution quips juxtaposed with Temple's fading into a Baudelairean vignette in three anapests and an iamb. In contrast, Faulkner offers the two finales of the titular "Go Down, Moses" in the register of simple, circumstantial description, Butch stripped and shaved before his execution, and Stevens commenting that he has been away from his office these past two days.

Still, it is not Stevens's last words but Butch's final sentence that grows richer in a reappraisal of the final section of the novel—"What will that matter to me?" In the atomistic terms of the hardman, it will not matter at all, for the death of the self is the end of history. However, it does not end there, because Butch does not end there. Stevens thinks it ends—"it's all over and done and finished"—when Molly Beauchamp sees her grandson "come home right."[80] That echo of Lucas seems as unlikely to resolve finally the racial and filial tensions of Lucas's own thoughts as he faces Zack: *"He will do something and then I will do something and it will be all over."*[81] Butch's death and homecoming are recorded in the paper, written down, but that cannot finish the matter completely. As the ledger section of "The Bear" emphasizes, and what the novel's reworking of Faulkner's previous themes of criminality and human agency demonstrates, what is written down allows for its own reading and rewriting.

It has become something of an accepted practice to read Faulkner as writing a sort of Southern history in Yoknapatawpha County. Toni Morrison, whose own work, like Faulkner's, shows a deep commitment to telling history, suggests that her investment in reading Faulkner and his "subjects had something to do with my desire to find out something about this country and that artistic articulation of its past that was not available in history."[82] In *Go Down, Moses,* in particular, that history and its writing simultaneously remain personal and extend into a broader cultural frame. Michael Grimwood does well in treating Faulkner's final version of *Go Down, Moses* as the author's redress for his negative stereotyping of blackness in some of the stories that, in their aggregate, served as an early draft of the novel.[83]

However, there is a larger history and broader acknowledgment the novel makes. A provocative passage from *Intruder in the Dust* proclaims that "not courthouses nor even churches but jails were the true records of a county's, a community's history," and the Gavin Stevens of *Requiem for a Nun* similarly locates "the history of a community" as being written in "the walls of the jail."[84] Those later novels demonstrate the racial expectation of criminality, as Lucas Beauchamp spends most of *Intruder in the Dust* anticipating a lynch mob motivated because he refuses to "*be a nigger,*" and Nancy Mannigoe is termed ten times over a "nigger dope-fiend whore" or variations thereof.[85] It is in *Go Down, Moses* that Faulkner offers his first and fullest account of the historical process criminalizing blackness, where social history in large part defined by race shapes human agency, from Butch's presumed criminality to the community that sees the executed criminal return home. In Faulkner's South, there are painful connections between lynching and execution, and between slavery and imprisonment. These too need to be put in the paper—so that, like Molly Beauchamp, we know where to look.

# 3

# Soul on Ice,
# Schizoanalysis, and
# the Subject of Imprisonment

> From the beginning, America has been a schizophrenic nation.
>
> —Eldridge Cleaver, *Soul on Ice*[1]

IN THE DECADES following the publication of *Go Down, Moses*, the history equating blackness and criminality that contributed to containing black men in prison in Faulkner's South became a matter not of region but of nation, even as Southern politics and problems became national matters in the 1950s and 1960s. The rise of the South might be charted in any number of ways, including Lyndon Johnson's presidency in 1964 as the first elected Southerner in ninety-two years, Texas Representative Sam Rayburn's extended tenure as House Speaker from 1949 to 1961, and, specifically regarding prison policy, the increasing Southern leadership of the American Correctional Association, formerly the American Prison Association.[2] Such Southern representation mandated its own difficult negotiation of regional and national conflicts, and Johnson capitulated to Southern states in limiting the civil rights bills he oversaw in 1957 and 1960 as Texas senator and majority leader. Thereafter, the national political implications of Southern racism, of social and electoral disenfranchisement, like the compromises of one hundred years before, could no longer be reconciled.

The divisions were most stark in the violence and riots of the first of the "long, hot summers" surrounding the 1964 Civil Rights Act and 1965 Voting Rights Act, the highest profile of Johnson's "Great Society" initiatives, enforced by federal troops, unlike the earlier toothless recommendations. The civil rights ruling, in particular, provided a constitutional basis for prison reform. For example, in 1970 the U.S. District Court in Arkansas ruled, in a culmination of a series of cases through the late 1960s, that the entire state's prison system violated prisoners' civil rights, constituting cruel and unusual punishment under the Eighth Amendment.[3] Prison history remains inseparable from the tension between the nation's racism and its ideals of liberty and equality.

The year 1968 and the decade that followed marked a fundamental change in the direction of the nation as embodied in the stories of its prisoners, according to both Cleaver's *Soul on Ice* and the views of prison officials as recorded in the annual conference meeting transcripts of the American Correctional Association, the nation's preeminent organization of prison administrators and policy makers. This chapter charts the shift from revolutionary possibility—from politicized racial and criminal identities and the social responsibility for them—to a nation exhausted by perceived threats of cultural change, race, crime, and plural identity. *Soul on Ice* documents the formation of the identity of a prisoner in a manner that gained Cleaver release due to the efforts of activist supporters, though he fled the country shortly thereafter following a violent confrontation between the Black Panthers and the police. In *Soul on Ice* Cleaver both witnesses and appraises. First, he testifies on behalf of prisoners, representing them to those outside, enacting a sort of habeas corpus in the cultural imagination. Second, Cleaver offers a strategy of cultural psychoanalysis to describe the racial divide in a manner resonant with what Deleuze and Guattari later termed "schizoanalysis." The prominence of Cleaver's prison writing in the late 1960s left its mark in history, which echoed in the discourse of those he critiqued, from then California Governor Ronald Reagan to the prison officials of the ACA.

However, in the years immediately following *Soul on Ice,* the nation experienced a radical foreclosure in the potential for alternatives to imprisonment, due to the expansion of criminalization and sentencing through the Rockefeller drug laws, the perceived lack of alternatives in treatment, and the fear of black militancy. This shift in criminal–justice practice contributed to the widespread imagination of prisoners as violent, dangerous, and evil, even as prisons grew over-crowded, filling with nonviolent offenders. Perhaps no one embod-ied this contradiction of black masculinity as criminally violent and necessarily revolutionary better than Cleaver himself: prisoner, Black Panther, best-selling author, and presidential candidate.

*Soul on Ice* is not an idiosyncratic account of imprisonment pulled from the dustbin of history, but is instead indicative, in the promi-nence at its release and resonance with the historical record of the ACA transcripts, of larger cultural trends both contributing to and affected by U.S. prison policy. Cleaver describes an identity forma-tion, a process of "becoming" in prison, taking place both in history and with his various and sometimes conflicting desires. While my argument makes some use of theoretical vocabularies, it is not an exclusively psychoanalytic account of the degree to which Cleaver describes his sense of self. Instead, my analysis shows how *Soul on Ice* offers vital testimony at a critical period in U.S. prison policy, a time when the possibility of radical change tilted first to progressive reform and veered then to an extreme expansion of incarceration. A rich history of the ACA conference proceedings remains to be written. What follows is, first, an account of discussions of race and social change at those meetings immediately after the publication of *Soul on Ice;* second, a demonstration of the similarities between Cleaver's writing and Deleuze and Guattari's description of schizoanalysis; and third, a demonstration of how the social psychoanalysis performed in *Soul on Ice* clarifies the reactions of ACA wardens and administrators to Cleaver's book. Reading from our own historical vantage point of decades later, we see more clearly the opportunities lost then to redefine the ruthless equation of criminality with black masculinity and, in the wake of the even more oppressive racial incarceration that has taken place since, the increased urgency of challenging that racism now.

Cleaver documents his tumultuous time in the unique register of *Soul on Ice:* alternately autobiography; literary criticism; myth; cultural theory; and a prison-cell view of the mid-1960s, the Watts riots, pro-tests of the Vietnam War, and the conflicts of race, class, and gender in the history of his now. It quickly sold more than a million copies and was named a Book of the Year of 1968 by the *New York Times.*[4] Cleaver leveraged such prominence to run for president with the Peace and Freedom Party, a cross-racial alliance between that group of largely young white radicals and the Black Panther Party. By 1979, he had swapped extremes, a wholesale switch from revolutionary to reactionary.[5] However, the Cleaver of 1968 looks to the hope of revolution and provides a critical account of his crimes and imprisonment as they relate to U.S. cultural history in the 1960s. He presents a book-length and arguably nonfictional testimonial of incarceration, even as such writing soon thereafter provided the basis for several Supreme Court cases concerning the development of U.S. prisoners' right to self-representation.[6] Like those plaintiffs, Cleaver contests *for* representation and *against* silencing, and his writing demonstrates an imperative to confront readers with history. Furthermore, like the officials of the ACA, Cleaver is shaped by his historical moment even as he writes the words that in part define that history.

His *Soul on Ice* is a difficult book. There is of course his immediate acknowledgment that "I've been a rapist"—and it is easy enough to stop there, and perhaps many readers do.[7] Moreover, to judge the book by its cover is to misread it entirely. The back of most paperback editions identifies it as a "spiritual autobiography" or "classic autobiography," while the front cover operates in the convention of a whole body of writing by black prisoners and former prisoners[8] which *Soul on Ice* is a both a part of and apart from: Cleaver's face in a close-up black-and-white photograph, a view similar to the most common book jackets of *The Autobiography of Malcolm X* (1964), George Jackson's *Soledad Brother* (1970), and Rubin "Hurricane" Carter's *The Sixteenth Round* (1974). *Soul on Ice,* however, is far more a work of cultural theory and criticism than it is any sort of conventional autobiography, its discursive legacy in Frantz Fanon more than in Malcolm X. Cleaver's identity of prisoner number A-29498—a conceit of prison identity repeated by Carter in his biography and by Himes in at least two short stories[9]—is the result of his incarceration, but its meanings and effects are offered less in personal than national history.

Of its four parts, only the initial "On Becoming" of "Part One: Letters from Prison" conducts even a partially retrospective account of the author's life in the vein of Malcolm X, and the subsequent eight letters are snapshots of the time of their writing, during 1965, offered out of chronological sequence. "Part Three: Prelude to Love—Three Letters" conducts a correspondence between Cleaver and his lawyer and is by far the shortest section, shorter than some of the individual chapters of parts two and four. The analysis conducted in those sections, the longest parts of the book, distances itself rhetorically from the "I" so prevalent in the letters of parts one and three, which feature a litany of "I was eighteen years old," "I was black," "I love you," "I hate you," "I declared myself for Malcolm X," "I seek the profound," etc. The identity of the perceiving eye of parts two and four is occasionally the first person, but rather than limiting itself to the close quarters of self-reflection, the expository gaze spans culture and history: youth activism, the racial connotations of boxing and literature, the Vietnam War and riot suppression as concomitant police actions, the legacies of slavery—all offered with wry wit in tracing their connections. To read *Soul on Ice* as Cleaver's life story is to undo its outward direction and to read the political as personal, cultural history as a person's past, and theory and criticism as autobiography, a reading that overturns the trajectory the text itself maintains, wherein the self is constituted in and understood through its social investments.[10]

Cleaver's self-declarative, autoperformative *prison sentence*—nine years, the time during which he "began to form a concept of what it meant to be black in white America"[11]—writes him into becoming with and through the very awareness that only in communication does a self-aware subjectivity emerge. There are poststructuralist resonances to that equation of language and the subject, but the wording of the Supreme Court ruling in favor of the authority of writ lawyers supports it as well. *Johnson v. Avery* (1969) upheld a district court decision against a prison regulation prohibiting writ lawyers (prisoners serving as legal representatives for other prisoners) because, according to the court, that ordinance had "the effect of barring illiterate prisoners from access to federal habeas corpus." In basing their ruling on habeas corpus, the court effectively equated one prisoner representing another's legal interests in writing with the actual physical presence of that prisoner in the courtroom. In that decision, Justices Hugo Black and Byron White dissented, suggesting that the writ lawyer was less "motivated by altruism rather than by self-aggrandizement, profit, or power." While an aside might note the circumstantial racing of the dissenting justices' surnames, the emphasis here rests with the majority ruling, the equation of subject and statement.

In 1968, not only Cleaver but also prison wardens and ACA leaders recognized the possibility of radical reform, viewed criminality often as a political matter, and emphasized the factor of race in incarceration. However, through the 1970s diverse strategies of rehabilitation widely disappeared as more frequent and longer sentences became standard, the term "political prisoner" met disparagement, and race dropped as a broad topic, replaced by the problems raised in the over-crowding brought about by increased imprisonment. The domestic "war on crime" effort that Johnson sponsored as the Safe Streets and Crime Control Act passed Congress in 1968 as the Law Enforcement Administration Act, with a $63 million budget that grew ten-fold by 1971 under President Richard Nixon. Nearly half of those increased funds were dedicated to corrections programs, and they dramatically expanded the ACA, while increasing crime rates and perceived failures of imprisonment drew national attention. The sense of social crisis in 1968, the simultaneity of hope and catastrophe, is as apparent in the discussions of wardens and other prison officials of the ACA as it was elsewhere in the United States. In his presidential address, the warden Parker L. Hancock describes the present in terms of radical change, claiming that "the pace of American social revolution is accelerating," and "the past blurs and the future seems uncertain."[12]

Hancock adopts a historically informed approach, claiming that more-severe punishments during cycles of increased crime are both transhistorically phenomenal and counterproductive. Instead, he observes that prisons are adopting a "more enlightened correctional philosophy," including community-based alternatives, increased access of inmates to education, work, and counseling. All told, "Cor-rections today is experimenting with programs that hold promise for the future."[13] He associates university protests with an evolving view of crime, and with the potential for transformation in national culture. "The revolt of youth, as seen in student demonstrations from New York to California," has caused crimes committed in the name of war protest, drug use, and civil protest against racism, and he concludes that "we must reaffirm our traditional values or create new ones."[14] The ACA, like the universities "from New York to California," seemed poised to consider broad cultural changes—specifically, a changed sense of criminality and how prisons might recognize and respond to it. The next few years saw the same points raised in nearly identical terms. A 1970 participant begins:

> It is difficult to speak about corrections today—indeed about any part of the administration of criminal justice—without reference to the massive social changes which are occurring in this country. Tensions

in the black community, a discordant youth culture, an unpopular war which is producing an increasing number of young men convicted of offenses essentially political in nature, raise profound questions about the limits, methods and aims of correctional activities.[15]

The overall tone of presenters during the social unrest between 1968 and 1971, reflective of this quote, was open to reform, optimistic toward change, and accepting of the possibility of broad-based transformation in prison practice.[16]

The beginning of that contentious period saw a split in the perception of criminality and race. In his survey of the representation of imprisonment in common U.S. periodicals, John Sloop identifies the popular view of black male inmates in 1968 as being at the cusp of change. His terms speak directly to characterizations of Cleaver. The view of black inmates as violent and irrational felons shifts to a divide between, on the one hand, revolutionaries and, on the other, irredeemably dangerous criminals, though potentially violent either way. In contrast, white male prisoners remain "forever open for rehabilitation."[17] The transcripts of the ACA largely follow that split perception of black inmates. In the years immediately following 1968, discussions of black inmates are polarized sharply between accounts that recognize a legitimate political grievance for black prisoners, and descriptions that are derisive and occasionally hysterical.

The more marginal view from the radical right includes a U.S. Army major and director of mental hygiene, who offers a sharply critical description of the "Militant Black: A Correctional Problem." The administrator portrays such activists in terms of generally lower intelligence scores, possessing "infantile, narcissistic needs," psychological disorders "of psychotic proportions"; to him activists are highly paranoid, a "primordial people using primitive functioning."[18] The director suggests that education in black history, group counseling, and role-playing can prove constructive for borderline cases, but that "the very militant inmate" is a lost cause, demanding psychiatric hospitalization and segregation.[19] In the major's view, the black militant cannot be a U.S. soldier, because he is already at war with the United States, a matter clarified when a later participant, an associate warden, describes Cleaver and those like him as having committed an "act of war against the state."[20] At this same time, the formation of a chapter of the Black Panthers at Angola State Prison prompted its associate warden to claim that "a certain type of militant or revolutionary inmate, maybe even a Communist type" must remain in constant isolation.[21]

That view from the radical right was not the norm in the ACA. A director of a correctional council in 1969 draws from empirical research to depict an "exaggerated" fear of crime in big cities, where those living in the safest neighborhoods are the most afraid of violent offenses. He criticizes the predominantly white and affluent citizens who make baseless demands that police begin "cracking down on black militants."[22] The next year, District Court Judge Leon Higginbotham asked, "Is Yesterday's Racism Relevant Today in Corrections?" The answer, he implies, is yes. The judge traces a Philadelphia prison superintendent's blame of a riot on "hard-core black militants" to the U.S. Constitutional Convention and the revisions to the constitution that allowed for slavery, then to the 1857 Dred Scott case, then to *Plessy v. Ferguson*.[23] From 1968 to 1972, the divide over the perceptions of black inmates' activism and the surrounding violence seems informed not just by a conservative or liberal bias, but by the degree to which those on one side or the other are prepared to situate contemporary problems in a historical framework.

The conflicting views came to a head in 1972, the first recorded meeting of the ACA after inmates revolted in Attica Prison in New York, September 9–13, 1971, where forty-three people died, eleven of them hostages, thirty-nine shot by the state troopers sent by Governor Nelson Rockefeller. Rockefeller's Goldman Panel, established to ensure prisoners' rights after the riot, cleared the authorities of any wrongdoing, and the ACA's 1972 panel concerning the "Rights of People" appropriated liberal rhetoric, employing the language of human rights in safeguarding prison authorities against criticism.[24] In 1973 a "tough on crime" posture fueled the changes in the criminal code for drug violations that Rockefeller implemented in New York, including broader criminalization, mandatory sentencing, and longer prison terms.

The revolt at Attica and the state troopers' violent incursion that concluded it galvanized both sides at the next ACA conference. A New York correctional commissioner recognizes that administrators must acknowledge the self-appointed political prisoners and the basis for their arguments regarding racial and class-based adjudication and sentencing. However, he immediately dismisses those concerns— while "the problem is there [ . . . ] it has no merit" for corrections.[25] The next speaker, an Illinois prison administrator, performs the same reversal, acknowledging that the system of justice is racist and economically discriminatory, but insisting that systemic injustice does not equate to political imprisonment.[26] A chaplain's paper titled "Attica: Anatomy of the New Revolutionary" first cites the prevalence of racism in prisons and the general failure of corrections, then characterizes and subsequently condemns black militancy at length, even including, verbatim, two pages of Black Panther Party materials.[27] The chaplain demands that corrections administrators not confuse legitimate criticism with revolutionary critique.

Other participants found those two inseparable. Also in 1972, Vernon Fox, a Florida State University criminologist, argues that prison officials must maintain an awareness of history—especially slavery—offering statistics of slave populations, quoting at length a deed of slave ownership, and identifying the 1964 and 1965 race riots as another iteration of regularly occurring conflict. Fox argues, "The majority of persons arrested for crimes are white, but the majority of persons sent to prisons in many jurisdictions are black. The social distance and the cultural differentiations have contributed to a new ideology of revolution and social change among many blacks, an ideology intensely resisted by the white power structure." He claims that a history of inequity produces contemporary racism in law enforcement, courtrooms, and prisons, thereby resulting in both an ideology of black resistance and a white reactionary response.[28] He concludes with a detailed account of the violence at Soledad Prison from 1970 to 1971 and its fallout, including the deaths of Jonathan and George Jackson, tracing the latter's shooting as the immediate reason for the riot at Attica. Fox proposes that the larger social causes of racism underlie incarceration patterns and can be addressed only through education involving cultural history both in and out of prisons. Several other papers in that session also support the necessity of understanding contemporary problems in prison as the product of a history of racism and implicated in broader social struggles outside of imprisonment.[29]

Cleaver is linked directly to the accounts of these administrators. Fox traces the politicizing of black prisoners to the writings of Malcolm X, Cleaver, and George Jackson. Another paper offers a similar reading list, citing *Soul on Ice* twice. The presenter points out how blackness becomes identified with criminality in the uncritical diagnosis that is part of the sociology of corrections.[30] Culturally sensitive education could address that matter, according to E. Eugene

Miller's "Necessary Preconditions to Achieving Cultural Awareness." He opens by mocking his very invitation to speak on that topic because he had worked with blacks and Native Americans and thus was presumed able to speak knowledgeably, giving a fifteen-minute synopsis of the culture of each. He interprets this very invitation as symptomatic of the white racist "paternalism" he argues against. He also mentions an ACA position paper published earlier that year acknowledging "that racism has and does exist in corrections." He argues for knowledge of and respect for cultural difference and ends with a call for an identification of an "us" between corrections administrators and a "them" of prisoners "without regard to race, color, or creed."[31] The call for such specific identification between prisoners and those who imprison is a rare one—though it repeats a 1929 participant who says of nonprisoners and prisoners alike, "All are brothers under the skin."[32] Miller's encouragement for culturally sensitive history paradoxically echoes the more reactionary army major's support of black history classes. Presumably the major does not envision them being taught by Cleaver, who led such classes in prison.[33]

However, as quickly as the storm of Attica raised discussion of race in the ACA in 1972, those voices almost entirely disappeared. The legitimacy of political prisoners had been a central issue in eight presentations from 1968 to 1972, but over the next seven years it faded to obscurity or derision.[34] However, in 1979, both plenary addresses deal centrally with race and imprisonment, including the keynote address, "Race, Crime, and Corrections" by Charles Silberman, and a follow-up by Higginbotham. However, the latter's speech, "Is Slavery Relevant to Corrections Today?," repeats almost verbatim, in its title, argument, examples, and language, his 1970 conference paper. Apparently, so few had heard the first time that the same material could serve again nine years later. Questions of race and social struggle were discussed broadly as underlying issues of prison policy and practice from 1968 through 1972. Thereafter, the vast majority of presentations ignored these matters, instead reflecting the national shift in favor of more-frequent and longer sentencing, which precipitated the overcrowding crisis. Numerous participants remarked that correctional systems were shifting away from a rehabilitative paradigm based on psychological classification and treatment, but that no new model had appeared to take its place. The rise of "just desserts"—flat sentencing irrespective of mitigating individual or social circumstances[35]—as the prevalent punishment matched the "tough on crime" rhetoric adopted by Rockefeller, Nixon, and others. They promoted broader and harsher criminalization and incarceration, and thereby initiated the dramatic expansion of imprisonment in the United States beginning in the late 1970s, an increase that has disproportionately affected black men.

*Soul on Ice* in 1968 offered a prescient analysis of the racial divide that saw its harshest expression in the prison populations expanding through the following decades. Cleaver's account of himself demonstrates the struggle to enter history, to communicate an identity beyond that of the prisoner, and he uses various discursive strategies in describing self-conscious identity formation inside prison walls. *Soul on Ice* writes the author as a tense reflection of a larger national history that is as much of two minds as the divided view of black militancy in the ACA. Cleaver writes, "From the beginning, America has been a schizophrenic nation. Its two conflicting images of itself were never reconciled": the white image of "freedom and justice for all" and the black image of oppression and resistance.[36] Cleaver employs "schizophrenia" as the popular misreading of multiple personality disorder. In the medical discourse of psychology and the study of disorders of the brain, schizophrenia is actually a dissociation from reality, the inability of the subject to engage the world around him or her. However, Cleaver treats schizophrenia in plural and racial terms that make explicit the power differential in culture, a disease of the *social* body that produces a failure to acknowledge the fault lines of history, the cultural differences that must be named and engaged. Though Cleaver generally views the term negatively, the more positive description in how Deleuze and Guattari theorize it clarifies aspects of *Soul on Ice*.

The titular aim of Deleuze and Guattari's *Anti-Oedipus* is the rejection of the oedipal "I," the autonomous, unified self, in which Oedipus is the offspring of Freud and Lacan, initiated in the divorce from totality in a psychoanalytic version of the paradox of the Fall. The loss of completeness is the split from the imaginary whole, the cause of the lack upon which the sense of self is predicated, the *manque-à-être,* the lack that is the "want-to-be."[37] Deleuze and Guattari turn to Friedrich Nietzsche and Antonin Artaud for a different sense of self: if *"every name in history is I,"* then "I have been my father and I have been my son."[38] "I" thereby loses its power. Their hypothetical schizophrenic says, "'I won't say *I* any more, I'll never utter the word again; it's just too damn stupid. Every time I hear it, I'll use the third person instead, if I happen to remember to. If it amuses them. And it won't make one bit of difference.' And if he does chance to utter the word *I* again, that won't make any difference either. He is too far removed from these problems, too far past them."[39] Writing against psychoanalysis means overwriting its privileged categories with those of the schizoanalytic: replacing the oedipal subject with the schizophrenic, the individual with the social, the symbolic with the concrete, the expressive with the productive, and the theatrical with the historical.[40] The schizophrenic is an ever-shifting body of "we's," and schizoanalysis is the project of tracing such various social investments.

Schizoanalysis works against oedipalization, an individualization that is less a matter of a Freudian sexual dynamic of desire for the mother than desire for the Other, the strategy by which selfhood itself is interpellated, brought into being through divorce from an imaginary whole and thereby defined by the lack of the whole it desires. Paranoia is a condition of oedipalization whereby the self misrecognizes its autonomy, a separate-but-equal individuality situated in a world of stable meaning. Paranoia thus describes a state in which meaning is one with fact, social structures are inviolable, and power maintains an a priori fixity not in institutions but through imaginary unity under a God-ordained leader. Schizoanalysis attacks the primacy of "I" and its stable singularities. Of course the joke is that "I" saturates their text and Cleaver's as well, and "I won't say *I*" doubly violates itself, invoking the forbidden as both the subject and the object of saying, of discourse. However, the contradiction does not make any difference for those who situate themselves beyond these difficulties, as such plural selves are accustomed to living with contradictions.

Cleaver describes identity in a manner that gains clarity when understood in terms of the Deleuzo-Guattarian schizophrenic. Cleaver writes, "I was very familiar with the Eldridge who came to prison, but that Eldridge no longer exists. And the one I am now is in some ways a stranger to me. You may find this very difficult to understand but it is very easy for one in prison to lose his sense of self."[41] Certainly for the prisoner, this claim is a self-serving dodge. Imprisonment rests upon the assumption that the person in prison is the same one who was determined in court to be a criminal; to be any other than the "Eldridge who came to prison" is to no longer need to be imprisoned, as he has been corrected, reformed. However, Cleaver's point is that the subject in history is ever in flux. For the self to be constituted in its social investments—in the first passage after the opening section, "On Becoming," these identities include being a prisoner, an African-American, and a convicted rapist, as well as having a "Higher Uneducation"[42]—is to shift in the ebb and flow of those partial and conflicting participations in the social. Imprisonment in its practice, as described in *Soul on Ice,* seeks to oedipalize; it individualizes, isolates, and alienates, produces paranoia and surpasses that paranoia, such that the question in the condition of Cleaver's imprisonment is not, Am I paranoid? but Am I paranoid enough? He resists that oedipalization, tracing different models of the subject in history, actor and acted upon, the subject *of* and subject *to,* a tension of identity and agency perhaps written most severely in the position of prisoners.[43]

Cleaver's prison writing of 1968 demonstrates the implication of imprisonment in broader historical and cultural contexts, the black man in prison as part of a larger network of misplaced desires. *Soul on Ice* functions to a significant degree as an integrated schizoanalytic critique as described in *Anti-Oedipus:* the combination of radical politics, aesthetics, and historical analysis, the synthesis of "the artistic machine, the analytic machine, and the revolutionary machine." In a definitive passage of such practice, Deleuze and Guattari turn to a letter from Vincent van Gogh to Artaud, an image of prison escape, a wall "penetrated with a file," where the effort is not escape but "at once the wall, the breaking through this wall, and the failures of the breakthrough."[44] The metaphor of imprisonment, the simultaneity of the wall and the breaking of it, and the integrated critique all aptly describe *Soul on Ice.* At a literal level Cleaver acknowledges that the political project of the book keeps him incarcerated: "If I had followed the path laid down for me by the officials, I'd undoubtedly have long since been out of prison."[45] The text itself, in its account of the radicalization that Cleaver claims prolongs his stay, is the wall, while the letters back and forth in and out of prison and his own becoming are the breakthrough. The failures of that breakthrough might be viewed as the lack of the transformation of U.S. domestic and foreign policy that Cleaver envisioned. The breakthrough and its failure are bound to the degree to which the self Cleaver writes is a subject constituted in history, even as he tries to rupture that history, not break from it, but fracture history itself—for what else is revolution, whether viewed by the ACA leadership or hailed by Cleaver, but the shattering of history?

Cleaver in 1968 was in search of revolution, a political project that superseded divisions of incarceration and race. He regularly identifies with the young white and black protesters of 1965, some of whom commit the political crimes described by the ACA, and points out his desire to "look with roving eyes for a new John Brown," claiming that Malcolm X would "accept John Brown [to the Organization of Afro-American Unity] if he were around today." Cleaver further claims that the "ghost of John Brown is creeping through suburbia," an image he returns to in his *Post-Prison Writings:* "a second Civil War, with thousands of white John Browns fighting on the side of the blacks, plunging America into the depths of its most desperate nightmare on the way to realizing the American Dream."[46] In an echo of Cleaver, Deleuze and Guattari draw relationships between, if not equate outright, the political radical with the black prisoner. In calling to "become black like John Brown.[,] George Jackson,"[47] blackness marks not abjectness or complex inferiority but revolutionary consciousness, even as it overwrites skin with politics. The degree to which race as a signifier slips from skin color to radical action is a gesture to the revolt against barriers of racial difference and oppression Cleaver views as epitomized in imprisonment. Speaking for himself becomes the means by which he can invite cross-racial identification.

*Soul on Ice* demonstrates Cleaver's effort to articulate himself, to speak his position in and view from prison and thereby reorient himself (and thereby those who identify with him) politically and personally, to put his individual situation in the larger context of U.S. racial history—the exact strategy engaged by Fox, Higginbotham, and others in the ACA. Much of *Soul on Ice* accounts for the acts of the self historically, and it often reads like a litany of pairings of the personal and historical: Cleaver's imprisonment and *Brown v. Board of Education,* his violently divided and raced sexual desire and the lynching of Emmitt Till.[48] The implied argument is that personal acts are best understood within narratives larger than personal history. The Cleaver of the book is schizophrenic, in Deleuze and Guattari's terms. His account of his psychiatric treatment in prison grows in focus and importance when viewed in the context of Deleuze and Guattari's exchange of the autonomy of Oedipus for the social subject in history:

I had several sessions with a psychiatrist. His conclusion was that I hated my mother. How he arrived at this conclusion I'll never know, because he knew nothing about my mother; and when he'd asked me questions I would answer him with absurd lies. What revolted me about him was that he had heard me denouncing whites, yet each time he interviewed me he deliberately guided the conversation back to my family life, to my childhood. That in itself was alright [*sic*], but he deliberately blocked all my attempts to bring out the racial question.[49]

This parody of psychoanalytic treatment, the tracing of all experience to the childhood relationship with the mother and the attendant blocking of the desire to address sociocultural concerns, demonstrates Cleaver's rejection of his oedipalization. He instead opts to understand himself in terms of "the dynamics of race relations in America" and a Marxist critique of U.S. capitalism.[50] Deleuze and Guattari describe that shift as the schizophrenic turn from "daddy-mommy" to the "economic and political spheres."[51] The oedipal self impedes the flow in the circuitry of the social, which, in the case of Cleaver, blocks the attempt to rupture the boundaries of skin color and prison walls, to act and write across lines of difference in terms of race and incarceration. In *Soul on Ice*, Cleaver writes against conventional psychoanalysis, as Deleuze and Guattari would later do, the latter even abandoning his personal practice for cultural critique.

Cleaver's rejection of his psychiatric session can be viewed in the comic tone he engages so often and so successfully, as when he applauds the revolutionary possibilities of desiring beefsteaks or prepares to describe the mystery of the holy Trinity as three-in-one oil.[52] However, tricksters regularly mask their masterstrokes in humor; keeping in mind the schizoanalytic imperative—the political psychoanalysis of desire in social bodies—foregrounds the richer implications of Cleaver's argument. Analyst and analysand must alike leave behind the reductive, isolated, and isolating interpretation of personal history for wider contexts. *Soul on Ice* effectively invites the racial history of now to get up from the couch and walk around the city in order to talk about its troubles. Cleaver adopts the theoretical approach of implicating the seemingly autonomous author and book in intertextual relationships with their historical and cultural situations.

The discursive impulse of such contextualization guides Cleaver's best writing in *Soul on Ice* and his short story "The Flashlight," which appeared in *Playboy* in 1969 and won an O. Henry Award. The story features the becoming of the main character, Stacy Mims. He transforms from leader of a band of petty criminals to a loner who uses the titular flashlight to interrupt drug activity in his neighborhood, to a participant in the gang of "Marijuanos." In her commentary in *Eldridge Cleaver* (1991), Kathleen Rout underreads "The Flashlight," missing its emphasis on the social. Overall, her book offers far more a critical (and metacritical) survey of Cleaver's primary writings than a biography, but the story merits less than a page and a half that describes it entirely as a coming-of-age story emphasizing the singular individual, replete with the stock psychoanalytic terms of Freud and Adler both, from "phallic symbol" to "self-assertion."[53] However, Cleaver takes pains to implicate the main character in a particular cultural space, written in social rather than personal history.

The initial description of Stacy is in terms of an incarnate social body composed of himself and his gang members, made in "knowledge of each other, the thick glue of the brotherhood of youth, of their separate selves bound into one."[54] The subsequent thick description of the main character emphasizes the neighborhood as a self-sustaining environment with its own history. However, Cleaver describes it as already receding into the past, both literally, as the dilapidated but historied houses are replaced by projects, and figuratively, as the nearby, diminishing wilderness is cast in terms of the pastoral, from the gang's hunter/gatherer activities there to its "Indian burial ground" and shepherds.[55] The middle passage describes Stacy's own poorly understood resistance to both his gang's criminal activities, which have lost their meaning for him, and the terrorism of surveillance he initiates on the drug users and dealers, until he becomes first their target and then their peer. Cleaver describes the process of becoming in terms of two warring voices in one body—resonating with DuBois's famous claim of "double consciousness," with Gavin Stevens's description of Joe Christmas in *Light in August,* and with a sense of the schizophrenic—as Stacy identifies himself as joining the users and dealers through the ritual of smoking (and presumably later selling) marijuana. "He had the sensation of being two disembodied beings fighting to inhabit one yielding body. His body, offering no resistance, became a battlefield on which two rival armies contended."[56] His identity at the close is that of "Marijuano," part of a different social body than his previous gang.

The story trades on the cachet of Cleaver's fame as a former prisoner and fugitive as of November 1968. The term *prison* appears on each of the first three pages of the story, and it is easy to do as Rout does and read Stacy as Cleaver, who in 1954 first went to prison for selling marijuana, then a felony in California. By 1969 the cultural climate had changed, and a cartoon in the same issue of *Playboy* features a doctor telling his patient, "I want you to lay off that alcohol and switch to pot, Mr. Fuller. Your kidneys are in terrible shape."[57] Also joining Cleaver's story in that issue is the article "Hunger in America" by U.S. Senator Jacob Javits, who had joined Senator and later President Johnson in supporting both the 1957 and 1964 civil rights bills. The story itself chronicles the sort of material and spiritual poverty that precipitates Stacy's pursuit of meaning, which is caught between his desire to act and to belong. In Javits's account, identity becomes a plural, social sense of selfhood defined in space, subculture as a place of mind, described as "that underground world, psychologically as far beneath the consciousness of a city's solid citizens as a city's sewerage system is beneath its streets."[58] Individuals and social groups both are collectives, and ghettoized communities become the cultural unconscious of the society that suppresses them. In a related vein, the two issues of *Playboy* immediately prior to the one featuring "The Flashlight" offer articles on "the demise of Freudianism" that survey psychoanalytic approaches less invested in personal history than in community. So the very psychoanalytic emphases on individuation and personal history that Rout reads in "The Flashlight" are resisted not only in the text itself, but also in the context of its original publication.

Cleaver's own most fully developed theoretical framework of sociohistorical analysis focuses on the racial difference and oppression he describes as blocked in his earlier parody of Freudian psychoanalysis. In "The Allegory of the Black Eunuchs" and "The Primeval Mitosis,"[59] he offers a structure of difference on the twin axes of race and gender, defining black and white men and women with respect to one another in terms of sexual desire, power, body, and mind, all key points of reference in *Anti-Oedipus* as well. Cleaver identifies four allegorical types. The white man as Omnipotent Administrator—the mind of systemic power suffering from the "negation and abdication of his Body"—is in dialectical opposition to the black man, the Supermasculine Menial. The white woman, as "beautiful dumb blonde" and Ultrafeminine, is desired by men black and white, but available only to the white, who, lacking the body, can never fully satisfy her. The black woman is therefore the abject object, Subfeminine, subordinate by gender and race, but nevertheless the "strong self-reliant Amazon." The image binding these types draws straight from confinement: the "two sets of handcuffs that have all four of us tied together."[60] The allegory escapes the symbolic for the concrete by being embodied in Cleaver's own desires, which are symptomatic of the history of racism and slavery in the United States that situates white men as conceiving of themselves as superior to black men. Given the economic circumstances of production, that superiority made black men the force of labor, body without mind to white men's mind without body. Black femininity twins and exacerbates this double hierarchy.

In Cleaver's description, the surrender of the body inadvertently relinquishes the (Freudian) phallus to black masculinity while maintaining social power (the Lacanian phallus), creating a network of blocked desire in a set of relationships of gender and race, the relationships that determine class and sexuality. Estranged from the body, white masculinity hysterically asserts dominion over the physicality the body lacks, and thus desires, in blackness. Black masculinity desires the white femininity from which it is barred, and is also separated from black femininity in the shame of its inferiority. White femininity can only be satisfied by the bodily engagement whiteness has surrendered, and black femininity "is lost between two worlds."[61] There are of course clear problems with this model, the greatest of which include how class becomes a symptom of race and gender, how homosexuality is denigrated, and how black women are doubly subjugated.[62] Still, that model has some critical use-value with regard to literary study, though only a few have noticed. As early as 1974, Robert Felgar points out in *Negro American Literature* how the theory might apply to Richard Wright's *Native Son*.[63]

Cleaver recognizes the introductory nature of his analysis. "Just how this [psychosexual dynamic] works itself out is a problem for analysis by sociologists and social psychologists on the mass level, and the headshrinkers and nutcrackers on the individual level."[64] The pejorative phrase *headshrinkers and nutcrackers* marks Cleaver's reiteration of his dismissal of conventional psychoanalysis, focusing instead on outlining study for "social psychologists on the mass level." He is less concerned with what such ideological structures *mean* than with what they *do*. Deleuze and Guattari would similarly challenge psychoanalysis in their own formulation of schizoanalysis. Cleaver's attention to indices of difference and the interplay among diverse textualities in *Soul on Ice* should be recognized in cultural-studies and postcolonial-theory approaches sensitive to history, identification, and alterity. Certainly his analysis is preparatory: "What we are outlining here is a perspective from which such analysis might be best approached."[65] Cleaver's heuristic is provocative because it develops a model of cultural psychology implicated in historical process; it is compelling because its deployment even acknowledges its preliminary role. Cleaver advocates a plural psychoanalysis in order to trace the historical causes of cultural conflict—specifically the national divides along lines of race, class, gender, and sexuality, of which, he argues, his own criminality and incarceration are symptomatic.

There were clear difficulties for some in treating violence as a symptom. In 1968, the year of the publication of *Soul on Ice* and the student strikes at Berkeley, where Cleaver was teaching an experimental course, California's governor, Ronald Reagan, warned, "If Eldridge Cleaver is allowed to teach our children, they may come home one night and slit our throats."[66] That year also saw Reagan contend for the Republican nomination for president against both Nixon and Rockefeller, even as Cleaver headed the Peace and Freedom Party. The oedipal fear demonstrated in the warning by the governor is generalized in the address of "our children," a generational anxiety that begs the sort of mass-level social psychology Cleaver advocates.

Reagan was not alone in pointing to Cleaver. Prison officials regularly commented on *Soul on Ice* from 1970 to 1972, and some did so as derisively as Reagan, even as they, like Cleaver, dismissed psychoanalytic inquiry—but without proposing an alternative, as he did. For example, one ACA presenter in 1970 suggests that penal practices are about to undergo a paradigm change, making the requisite gesture to Thomas Kuhn. The participant suggests that the rehabilitation model of the individual is "attributable to Sigmund Freud," but it is about to change to a model of a community of citizens.[67] However, that speaker then specifically distances himself from the primacy on social environment and its history maintained in *Soul on Ice*. "Eldridge Cleaver tells his followers that crimes committed by members of the Black minority are not crimes at all but protests against and compensation for deprivation. Of course this rationalization will not do."[68] The speaker does recognize a need for change and recommends a social renewal akin to Johnson's "Great Society" in broad-based programs, but in his view, the present and the past, and the social and the particular, cannot have any bearing on one another.

The year after Attica saw the divided image of the black prisoner as incorrigible and revolutionary further separate. The split is reflected in the perceptions of Cleaver. For instance, the San Quentin associate warden, an ACA participant, dismisses both psychoanalysis and self-proclaimed political prisoners: "During the 50 years of the psychoanalytic fad, prisoners became quite skilled in tracing their aberrations to unhappy early experiences." The associate warden goes on to make a joking reference to prisoners exchanging the oedipal epithet—likely the only reference to "motherfucker" in the 137 years of the ACA proceedings.[69] In addition, he claims contemptuously, "Handsome rewards have been furnished men who gave themselves whole-heartedly to the role of 'political prisoner,'" a part he links specifically to Cleaver. The warden's anxiety, like Reagan's hysterical fears, is inspired by Cleaver's fusion of his various identities of black man, convict, political prisoner, writer, teacher, political leader, and candidate for office (at various times, Cleaver campaigned for president, senator, mayor, and city council member). That social fear was the sort of phenomenon for which he offered an investigative approach.

Some participants in the annual conference recognized aspects of this. Two participants suggest *Soul on Ice* to prison administrators because it describes contemporary "racial questions." One, a sociologist, recommends the book twice and describes how a colleague "became physically ill for three days because of his reaction to reading" it.[70] The individual body's illness itself becomes symptomatic of its social investments, a description of physical sickness that has its own parallel in *Soul on Ice,* when Cleaver's bodily illness is the response to the estrangement of and challenge to racial expectation.[71] That anonymous prison sociologist's violent reaction to the book is a physical embodiment of the "convulsive spasms of change" perceived as imminent in the United States in 1968, according to both the ACA president and Cleaver. Personal and social bodies and their violent reactions are understood best historically as part of not the personal past but the larger cultural histories of difference and conflict.

In his own analysis, Cleaver's utopian vision for fulfilling that struggle is one in which the bodies of black men and women are the "wealth of a nation," the "human raw material upon which the future of society depends and with which, through the implacable march of history to an ever broader base of democracy and equality, the society will renew and transform itself."[72] Those mechanics of a cross-gender Marxist vision resemble the future articulated by George Jackson in *Soledad Brother* and *Blood in My Eye*. Though Jackson is far less optimistic than Cleaver regarding the inevitability of transformation, he also links gender equality to revolutionary change: "The black man and the black female must be, as I have mentally ordered things, completely joined in the act of liberation." In a letter to Angela Davis, Jackson reiterates his position on a "woman's role" in revolution: "the very same as a man's."[73] The necessity of cross-gender unity in reading race struggle in terms of class highlights the degree to which black masculinity relates to black femininity in its formation. Jackson describes this most completely when he claims, "The strongest impetus a man will ever have, in an individual sense, will come from a woman he admires." With some of his correspondence with women, Jackson acknowledges an unbridgeable gulf in gender difference: "As a woman, you just do not (and I guess never will) understand what it means to be a man in this particular situation here in the U.S." However, with Davis, Jackson acknowledges that in "generalizing about black women I could never include you in any of it that is not complimentary." Perhaps Jackson's highest accolade for Davis comes in a near aside, in which he places her along with other Black Panther leaders: "The leadership of the black prison population now definitely identifies with Huey, Bobby, Angela, Eldridge, and antifascism."[74] Jackson's final position on gender difference with regard to race in those letters seems to be akin to Cleaver's before him, and to Deleuze and Guattari's after: revolutionary politics overwrites differences of identity, whether gender or race.

At the close of *Soul on Ice,* Cleaver's rosy Marxist version of the future gives way to a utopian romance in the subsequent and final ending of the book, in which Cleaver invokes the black woman to claim her place not as Subfeminine but as sovereign: "Put on your crown, my Queen, and we will build a New City on these ruins."[75] While previously adopting the social and historical sense of self that Deleuze and Guattari type as schizophrenic, he remains enamored with the individual autonomy that is quite literally Oedipus, the singular king to match the queen. It is difficult to sort exactly to what degree desire here flows away from the postulate of a social subject, to what extent the allegorical singular is part-for-whole, or a retreat to imagined autonomy. Likely the problematic final section so at odds with much of the rest of the book is, in some measure, an apology for the third part, the letters to and from his white female lawyer, letters that Ishmael Reed dismisses in his preface to the book as "gushing" and "cloying."[76] Jackson is at times equally gushing. He writes to his black confidante Davis in the same manner that Cleaver relied on his white lawyer, Axelrod. "I'm thinking about you," pens Jackson. "I've done nothing else all day. This photograph that I have of you is not adequate. Do you recall what Eldridge said regarding pictures for the cell?"[77] Of course, what Cleaver said about pictures of women on cell walls is a bit complicated, as he makes his "pin-up girl" his wife, to "fall in love with her and lavish my affections upon her."[78] However, it is this picture of a white woman that prompts Cleaver's self-described "nervous breakdown," which subsequently leads to his heightened consciousness of race and gender.

It is thus possible that the final conclusion of romantic adoration of black women in *Soul on Ice* is Cleaver's effort to write over that earlier conflict and his own attraction to Axelrod. The move is less a bait and switch of individual and social subjects than a consequence of the book's difficulty: Cleaver shifts so rapidly among various approaches, including conflating the personal and the historical, that he often (though not always) substitutes vitality for rigor. He clarifies that his theorization of race, class, gender, and sexuality in "The Allegory of the Black Eunuchs" and "The Primeval Mitosis" is preliminary, and like subsequent literary critics of a historicist bent, he ranges among documents literary, historical, and popular to provide the basis for his cultural critique. However, he does so in a wide-ranging rush and with a reliance on the extended quotation of others that at times borders on bricolage and can be hasty or wrong.[79]

Most often, though, he is successful. One of the final sections of the book, "Convalescence," is a culmination of the earlier theorization of the raced and gendered split of mind and body. It reads like a Birmingham School cultural-studies polemic, starting with *Brown v. Board of Education* and continuing through an analysis of 1950s and '60s popular music and writing inflected by racial critique, a litany of injustices that include the lynching of Emmett Till, and a reading of the Beatles as minstrels playing a black Jesus performing the Eucharist.[80] This approach is so broad as to seem scattered, though it is held together by Cleaver's fierce style and wit and remains a powerful and playful model of cultural criticism as a capstone to a book that has a too-unremarked place in the history of theory. As the investigations

Cleaver engages have taken firmer root and seen tremendous elaboration in historically nuanced cultural studies, critics have mistakenly passed over his work that adopts, combines, and deploys what were at the time largely nascent lines of inquiry in U.S. letters. *Soul on Ice* is valuable strictly in this regard. As an adaptation of Marxist historicism, Cleaver's book is part of a tradition that transformed Marx's single gravitational point of class to a more complex system of race, gender, class, and other categories of human experience, the fault lines of history.

In addition, his indictment of 1960s U.S. geopolitics speaks directly to the history of now, at the start of the twenty-first century, when critics regularly compare current international conflicts to those of 1968. Cleaver argues that a conservative presidency and Congress can "manipulate the people by playing upon the have-gun-will-travel streak in America's character."[81] His point about Vietnam echoes in the United States today, with its international and domestic policies of violence and domination, particularly with regard to the war in Iraq and the limits on civil liberties: "Justice is secondary. Security is the byword."[82] Furthermore, catalogs and studies of prison writing in the vein of Chevigny's and Franklin's demonstrate the tendency to autobiography and to testifying on one's own behalf. *Soul on Ice* expands on this tendency to include not only the prison writer's *self-reflection*—or mirroring of the culture that incarcerates—but also his reflection *on* that culture, situating the condition of imprisonment in a much larger cultural history. For Cleaver, celebrating those efforts faces its own difficulties, given the crimes of theft, assault, and rape that preceded his imprisonment, and the degree to which he argues that those criminal efforts were part of his will to become. The most vituperatively dismissive critics of *Soul on Ice* read it as if the book were an apologist autobiography, a blame-casting story of "I." For example, the conservative nonprofit Intercollegiate Studies Institute places it, along with Mailer's *Armies of the Night,* among the fifty worst books of the twentieth century.[83] However, Cleaver far more often writes against that sense of self. Speaking for himself becomes Cleaver's strategy of testifying to larger scars of history.

At a quite literal level of identity, Cleaver ceased to be a prisoner through writing, as his writing encouraged the activist efforts (including Mailer's) that saw his release. In a more theorized sense, Cleaver's model of self produced discursively most often resembles a social subjectivity, the self that extends past the skin to create space for radical consciousness beyond the isolation of individuality. It is not just that Cleaver assigns too much responsibility for his criminality to social and historical forces. *Soul on Ice* provides more space than that for the multiple points of view of lived experience situated in history, as opposed to the rhetoric of singular autonomy, of the individual versus history. There is a tension in the relationship between the singular and plural, the both-and of the subject in history. For Cleaver, this is manifest in how sexual desires of the body are shaped by the sedimentary history forming the social, how his desire for his white lawyer and his desire *to desire* the allegorical black woman belong both to him and to a broader culture in which he, she, whiteness, and blackness are all constituted.

In 1968 many readers of *Soul on Ice* were prepared to view the prisoner, particularly the black male prisoner, in political and historical terms. As exhibited in the ACA transcripts, even some prison officials could accept the book and its author as resisting U.S. racism, understanding both as revolutionary. Leading prison administrators held the perspective that historical and social forces shape incarceration. However, through the 1970s the ACA focused on keeping up with the radical expansion of imprisonment, irrespective of mitigating factors or alternative judicial responses. The decade following the appearance of *Soul on Ice* marked diminishing possibilities in the condition of prisoners as subjects of and representatives for the United States. The 1970s saw the radical foreclosure of possibility for discussions of race, criminality, and incarceration. Many factors contributed to the change, including the expanded imprisonment of drug users, the demonization and dismantling from inside and out of the Black Panther organization, the misrepresentation of the revolt at Attica, the failure to account for alternatives to imprisonment, and the notoriety of violent, apolitical prisoners such as Jack Henry Abbot—and, as we will see in the next chapter, Gary Gilmore. Incarceration became the sole solution to nearly every criminological problem, and blackness equated to criminality without any sense of social or historical factors, even as imprisonment, in its widespread imagination, presumed guilt of violent, most often murderous crime. Cleaver named the problem and began a strategy of analysis that his readers, even those among prisons' top administrators, recognized in the late 1960s and early 1970s. Given the tremendous expansion in imprisonment in the intervening decades and incarceration's increasingly stark differences of race, how can we not return to his analysis now?

**4**

# The Executioner's Song
# and the Narration of History

> He had come to decide that the center of America might be insane.
>
> —Norman Mailer, *The Armies of the Night*[1]

ONE OF THE activists who helped arrange Eldridge Cleaver's 1966 release from prison was Norman Mailer. It was one of his several associations with prison writers over the decades, most infamously his work to see convicted murderer Jack Henry Abbott published and freed—only to have Abbott kill again and return to prison. However, it is neither his work with Cleaver nor his work with Abbott but his story of convicted killer Gary Gilmore that became his most acclaimed writing, the Pulitzer Prize–winning *The Executioner's Song*. Like *Soul on Ice,* Mailer's text faces challenging questions of genre between biography and history, between nonfiction and fiction, and how the book speaks for itself cannot determine the matter. The back cover of the 1998 Vintage International Edition[2] splits the difference, as its category code lists it as "Literature/Current Affairs." The accompanying praise from the *Miami Herald* identifies it as "literature of the highest order," but Random House broadens that claim to begin the jacket summary with the phrase "in this monumental work of journalism."[3] The ambiguity is a consequence of Mailer's method, wherein the narration of history is as much a subject of the book as the imprisoned and executed Gilmore, a national history written in the story of its then most famous prisoner.

The years 1968 through 1979 marked a fundamental shift in the direction of cultural change for the nation as embodied in the stories of its prisoners, a shift from revolutionary possibility, from politicized racial and criminal identities and the social responsibility for them, to a nation exhausted by perceived threats of change, race, crime, and plural identity. The shift in corrections practice contributed to the widespread imagination of prisoners as "not only violent but dangerous and bad"—as Gavin Stevens reads Butch Beauchamp—even as prisons grew overcrowded, filling with nonviolent offenders such as drug users. Like *Soul on Ice, The Executioner's Song* testifies on behalf of prisoners, makes the accused present in the court of public opinion, and also like Cleaver, Mailer uses the term *schizophrenia* to describe social contradictions. However, representative of the shift in the treatment of prisoners, instead of Cleaver's cultural and political "we," there is Gilmore's alienated and apolitical "I." Nevertheless, the bleakness of the latter's autonomy is undermined, as Mailer simultaneously implicates Gilmore in history and documents its narrativization, the process by which the past "becomes." This chapter shows that Mailer writes national history in Gilmore's story. The writer identifies not with his ostensible subject in the prisoner, but with the producer Larry Schiller and thereby with the process of telling history. *The Executioner's Song* presents Gilmore's double bind, his wish to "not be" that represents the impossible desire both for autonomy and for opting out of history, a desire the book itself thwarts. In that tension Mailer describes the diminishing possibilities of prison history, and thereby national history, in 1979; in the place of a Black Panther who ran for president a decade before, the nation focused on a racist white sociopath fighting for his own execution.

The 1972 *Furman v. Georgia* decision regarding the death penalty ended a decade-long series of appeals, ruling in favor of three black men sentenced to death in the South, one for murder and two for rape. In their decision, the Supreme Court placed a moratorium on the death penalty because the racial bias of its practice violated not only the Eighth Amendment but also the Fourteenth, the latter enacted after the Civil War to protect the newly established rights of black Americans.[4] However, while the court's decision sanctioned what had been an unofficial moratorium since 1967, the ruling also laid the grounds on which states could make the death penalty constitutional. The Supreme Court ruled on the constitutionality of those revised codes in 1976, and the ten-year hiatus ended in 1977 with Gary Gilmore's voluntary execution, a matter that drew the nation's (and Mailer's) attention.

Mailer goes further than Cleaver in exploring how "modern life is schizoid." *Schizophrenia* is one of Mailer's preferred words, which he associates variously with "modern life"; with an "American public" in its view of Nixon, its view of international wars and domestic race relations, and its view of policemen and criminals all the same; and with the American dream, activist students, and the popular perception of the Vietnam War.[5] Mailer is not particularly consistent in his use of the term, nor rigorous in his pursuit of it—it is among his favorites, after all, so he wears it in a wide range of fashions. Still, like Deleuze and Guattari's schizophrenic, the narrated "Mailer," the "reporter" of both *Miami and the Siege of Chicago* and *The Armies of the Night,* is constituted in his partial and conflicting investments with various groups. He is both a part of and apart from the cocktail party of liberal academics, the marchers at the Pentagon, and his fellow protesters in jail in *The Armies of the Night.*

In particular, racial conflicts are cast in the terms of the "schizophrenia" he describes in *Miami* and *Armies* as the "ranch-house life" divided on cultural lines, the normalcy of the American dream concealing sharp divides between black and white.[6] He documents his own participation at the line of that very division at the Chicago Democratic Convention. He distances himself from sharing ideals with black leftists until his guilt gets the better of him when, onstage, "some young Negro from the Panthers or the Rangers or from where he did not know" raises their black and white hands clasped together, and Mailer feels "rueful at unkind thoughts of late." These thoughts include Mailer having admitted earlier, albeit grudgingly, that "he was getting tired of Negroes and their rights."[7] Like the Cleaver early on in *Soul on Ice,* both loving and hating white women, the Mailer of 1968 proves deeply divided in his allegiances. Unlike Cleaver, and unlike Deleuze and Guattari, Mailer is less prepared to allow a tenuously shared radical project to supersede race in identification. There is no ghost of John Brown circulating in Mailer's writing.

Eleven years later, *The Executioner's Song* produces, rather than claims, this sense of the schizophrenic, though the nation fulfilled the writer's expectation of exhaustion at the questions of race and revolution. Mailer's use of "schizophrenia" in 1968 describes lived contradiction; his writing in 1979 embodies it, as it shifts from the individual point of view to the social. *Armies of the Night* opens with *Time* magazine's account of Mailer's speech at the Ambassador Theater and then his arrest at the Pentagon,[8] a shred of the historical record the book in its entirety retells and expands. The point of view may be the third person, but the author remains the first character, his unspoken "I" the reader's eye, his point of view the guide as much as Cleaver's in *Soul on Ice*. In contrast, Mailer is absent as a character in *The Executioner's Song,* and the entire work consists of competing points of view, incorporating diverse documents to record not only history but also its narrativization, the way those who tell the story shape the events even as the participants do. The book, in both topic and focus, capitulates to the virtual abandonment of racial questions, cultural change, and plural identity that characterizes the shift in national tenor from eleven years before, instead emphasizing an antisocial and apolitical Gilmore's relentless quest for the death that asserts his individual autonomy. However, the ways that Mailer narrates the desire to *not be* demonstrate that there is no path out of the sociality of history and its conflicts, in which individuals embody political positions, and narrativization is at once a matter of personal identification and the retroactive production of contradictory views.

Such contradiction defines the novel's fragmented and episodic narrative of a multitude of perspectives. Toward the end of the book, at Gilmore's execution, the warden reads what one viewer describes as "some official document," which he hears only as "blah, blah, blah." Mailer overwrites the official papers of that business with competing responses to Gilmore's own words, "Let's do it." Gilmore's uncle, Vern Damico, views the statement as demonstrating the "most pronounced amount of courage," but the lawyer Ron Stanger sees instead that his former client "couldn't think of anything profound."[9] Such accounts are not merely different interpretations of the same event but are exactly opposite, the conflict in perception rendered visible as Mailer offers some twenty competing fragments of seven points of view of the execution. Mailer critic Robert Merrill, in an otherwise excellent analysis of the novel, reads this episode as "perhaps the most powerful in all of Mailer's writing," which may or may not be the case. He also identifies the scene as "perceived in much the same way by everyone present," which is not accurate.[10]

The assessment of the *literary* execution of the scene is pertinent to the resemblance between the writer of the book and its primary character. Two of Gilmore's writers, Barry Farrell and Larry Schiller, agree that when Gilmore describes the murders he committed, he adopts the "same narrative style every hustler and psychopath would give you of the most boring, or the most extraordinary evening [ . . . . ] Episodic and unstressed."[11] It is a rhetorical gambit on Mailer's part in that if his own highly episodic narrative is similarly unstressed and flat in its account of both the boring and the extraordinary, then the narrator of the novel is as psychopathic as Gilmore. Mailer's biographer Mary V. Dearborn misses this point when she lauds the "equal emphasis" of "each detail of the story," particularly surrounding Jensen's murder.[12] Regardless, *psychopath* is not a term from which Mailer—once arrested for stabbing his wife—necessarily would withhold in describing himself.

Multiple perspectives define the second half of the book, which incorporates not only transcripts of interviews but also excerpts from newspapers. Two lengthy accounts that follow the execution include stories carried by the *Salt Lake Tribune:* "ACLU Calls Hansen Murder Accomplice," and "Justice Has Been Served, Hansen Says of Execution."[13] Again, the juxtaposed articles offer diametrically opposed perspectives of the same event. The contradiction resembles aspects of *Soul on Ice,* wherein Cleaver describes his simultaneous love and hate for white and black women—and his racial desires and crimes—as symptomatic of larger cultural divides. Mailer mostly dodges the issue of race and desire in depicting such divisions. Schizophrenia in *The Executioner's Song* functions as a social negative capability, wherein it is not in an individual's capacity to sustain mystery or contradiction; rather, it is a society's ability to do so and not tear itself apart.

Such deliberate social commentary in the novel has not escaped critique. Jonathan Dee focuses the problem of genre, suggesting that the blurring of story and history imagines that "the chasm between action and self—between the record we leave behind on this earth and the hidden complexity of the living mind—has been closed. We can call it, for lack of a better term, the birth of the psychohistorical novel."[14] Dee condemns this impulse, concluding that such works signal the surrender of the novel's "unreal power to apprehend, and meditate on, the nature of our existence."[15] Dee's use of the term *unreal* emphasizes both fiction's extreme power and lack of the real. In effect, constructing the interiority of actual people based on their historical documents represents a disavowal of the novel's proper authority, a slip from meditation to mediation, from philosophy to history, from imagination to psychology.

However, the differences between these categories have grown complicated in the wake of deconstruction and other aspects of postmodernity in the writing of fiction and history, and in the analysis of each. Furthermore, this book focuses on texts that challenge distinctions between personal and social history, restlessly and relentlessly trafficking back and forth between imagination and history. In addition, Mailer's method of writing Gilmore by integrating various textualities has as much to do with illuminating Gilmore as it has to do with the writer's own dissimulation. Mailer encounters the difficulty of representing imprisonment defined by concealment, and the text regularly features the subterfuge and mediation of television producers, journalists, lawyers, and others attempting to interview Gilmore, often thwarted by prison policies and Supreme Court rulings such as *Nolan v. Fitzpatrick* (1971) and *Pell v. Procunier* (1974), which allowed and then limited such contact. However, Mailer's meticulous account and his formidable sources are also vain efforts to conceal his discursive authority in a surfeit of documents, the effort to write a story of man and nation with an invisible hand.

Because of that effort, contextualizing *The Executioner's Song* within larger fields of discourse seems a little redundant, particularly with regard to documents of law and history, as those tactics of literary scholarship with a historicist bent are already part of the discursive strategy of the novel. There is the author's general treatment of history as a novel and the novel as history, the declared subtitle of *Armies of the Night* and undeclared assumption of much of his work, most especially the "true life novel" account of Gilmore's difficult end. These are not actual events rewritten as fiction in the vein of John Dos Passos's *U.S.A.* (1937),[16] or, regarding crime and punishment, *Native Son*. Richard Wright acknowledges in "How 'Bigger' Was Born" that "the newspaper items and some of the incidents in *Native Son* are but fictionalized versions of the Robert Nixon case and rewrites of news stories from the *Chicago Tribune*."[17] Mailer interweaves his piecework account of Gilmore with headlines and opening excerpts from the *Salt Lake Tribune* and other papers and their account of events Mailer sees as related to the episodes of his text.

For example, one page incorporates a letter from Gilmore to his lover Nicole, a narrative account of the Utah attorney general's citation of *Pell v. Procunier,* and a newspaper excerpt on Gilmore's execution status complete with a neighboring headline, "Carter Wins Election."[18] Mailer in his text offers a flurry of claims and counter-claims for the reader to sort. However, juxtaposition is not analysis, and Mailer acknowledges in the afterword that his hand has shaped the material not only in selection but also in choosing for and against competing accounts, reorganizing, rewriting, and entirely re-creating certain moments.[19] To some degree, Mailer's effort to write himself out of *The Executioner's Song* functions as a response to the excesses of *in propria persona* in *Armies* and *Miami,* where he speaks too much for himself.

In comparison to both Mailer's earlier work and to *Soul on Ice,* where Cleaver at times testifies for himself, *The Executioner's Song* seems to offer a much different puzzle, as it attempts to efface the author's view in a meticulous documentary narrative through which to locate Gilmore. That effort bears on the central question here of testimony and the competing forces of the want to not be and the will to become, of unwriting and writing the prisoner as a sub-ject in history. Mailer, in incorporating hundreds and hundreds of "interviews, documents, records of court proceedings, and other original material,"[20] creates a pastiche of competing scripts regard-ing Gilmore's plotted execution. Still, Mailer's involvement is bound inextricably with the work of Schiller, who purchased the media rights to Gilmore's life and death, and is thus the proprietor of the records and the recorders. Mailer acknowledges in his postscript his debt to the interviews Schiller conducted with Nicole, the basis for the narration of "this factual account—this, dare I say it, *true life story,* with its real names and real lives—as if it were a novel. [ . . . ] Without Schiller, it would not have been feasible to attempt the sec-ond half of *The Executioner's Song.*"[21] The Schiller of the text offers more than an indispensable source for the narrative; in his obsession with recording the truth through documenting history, he becomes a stand-in for Mailer. In the attempt to write Gilmore (and the United States), Mailer instead writes himself in the mirror of Schiller; Mailer misrecognizes himself in Schiller, perhaps because he expected but failed to do so in Gilmore. The shift occurs to some extent because of the schism between Mailer's schizoanalytic method and his desire for a romantic subject, a unified self that finally proves impoverished in the face of historical process and its narrativization that thereby shapes subsequent history.

Mailer works from a diverse set of texts in writing the bulk of *The*

*Executioner's Song,* three-quarters of it set in jail and prison, and thus having the most in common with *Soul on Ice.* It is the second section that has seen less critical review,[22] and this bulk of the novel features the excerpts from local and national media accounts. Many of those newspaper, magazine, and television descriptions were regulated by Schiller and Gilmore: the photocopied letters, the interview questions and transcripts, their piecemeal publication in *Playboy,* the reports Schiller's team leaked to the press or the reports from journalists who accessed Gilmore despite Schiller's best efforts.

The writer Schiller contracted for that *Playboy* article, Barry Farrell, began the role of writing Gilmore, a role that Mailer plays more fully in *The Executioner's Song.* What Mailer writes of Farrell he could as easily write of himself. Gilmore "was being his own writer," but Farrell "was being given the Gilmore canon, good self-respecting convict canon," and "was loving the job even more than expected [ ... ] What a delight to be altogether out of himself. By God, Barry thought, I have all the passions of an archivist. I'm proprietary about the material."[23] Drawing upon the prisoner's own letters to write the prisoner resonates with the expansion of habeas corpus in *Johnson v. Avery,* but unlike the writ lawyers Cleaver describes, Farrell is not in prison. The thought Mailer locates in Farrell here is a provocative one: there is an attitude of ownership in Mailer's use of "proprietary," balanced by the abandonment of Farrell's own identity in being "altogether out of himself." The textualization of the prisoner charts a discursive space in between, and mutually occupied by, Gilmore and his writer, two men who have never met but whose language together produces "Gilmore," who is thereafter shaped by Mailer.

*The Executioner's Song* conducts, in the register of fiction, a historiography of its present as it simultaneously conducts and reveals the historical narrativization in the stops and starts of multiple channels of communication. For example, there were the questions invented and revised by Farrell and Schiller, posed to Gilmore by the lawyers Bob Moody and Stanger, answered by Gilmore, recorded on tape by the lawyers, and transcribed by Schiller's secretaries. These questions and answers became documentation that served as a sort of raw material first for Farrell and then for Mailer, even as Schiller released pieces of the story to the news agencies in an effort to control the wider representation. Critics too quick to underwrite that mediation thereby *over*write the relationship between Mailer and Gilmore.[24]

In 1976–77 Gary Gilmore offered Mailer a true-life Stephen

Rojack, from *An American Dream,* to make it real, a proxy for "the themes I've been dealing with all my life,"[25] but a person other than the author so that he could try his hand at writing himself out of the story. As he does for Schiller, Gilmore presents for Mailer the opportunity to render history through writing a person (other than himself) in history. Mailer does face a problem, in that he admits: "When I started *The Executioner's Song,* I thought I would like him [Gilmore] more than I did."[26] Mailer was not alone in that response, as the various writers involved in the process of collaborative narration regarded Gilmore similarly, including the convict himself, Farrell, and Schiller. Gilmore regularly recognized himself in negative terms, harboring uncontrollable, sourceless violence, though he repeatedly blocked any desire to trace that criminality to any childhood cause.[27]

Others attempted to resolve that difficulty in searching for a conventional psychoanalytic causality for violence. According to Farrell, "The key to every violent criminal could be found in the file of his childhood beatings, but Gilmore claimed his mother never touched him, and his father never bothered to."[28] Like Farrell, Schiller turns to such an oedipal model as an interpretive framework when he questions Gilmore with regard to his childhood relationship with his mother, offering, in that interrogation, the recognition: "Maybe that's psychoanalytic bullshit, and if so, I stand accused." Gilmore's mother, Bessie, is more circumspect, suggesting that, regarding her son, she did not know "how much was her fault, and how much was the fault of the ongoing world."[29] From the late 1960s through the 1970s, Cleaver, ACA prison officials, and even *Playboy* may have begun acknowledging that Freudian and Adlerian emphases on childhood history were limited and limiting, but in 1979 journalists and producers were still testing those worn paths of inquiry.

Even Mailer himself occasionally turns to such psychoanalytic expectation, as the first of the book's three endings turns back to Gilmore's mother saying that she has the same guts Gary has, before turning to himself with his own prison rhyme, then his apologia.[30] However, Mailer more often turns away from the psychoanalytic, using the personal as a springboard for broader inquiry. For example, Nicole Baker once asks Gilmore if he is the devil, a comparison her sister makes as well, and in a long letter to her, he writes, "I might be further from God than I am from the devil," a letter that concludes with his referring to her as "Angel," a repeated nickname.[31] The psychoanalytic talking cure of such free-form letters becomes a methodological starting point for exposition extending well beyond the personal. Rather than leave the devils and angels in the realm of the imaginary, expressive of the personal, Mailer makes them concrete and social. He titles chapter 32 "The Angels and the Demons Meet the Devils and the Saints," which focuses not at all on Gilmore directly but entirely on the legal struggle, the contest among many groups for determining Gilmore's fate. Mailer sees in the person of Gilmore a center of gravity by which to organize the claims and counterclaims, the Eastern and Western Voices that are the two halves of the book and the nation.

In the process of writing how Gilmore, in his celebrity, becomes a screen for the nation, it is not Gilmore but the producer Schiller who becomes Mailer's proxy in the text. Mailer repeatedly describes Schiller as obsessed with recording history, in part for personal prestige, to be a man of truth. Schiller tells himself, "You recorded history right. If you did the work that way, you could end up a man of substance."[32] More often, however, Schiller's attention is less to his own "substance"—what he is made of—and more to the stuff of the real, history as truth. In a telegram Schiller writes to Gilmore, the former states, "I am here to record history, not to get involved in it," a claim he immediately overturns in acknowledging that he is already in the story.[33] To the lawyers, Moody and Stanger, who become the interview mediators Schiller uses to communicate with Gilmore after being banned from the prison because he is a film producer, Schiller says, "Forget Larry Schiller the businessman . . . That's a side of me, but we're forgetting it. We have history here. We have to get that. [ . . . ] It's all part of history." When he tells himself the story of what he is doing, Schiller says, "For the first time, Schiller, you can't fictionalize, you can't make it up, you can't *embroider*," as such embellishment would run counter to his "desire to record history, true history, not journalistic crap."[34] Schiller obsesses over how he might maintain a posture of objectivity, capturing history and placing it on view like a curator, accessing and representing an unmediated real. Like the character of District Attorney Gavin Stevens at the end of *Go Down, Moses,* who no longer narrates out of hand but must turn to the "papers of that business" and meet with the newspaper editor to track down what has happened to Butch, Schiller wants not to tell a story but to reveal it, even as he orchestrates the revelation. It requires some interpretive acrobatics not to read Schiller's account here as a proxy for Mailer's own purposes in the book, particularly after the incessant self-aggrandizement of *Armies of the Night* and *Miami and the Siege of Chicago.*

The proposition that Schiller's and Mailer's points of view are deeply implicated[35] becomes more compelling in the face of the later history of their collaboration. Schiller directed the television film *Master Spy: The Robert Hanssen Story* (2002), from Mailer's screenplay, based on the life of the FBI agent and Russian spy, and Schiller subsequently authored the novelization of Mailer's screenplay. The working title of the project was *Into the Mirror,*[36] richly suggestive of the degree to which the discursive work of each reflects the other. The mutual identification that began in their collaboration in the case of Gilmore also shows their twin tendencies to write national tragedy in particular biographies. Both are obsessed with reading U.S. national culture in the lives of its imprisoned antiheroes. For instance, in addition to collaborating with Schiller on the stories of Gilmore and Hanssen, Mailer wrote the screenplay adaptation of Schiller's book account, cowritten with James Wilwerth, of the O. J. Simpson trial, *American Tragedy* (1996). Then, too, Mailer has his *Oswald's Tale: An American Mystery* (1995), while Schiller interviewed Oswald's killer, Jack Ruby, on the latter's deathbed. Schiller titled his film on Dennis Hopper *The American Dreamer* (1971), and there is Mailer's fictional novel of celebrity murder, *An American Dream* (1965). Furthermore, Mailer considered titling *The Executioner's Song* "American Virtue."[37] In their mutual fascination with imagining the dream of America told in the representation of its antiheroes, and through their frequent collaboration, even to the extent of rewriting one another's work, Mailer and Schiller offer a reversal of the popular misreading of schizophrenia as multiple personality disorder, two voices in one body. Instead, the voices of their two bodies become one.

At stake in those various "true" stories around which they grouped their often collaborative efforts is the ability of a criminal case to represent a sort of national consciousness. Mailer had grappled with these questions before. In an overall negative review of Mailer's *Of a Fire on the Moon* (1969), Richard Poirier quotes Mailer's claim that "there is an unconscious direction to society, as well as to the individual."[38] To a far more successful degree, *The Executioner's Song* uses Gilmore's death sentence to conduct its narration of a nation's fears and desires through the diverse array of texts that Mailer employs to write the novel. Steve Shoemaker suggests that Mailer's "The White Negro" (1957), in its cross-cultural observation, serves as a proto–

New Historicist examination in an anthropological vein.[39] In that essay, then, Mailer offers a sketch of a method for interpreting the subject *of* culture through the subject *in* culture.

Eleven years after "The White Negro," in *Armies of the Night* Mailer extends that project to understanding cultural history in a novel form, the history of now as written by the author participating in it. And eleven years after that, *The Executioner's Song* refines that historiographical imperative by writing the author out of the book, though Mailer cannot help but read himself in Schiller. The evolution of discursive technique represented in these three works also marks the high points of Mailer's oeuvre in terms of critical acclaim, as the first is among his most anthologized essays, and the two books won Pulitzers for nonfiction and literature, respectively. Like Cleaver, then, Mailer works best when blurring distinctions between narrative and critique in the challenge of tracing the outline of the subject constituted in history. Like Schiller, who does "get involved in it" and becomes one of history's characters whose choices affect the narrative, Mailer also plays his part in describing how the narrativization itself changes the course of the action.

The game of finding Mailer is of interest in its own right. However, that effort takes on greater meaning when keeping in mind the degree to which the schizophrenic self emerges in its participation in history. Mailer is like Gilmore in that he may "like language" but is committed to "tell the truth." However, unlike Gilmore (and far more like Schiller), the Mailer who drafts *The Executioner's Song* recognizes that the truth of history is multiple and conflicting, and is shaped in the telling. It is Gilmore who tires of the sounds of others and Mailer who reproduces that noise in the competing scripts. That incessantly multiperspectival narration is at odds with the object of his analysis, with Gilmore's effort to gather himself at the culmination of his violent and aimless personal history that, in retrospect, fulfills his deathward trajectory. He admits, upon returning to jail for the two murders, "I am in my element now," and later tells his lawyers-cum-interviewers, "I figured I'd probably spend the rest of my life in jail or commit suicide, or be killed uh, by the police."[40] Paradoxically, all of those ends reach fulfillment when Gilmore calls the state's hand in his death sentence, resists the stays of execution purposed on his behalf, and faces the riflemen.

That will to death contrasts with the lack of clarity he has regarding the crimes themselves,[41] a reverse of the case of Wright's "Bigger"

Thomas, whose life gains focus in killing even as social and histo-
rial machinations orchestrate his fatalistic trajectory toward execution. Gilmore looks even less like Cleaver, who views his criminality
largely as the product of the forces arrayed against him. As a prisoner,
Gilmore instead resembles Butch Beauchamp, described by Gavin
Stevens as "some seed not only violent but dangerous and bad," just
as Gilmore is frequently violent and describes himself as "vicious"
and "not a likable person."[42] However, the execution of the character
Butch comes at the culmination of a genealogical history providing
coherence for much of the prior episodes of *Go Down, Moses.* The
nearly one thousand pages before the scene of Gilmore's execution
do not provide a similar sense of cause situating the personal in a
broader social history.

The book has less to do with tracing cause for effect—Gilmore's
personal history or cultural difference leading him to commit senseless
murders—than with the complication of causality, of agency, of personal and social history. Just as acts are never entirely ours, they affect
more than just us. Documenting "true history" in *The Executioner's
Song* is not as much about meditating on the nature of Gilmore's
crime as it is about recording the mediation: the media flurry surrounding his impending execution, the reporting that consequently
affects the case. Writing history produces a version of events that, in
its telling, shapes subsequent events, and Mailer represents the process
of that narrativization and its effects. In response to a *New York Times*
front-page article on Gilmore, David Susskind, who early on competed with Schiller for the rights to Gilmore's story, recalls a story by
his friend Stanley Greenberg, which Mailer puts forth this way:

> Stanley had written a TV story fifteen years ago about a man await-
> ing execution. The man had been so long on Death Row that he
> changed in character, and the question became, "Who was being exe-
> cuted?" Metamorphosis the play had been called, and Susskind always
> felt that it had had some effect on the end of capital punishment in
> New York State, and maybe even a little to do with the Supreme
> Court decision that saved a lot of men's lives on Death Row.[43]

The teleplay was a script for the series *The Defenders,* and the
Supreme Court decision at hand is *Furman v. Georgia,* a moratorium
on executions that ended with Gilmore's death sentence. The assumption is that telling a "true" story can affect history. In a discussion

between Susskind and Greenberg regarding a television or film account of Gilmore, the latter says, "I even think that reaching a large audience can probably save the guy's life."[44] Early in the development of his case, popular representation of Gilmore might have made him sufficiently recognizable or sympathetic so as to offer reprieve. However, that hope quickly gave way to the emphasis on a voluntary execution to end the ten-year hiatus, a more valuable media event than a life sentence. The turning point came at a press conference featuring Farrell and Dennis Boaz, Gilmore's lawyer prior to Moody and Stanger.

> "Don't you think," said Barry Farrell, "that if Gilmore isn't executed, he'll slip right back in with four hundred and twenty-four other condemned men and women? A lot of them may have more tragic stories than Gilmore."
>
> "Gary is the only one," said Boaz, "who has the courage to face the consequences of his act."
>
> "How," asked another reporter, "is Susskind going to do the film?"[45]

Farrell and Boaz's dialogue emphasizes the tension between individual agency and social identification, foregrounding one of the central questions of *The Executioner's Song*. The immediate transition to the reporter's banal question, which undercuts their debate, is one of the book's most powerful moments. In *The Armies of the Night* or *Miami and the Siege of Chicago,* such a disjuncture between history and its narration, between a man's death and the film style of its narration, between the high and low of human possibility, likely would merit an extended expository rant. Here, the sharp turn is not even emphasized with a line break. For once, Mailer seems prepared to let the seeming artlessness in his words speak for itself. However, it would be too easy and inaccurate to cast the reporters as the ones whose participation makes Gilmore's life or death a matter of publicity, ratings, and money. When *Newsweek* put Gilmore on the cover, they captioned his mug shot with "DEATH WISH." His lawyer, Moody, "felt it gave a big push to the bidding [for his story]."[46] The lawyers themselves, Moody and Stanger, were as much Schiller's link to Gilmore as they were Gilmore's own legal representatives, transceivers in a network that included Gilmore, Schiller, lawyers on both sides of the case, the Utah attorney general, the reporters, and the larger media networks themselves. The prison administration was involved as well. Director of Corrections Ernie Wright, for example, insists, "No movie producer is going to make one dime out of Gilmore." Gilmore's lawyers—one of whom was a member of the State Building Board, which approved prison-construction expenditures—contest that claim, demanding the written policy preventing it. "Oh, it isn't written," Director Wright responds, "it's prison policy."[47]

Of course, as the ACA transcripts demonstrate, some policies *were* written, but the director's complaint saw partial fulfillment: producers such as Schiller may still have profited, but most prisoners did not, as cases such as Gilmore's encouraged state laws passed in the 1980s barring prisoners from accepting royalties.[48] Different versions of events competed with one another as newspapers picked and chose among reports, and Schiller carefully selected the reporters with whom he worked and what he told them: "A pipeline into the biggest local paper could enable him to affect the output on the AP and UP stories." However, not all papers made use of the material in ways the producer anticipated. What Gilmore's earlier lawyer Boaz says regarding himself to reporters is also true of Schiller; he is "a character," "being acted upon by the real author of these events."[49] In the "true life story" Mailer authors, Boaz and Schiller are two of many in a narrative in which they have partial but not complete agency.

So it is for Gilmore as well, though his stakes are far higher. His desire to opt out of the social sphere becomes his definitive characteristic in the second half of the novel, and it is part of the narrativization that subsequently scripts his acts. Farrell, as quoted above, asks whether Gilmore, if he appeals, will "slip right back in with four hundred and twenty-four other condemned men and women." Later, he suggests that "if less attention had been paid to Gilmore he might have changed his mind and looked to avoid his execution. Now Gary was trapped in fame"[50]—no execution, no film, no book. In a paradoxical and quite literally antihumanist reversal of the Lacanian subject—the subject constituted in the symbolic order of language—in order for Gilmore to enter language, he must die. Becoming "Gilmore" means no Gilmore. His narration is predicated on the certainty of his death. Gilmore's self-erasure offers his only means of self-presentation, of establishing an identity differentiating him from others in his similarly fraught position; his urge to be an individual trumps the desire to be alive. In Farrell's view, scripting his own death validates Gilmore's life more than the living of it, but

Farrell (and Schiller) has time and money invested, while the prisoner has his life in the balance. Anthony Amsterdam, a consulting lawyer to Gilmore's brother and counsel in *Furman v. Georgia,* suggests that "discharging a competent lawyer, when you are under a death sentence, is a form of suicide in itself. Gary had raised questions about free will and self-determination."[51]

Gilmore in effect accepts the very same existentialist model of subjectivity that Lacan rejects in his trope of the prison in "The Mirror Stage," in which liberty "is never more authentic than when it is within the walls of a prison," when "a personality realizes itself only in suicide."[52] Whereas Cleaver writes in order to save himself, and his prison sentence is the time during which his reading and writing are the means of his becoming, Gilmore's entry to history as written by Mailer depends entirely on his literary execution as a historical fact. Willing the death of the self becomes a gambit to realize that self and to escape the formative processes of history. Owning his death to the extent of orchestrating it resists the implication that in his life he is subject to forces beyond his ken, whether impulses from within that he cannot control or historical forces from without.

However, as Deleuze and Guattari make clear (and as Lacan suggests), there is no subject outside of history, and such is the case for Gilmore. Gilmore believes that his execution fulfills his own individual will, but Mailer writes that, according to Richard Giauque, another lawyer peripheral to Gilmore's case, "Gary was being used by many people." According to Giauque, the attorney general, and others, "A great many other conservatives obviously wanted to use Gary's willingness to die for their own political ends [ . . . ] Right now, to recognize one man's right to die could have a deadly effect on four to five hundred lives in death row."[53] The fear then becomes that Gilmore's will to death could legitimize a broader sense of the righteousness of the death penalty, execution as a fulfillment of the prisoner's own intent. Mailer offers the similar view of ACLU representative Shirley Pedler: "Capital punishment was not only wrong, but his execution might touch off others, for it would demystify the taking of life by the state. [ . . . a] methodical, calculated turning of the machinery of the State against the individual."[54]

Still, Mailer records Farrell's consideration of the exact opposite possibility, that "if Gilmore were not executed, a major wave of executions might be touched off. Every conservative in America would say: They couldn't even shoot this fellow who wanted to be shot. Who are we ever going to punish?"[55] Farrell's position seems far less likely, though Mailer's inclusion of his stance emphasizes the simultaneous and competing points of view in the participatory spectatorship that is culture. The larger social context of competing ideological positions demonstrates that the potential effects of Gilmore's execution extend beyond his own life and death; like it or not, agree with it or not, he is part of a larger body of death row prisoners whose fates are attached to his. Also embedded in the available responses—either Gilmore's execution or its stay will set off a string of executions, depending on whom Mailer records—is a sense of the schizophrenic, where instead of the individual's life until death as a single vanishing point, life and death both offer disjuncture and undecidability.

Unlike Cleaver, who constantly places his own imprisonment in the context of allegiance with other prisoners, Gilmore himself resists the political implications of his execution by contesting his own representativeness. When the ACLU and NAACP turn to Gilmore's case as a point of leverage to maintain the moratorium on executions, Gilmore's response is immediate and vituperative. The *Provo Herald* published his open letter to the NAACP: "I'm a white man. Don't want no uncle tom blacks buttin [*sic*] in. Your contention is that if I am executed then a whole bunch of black dudes will be executed. Well that's so apparently stupid I won't even argue with that silly kind of illogic. But you know as well as I do that they'll kill a white man these days a lot quicker than they'll kill a black man."[56] History proves Gilmore wrong with regard to raced execution,[57] and this is only one of Gilmore's many racist comments. However, the prognostic veracity of Gilmore's claim is less significant than Mailer's curious narration some pages later. Gil Athay is a lawyer who involves himself in contesting Gilmore's execution not for Gilmore, but for death row inmate Dale Pierre, a black man he believes to be innocent, convicted "because he was black, a condition to avoid in the state of Utah."[58] Working for Gilmore's stay would help maintain the moratorium of *Furman v. Georgia,* staying Pierre's execution as well. For Athay, the presence of both of them on death row was a more-important bond than the difference in their races—or even than one's admitted guilt and the other's believed innocence. The social category of condemned prisoner necessitates cross-racial identification; the death sentence writes over color. Athay's involvement, which began with his unwilling court appointment as a defender, cast him as lenient on crime and thereby cost him the race for attorney general versus the "tough on crime" Bob Hansen, who pursued Gilmore's execution.

In an odd passage, Mailer describes Athay supporting Pierre because he saw him as innocent, and as "a complex man, a difficult man, but now, to Gil Athay, rather a beautiful black man, and besides, Athay had always hated capital punishment."[59] Mailer is quick to insert the attribution *to Gil Athay* between *difficult* and *beautiful*, writing in the quote to attribute the description to an interview transcript rather than to himself. Athay's perception of "a beautiful black man" possibly speaks to the race slogan of the linguistic reversal, "Black is beautiful" —or it is some other recognition of Athay's, or just one of many words offered in an interview that Mailer seized and rewrote. Regardless of what the description *means,* what Mailer's direct attribution *does* is distance Athay's view from his own. Athay views a black man as innocent, complex, and beautiful, but Mailer had grown even more tired of race since he stood on a platform eleven years before and clasped hands with a young black man moments after telling his assembled audience, black and white, men and women, "You're beautiful."[60]

Athay is just a bit player in the proceedings, and Pierre never appears directly. Black characters are scarcely present in *The Executioner's Song,* largely mentioned only in racist comments by Gilmore as he attests to the overrepresentation of black men in prison and thereby their local superiority there. The cross-racial identification Athay engages is absent in Mailer and Gilmore. The racism of the latter, coupled with his adherence to imagined autonomy, means that he cannot, will not, ally himself with a larger social body of prisoners—so many of them black men—and it is Gilmore's story that Mailer tells. It would be historically inaccurate to suggest that Gilmore was or is representative of U.S. prisoners in general or death row prisoners in particular. Mailer's chronicle makes exceptional what was in 1977 already a special case, given that his would be the first execution following the *Furman v. Georgia* decision. And in a final analysis that extends after *The Executioner's Song,* Athay's fears, as well as those of the lawyer Giaque and the ACLU, seem justified, as Pierre was executed in 1987, ten years after Gilmore, and the number of executions increased in the 1990s to the levels of the 1950s. Perhaps if Mailer had written about Dale Pierre instead of Gilmore—but there is no place outside of history from which to judge that conjecture, and at the end of the 1970s, Mailer and the majority of the ACA (and America?) had grown weary of racial questions.

The historical events and the actual people participating in them as narrated in *The Executioner's Song* quite literally know that they are the book's characters, taking part in the various actions that are its story. That awareness shapes the telling. Before his execution, Gilmore tells his brother Mikal that he does not know how to conduct himself for his execution. "Maybe that's why I need Schiller," he says. "He'll be there recording it for history, so I'll keep cool."[61] Schiller in the story and Mailer in the account of it—so dependent on Schiller's own interviews—set the stage for the "true history" of this "true life story" to be performed, and its very pretense of objectivity scripts the roles for its characters. Gilmore will "keep cool" so that his posthumous representation meets his expectations of how a man should behave. Given that Schiller functions as Mailer's proxy in the novel, the last exchange between written subject and writer is especially telling: when Schiller says good-bye to Gilmore at the execution, he shakes hands and says, "I don't know what I'm here for," to which Gilmore replies, "You're going to help me escape." Schiller responds, "I'll do it the best way that's humanly possible."[62] Where Cleaver writes in order to save himself, Gilmore paradoxically opts out of events to become the story by which Schiller, via Mailer, will write him into history. Writing Gilmore offers him bodily escape from participation in the world.

Except, of course, it does not. Gilmore's will to not be—as orchestrated and contested by the condemned himself, the Utah judicial system, the ACLU, the prison officials, the NAACP, and the U.S. Supreme Court, and as rendered by his double narrators, Schiller and Mailer—makes his unmaking not his own, but the result of a cascade of claims and counter-claims. And in the final analysis, Gilmore's effort to escape the prison system capitulates to the very ends of that system: his ultimate silence and erasure, historically two of the primary functions of incarceration in the United States. Gilmore's case as offered by Mailer in *The Executioner's Song* at one level perpetuates a dangerous myth, a myth alongside the myths of prisoners who are universally guilty of violent crimes and of blackness and criminality as equivalent—the myth that death row, the most final expression of incarceration, fulfills the self-erasure those imprisoned are themselves seeking.[63] The prison system may have made Gilmore and may control his life, but he maintains some control over his death, first in not appealing his execution, and second in trying twice to kill himself more directly, via suicide. Determining one's own death, however, is perhaps the bleakest of all spaces for human agency and possibility. Deleuze and Guattari argue that schizoanalysis seeks to allow desire to circulate freely by destroying the unified oedipal subject. Gilmore's want to not be perversely capitulates to their thesis, as his desire for a unified, autonomous sense of self can be fulfilled only in his death.

However, it is not Gilmore but Mailer who has the last word, and Mailer's multivalent narration of Gilmore locates him in a set of relations outside of himself. Mailer through his proxy, Schiller, at once abets Gilmore's escape, by writing him into *The Executioner's Song,* and blocks Gilmore's attempt to escape, to opt out of history as the course of human events, the condition of being subject to forces beyond one's self. Farrell observes that Gilmore is "trapped in fame," but Gilmore, Farrell, Mailer, and Schiller—writers all—are implicated in the media operations that are simultaneously the trap and the means of fame. Gilmore's celebrity status relies on and thereby perpetuates his demand for his own execution. That desire stems from how tired Gilmore is of the "noise" of prison, the sounds of other competing voices, the sum of everything ever said and done that is history. However, these are the very noises that fill the book, including, at the end, the rifle shots, the babble of Gilmore's lawyers and writers, the doctor's chatter during the autopsy, the conversation over drinks among the executioners, the conflicting newspaper accounts. Executed, Gilmore does not somehow ascend bodily into social memory like Joe Christmas; Mailer's entire effort has been to sing the executioner's song that assembles the readers to view what it means for the state to kill a man. Just as Butch is the product of a town's, a community's, history, Gilmore is part of a larger national self-image, its schizophrenic sense of itself written in its death sentences.

Mailer's account of the prisoner's participation in his individuation is encapsulated nicely at the end of chapter 17 of the second half, "I Am the Land Lord Here." Like most of the chapters, it re-creates many perspectives and textualities, including excerpts of Gilmore's letters, many conversations, a fragment from the local newspaper, part of an interview transcript, and a poem by Gilmore, which closes the chapter and from which the chapter takes its name. Gilmore answers one of Schiller's questions with, "*Right now, I'm a prisoner of my own body— / I'm trapped in myself— / Worse than jail!*" In Gilmore's poem, written a few years earlier, the speaker goes inside himself to see "*A mirror of me reflecting myself.*"[64] Despite the harsh litany of sins and evil represented, "*There was no scorn to menace here,*" because

> *I built this house      I alone*
> *I am the Land Lord here.*

The poem is subtitled "an introspection by Gary Gilmore," so the speaker and author, like the "Mailer" as narrator and author of *The Armies of the Night* and *Miami and the Siege of Chicago,* are implied to be the same. There is a tension between the poem's ownership of self-as-body and the response of feeling "trapped" in the body. Gilmore in prison stops at the skin but does not want to, his individuality limited, limiting, and inescapable.

In telling contrast, in his short story "The Flashlight," Cleaver describes the body as at once a prison and an extension beyond the self. He initially renders the main character as feeling like "a dynamo imprisoned in the blood, the flesh and bone of his own body," a limit of bodily self which thereafter becomes his school and his gang, which seem like prisons as well.[65] Where Gilmore accepts the prison of his individuality, Cleaver challenges it. The point of view character, Stacy, likens his "own body" to a prison, but his body and the social body of his gang are described as mutually constituting composites, "separate selves bound into one." Comparing social organizations thereafter to prisons speaks as much to the duality of personal and social bodies as it does to the likeness of an organization with an excessive sense of its autonomy to a repressive state.

The distinction between the two is summarized in Foucault's argument, in *Discipline in Punish,* that the body is not the prison of the soul, but "the soul is the prison of the body."[66] The rhetoric of individual autonomy enacted by Gilmore represses the ability of the subject to participate in a social identity extending beyond the self, the social subjectivity Cleaver represents. It is worth noting that in these instances both Cleaver and Gilmore write in terms of figurative imprisonment, a tendency critiqued in chapter 1 of this book. However, prison as a metaphor for those themselves incarcerated is a slippage that means something different than it does when nonprisoners use it. Just as "Black is beautiful" served as a rhetorical reversal of racism in the 1960s, metaphors of incarceration, like pejorative terms of identity, are reappropriated and thereby transformed, such as when black rap artists Tupac Shakur, DMX, and Eve all employ the call and response of social belonging by rewriting a pejorative term as positive (if problematic) social belonging: "Where my niggas?" Identity not only is in flux in the tension between subject and history, but is also changing as historically transitory associations and meanings themselves alter. Words may carry with them the places they have been, but the street makes its own use of them as well.

The situational meaning and use of metaphoric imprisonment, like the racial epithet, change depending on who employs it.

Cleaver's *Soul on Ice* and Mailer's *The Executioner's Song* chart reversed readings of the process of identity formation in prison, a becoming and an erasure. At a quite literal level of identity, Cleaver ceased to be a prisoner through writing, as his writing encouraged the activist efforts (including Mailer's) that saw him paroled, while Gilmore ceased to be a prisoner through his execution. In a more-theorized sense, Cleaver's model of self produced in his narrative most often resembles a social subjectivity, the self that extends past the skin to create space for radical consciousness beyond the isolation of individuality, while Gilmore's desire to be an individual and to die are one and the same. The difference does not resolve neatly into Cleaver assigning too much responsibility for his criminality to social and historical forces, and Gilmore taking too much responsibility for his. Both books provide more space than that for the multiple points of view of lived experience situated in history, as opposed to the rhetoric of singular autonomy, of the individual versus history. Cleaver's book regularly implicates the self in history, and though Gilmore opts for a more-impoverished model, Mailer's narration testifies to the inadequacies of imagined autonomy. There is a tension in the relationship between the singular and plural, the both-and of the subject in history, and for Mailer, the tension is even sharper in his multiperspectival, schizophrenic account of an individual autonomy that can only fulfill its desire in its death.

In 1968, readers of *Soul on Ice* were prepared to view the prisoner, particularly the black male prisoner, in political and historical terms. As demonstrated in the ACA transcripts, even some prison officials could accept the book and its author as resisting U.S. racism, understanding the book and its writer as revolutionary. In 1979 *The Executioner's Song* met a different readership, and there is nothing political in Gilmore's defense for his murders of Ben Bushnell and Max Jensen, no larger historical injustice testified to in the narrative. His irredeemably criminal character matched the increasing pessimistic belief that when it comes to rehabilitation in prison, nothing works. The expanded criminalization and sentencing for drug crimes largely began in New York under Governor Rockefeller. That approach dismantled the state's extensive treatment program and signaled a departure from the rehabilitation the governor seemed to have endorsed just a few years before. That is, in 1967 Rockefeller had established a special committee to recommend transformations for the state's prison programs, and that committee conducted a survey of the best rehabilitative practices. Sociologist Dr. Robert Martinson had the review ready for publication in 1969, but the state suppressed the findings until a subpoena released them.[67] It was a curious move, since Martinson's research seemed to offer a dim view of rehabilitation. In the mid-1970s the findings were interpreted to support Rockefeller's more extreme sentencing platform. According to Martinson, Nixon's attorney general, William B. Saxbe, and many newspapers inaccurately distilled the findings to "nothing works,"[68] for which Gilmore seemed to offer a case in point.

When Mailer claims, "The public could live with a killer who was crazy, mixed-up, insane," the "public" to which he refers is as much the one initially reading the "true life novel" as the one inside the book.[69] That particular observation of what "the public" can accept appears in a fragment sandwiched between two of Schiller's perspectives but without direct attribution to anyone in particular, thereby situating the view as ambiguously Schiller's and Mailer's, as is much of the latter half of the book. The gulf between expectations of prisoners in 1968 and in 1979 offered in these two books parallels the discussion of actual imprisonment policies and practices. *Soul on Ice* and *The Executioner's Song* mark diminishing possibilities in the condition of prisoners as subjects of and representatives for the United States. The films of the next three chapters all represent these matters of race, representation, and imprisonment in ways that directly address the tensions between history and its narration as explored in *Soul on Ice* and *The Executioner's Song*—and the bleak history that followed them. In the last two decades of the twentieth century, the number of people incarcerated in prisons and jails ballooned from less than five hundred thousand to nearly two million, and rates of incarceration increased almost fourfold, while the "war on drugs" targeted inner-city communities largely composed of black and Hispanic citizens. Even as early as 1977 and 1978, keynote speakers at the ACA conferences cite overcrowding as the most significant problem facing prison administration. Anthony Travisono, the ACA's executive director from 1975 to 1990, titled a 1977 article in *The American Journal of Correction* "Prison Crisis—Over 280,000 Men and Women in Our Nation's Prisons."[70] Presumably, if that number presents a crisis, then its more than fourfold increase by 1999 is a disaster.

# 5

# The Contradictions of "Documentary Realism" in *American History X*

> The cinema provides us with an understanding of our own memory. Indeed we could almost say that cinema is a model of consciousness itself. Going to the cinema turns out to be a philosophical experience.
>
> —Henri Bergson[1]

NORMAN MAILER'S *The Executioner's Song* stands as one historical landmark in U.S. audiences' attention to accounts of imprisonment that blur the difference between fictional and actual. The story of Gilmore in prison seeking his execution was told several times, suggesting both book and television audiences' interests and producers' efforts to capitalize on related properties through multiple media. Gilmore's sentence, after all, appears in Mailer's Pulitzer-winning novel and Larry Schiller's 1982 television film starring Tommy Lee Jones and Rosanna Arquette, as well as in Gilmore's brother Mikal's own version in his book and its HBO film adaptation, both titled *Shot in the Heart*.[2] Two decades after Mailer's novel, three prison films have further complicated the difference between reality and imagination in representing criminality and imprisonment. *American History X, The Hurricane,* and *The Farm: Life Inside Angola Prison* span the spectrum from realistic fiction to biographical picture to documentary, and they demonstrate how incarceration functions as a field that organizes race and masculinity in the transformation of criminal character.

Before demonstrating how *American History X* represents criminalization, incarceration, and cross-racial redemption, this chapter begins with a description of how and why the prison population expanded in the 1980s and 1990s, and how the ACA responded to that transformation. Next, I show how changes in the movie industry with regard to production and reception situate films in a highly problematic tension between the cultural imagination and historical actuality. Then this chapter as well as the subsequent two show that the court-determined guilt naming the subject a criminal initiates the identity of the prisoner, which all three films describe as man-making irrespective of the commission of crime. In these films, racial conflict directly leads to incarceration, and all three point out that to identify blackness is to misrecognize violent criminality. The process of imprisonment thereafter functions as a sign of redemption, whereby even men innocent of their crimes are personally improved while incarcerated, and cross-racial identification among inmates is the irreducible sign of transformation, wherein a raced "I" becomes "us." The fallacy of these prison films' redemption narratives lies in their implicit endorsement of the legal system that they suggest unjustly imprisons, but nevertheless improves, black men. That fallacy becomes more pernicious when one places these three films in their historical context. All three appeared in the last years of the twentieth century, a time when the United States' three-decades-long experiment with incarceration reached enormous proportions, creating a system dramatically overrepresenting black men. That history is crucial for films making claims to the real. Even as fictions trade on the cachet of true-life stories, historical records such as documentary films can conform to the shape of prior imaginings—just as stories such as *The Shawshank Redemption,* a phenomenally popular film that consolidates nearly every component feature of prior movies set in prison, affect the narratives of subsequent films with far greater stakes in historical actuality.

The nation's incarceration rates nearly quadrupled between the end of the 1970s and the release of these three films at the end of the century, largely because of increasing sentences for offenses that previously had not even merited prison terms, and the racial differences in those prison populations grew stark. Critical comment did not always accompany that expanding disparity, and the ACA Presidential Address in 1980 acknowledges the disproportionate increase in black inmates, only to then equivocate: "I will not attempt to explain the reasons for the racial imbalance. Suffice it to say that they are complex and varied."[3] The problems and their "complex and varied" causes only expanded in the next two decades. The nature of the crimes yielding prison terms changed dramatically between 1980 and 1999, according to the U.S. Department of Justice Bureau of Statistics. Adjusted for the population increase between 1980 and 1999, the number of sentences for violent crime increased by 265 percent, property crimes by 221 percent, both more than doubling. However, during that same period, rates for both property offenses and violent crime actually *decreased,* property offenses steadily declining since the mid-1970s, violent crime remaining steady until 1994, at which point it decreased sharply each year.[4] Even more significant, the number of sentences for drug crimes increased more than tenfold, and the number of offenders imprisoned for public-disorder offenses increased by a factor of nearly eight.[5] Compared with violent crime and theft, the proportionally far greater increases in prison sentences for drug and public-order offenses are the defining factor in the rapidly expanding prison population. More than 30 percent of prisoners were incarcerated for offenses in 1999 that in the 1960s and early 1970s might have led instead to treatment programs, a matter driven home by the likelihood that, according the *Atlantic Monthly,* approximately 10 percent of offenders have a mental illness.[6] Those increases meant that in 1999, there were 476 people in prisons for every 100,000 U.S. citizens, a number that had increased every year since 1980, doubling in each passing decade.[7]

That increase has not been race-neutral. In 1999 there were 3,408 black men under state or federal jurisdiction for every 100,000 black men in the United States, 1,335 Latino men per 100,000, and 417 white men per 100,000.[8] That overrepresentation of black men in prison means that more than one out of every four black men likely will be incarcerated during his life, compared to a one in twenty-three chance for white men.[9] While white and black men reportedly use illegal drugs equally, black men are five times more likely to find themselves arrested for it, and U.S. prison historians and journalists describe white offenders as receiving a greater availability of alternatives to imprisonment by a prejudiced judicial process.[10] Indeed, the reported narrowing of the wage gap between black and white men of the 1980s and 1990s is inflated artificially due to the uncounted joblessness of incarcerated black men.[11] These are difficult numbers for a nation dismantling many affirmative action programs, locating its racism in the past. Imprisonment became the same response to a broad array of offenses, many of them so-called "victimless crimes" and matters that had previously meant drug treatment or alternate custody such as that administered by halfway houses. Such a total solution meant that the increasing construction of prisons still failed to address overcrowding. If crime rates dipped, it was because of prisons, so more were needed; if crime rates increased, more prisons were needed. As Franklin E. Zimring, director of the Earl Warren Legal Institute, points out, regardless of the question posed to the criminal justice system in the past thirty years, "Prison has been the answer."[12]

Throughout the 1980s and 1990s, prison officials returned to a model of inquiry—"what works?"—as opposed to the "nothing works" approach that emerged in the 1970s. The reason for the shift is clear: the overcrowding that began in the mid-1970s rapidly accelerated thereafter, and prison administrators searched for alternatives. The keynote addresses of the ACA during these two decades remain as generally progressive as in the past, emphasizing shared responsibility for social inequity and long-term solutions to problems of crime.[13] For example, in 1982 Houston, Texas, Chief of Police Lee P. Brown argues, "Crime is the natural consequence of the social, economic, and political systems of this country; and as long as unequal means of achievement exist, there will always be crime." His criticism of national policy gestures to the rhetoric of war so often characterizing imprisonment: "President Reagan leads us in the crime battle, but in the wrong direction"[14]—a reference to the administration's policies treating criminality as an innate matter of morality.

However, unlike during the 1970s, the willingness to treat crime and punishment as social phenomena is apparent not only in the plenary addresses but also in many of the general-session papers, such as a rehabilitations commissioner from Atlanta evoking a "we" who understand that "poverty, discrimination, lack of opportunity and poor education cause crime."[15] As prison populations soared amid dipping crime rates, the professionals most experienced with imprisonment saw firsthand the failures of the system. Presentations in the 1980s and 1990s suggest expanding parole options and call for alternate facilities such as community-based corrections. At the same time, national legislation dismantled parole at the federal level, and the furlough programs came under harsh attack following the Willie Horton debacle. Prison officials of the late 1980s and early 1990s regularly repeat, "America can't build its way out of the crowding problem."[16] However, state and federal lawmakers continued to try to do so, which identifies the political root of the dilemma. A survey of each state's director of corrections in 1988 led the researchers to conclude that "the political climate clearly does not support" scaling back the increases in sentencing and reductions in parole.[17] Prison officials initiated stopgap measures to an escalating problem that they viewed as a consequence of at best uninformed and at worst pernicious legislation.

In the 1990s, the ACA intensified its criticism of the policies that increased the prison population. Its president in 1993 points to "unjust sentencing" and excessive criminalization and imprisonment; the Pennsylvania corrections commissioner that year identifies that the "fiscal and crowding crisis is the result of our having politicized the issue of crime around a 'war on drugs.'"[18] At the same conference, the chair of the U.S. Sentencing Commission suggests scaling back mandatory sentences, and a senior circuit judge recommends their immediate reduction.[19] The 1994 ACA president remarks in his keynote address that there is "a widespread pattern of distortion and exaggeration concerning the nature and consequences of criminal behavior," an illusion to which "the politically ambitious often deliberately contribute."[20] He cites a May 1994 *U.S. News & World Report* editorial that claims, "We are at war today. The enemy is the criminal." President Perry M. Johnson discounts these hysterical accounts. He points out that crime is not the result of "some 'other'—some 'them,'" suggesting instead that criminality is not distinct from but part of a broader social world. Like a much earlier participant, Johnson cites Churchill's oft-quoted "never, never, never" speech regarding giving in to the enemy. However, unlike that earlier participant, who resists giving in to the supposed criminality of black militancy, Johnson proposes a struggle against the forces that make criminality a tool for political gain.[21] In 1996 a Virginia Democrat reiterates calls from the late 1960s and early 1970s for a long-term commitment to social programs of prevention rather than to political expediency, and an ACLU director and a Southern juvenile-facility administrator both sharply criticize the political failures of escalating "tough on crime" rhetoric.[22] A Republican senator's general address that year is substantially less clear in its criticism and offers the requisite paean to family values; nevertheless, he pushes for gun crime to be the top federal priority, a tacit departure from the emphasis on drug crime at the time.[23] At the ACA conferences of the 1990s, critique of wholesale incarceration proved cross-regional and occasionally bipartisan.

Among the best approaches to posing the question of what works is voiced in 1997 by ACA President Reginald A. Wilkinson. He offers a series of perspectives of those involved in corrections, evoking points of view of staff, administrators, and inmates, an unconventional rhetorical strategy surveying equally unconventional practices. In terms reminiscent of Deleuze and Guattari's Nietzschean turn, he provides a litany of the pronoun *I:* "Imagine that I am a records office supervisor"; "I have been a member of a street gang"; "I am a state probation officer"; "I am a fifty-six-year-old inmate"; "I am a lifer at a large prison for women."[24] If every name in history is I, then I am a prisoner and I am a warden. His recognition of alternate practices for corrections and his rhetorical approach are both innovative, and he acknowledges that it is "a risk to step over known boundaries." Nevertheless, he proposes that such approaches are necessary to depart from increasing incarceration.[25]

However, the descriptions of the ACA president's speech were not the only imaginative construction of prisoners. As Wilkinson makes clear in his 1998 address, television and the "silver screen" shape the perception and thereby the actuality of incarceration.[26] At the close of the twentieth century and the beginning of the twenty-first, the ACA itself capitulated to the power of media presentation, as keynote speakers from 1999 to 2001 departed from past tradition. Attorney General Janet Reno and Sarah Brady, chair of the handgun-control lobby, spoke in 1995, and the ACA president and Michigan governor gave the general address in 1998. However, in 1999 CNN's Greta Van Susteren and ABC News' Hugh Downs of *20/20* offered the keynote addresses. The next year saw such speeches by singer Tony Orlando and a New England Patriots football player turned motivational speaker, as well as Patty Duke. In 2001, the general assembly was addressed by Hunter "Patch" Adams, the doctor whose biography informs the based-on-a-true-story film *Patch Adams* (1998), starring Robin Williams and featuring a villain played by Bob Gunton, the evil warden of *The Shawshank Redemption*. That speech was immediately followed by one from Burl Cain, the warden of Angola, the Louisiana State Prison where the documentary *The Farm* is set and in which Cain features. The year 2002 featured the host of the television show *America's Most Wanted.* So it is not only *American History X, The Hurricane,* and *The Farm* that blur distinctions between actuality and imagination; it is also ACA speakers themselves who complicate the differences between news and entertainment.

The actuality of prison practice shapes films that leverage the cachet of the real, even as such films also capitulate to the historically inaccurate fantasy that all prisoners are guilty of violent crime, typically murder. In *Shots in the Mirror: Crime Films and Society,* Nicole Rafter suggests that the bleak history of the past three decades of actual imprisonment sharply divides the two sorts of prison films, "commercial entertainments and [ . . . ] political truth-telling," and that the "two may eventually merge in some way."[27] All three of the films I cover demonstrate this merging and its ramifications. *American History X* quotes directly the racial overrepresentation of incarceration patterns, though twisted to serve the interests of white supremacist characters. Raced criminality and imprisonment is the background to Rubin Carter's story in *The Hurricane,* and the contemporaneous history of racial profiling and the overrepresentation of black men in prison give its 1999 release further relevance. *The Farm's* occasional voice-over recounts racial statistics of imprisonment even as the camera records black men of dubious guilt behind bars. All three films make claims to the real in representing imprisonment. This chapter and the next two emphasize these films' deployment of the identity of the prisoner with conflicted purpose and dubious historicity. However, I am less invested in sorting truth from fiction, in questioning the veracity of the statistics Vinyard offers in his racist rants, in pointing out where *The Hurricane* deviates from the "real" biography of Rubin Carter, or in challenging the representativeness of *The Farm's* six inmates. Instead, I am interested in demonstrating a far more vexed relationship of history and imagination in their account of the differential tensions between black and white men, people in and out of prison, and individual autonomy and social belonging.

These films are not only part of the historical and cultural landscape in which viewers situate themselves,[28] but are also self-consciously crafted as such, not with the sly wink-and-nudge of late-twentieth-century irony and self-reflexive pastiche, but in the service of earnestness. They signify their own effort to tell the truth. They assert that claim to the real—in all three cases, of criminality and imprisonment as formative of selfhood—through narrative techniques and film technologies that fracture a sense of unbroken reality. Non-linear, fragmented, multiperspectival accounts stake claims as *really* real, a contentious matter given that the fictions and fictionalizations shape the patterns of prison-film narratives, including documentary. The identities of prisoners produced in these films draw attention to raced incarceration, but the films in attesting their truth-value thereby locate the resolution to that injustice within the reality constituted in the film. *The Hurricane* and *American History X* fulfill this logic, sharing a secret knowledge with viewers: we know the system of justice is racist, but in watching this film, and seeing justice be done in this film, we believe there is in fact social justice. That feature films fulfill culturally normative roles—what leftist critics a generation or two ago might have described as "bourgeois"—is not news. However, the stakes are higher for films attesting to their historical accuracy in a cultural climate where audiences increasingly encounter "reality" entertainment. Therefore, before engaging the production of the identity of the prisoner in each film, it is necessary to note how recent industry changes have fundamentally altered how films operate in the contexts of their production and reception. In addition, each of these films has been strategically screened to particular audiences, demonstrating a consequence of their claims to historical actuality and social relevance.

The space of prison, more than most places, defines the position of its population. For prisons films, in which the subject characters are incarcerated and thus relatively immobile, the camera creates the sense of movement. In terms of de Certeau and Deleuze and Guattari, inmates may not be out for a walk in the prison, but the camera is, and the fragments of shots are pieced together in editing like jigsaw pieces connected to the larger blocks of scenes in a puzzle whose overall shape and size are determined largely in editing. That in itself has held true for movies for most of the twentieth century, but due to transformations in development and distribution, films themselves are freed from the theater and circulate in space in a manner that invites various ways of viewing. A common way of viewing film in academic inquiry has been psychoanalytic inquiry, the study of how fear and desire operate in identification, the misrecognition of the self vis-à-vis the screen.

It is not difficult to see how this became the case. The vocabulary of psychoanalysis and the technology of film developed concurrently. The interpretation of dreams structured early Freudian analysis, and theatrical film could be addressed as shared dreams, the audience seated in darkness, alone, together, watching the projections of the fantasies they had paid to see. However, industry restructuring of the past two decades, coupled with technological developments, radically transformed the ways in which films are made as well as their conventional viewing experience, changes that include the horizontal and vertical integration of the film industry, the expansion of cable networks, and the development of VCRs and then DVD players. Therefore, while I occasionally make use of Lacanian and Deleuzo-Guattarian terms to describe film characters, I am also interested in drawing attention to how desire functions as a social and market force, and my attention is thus focused at least as much on production history and movie-industry mechanics as on the mechanisms of identification on and across the screen.

*American History X* was produced and distributed in the United States by New Line Cinema, a Time Warner company. New Line Cinema grew to prominence as a factory for 1980s "slasher" films, and then became the parent company's second-tier distributor for specialty markets, including prestige, horror, teen, and black films. Throughout the 1980s, the company thrived on the *Nightmare on Elm Street* franchise, but with the profit ratio of *House Party* in 1990 and its sequels in 1991 and 1994—the initial film grossed $26.4 million on a budget of $2.5 million—the company increasingly developed films with largely black casts to capitalize on the market share of African-American audiences, who historically have high numbers in theater ticket sales. *Friday,* the Ice Cube franchise of hood comedies from 1995 to 2002, offers another example of New Line's production and distribution in this genre. In the late 1990s, the production company expanded its role in the prestige-film market of hot new directors, ensemble casts, and unconventional narrative, producing director Paul Thomas Anderson's critically acclaimed work. New Line's production and distribution of *American History X*—with its subject of racism, its ensemble cast, and its first-time director, Tony Kaye—occurred, then, at a point when the company had a recent history of racially topical themes and was increasingly packaging medium-budget projects of established actors with new directors aimed at Academy Award recognition to build industry prestige and expand its market share.

The production company is just one of many interrelated components of the process of development and the chain of distribution.

A viewer might first have encountered *American History X* in its 1998 theatrical debut; rented or bought the videotape or DVD as a Warner Home Video release; watched the film on the movie stations HBO or Cinemax (both of which are Time Warner companies), or on regular cable stations such as Time Warner's TBS or TNT; or seen an advertisement or read a review in *Time, People,* or *Entertainment Weekly,* all Time Warner magazines.[29] The film failed to break even during its domestic theater run, for which the common response of distributors is to recoup such losses in overseas exhibition, cable, and rental sales. The Time Warner media conglomerate was in a position to exploit its vertical and horizontal control (producing and distributing the film, overseeing first-run theaters, owning not only the premier and standard cable companies but the material cable network itself) by releasing the film over many of its ancillaries, from pay-per-view services to the specialty movie channels to standard cable networks.

That saturation means that the film can play on any number of stations in various time slots. Viewers might watch a segment of it as they scan through hundreds of channels, or it might play in part or in its entirety while a potential spectator works from home, studies, eats, does housework, or participates in any number of household activities—or it might be viewed in another context entirely. In 2003, for example, I saw part of *American History X* muted but closed-captioned on a large-screen television behind a bar in Austin, Texas, in between live band sets. Rather than pay for a film one intends to see, a viewer can see a film by accident in unexpected public locations. Films leave the interior seclusion of traditional spectatorship and become part of a larger network of sensory stimuli where they compete for attention.

Filmmaking has both contributed to these transformations and responded to them. Editing practices such as rapid-fire cutting between shots and alternating color footage with black and white (*American History X, The Hurricane,* and *The Farm* all employ the latter method) demonstrate the influence of the short-format commercials and music videos where directors such as Kaye get their start. Black and white spliced with color has, since *The Wizard of Oz* (1939), differentiated reality from fantasy; Kansas, after all, is in black and white, the film of dream in color. Films such as *The Purple Rose of Cairo* (1985), *Pleasantville* (1998), and *Mumford* (1999) maintain the distinction even if some reverse the signification. Black and white is also a device signifying the past, either personal memory shared in its telling or public history, and the piecing together of that past leads to a disjointed narrative that is *really* real (because it is in black and white and is fragmented), even as its reconstruction demands viewers' engagement.

Incorporating black and white with color is then both an aesthetic gesture—particularly for films engaging race as a topic—and a preventive measure against channel switching. Furthermore, the increasingly digital format of video, coupled with transformations in computer technology and the expansion of file-sharing networks, has changed the ways that people access and view film and television programs. Audiences for major features such as *American History X* might, after the theatrical releases end, view them on cable. Or they might purchase a DVD or illegally download the digital files from any number of newsgroups or file-sharing networks to watch on a laptop computer at their leisure. Video becomes something that moves with viewers, seen in transit, stopping and starting at the convenience of the audience. Instead of Hollywood as a dream theater, films can become akin to the video billboards of the futuristic Los Angeles of *Blade Runner* (1982), viewed in medias res, part of a saturated cultural landscape.

Film viewing in these contexts has less in common with the Freudian or Lacanian analysand on a couch than it does with Deleuze and Guattari's schizophrenic on the move, de Certeau's sense of subjectivity as demonstrated by a walk in the city, an urban landscape one might read. Just as the setting of the psychoanalytic subject (the couch, the narration of personal history) foregrounds its investments in individualization, the schizophrenic in the city foregrounds the investments in mobility, collective identity, and larger social history—all key elements in these films set in prison at the close of the 1990s. And, more than either model, desire as a market force proves paramount—how directors and producers work to meet, manufacture, and challenge audiences' sense of the real and how films produce it. People moving through the city sometimes situate themselves vis-à-vis that reality through the reference points of fictional films. For example, Loren Hemsley, a bail bondsman in Los Angeles, describes conducting a home visit at Normandy and Crenshaw: "In case you don't know," he says, "that's the neighbor hood Ice Cube and Chris Tucker lived in the movie *Friday*."[30] The shared cultural imagination of the mediascape becomes a city à la de Certeau, one by which people relate to one another, and films serve as imagistic reference points viewers can use to locate themselves and others in the space and time of culture and history. As the opening epigraph for this chapter from

Henri Bergson suggests, film becomes a model for an "understanding of our own memory." Prison writer Abu-Jamal plays this trope when a sound from prison "merges into the mind's moviemaking machine, evoking distant memories."[31]

Race, place, and memory shape the landscapes of all three of these films determined by the prisons prominently featured as their settings, prisons populated by white and black men—the latter often of dubious guilt. In *American History X* the black-and-white flashback that recounts the main character's incarceration is the most significant stretch of the film's narrative, while Jewison shot much of *The Hurricane* on location in Ralway Prison, and *The Farm* takes place almost entirely inside the Louisiana State Prison. The first two films chronicle main characters arrested for race-related murder, imprisoned, and thereafter released; *The Farm* is organized around two white and four black inmates and depicts their day-to-day existence in the prison. The confined space of the prison is the most important place in all three films, just as racial difference defines each of their characters.

The claims of incarceration and race offered in the register of the real in *American History X* affect its reception and the use specific audiences make of it. The film is advertised, reviewed, and analyzed with this or that agenda by one group or another, matters of reception cued by its complicated production history. First-time feature director Tony Kaye filed a lawsuit over *American History X* against New Line Cinema and the Directors Guild in 1998, claiming that the film listed him as director against his wishes. During postproduction, New Line assumed control of piecing the film together after Kaye had spent some year and a half and still did not have a completed film. Edward Norton, who plays the role of the reforming white supremacist Derek Vinyard, reportedly oversaw the editing of the final cut, becoming the film's centerpiece. Kaye had filed to have his name listed in the credits as "Humpty Dumpty," suggesting that all the king's men could not put together a two-hour film from its many pieces, but the U.S. District Court dismissed the case, in 2000, "with extreme prejudice," denying appeal.[32] The court's ruling resonates with the film itself, given its chronicle of Vinyard's racist crime, his time in prison, and his subsequent dismissal of his own extreme racial prejudice.

Despite that disavowal, the film is equivocal in its depiction of racism, particularly the causes and effects of raced criminality. Reviews of the film are split fairly evenly between, on one hand, reflecting the

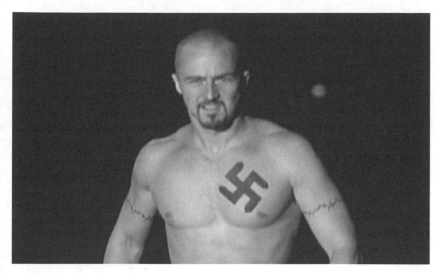

**Figure 1**
**Hard Aryan youth.** Derek Vinyard's (Edward Norton) steeled masculine body early in *American History X* matches Hitler's call in *Triumph of Will* (1935) for "this people to be hard, not soft, and you must steel yourselves for it in your youth."

film's ambiguities or even subtextual endorsement of white supremacy and, on the other, praising its realism and tour de force acting.[33] The divide largely can be attributed to the film's postproduction history and Norton's hand in the editing, which likely emphasized his charismatic performance, thereby facilitating the critical accolades he received. He was nominated for an Academy Award for his role, and named Best Actor by the Southeastern Film Critics Association and the Golden Satellite Awards. The film also was nominated for the "Peace" Award offered by the nonprofit Political Film Society, slated for use as an educational tool by Amnesty International USA, and taught in some schools.[34] The "Peace" Award in particular seems possibly out of place for a film whose style pays homage to Leni Riefenstahl as it attempts to explain Norton's neo-Nazi character so persuasively that it can be read as glorifying him, a film that sees every black man a criminal, prisoner, or former offender. It seems likely that the film's difficult delivery produces some of its ambiguity; after all, the film is the problem child of two men, Kaye and Norton (or three, if one counts the screenwriter, David McKenna), one of whom denied paternity, and its message of racial harmony is largely organized through the triumph of Norton's will.

*American History X* is at once brilliant and deeply flawed, a triumphant failure of excellent acting depicting a charismatic racist's prison transformation.[35] The film focuses on a white family, the Vinyards, especially the two sons, Derek (Norton) and Danny (Edward Furlong). Derek is a prominent young leader of a white supremacist gang in Venice Beach, California, the DOC (Disciples of Christ). Three black men attempt to steal his truck from outside his house; he shoots two, one of whom is only wounded, and is then killed by Derek in an a scene of almost-unwatchable violence. Derek spends three years in prison, where, through contact with two black men—the coworker Lamont, whose imprisonment is far out of proportion with his minor crime, and his former English teacher, Dr. Sweeney (Avery Brooks)—he learns to repudiate the racism that caused his crime. Released from prison, he spends a day trying to undo the racial conflicts he has helped to propagate, including violently rejecting DOC patriarch Cameron (Stacy Keach), leaving the group, and severing his younger brother Danny's participation in the white gang. Those efforts take place during a skinhead rally edited in a sequence that has Kaye's thumbprint, a frenetic montage described in *Sight and Sound* as one of "documentary realism," suggestive of the film's overall look and feel, described by industry trade *Variety* as one of "truthfulness and integrity," its style one of "heightened realism."[36] The claim to the real is a defining feature of the film.

Much of the narrative is told by Derek to Danny or by Danny to the audience. On the day of Derek's release from prison, Danny has submitted a paper in his English class treating Adolph Hitler as a civil rights leader, landing him in the office of the principal, Dr. Sweeney. Sweeney assigns a new paper to Danny, a paper titled "American History X," in which he is "to analyze and interpret all of the events surrounding Derek's incarceration," in order to demonstrate how those events shaped Danny's current view of contemporary culture. That history is largely the assembly of memory in black and white, either Danny's or Derek's flashbacks, the latter offered as the elder brother narrates his prison experience as an explanation for why they both must reject the false consciousness of their racism. The chronology of events thus is out of sequence: a black-and-white first-person shot from the point of view of one of the prospective car thieves opens the film, followed by first Derek's and then Danny's perspective of the two murders. The film thereafter regularly features the flashbacks—the events leading to the incarceration—as they are invoked by the two brothers' activities through the first twenty-four hours after Derek's release. The narrative is fairly complex, both a cause and a result of the crisis over the editing involving Kaye, Norton, and New Line. The fractured sequence allows the graphic shot of the particularly grue-some murder to take place midway through the film, after audiences have had an opportunity to compare Derek's persona before and after his incarceration.

Memory serves as the narrative device linking chronologically dis-jointed scenes. Danny's point of view memories are triggered in two ways: either as he writes the paper to fulfill his assignment or as he walks through Venice Beach and is reminded by aspects of the land-scape. Furlong's character presents both the conventional analysand performing a talking cure in his voice-over as he reads his writing of the paper, and the subject taking a walk in the city. He pauses at the municipal basketball court, which calls up the memory of the black-versus-white game that loosely instigated the carjacking and subsequent murder, landing Derek in prison. Danny runs past dilapi-dated storefronts on his way home, his rapid pace and destination a parallel to the end of Derek's three years in prison and release that day, leading to the memory of the elder brother's return that morning in the accompanying black-and-white flashback of his welcome by the family. The beachside Southern California city where the film was shot on location is offered visually several times as a broader context for "the events surrounding Derek's incarceration" as perceived by Danny. Furlong takes a walk in a city, amid the ethnic diversity of its pedestrians, its graffiti, and its crime, the "stylistic procedures" that de Certeau suggests resist textualization.[37] Those "pedestrian practices" trigger vignettes of memory, implicating the relationships of past and present—and between Danny and his brother—and shaping the essay he writes upon his return home.

Making sense of the racial (and narrative) difficulty of his brother's development is thus the job of Danny in the film; the paper he writes is effectively the film itself, so interpreting it is the viewer's job as well. The film foregrounds this fact when Danny begins writing the essay. He sits at his computer and types the name of the film and essay, then types repeatedly, "Analyze and Interpret," until it becomes "Anal sex and"—a bit of foreshadowing, as Derek's anal rape in prison by white supremacist gang members plays its significant part in his reformation. Then Danny writes that when people look at him, they see his brother—much as Danny himself has, misrecognizing in his brother a coherent self he yearns for and strives toward. The film self-consciously fashions itself as an object to analyze and interpret here, perhaps anticipating its own later role as a teaching tool in classrooms, where actual students might write their own essays (or professors, books) about it. There is a cued earnestness in the scene; just as Danny stops his own linguistic play to get serious, the film invites audiences to take the movie seriously, as Danny writes a fusion of his brother's and his own diagnostic biography, which viewers watch played out on screen. Regarding the essay, Dr. Sweeney tells Danny, "I will be the only one reading it," but he is wrong on two counts: Danny reads as he writes the film that viewers are deliberately hailed to "read" as well.

The fusion of the two brothers means that they both can—and do—change their racist views, Derek during his prison sentence and Danny during the time it takes the older brother to offer a thick description of that time served. The brothers are sufficiently doubled, so that audiences can look at one and see the other as well, meaning that it does not really matter which one of them gets killed to close the tragedy. Derek walks Danny to school and, on leaving, looks back, seemingly hearing the "threat score" of rising violins, which predicts violence, the precursor to the deadly retribution that befalls Danny at the end. A black student shoots him in the school bathroom for a minor slight earlier in the film, providing the fulfillment of the film's moral: racial violence only begets more of the same.

However powerful that moral may be, the racial logic of the film is deeply flawed. There is not a sufficient narrative basis within the film for the black student to kill Danny—Danny's brief altercation with the unnamed student earlier in the film is no motive, and there is no indication that when the character shoots him, he is looking at Danny but seeing his brother. In effect, the character is signified only by his blackness, and any black character might do as well as any other. Similarly, at least one of the three would-be car thieves loses to Derek and members of his gang in a racially charged black-on-white basketball game, but it is not clear if their crime is motivated by anything more than the loss of the game, such as Derek's leadership in the DOC. The two prominent black male characters of Dr. Sweeney and Lamont are relegated to helping the white Derek become who he needs to be to fulfill the story.[38] Derek and Danny's father, Dennis, was a firefighter shot on duty by a black man, and even Dr. Sweeney suggests having spent time in prison. Crime and incarceration are

connected to every single black man mentioned in the film. Furthermore, there are virtually no black women, as Sweeney's secretary,
a black woman, is seen only partially and fleetingly, though several
white women have prominent roles.

That exclusion is produced largely by the focus on the Vinyard
family, which makes racism a family and an oedipal phenomenon:
Derek learned it from his father, and with the death of the father
and the son's assumption of the father's place, Derek teaches it to
Danny. Any mention in the film of the broader causes of racism, such
as economic disparities and historical disenfranchisement producing
segregation, as well as a social psychology of racial fear, are either
voiced by Derek or Danny and twisted to substantiate their racism,
or immediately dismissed by the brothers as irrelevant. For example,
Derek says, "One in every three black males is in some phase of the
correctional system. Is that a coincidence or do these people have, you
know, like a racial commitment to crime?" He speaks the unspeakable
in racializing criminality, the blatant "natural" or ontological racism
so often politically decried while social welfare programs are dismantled and racial profiling has been until recently de facto police
protocol. Derek rallies his gang members around him with rhetorical
and physical flourishes that are offered so as to seem persuasive to
other characters in the narrative, and that thereby foster the credibility
viewers might hold for his character. The effectiveness of Norton's
performance (around which he edited the film) becomes a sizable
obstacle for any efforts of *American History X* to address a larger causal
framework for racism and racial criminality.

Derek's racially motivated murder of the second would-be car thief
depicts the crime that is the clearest origin of his imprisonment. The
camera shot of the near decapitation of the wounded man features
plenty of warning, including Derek's shirtless slow-motion approach
to the camera, pleas from both the victim and Danny, and the ubiquitous crescendo of violins. Audiences are prepared so ruthlessly for
the ultraviolent moment that they can look away, and likely many
do—and the close-up of the terrorized black male character cuts to
a long shot of the murder from Danny's vantage point in which the
victim is barely visible. Therefore, the scene of Derek's crime that
is the culmination of his racism, the crux of the film, and the one
most commonly cited by viewers and reviewers, is quite literally *not
seen* by many. His sentencing, or any other jurisprudential proceed-
ing, is not shown at all, and there is only a faceless parole officer

occasionally mentioned. The naming of Derek's criminality as distinct from his criminal act thus is offered only obliquely when Danny offers his testimony, "It would have been life if I had testified," a sentence he types and promptly erases. Sweeney will not be reading this sentence, but Danny and viewers do.

Derek's imprisonment, which constitutes the longest stretch of unbroken narrative in the film, is organized around two inverse social arcs, a series of increasingly friendly discussions with his black coworker, Lamont, and Derek's deteriorating relationship with the white supremacist prison gang, which culminates in their raping him. Both function as processes of prison rehabilitation. The rape scene has its own ominous approach, a gradually emptying shower, the disappearance of the lone guard from the scene, and more of the camera's adoring gaze, the slow motion of Derek's naked skin. This moment of violence is paired with the earlier one, punishment matching crime in black-and-white flashback, the parallel complete down to the slow-motion hyperreality of impossible clarity as Norton approaches the camera to commit murder, as individual drops of water fall from his face in the shower. Furthermore, the earlier sequence opens with Derek having rough sex with his girlfriend, ands its corresponding scene closes with Derek's own violent rape.

However, the Motion Picture Association of America ratings system has greater leniency for the graphic depiction of violence compared to sex,[39] which means that Derek's rape is represented with even more discretion and is thus watchable in a way that his crime is not. Derek's victimization by white supremacy becomes more narratively significant than the victimization of the black man he killed. The greater importance is underscored by Norton's extended time on camera—whether shirtless and triumphant in a reverse dunk on the basketball court; rallying his gang members by citing immigration and incarceration statistics; after his reform in prison, using his power to reject his racism in assaulting the patriarch of the white gang and disarming one of its soldiers; or persuading Danny to surrender his own prejudice. Understanding the rape as Derek's real punishment in the film reflects what prison historians describe as the "just desserts" model of punishment prevalent since 1975.[40] It is also a bodily punishment, a throwback to what Foucault deems *old regime* practice, except that rather than the state fulfilling the bodily torture, inmates themselves conduct it. And just as Foucault claims that the visibility of public torture such as that of Damien the Regicide sparked unintended sympathy for the criminal, the spectacle of Derek's rape deliberately elicits sympathy for him from the audience.

Norton, arguably one of the finest actors of his generation, effectively does too good a job in portraying a charismatic bigot, and the two-hour edit of the film he largely oversaw organizes itself around his character, highlighting the actor's physicality, built for the film and deployed in a visual rhetoric of power. Norton's character is language and body, and inadequacies in one can be compensated for by the other. When a potential suitor of his mother challenges him over a family dinner, Derek can support any insufficiencies of argument by taking off his shirt, the swastika tattooed above his pectoral a threat to the Jewish teacher, an excess of visibility that appears repeatedly in various flashbacks, the black and white highlighting Norton's musculature. Within the context of the narrative, the physical threat he poses is daunting to other characters; extranarratively, the camera loves him, and he gets the best lines. In the absence of any competing discourse, his language of hate is fetishized narratively and visually, and there is no competition. The mother, Doris Vinyard, is played by Beverley D'Angelo in a largely understated, if powerful, performance, and the suitor—and history teacher who sends Danny to Principal Sweeney—is a bit part for Elliot Gould as Murray Rosenberg. D'Angelo's and Gould's characters proffer liberal rhetoric situated as outmoded and nostalgic, Doris even in a flowered minidress shot in soft focus outside her 1950s-era home. Sixties liberalism is not prepared to deal with harsher 1990s "reality."

Coupled with Furlong and Norton, D'Angelo and Gould offer performances that help the casting itself create the opportunity for complex white characters to be nuanced and convincingly portrayed, with backstory to provide cause for their behavior, while black characters serve as background. Brooks is a polished, charismatic actor, but he has little room to maneuver while playing an urban saint. Both his role and the role of the character Lamont are undeviating, guiding Derek, and the other positions available for black men in the film, the basketball players fouling with violence, the car thieves, prisoners, and school-bathroom shooter, are all cardboard cutouts with crime on their minds and few to no lines. The film fulfills the equation of black masculinity with criminality that has proven so prevalent historically in the cultural imagination. Though Norton's character, Vinyard, claims that one out of every three black men will enter the criminal justice system, the film itself gives far better than even odds.

**Figure 2**
**Look, a white man!** In a scene that reverses Frantz Fanon's recognition of raced blackness, Derek Vinyard (Norton) sees that others recognize him as the only white prisoner on the cell block.

A contributing factor to the film's latent bias is the degree to which the writer and director try to break the ontological category of race and make it a free-floating signifier. When Derek abandons the Aryan gang during a party the evening he is released from prison, his former girlfriend Stacy repeatedly screams that he is a "nigger." In the extended flashback in which he relates his prison experience to his younger brother—and by extension, the audience—viewers see how a Latino guard names Derek's own whiteness as an epithet, which is contextualized later when Lamont tells him, "In the joint, you the nigger, not me," and goes on to use the term to hail Derek several times. The rape scene is situated vaguely as a response to Derek's first disavowing the Aryan gang in the prison for their political inconsistency and then, after becoming friends with Lamont, playing in a mixed-race basketball game. The Aryan leader says, "Want to be a nigger? We'll treat you like one." Race is the X factor of American history; who is white and who is black can be reorganized easily as power structures are rearranged. The overrepresentation of black men in prison can create localized reversals of racial authority among prisoners, a claim Mailer's Gilmore also makes to provide a basis for his own racism. *American History X* presents a Hegelian recognition of the other recognizing the self: "you the nigger."

However, the limits of such a racial reordering in U.S. culture, whose history often is predicated upon assumptions of racial difference, possibly contributed to the film's failure at the box office. That is, the film can be understood by genre as a variation on the hood film, a white gang movie in the vein of John Singleton's *Boyz n the Hood* (1991). Both feature the constitutive elements: gangs organized on lines of racial identity; violence criticized within the narrative but extranarratively more ambiguous in the degree to which it is glorified; the scarce father figures; the cult of masculinity in which manliness is activity, the violent subordination of others, and invulnerability; and the family largely supplanted by gangs but offering the saving grace for the main character's rejection of violence, which occurs too late to save brother figures. The most visible difference between *American History X* and the hood gangster films is one of race. *White* masculine youth culture so subaltern as to turn to violence—with violence's attendant crime, imprisonment, and vengeful murder—possibly proved unmoving for audiences more accustomed to seeing gangs of young *black* men as a menace to society, doomed to incarceration and violent death.

*American History X* does not know what sort of movie it is, which is one way of saying that the overlapping audiences of popular moviegoers and film critics disagreed among themselves what to make of it. According to popular viewers recording their votes on the Internet Movie Database (IMDB), the film was the forty-second best film of all time at mid–2007, placing it above *Chinatown* (1974, forty-fifth) and *The Maltese Falcon* (1941, sixty-third).[41] One might dismiss this ranking as unrelated to more "elite" valuation, but typical distinctions drawn between "high" and popular culture are challenged by the close parallels between the IMDB rankings and the one hundred best films as ranked by the American Film Institute. *American History X* was released too late to be considered for the AFI 100 in 1998 and was not included on the 2007 revised version, but in general there is a high degree of correlation between the AFI and IMDB lists, especially taking into account the IMDB inclusion of foreign films and overemphasis on recent films. Of the AFI top 50, 19 appear in the IMDB top 50; 30 appear in the IMDB top 100, and only seven films do not appear in the IMDB top 250.

Users of the movie database can rank a film and post comments, and *American History X* has generated fierce discussion among participants. Through the end of 2003, more than eight hundred IMDB

**Figure 3**
**Interracial friendship as salvation.** In *The Shawkshank Redemption,* the friendship between Andy (Tim Robbins) and Red (Morgan Freeman) saves both of them.

members had made online contributions, more than each of the AFI's top three of *Citizen Kane* (1941), *Casablanca* (1942), and *The Godfather* (1972), all of which were ranked in the top twenty-five by IMDB voters as well. *Real* is the primary term of contention among the online posts, which are roughly split as to whether the film is realistic or not, though applause for Norton's acting performance is another focus. Professional film critics are similarly divided and in identical terms, recognizing the ambiguities of the film's representation of racial conflict while celebrating Norton's acting and the film's look and feel. Norton's performance is "history-making" in the *National Review;* the industry trade *Variety* praises the story's "truthfulness" and Kaye's on-location direction as "gritty," suggesting that it adds to the "heightened realism of the film's style."[42] The perceived visual quality of *American History X* is bound to the contention regarding its symbolization of the real, with the historical traumas of racism and incarceration.

For these overlapping groups of popular audiences and critics, what makes the film great is its thematic and visual participation in

**Figure 4**
**Redeeming American history.** In *American History X,* friendship with Lamont (Guy Torry) protects Derek (Norton) from racial violence.

a code of realism: its willingness to name and represent racial conflict without easy resolution in its substance, coupled with its stylish cinematography and location shooting. When Danny (Furlong) walks along Venice Beach, the long shot substantiates the actual setting; when he dies at the end, the possibility of a happy ending is frustrated. This is not the sacrificial death at the close of *Cool Hand Luke* (1967), Paul Newman's pose of crucifixion signifying sacrifice and transcendence. Furthermore, the prison of the central section of the film is steel bars and dirty blacktop rather than a studio fantasy of technofetishism, as in Stanley Kubrick's *A Clockwork Orange* (1971) and John Woo's *Face/Off* (1997). Neither prison nor city is a utopian fantasy of racelessness, without distinction between black and white. The filmic world of the real is represented as isolated, nasty, brutish, and short, where people are born, suffer, and then are murdered at street curbs and in high school bathrooms because of racial hate. The camera's unflinching gaze on that very unpleasantness and grittiness is symptomatic of its integrity and "documentary realism."

*American History X*'s initial box office failure followed by subsequent positive critical and popular reception means that it parallels Darabont's *Shawshank Redemption,* which disappointed similarly at the box office but garnered seven Academy Award nominations and became a cultural phenomenon in its popularity and ubiquity in cable rotation. The similarities are curious given the degree to which *American History X* attempts to challenge *Shawshank*'s romantic narrative, lyrical style, and escapism with a stark, gritty look and feel to complement its bleak story. Nevertheless, both films capitulate to similar racist expectation and fictions of redemption, wherein black men are criminals whose rehabilitation involves helping white characters become who they need to be. In contrast to *Shawshank Redemption,* which I find compulsively watchable but ideologically bankrupt, I find the skillfully written and directed *American History X* well-intentioned but deeply problematic. I appreciate the film's style and applaud its excellent acting and unglamorous representation of imprisonment, but am cautious of its exclamatory realness of white men in prison, when the historical account reads much the opposite.

# 6

# "Based upon a true story"

## The Hurricane and the Problem of Prison Redemption

> Most of the Jamesburg kids had only committed the same violations of rules as had endeared Huckleberry Finn to millions of people, but in us society found these deeds intolerable.
>
> —Rubin "Hurricane" Carter in *The Sixteenth Round: From Number 1 Contender to #45472*[1]

THE WHOLESALE fiction of *American History X*'s "documentary realism" gives way to the "invented characters and fictionalized events" of *The Hurricane,* based on the true story of Rubin "Hurricane" Carter. The question of reality versus its absence as well as championship acting are similarly touchstones for the critical response to *The Hurricane.* Whether or not it tells the "real" story is similarly at stake among viewers posting comments to its IMDB forum. Like Edward Norton, Denzel Washington, with his portrayal of Carter, garnered an Academy Award nomination for Best Actor, and his failure to win that year prompted discussion as to whether his 2002 Best Actor Award for his performance in *Training Day* (2001) was at all informed by white guilt.[2] Critics in the major weeklies and dailies roundly praised Washington's portrayal as "splendid," "his best role," a "knockout," and "a moving, fiercely compacted performance."[3] The latter of these two speak directly to the middleweight Carter himself, a gesture underscored by the director, Norman Jewison, in his hyperbolic praise that he could not tell the difference between the actor and the former boxer.[4] Feature articles in the magazines *Ebony* and *Jet*, both geared to black audiences, further highlight the film's claim to the real, the latter by including a set photo of Washington-as-Carter with the actual people of Carter's life.[5] Such reviews juxtapose pictures of Carter boxing with film stills of Washington in the ring and count on audiences to tell the difference. However, reading the history produced in the film presents more-significant challenges than telling the two men apart.

Like *American History X*, with *The Hurricane* it is difficult to sort the difference between actual events and their imagination, both in its story and in selective contexts in which groups have screened the film. In addition, like the earlier film, *The Hurricane* features the cinematic construction of the identity of the prisoner: crime or its lack, the declaration of criminality, and imprisonment as transformative, even redemptive. The film incorporates a wide variety of sources of varying adherence to actuality, from Carter's autobiography (written while he was still in prison) to wholesale inventions, and much in between. Furthermore, as with *American History X*, matters of criminalization are linked inextricably with race, though this time the falsely presumed guilt of black men proves far more central to the film. This chapter first demonstrates the narrative and extranarrative efforts to equate Carter and Washington and the problems in doing so, and then describes the film's rendition of racist criminal justice and the director's efforts to complicate an overly simplified version. Next, I point out the rich psychoanalytic implications of Washington's performance of Carter's story, wherein a self divided cannot stand any more than an imagined unity of self. Instead, the film advocates a social identity, a "we"—paradoxically, an "us" that includes the judicial process initiating the same imprisonment that the U.S. Supreme Court deemed unjust.

On February 26, 2001, a group of student organizations at the University of Southern California sponsored the screening of *The Hurricane*, Jewison's film account of Rubin "Hurricane" Carter's life, from a tempestuous young man to the up-and-coming boxer imprisoned for a crime he did not commit, to his years behind bars and the efforts of lawyers and activists that finally freed him. The flyer for this screening lists the student organizations in small type across the top, including the Black Student Assembly and the Student Senate Minority Affairs. The banner just below reads, "RUBIN HURRICANE CARTER," the nickname and film title in larger letters, conflating man and movie; all of the text is white on a black background, including the date and location of the screening, which are listed at the bottom. The primary images of the flyer are three vertical frames, a triptych. The leftmost panel features a photo of Carter wearing boxing gloves, fists low, facing the camera, his torso and head visible. The rightmost panel is a closer shot of the man playing the role of Carter in the film, Washington, his brow furrowed, eyes on the camera, one fist ungloved but taped, a more-guarded pose than its twin. The center panel dividing the stills of Carter and Washington is white, blank. That gap might emphasize the difference between the images of subject and actor, or possibly its whiteness framed by blackness reverses the racial politics of the film—or perhaps the photographs merely balance better that way. Two months later, the film screened at the University of Texas at Austin as part of the Sweatt Symposium on Civil Rights.[6] John Artis, Carter's codefendant and also a prisoner for sixteen years before a federal judge voided the earlier decision, delivered the keynote address for the conference, his presence and personal experience with the racial inequities of the judicial system guiding the reception of the film. The film cliché of the wrongly imprisoned protagonist assumes a greater urgency and authenticity when situated in the context of historical actuality and civil rights, with Artis there to tell the difference.

The conflation of historical documentation and fictionalization poses risks to the apprehension of history, both the claim to history and the anxiety over its misrepresentation. Before the film has even begun, it offers the obligatory disclaimer that frames its subsequent criticism: "While this picture is based upon a true story, some characters have been composited or invented, and a number of incidents fictionalized." The inventions far surpass Mailer's writing a dream and inserting it into the unconscious of one of Gilmore's analysts, as the systemic racial bias in the judiciary that imprisoned Carter collapses into one white detective with a vendetta, Della Pesca (Dan Hedaya), a heavy fictionalization of Lieutenant Vincent DeSimone.[7] The *Nation*'s review praises Washington's performance, but is highly critical of the film's overwriting of "truth," a claim to the real the article itself embodies in being written by Lewis M. Steel, a member of Carter's legal team—who, incidentally, is left out of the movie. Unlike Gilmore's lawyers, whom Schiller dismisses as "hopeless as journalists,"[8] Steel rises to the occasion. If filmmakers are going to write history, then lawyers will review their films.

This is not the first time that a Washington role has been at stake in questions of historical actuality and its film depiction. He plays South African activist Stephen Biko in Richard Attenborough's *Cry Freedom* (1987); a Union soldier in Edward Zwick's *Glory* (1989), a film based on an actual colonel's letters; and Malcolm X in Spike Lee's so-titled film (1992).[9] There has been a flurry of criticism regarding historical docudramas such as these,[10] challenges that are pertinent to this film as well. *The Hurricane*'s collapse of systemic injustice into one rogue cop is a conventional narrative pattern, effectively an individualization of institutional power that whitewashes more-endemic problems. Such fictionalization is one half of what Hayden White, among others, describes as "postmodern history," where fiction is framed in a "real" context even as the real employs cues of the imagination.[11] The decisions made by cable-network programmers offer an example of the complicated relationship of real and imaginary in such postmodern history. For example, the Court TV Channel is part of many standard cable packages, and grew to prominence with the trial of O. J. Simpson, featuring largely news and documentary programming related to the legal system, from live trial coverage to a talk show hosted by former district attorney and judge Catherine Crier. In the never-ending effort to fill its schedule, the channel began showing syndicated fiction serials with law-and-order themes, so whether a real judge or actor or former judge turned host appeared on camera may have been difficult for viewers of Court TV to sort, depending on the time slot.[12]

*The Hurricane* would fit such programming quite nicely, with its many prominent courtroom scenes, prison settings, and "based upon a true story" legal battles for justice. The film assigns a three-part structure to Carter's biography. The first follows the boxer's life from childhood until his arrest (with Artis) for a triple murder in Paterson, New Jersey, in 1966, a period defined by both Carter's repeated unjust incarceration and the meteoric rise of his boxing career. The second, initiated by his 1967 sentence to life in prison, features his resistance to incarceration through performing his own autonomy, refusing the trappings of prisoner because to assume them would, in his eyes, admit the criminality he disavows. He will not wear the uniform of the prisoner, or eat prison food; he keeps largely to himself in his cell, writing his autobiography, *The Sixteenth Round*, and reading philosophy, literature, and law.

The third stage of the story introduces Lesra Martin (Vicellous Reon Shannon), a teenage black youth from Brooklyn who is the ward of three white Canadians, Lisa Peters (Debra Unger), Sam Chaiton (Liev Schreiber), and Terry Swinton (John Hannah). They effectively adopt Lesra in order to facilitate his education, teaching him to read and preparing him for college. At a book sale where the youth is the only nonwhite, he stares at a box full of books and focuses on *The Sixteenth Round*, its jacket prominently featuring Carter's black male face. In an invitation to participate in the identification, the point-of-view shot equates the camera's gaze with Shannon's, and his hand that extends to select the book in which he recognizes himself is thus the viewer's hand. After reading the book, Lesra, along with the Canadians, meets Carter in prison and reignites the legal campaign to free him. After nineteen years of protesting his innocence, Carter becomes a free man.

In a manner similar to scenes of remembering in *American History X*, *The Hurricane* opens out of chronological sequence. Where the prior film uses the pair of brothers as narrators, memory coupled with the writing of the titular essay invoking flashbacks, the connections in the puzzle of Carter's life maintain largely thematic links established by the director, Jewison. A black-and-white episode of a 1963 boxing match cuts to Carter in color preparing to fight prison guards in order to maintain possession of his prison manuscript in 1973, then cuts to faceless men committing the 1966 triple murder in Paterson (although casual audiences are unlikely to know this, Jewison shot the scene at the Lafayette Bar and Grill in Paterson, where the actual murders occurred), and then to Carter and Artis being pulled over by the police. Conflict organizes the coherence among the opening jump cuts connecting disparate moments in history.

That device is replaced by literacy for the duration of the film, as shots of Lesra reading Carter's biography cut to Washington's portrayal of that life. The emphasis on literacy underscores the degree to which such editing emulates some of the conventions of the high-modernist literary novel in the first half of the twentieth century, replacing the sequence of chronology with narrative movement triggered by characters' personal memories and historical reconstruction, strategies that arguably see their ur-example in U.S. writing in Faulkner's novels from *The Sound and the Fury* to *Go Down, Moses*. Like Shreve's "let me play" of *Absalom, Absalom!*, such fragmentation, discontinuity, and multiplicity engage audiences in actively constructing the narrative, piecing together the puzzle. Late-twentieth-century U.S. films situated as art draw from this literary tradition as well as from documentary style, jump cuts, the mix of color and black and white, and other techniques borrowed from French new-wave cinema of the 1950s and 1960s and expanded in music-video shorts and commercials in the 1980s and 1990s, substantially altering the narrative styles of late-twentieth-century U.S. films.

Both *American History X* and *The Hurricane* make literacy itself a narrative device. In the latter film, the reading of *The Sixteenth Round* by Lesra and Lisa and the epistolary exchange between the two of them and Carter provide the basis for the film's movement in and out of prison, just as the letters between Cleaver and his lawyer and between Gary Gilmore and Nicole Baker pass back and forth. In *The Hurricane*, a scene of Lisa reading the biography aloud cuts to Carter in prison, or a shot of Carter reading a letter from Lesra cuts to Canada. Like *American History X*, then, writing and reading one's own life vis-à-vis the life of the "other" of the prisoner serves as both a structural and a thematic device. Danny's voice-over speaks his essay, writing how his perspective has been shaped by his brother's incarceration. Much of Washington's dialogue, by comparison, comes directly from Carter's book, and that actual prison writing, with its attendant emphasis on testimony—on relating the reality of imprisonment to those not themselves incarcerated—thus finds its way into this film largely set in prison. Re-created prison scenes frame actual prison writing.

Like the narrative of Kaye's film, the sequencing of *The Hurricane* is informed by treating reading and writing as fundamental to its story. Such a basis does emphasize the centrality of both Carter's book and the account offered by two of the Canadians, Chaiton and Swinton's *Lazarus and the Hurricane* (1999)[13]; both are primary sources for the film's screenplay. The narrative organization of the film, however, belongs to its director, Jewison, and his own effort to assemble the pieces in supervising the editing and telling the "truth." He achieves this organization of the story's parts through first an arrest and then three critical court scenes corresponding to the three parts of Carter's life, with visible and invisible cues to the historical actuality of the events depicted, gestures that complicate their own historicity.

**Figure 5**
**The policeman's call: "Hey, you there!"** A police car pulls over Rubin "Hurricane" Carter (Denzel Washington) and John Artis (Garland Whitt) and leads to this shot/reverse shot sequence. The officer says, "We're looking for two Negroes in a white car"; Carter replies, "Any two will do?"

The most crucial scene of the film occurs when the police pull over Carter (Washington) and Artis (Whitt). Artis, the younger man, drives the boxer's car and acts very nervous. Carter remains calm, and as it turns out, he and the first officer to approach the car know one another. The police officer says, "We're looking for two Negroes in a white car," to which Carter responds, "Any two will do?" The moment is one of twin recognitions, not only Carter and the officer recognizing one another, but also the officer recognizing Carter first as a black man and then as a particular celebrity, "The Hurricane." That initial recognition provides the first elaboration of the judicial racial bias that results in Carter's life sentence, and the court's recognition of that bias nineteen years later is the basis for his release.

The policeman's declaration, "We're looking for two Negroes," makes the search akin to Faulkner's description of the town of Jefferson's desire for Joanna Burden's murder to be a "negro crime committed not by a negro but by Negro."[14] The police in this scene, like the lynch mob, are looking for blackness as criminality, and they find it where they see it: Carter and Artis are stopped, arrested, and imprisoned. The scene very nearly appears twice in the movie, thereby emphasizing its importance. Later in the film, another black-and-white boxing sequence fades through a sly edit of a close-up of a red light that is not a police siren but a nightclub illumination, and Carter and Artis depart from the club only to be pulled over. The club they leave is an actual bar in Paterson, creating an invisible claim to historical actuality for the subsequent arrest. That arrest is the quintessential Althusserean moment, the policeman's call of "You there!" hailing the subject.

The policeman's call is the first scene of several in the film presuming Carter to be a criminal, and it sets the stage for the three times he is interpellated in court, named in the first and second instances as a criminal and in the third as innocent. All three identifications directly relate to his race. In the first, he is a child (played by Mitchell Taylor Jr.) accused of trying to rob an older white man, though the film situates him as first protecting his friend from sexual assault and then defending himself against murder. The white judge who addresses him wishes he could try the black boy as an adult and sentences him to reform school until he is twenty-one.

The scene directly follows Carter's interrogation conducted by his nemesis in the film, the detective Della Pesca (Hedaya), whose name roughly translates from Italian as "a catch" or "fishing for something." Pesca, upon initially seeing the child, says, "I see a nigger with a knife." That equation of blackness with violent criminality lays the basis for its numerous reiterations throughout the film, and it makes Pesca the face of racial bias. Carter's race and criminality are called out repeatedly, police officers referring to him as a "black son of a bitch" and "a life criminal" before the murders for which Carter is later accused even occur. The detective is present in every courtroom and in the initial interrogation; he garners false testimony from witnesses, and, upon arresting Carter after the latter's escape from reform school and stint in the military, says, "You still owe *me* time" (emphasis added).

Pesca functions as a personalization of the state, Carter's years a debt to be paid directly to him. Jewison admits, "I love dramatic confrontations like this, the standoff between two actors,"[15] and such standoffs are the "composites" that are "fictionalized," to both the distressed and apologist reviews of critics. Steel criticizes the "cinematic crime" committed by a "false Hollywood," while Roger Ebert doubts that a chronicle of a "complex network of legal injustice" would have made *The Hurricane* a better film.[16] In a *Newsweek* article that is at once about the story of Carter's battle with racism and Washington's fight against racial typecasting—another superimposition of subject and actor—the reviewer cannot decide if the blame for such narrative shortcuts lies with producers or audiences. The review offers, on one hand, that "audiences like their villains unregenerate"; on the other, it maintains that it would be better if the film "trusted the audience to swallow a less simplistic view of reality."[17]

Jewison does make some directorial effort to broaden the blame, cinematically representing the systemic racism arrayed against Carter. In the second courtroom scene, which concludes with the sentencing for the triple murder, the first shot is outside the courtroom, and the camera pans down from sky to white marble. There is a cut to the inside of the courtroom, a long shot from the entry that frames the assembled audience before the judge, then a cut to the national seal on a white wall, then downward to a medium shot of the white judge, who says that the defendants have been tried by a jury of their peers. There is then a cut to a brief shot of the all-white jury for a black man. That montage seems an effort on Jewison's part to implicate nation, institution, legal system, and whiteness in a network of forces differentiating the accused on the basis of blackness and isolating him in his criminality and attendant imprisonment, thereby fulfilling judicial racism's "defeat in detail" (cf. chapter 2). In an all-or-nothing bid, Carter and his legal team opt to take their case above the state of New Jersey to a federal hearing, arguing that the state trials were conducted improperly. The judge in the third courtroom scene overturns the verdict for the film's climax, and that moment is paired with the earlier one through a set of visual cues in order to demonstrate that the subject's rights and the state's wrongs can be redressed. The third scene similarly opens with a montage of the U.S. flag, the courtroom shot from outside, a close-up of the bas-relief of Justice, then Carter bidding farewell to fellow prisoners, and then to the lawyers' arguments inside the courtroom. Those arguments culminate in Carter speaking for himself before the court, then in the judge's decision to free him.

For the viewer schooled in the background of Carter's actual case and the film's production, the scene is a surreal composite of multiple historicities. The judge is named Sarokin, the arbiter of the actual trial. Sarokin is played by Rod Steiger, the bigoted sheriff from Jewison's *In the Heat of the Night* (1967), and now he rules that a racially biased prosecution violated the defendant's constitutional rights. His character recuperation is joined by that of an accommodating white guard, Jimmy Williams (Clancy Barnes), the sadistic prison officer of *The Shawshank Redemption,* who in this film aids Carter and then applauds Sarokin's ruling. The judge's ruling exculpating Carter quotes verbatim from the actual decision, and Jewison recorded Sarokin on videotape rehearsing his own role. The director liked the rendition, but preferred Steiger, who then rehearsed with the record of Sarokin's own rehearsal, taped almost fifteen years after the latter's real courtroom performance. In the actual hearing, Carter was not present, but Jewison felt the scene would work better with Washington in it. Washington's lines quote directly from Carter's biography, published eleven years prior to the actual hearing at which his speech is set. The shots are fairly still and lengthy during that monologue, the editing subtle, lending "a reality to it," according to the director. While Carter and Lesra wait for the judge's decision, they talk, with Washington and Shannon's dialogue offered in shot/ reverse shot with the bars between. This is an iconic shot so de rigueur of prison in film, photography, and experience that when Bob Dylan visited Carter in a minimum-security facility in 1975, an unused steel grille had to be appropriated to play the role of bars for a press photo.[18] Jewison describes the last of the film's many through-the-bars scenes between Washington and Shannon as "too real."[19] To top it off, black-and-white footage of the actual Rubin Carter closes the film. The combination of scenes culminating in Carter's freedom is postmodern history at its best or worst, depending on how separately one likes to account the imagined from the actual.

Again, I am less interested in sorting truth from fiction in the film than I am in suggesting how the difference between the two becomes one that is told, occurring in the narrativization. Jewison, as well as the screenwriters, Armyan Bernstein and Dan Gordon—the latter also responsible for writing another "based upon a true story" film about injustice in prison, *Murder in the First* (1995)—draw from a variety of narratives and documents. These include biographies of Carter, whether written by the man himself or coauthored by two of the Canadians; the transcripts of the trials themselves; and news footage of Carter, Dylan, and other actual figures involved in the case. The staging of shots simulates the events of the two and a half decades before: the faces of the murderers are not shown in the early sequence, and the film offers the points of view of witnesses as similarly limited. The undecidability of history nevertheless demands decision. The film reproduces Sarokin's actual verdict, which reached its conclusion of prior judicial bias, a decision that, like the film, simultaneously recorded and invented history, retroactively determining what had already happened. In the federal district court of 1985, that meant dismissing the 1967 verdict as racially prejudiced, a dismissal that was later upheld by the U.S. Supreme Court in 1988. In 1999 that meant concluding the film with Washington on courthouse steps followed by 1993 footage of a free Carter. The judicial process of indictment, incarceration, and exoneration offered as a "true story" in *The Hurricane* becomes part of the cultural imagination, even as its story of a prisoner's identity is one of personal transformation that has its own contemporaries and precedents in narrative film.

In *The Hurricane*, resistance and redemption define Carter's identity as a prisoner in visual and narrative terms strikingly similar to those of *American History X*. The images of masculine power as body and language offered in black-and-white flashback in the latter film similarly occur in *The Hurricane*, as viewers see Washington's year and a half of physical training displayed in brightly lit boxing scenes. The frequent displays in each film thus offer chiaroscuro impressions of masculine hardness, of power and indomitability. Black-and-white segments in these instances function as a historical conceit, locating their scenes as having taken place before the primary narrative. In *The Hurricane* the historical anteriority of those scenes associates them with the *really* real, as black-and-white footage of Carter boxing occurs alongside actual documentary black-and-white footage of 1960s civil rights demonstrations and the protests of Carter's imprisonment ten years later. However, unlike the Lafayette murder, the nightclub, and the prison scenes of *The Hurricane* shot on location, those boxing scenes were recorded on a Toronto set. Furthermore, Vinyard's rhetoric of racial hate, as offered to a television reporter before his incarceration, pairs with Carter's offhand comments to a newsweekly reporter, a mocking suggestion to shoot the "nigger-hating cops" beating protesters.

In prison, both men learn to disavow retributive violence, and each

**141**

leaves transformed. Lamont, one of the instruments of Vinyard's salvation and the reason that he even survives prison, calls out for him on his departure to remember "the brothers!" In one sense, that brother is Vinyard's younger brother, Danny (Furlong), and each brother spends a fair portion of *American History X* remembering the other in various flashbacks. In another sense, "the brothers" are black men, and in a film structured on the idea of male siblings as mirrors for one another, Lamont's call is one for cross-racial identification. In *The Hurricane*, Carter at first denies the prison, refusing to conform to its identification of him as a prisoner, but even his very resistance capitulates to the self-negation that imprisonment intends. The dialogue quotes directly from the last words of Carter's biography: "In the end, there is no prison, no more Rubin, no more Carter—only The Hurricane. And after him, there is no more."[20] Autonomy produces the narrative destined for erasure; like the character of Butch Beauchamp, the character of Carter is a masculine identity of invulnerable mastery predicated upon autonomous individuality, wherein death is the end of history.

A pair of scenes in the film captures the initiation into that autonomy as a practice of psychological resistance against the isolation and individuation of imprisonment, and then the repudiation of that isolation in favor of a social identity. Carter arrives at prison after his conviction for the Lafayette murders and meets the warden as a personification of the prison. The warden demands that he assume the position of prisoner, that he strip to wear a "standard inmate uniform with your number sewn on it so we can identify you." Carter's refusal merits him ninety days in solitary confinement. Jewison offers that isolation in a montage of Washington in a series of shot/reverse shots—the camera's *fort-da*—in which the camera's gaze on the subject cuts to what the subject sees. After isolation for days, marked by growing facial hair and Carter's increasing despair, he begins hearing another voice, and there is another Carter in the cell, an angry mirror who proclaims that he is the tyrant of self: "I'm running shit." The plaintive Carter replies, "What are we gonna do now?" and receives the reply, "Feel the hate," and the oedipal epithet *motherfucker*, which causes the first Carter to cry in solitary. He imagines a more complete version of himself in this doppelgänger, thereby emphasizing the lack, the inadequacy of the self on his side of the mirror.

Later, the Canadians visit for the first time, and Carter cuts their

**Figure 6**
**A caged black militant.** Denzel Washington's performance of Carter in solitary con-
finement for refusing to obey prison rules appears visually reminiscent of Eldridge
Cleaver, also in prison in 1966, the historical setting of this scene.

visit short, angrily denying their ability to identify with his situation:
"None of you can judge what I've been through. [ . . . ] What do you
know about being in this place?" Washington's dialogue in the scene
draws largely from Carter's *The Sixteenth Round,* and he declares that
he is free in prison because there is nothing he wants. Separating
himself from visitors means walling himself away from desire; wanting
something means that there is something the prison can take away.
Desire becomes its own instrument of punishment in a reversal of
Lacanian lack, as desire is not predicated on lack but itself produces
the possibility of lack.[21] Carter leaves them, and a crane shot rising up
past levels of cells tracks space in the prison, the distance between the
*here* of the visiting room and the *there* to which they cannot go, the
cell itself. Alone in his cell, Carter hears a litany of *don't trust 'em*s
from his other self.[22] However, he decides that it is time to participate
in a world outside his autonomy, and dismisses his double with, "It's
time for you to go." The other Washington shouts, "Don't you turn
your back on me, nigger!" but the camera returns to the shot/reverse
shot across the bars, Carter warming up by shadowboxing to the
ubiquitous rising violins—signifying emotional import—ready again
to fight for his freedom. A high shot from inside the cell emphasizes
the light illuminating the typewriter. Given that gesture to writing
oneself away from violence—communication with another to avoid

the tyranny of one—it is worth noting that the scene draws directly from Carter's autobiography.[23]

These are the only two scenes in the film where Carter experiences what might be understood as a schizophrenic episode, and they read as an amalgam of Deleuze and Guattari's *Anti-Oedipus* and the American Psychiatric Association's *Diagnostic and Statistical Manual of Mental Disorders*.[24] The medical condition of paranoid schizophrenia is understood as consisting of brain abnormalities that cause mental disassociation, cognitive dysfunction, and verbal memory loss—though it also carries with it the popular misunderstandings of the "someone is out to get me" perception coupled with multiple personality disorder. In *Anti-Oedipus*, schizophrenia is the self divided, constituted in multiple social investments and thereby positioned against the model of individual autonomy. Carter's extended isolation is an alienation from a world outside the self, fracturing his thinking, disconnecting him from any shared reality, precipitating anxiety and hallucinations. His delusions of persecution are, in the context of the film's narrative, true, and the question—as in *Soul on Ice* and *The Executioner's Song*—is not, Is the prisoner paranoid? but Is he paranoid enough? Washington plays the rest of the symptoms of clinical paranoid schizophrenia in a scene Jewison describes as "probably some of the most brilliant film acting" he has shot—heady praise, given that he has directed three Oscar-winning performances.[25] Jewison identifies the subsequent scene as one of his "high emotional moments as a director," as Carter participates in communication and trust across racial and correctional boundaries. In solitary confinement, the isolated, individualized subject (Carter) "others" the self as a response to alienation. Isolation divorces him from the world, so the self fragments to create the multiplicity and conflict that constitute subjectivity.

That first episode, where Carter envisions an angrier, more complete self, matches Deleuze and Guattari's description of the false autonomy of the oedipal subject and the paranoia attendant to the self's misrecognition of its singularity; Oedipus is a tyrant and a "motherfucker." Separated from the world, the self will imagine itself to death. Jewison views Carter's character in the first schizophrenic episode as suicidal, the step toward death that within the confines of individual autonomy means the end of history. The second episode, dismissing that other Carter, demonstrates the reinitiation of the subject to a social order, where the self is, in Deleuze and Guattari's terms, reterritorialized, reinscripted with desire—in this case, to participate in a world beyond both the prison and the myth of isolated autonomy. This second episode immediately cuts to a scene of Lesra and the Canadians in Toronto, with Unger's voice-over of Lisa's letter to Carter: "We get a rich, deep feeling of experiencing your presence here." The camera and the careful editing perform a material reterritorialization, relocating Carter in the sequence. The Canadians feel him "here," and the cut between the shots takes the audience "there" before returning to Carter looking at a picture of the scene as his refusal to want becomes a desire to be in the world, the linguistic participation that the typewriter allows.

His return to history occurs through a chain of identifications. The first moment of such self-recognition occurs before his false imprisonment for the triple murder, when he watches race riots on television in a bar and locates himself as part of an "us," a black identity larger than himself. Jewison acknowledges that this moment is when the picture "takes a turn." It is a historical turn. Prior black-and-white sequences in the film feature footage of Washington boxing in a ring, scenes shot on a set in Toronto; these black-and-white riot images are from historical footage of policemen beating black protesters. Carter as he is performed in the film views documentary footage of a civil rights protest that invokes in him an "us," a transsubjective identification, a participation in an identity that is the link between "I" and "we," between personal and social history. In the film, however, Carter does not act on the recognition. The slip in difference between self and other occurs later, in the mutual recognition that takes place between him and Lesra—and, by extension, his white Canadian guardians. Lesra identifies himself in Carter, first in choosing *The Sixteenth Round,* then as he reads the biography, proclaiming, "This book's about my life!" In writing the prisoner a letter, he initiates the chain of communication that will see Carter finally freed.

For Carter, recognition is not intersubjective identification, but a broadening of selfhood, a participation in the world beyond the self, which is constructed cinematically through cuts between shots in and out of prison and is linked by speaking the other's words in the letters between them. Later, after Carter has participated through letters and visits with the Canadians, and thereby with the world outside of prison, a court appeal that he hopes will free him fails. He attempts to repudiate the outside connection, asking them to no longer write or call him, a break described in terms of renouncing any self outside of prison, fully assuming instead his identity as prisoner: "My number is 4572," he says—dialogue emerging from an actual letter of Carter's and matching the move made by Cleaver and others. That renunciation prompts a last-ditch effort from Lesra, who sends his high school diploma to Carter and a photo of himself with his girlfriend. Shannon's voice-over accompanies Carter reading in prison. Slow, rising draws of violin strings score Washington's composure cracking. It is a cinematic cheap shot in terms of audience identification, cuing viewers exactly how to respond emotionally by making Washington's feelings a model for the audience. However, it initiates Carter's return to a world beyond the self, a plurality the film locates in the Canadians' full-time bid to see him released.

*The Hurricane* and *American History X* both offer prison as a transformative place—educational, redemptive—where male characters repudiate race-based thinking and hard autonomy in favor of participating in a larger social world of emotional connection that is initiated and sustained through communication and cross-racial identification. There are clear precedents in films of the prior decade, particularly in Spike Lee's *Malcolm X* and Darabont's *The Shawshank Redemption*. The former already has a multilevel relationship with *American History X* and *The Hurricane*. Like *The Hurricane* it is a biopic starring Denzel Washington. Jewison actually was listed to direct *Malcolm X* before Spike Lee drummed up opposition to a white director telling the story and took over the project himself. Jewison makes a wry comment to this effect in shooting a scene of Washington reading a letter in a cell with a poster of Malcolm X visible on the wall in the background. The poster is actually a picture of Washington playing Malcolm in the film, a sly wink and nudge to the confluence of reality and imagination, as well as to the director's own personal history. He gets to film Washington portraying Malcolm after all.

*American History X* not only features the titular gesture of race as the X factor, but at one point the character of Sweeney (Brooks) also refers to Norton's Vinyard as the "shining prince" of white supremacist patriarch Cameron, an allusion to actor Ossie Davis's eulogy for Malcolm X.[26] In the autobiography from which Lee's film is adapted, one of the chapter's chronicling Malcolm X's imprisonment is titled "Saved," and it includes his growing literacy and letter writing, which feature prominently in the film version. Indeed, the period of incarceration plays as the film's second act, preceded by Malcolm X's early life of crime and his ignorance of racial politics, and followed by his life and end as a leader, an act culminating in footage of young children standing and identifying themselves in intersubjective terms of (mis)recognition: "I am Malcolm X!"

*The Shawshank Redemption* does not make the gesture to actuality but it does to literacy, and the development of the prison library and a prisoner learning to read play their parts in the film's tale of the mutually redeeming friendship between a white man guilty of no crime beyond not loving his wife enough and a black man who did commit murder but has paid in decades of time. The titular redemption belongs to Andy Dupuis (Tim Robbins), who learns to love again, though the object of his affection is Red (Morgan Freeman). The relationship is cast as homosocial rather than erotic, and the final shot of the film is pure Hallmark, a high, long shot, in soft focus, of the two men approaching one another and embracing on a beach in afternoon light, sun glinting on the water. That film and *The Hurricane* share the happy ending of the uncomplicated "triumph of the human spirit" film, though the turn to footage of the actual Carter, overlaid with rolling text documenting events after his release, substantiates the historical truth of the latter film's exultant denouement.

Within a year of their respective releases in 1992 and 1994, *Malcolm X* and *The Shawshank Redemption* were either financially or critically successful, and the latter in particular set the stage for would-be high-concept films set in prison. The earnings of Lee's film doubled its budget during its domestic theatrical release, not even counting overseas distribution sales and Time Warner's subsequent rental and cable earnings, and it merited two Academy Award nominations. *The Shawshank Redemption* was advertised weakly and consequently did poorly at the box office, recouping its estimated production costs but not marketing expenses. Nevertheless, its Academy Award nominations and, more important, its word-of-mouth accounts made it the number one video rental the subsequent year, and it continues to be screened exhaustively on myriad cable outlets. Furthermore, it is the second-highest-rated film ever among IMDB users, as of early 2007, behind only *The Godfather*. It has been referenced or parodied in more than thirty subsequent films, and spawned a documentary in 2001 chronicling its emergence as a cultural phenomenon.

Its success speaks to the degree to which it meets audiences' expectations—as cited in the preface to this book—how the film fulfills an audience's sense of "how it must feel to be behind bars," that recurrent place of fascination in the cultural imagination. *The Shawshank Redemption* draws from the two most notable prior prison films, *I Am a Fugitive from a Chain Gang* (1932) and *Cool Hand Luke,* in offering wardens and guards as unremittingly evil caricatures,[27] consequently fostering an us–versus–them community among male inmates. In *Captured on Film: The Prison Movie,* Bruce Crowther points out that, along with the main character's innocence, these are some of the fundamental characteristics in the development of prison films.

However, in a sharp departure from the wholesale cruelty and punishment of earlier fictive prisons, in *The Shawshank Redemption* homosocial bonds across race and personal transformation become crucial factors in imagining incarceration. Writers, directors, and producers imagine that prisons somehow simultaneously fulfill the self-destruction prisoners seek and provide a humanistic personal improvement. The contradiction should come as little surprise, as actual prisons historically have been intended, somehow, to simultaneously separate, punish, and rehabilitate. In late-twentieth-century films set in prison, the crucial differences from these two influential predecessors (which are also, incidentally, along with *The Shawshank Redemption* and *American History X,* part of the Warner film library) are the interracial milieu and the titular emphasis on redemption. Prisons are settings for conversion narratives, where white and black men learn to love one another and thereby to fulfill their respective destinies after prison, becoming whoever they need to be. *The Shawshank Redemption* made such male romance narratives[28] organized around an actor with box office success the blueprint for subsequent prison films of the 1990s, not only for Frank Darabont's next direction, *The Green Mile* (1999), but also for *American History X* and *The Hurricane.* Framed as such, the degree to which such narratives represent actual imprisonment becomes beside the point. Films set in prison in this style are male romance, with plots of spiritual redemption brought about by interracial and homosocial (though not sexual) love, scored with rising violins and featuring close-ups of the tears of the men who are the focal characters in order to cue viewer responses. These films would not be expected to offer the "reality" of imprisonment any more than Harlequin historical romance novels might describe a "real" eighteenth century. Each genre reveals much more about the audiences that seek them than they do about their settings.

Prisons in films seem more likely to reinforce existing cultural norms. Such an endorsement is apparent at the close of *The Hurricane,* after Sarokin has declared Carter's freedom. A long, slow shot frames the golden sky in soft focus, and then the marble edifice of

**Figure 7**
**"A hurricane is beautiful."** Rubin Carter (Washington) experiences freedom after 19 years. Like Derek Vinyard's (Norton) own transformation, he leaves prison older, wiser, and more peaceful—and both lack the shaved head and traditional masculine hardness with which they entered.

the courthouse fills the screen, its motto extending past even a theatrical ratio 1.85:1 screen: "The administration of justice is the firmest pillar of good government."[29] Carter (Washington) stands amid a crowd of reporters on the courthouse steps, and there is a close shot/reverse shot of one reporter asking Carter if he will remain the "Hurricane." The freed man replies, "I'll always be the 'Hurricane,' and a hurricane is beautiful." The line might imply the historically and politically resonant racial rhetoric of "Black is beautiful," but the camera—like the two court shots preceding it—locates authority not in the language of revolutionary identity, but in the judicial system metonymically referenced in the marble monument that dwarfs the people on its steps. Social justice for Carter occurs through relying on the same legal apparatus that placed him in prison almost two decades earlier; the redemption that takes place is that of the judicial system itself.

Watching the film, some viewers (myself, for one) may want Carter to be angry, violently angry at so many years in prison, but the orchestral score builds while the high and long shot situates Carter beneath the imposing courthouse, and then text on a black screen relates a series of victories for the real-life characters. The state of New Jersey, we learn, appealed the case to the federal Supreme Court and lost, while Lesra became a lawyer, and Carter and Artis went on to serve as civil rights advocates—and Carter was awarded an honorary title by the World Boxing Association. The gestures to historical actuality legitimize the nearly two decades of judicial appeal radically telescoped to fit the cultural constraints of a two-hour feature film. Judicial institutions trump revolution to fulfill mainstream ideology in fictionalizations geared to profit from a thirty-million-dollar investment.

The amount of money invested in the story grows in its other incarnations. *The Hurricane* was produced and distributed by Universal Pictures, a property of NBC Universal—itself 80 percent the property of General Electric as of October 2003. The book publisher Houghton Mifflin, which NBC Universal acquired in 2001, released James S. Hirsch's *Hurricane: The Miraculous Journey of Rubin Carter* (2000). The soundtrack for the film is an MCA property, which is also an NBC Universal company, and the album features numerous artists also distributed by MCA. As the parent company also owns the NBC network and USA cable channels, it is in a position to exploit the related properties among its multiple media outlets of film, DVD, television network, cable, music CD, and trade paperback.[30] The consolidated ownership of these properties and the high cost of their mass distribution may contribute to both a normalization of their stories and a capitulation to a previously successful narrative such as *The Shawshank Redemption*. Couple that with the similarly profitable appeal of the movie's being based on actual events, and critical audiences encounter an increasingly familiar story: black men are imprisoned unfairly but nevertheless improved, a state of affairs that redeems them and the courts that imprison them. In the face of actual incarceration patterns, fact and fiction merge in a disturbing and long-standing trend with possible consequences, "reel" effects. Such films at once imagine the real and realize the imaginary in a wish fulfillment that may well affect actual prisoners.

# 7

# The Farm

## "This is no dream
## or nothing made up, this is for real"

> Serving time is just like a puzzle, a two-thousand-piece puzzle. There it is,
> throw it to you, and it's scattered every which way. Now, put it back together.
> That's the way your life is. When you are sentenced to a penal institution,
> your life is scattered. You is the one who has to put it back together.
>
> —Eugene "Bishop" Tannehill in *The Farm: Life Inside Angola Prison*

THOUGH TONY KAYE shot *American History X* on location
in Venice Beach, California, the characters projected there are
simulacra, copies without originals. And while Rubin Carter's historical actuality is cast in Denzel Washington, the events of his life
are rewritten to fulfill the narrative structure of a high-concept Hollywood production, a multimillion-dollar package organized around
the proven assets of its director and star, with its story of a boxing
champion wrongly imprisoned easily pitched to producers and then
to audiences. It would seem that a largely cinema vérité documentary
such as *The Farm* could resolve the tension between imagined and
real imprisonment in film. After all, its cameras circulate through the
corridors of the actual Louisiana State Prison, its characters the real
prisoners, guards, and administrators. The film is part of the historical

record, an actual documentary and not simply shot in a documentary style; it is a true story rather than merely based on one. However, it shares with *American History X* and *The Hurricane* the sense that racism contributes to the imprisonment of black men who are nevertheless redeemed in prison, and cross-racial identification transforms prisoners, even if it does not necessarily free them. This chapter shows how *The Farm,* like many documentaries, sometimes conforms to conventions of fictional narratives in its effort to represent its reality, in this case one of imprisonment. Nevertheless, this film more than the others most fully separates its representations of prisoners from popular imaginations of criminal justice and incarceration, largely because of the personalities of the prisoners themselves, their own statements of what freedom and imprisonment—and life and death—might mean.

*The Farm* is a documentary directed by Liz Garbus, John Stack, and Wilbert Rideau, the last of whom was an inmate at the Louisiana State Prison during the filming—a new trial freed him in 2005.[1] As of 1999 Louisiana joined the nation's capital with the highest rate of incarceration in the United States, placing one out of every hundred people in prison or jail, according to the U.S. Department of Justice.[2] The film's representation of the maximum-security facility is organized around six inmates: George Crawford, a twenty-two-year-old black man beginning a life sentence; John Brown, a thirty-five-year-old white man on death row for twelve years, executed during the film; George "Ashanti" Witherspoon, a black man in his forties, twenty-five years into his seventy-five-year sentence; Vincent Simmons, a forty-five-year-old black man who has served twenty years of his sentenced one hundred; Logan "Bones" Theriot, a sixty-one-year-old white man, twenty-six years into his life sentence, who dies of lung cancer; and Eugene "Bishop" Tannehill, a sixty-five-year-old black man, thirty-eight years into his life sentence. Innocence and redemption are common themes in their representations. Crawford and Simmons deny their guilt, the latter becoming a writ lawyer in the effort to appeal his case. Witherspoon too becomes a writ lawyer and regularly leaves the prison to perform community outreach and teach CPR, while Tannehill leads church services in the prison. The film emphasizes the inmates' experience of routine days, their isolation from their lives prior to prison, and, in the case of those who have already served many years, the dramatic difference between their current lives and the criminality that precipitated their incarceration.

The film received a nomination for an Academy Award and won

broad critical acclaim.³ *Variety* describes the film as a "matter-of-fact—and, therefore, all the more devastating—indictment of the U.S. penal system."⁴ However, the film also has been "roundly praised" by the Louisiana governor's office and prison administration, which expressed interest in using the film in its guard training.⁵ The video is for sale at the Louisiana State Prison Museum, along with prison T-shirts, hats, pens, hot sauce, and other memorabilia. That the film means different things to different people is a banal observation. That the documentary is perceived in such diametrically opposed ways is a matter for analysis, given that its frequent employment of cinema vérité style—what Angola is "really" like—nevertheless leaves available competing uses: scathing depiction, training aid, cultural kitsch.

The film's supratext, like those of *American History X* and *The Hurricane,* draws attention to the ways movies are directed not only by directors but also by and to specific audiences. *American History X* has seen critical indictment for its account of race relations even as others have nominated it for human rights "Peace" awards; *The Hurricane* was used as a teaching tool by university civil rights organizations, and prison administrators considered employing *The Farm* to train new guards. These strategic projections of the films exemplify ways of viewing that emphasize the rhetorical—not what a text means, but what it is for, what it does, what it produces. In these films' claims to the real, they produce history, repeatedly attempting to substantiate the actuality of their representations of prisons, race, and masculinity.

In directly psychoanalytic terms, documentary filmmaker and theorist Jill Godmilow suggests, "Unconsciously embedded in these forms called documentary is the conceit of the 'real,' which substantiates the truth claims made by these films."⁶ Producers and audiences alike participate in the sense of documentary films as, if not the stuff of the real itself, then at least less mediated, less constructed than fictional narratives of "documentary realism" or narratives based on a true story. However, as Godmilow also points out, historically documentary has borrowed from the conventions of dramatic narrative film.⁷ Nancy F. Partner raises similar questions,⁸ and Paula Rabinowitz emphasizes that documentary films typically maintain a reliance on both a political agenda and the narrative strategies of fictional film, which results in their "reinforcing dominant patterns of vision."⁹ Documentary films then capitulate to mainstream expectations similar to those for would-be blockbusters.

What this means is that even as the "conceit of the 'real'" is embedded in the historical records of documentary film, narrative conceits of fiction help to shape their production. In an extended interview, Garbus claims that in the production of her work, the film is "something I came to very organically, rather than with a lot of intellectual ideas," and that "story and character" are "paramount to the formalistic concerns."[10] It is easy to conceive of that organic process of storytelling as an approach to history itself informed by previous narrativization, through what Jameson terms "the political unconscious." History as the sum of actual lives exists in a surplus to its narration, its vagaries exceeding the conventions of representation. For example, in the two years that *The Farm*'s outside directors, Garbus and Stack, visited the prison of more than 5000 inmates, they shot over 150 hours of film, which they distilled to 100 minutes organized around six characters. Garbus acknowledges that the film "was really made in the editing room,"[11] a claim that is equally true of *American History X* and *The Hurricane*.

Memory and history serve as the scattered pieces of a puzzle that viewers assemble together in the watching. Even as the editing of *The Farm* shapes the depiction of recorded events, the recorded events are themselves shaped by the presence of the camera. Of inmates with life sentences lacking the possibility of parole, Garbus says that they "see a camera and they think 'there's a chance.'"[12] Godmilow addresses the related case of a documentary account of the Romanian revolution, in which revolutionaries acted for their own camcorders in order to "play well on TV and produce a useful political record."[13] This is the other half of Hayden White's conception of postmodern history: not only does the imaginary code itself as real, but also the historical is offered with the grammar of the imagination. *The Farm,* like *American History X* and *The Hurricane,* is shaped by the cultural expectations that are, in part, produced through the prison films that precede it, where prison is a place of redemption, and where predominantly black men are condemned, many unjustly, but are nevertheless transformed—where the criminal violence of black and white men is converted to homosocial love, and autonomy gives way to a social identity.

*The Farm* offers a predominantly synchronic account of the Louisiana State Prison, "a slice of life" more attuned to space than time, an impression of the place shot over two years in bits and pieces of footage thereafter organized around six inmates. The opening montage of brief clips and dialogue from later in the film sets the stage in medium shots of the inmates acknowledging their hopes, black-and-white mug shots, an Angola road sign, a hearse and burial, and a score of harmonica blues underlying bits of dialogue: "God still exists behind prison bars"; "I am an innocent man"; "The slaves that worked these fields came from Angola in Africa and it picked up its name from there." The measured tones of the narrator, Bernard Addison, introduce the place: "Down in Louisiana lies America's largest maximum-security prison," where most inmates serve life sentences—a place where the vast majority, 85 percent, will die behind bars. Addison then offers the film's narrative thrust: "This is the story of six men trying to overcome the odds." There is some tension between that organization around character and the film's emphasis on setting and on the broad experience of thousands at the nation's largest maximum-security prison. Representation is one means of bridging the gap, and the six men roughly match the racial breakdown of the prison, where 77 percent of the more than five hundred new inmates admitted each year are black men—Crawford, Simmons, Tannehill, and Witherspoon are black, and Brown and Thierot are white.

The first narrative sequence uses the admission of Crawford as a means into the story of the prison, and even before viewers meet him, a white female guard overseeing processing points out that many new inmates arrive every Monday: "We're all guaranteed a job, we have good job security." Her matter-of-fact tone, lacking any irony, introspection, or critical distance, is maintained in most of the film's account of Angola's 100 percent white administration. There are visual cues such as the red, white, and blue pen with which Crawford signs an admittance form, and prison guards later practice for Brown's execution, joking with one of their own playing the role of the condemned. During Crawford's processing, the color footage gives way to a black-and-white still, a mug shot, a gesture to the official declaration of criminality, the initiation of the prisoner's identity and a conceit maintained for the other five inmates.

After the new inmate's arrival, there follows a brief scene of Witherspoon conducting orientation during Crawford's processing, but the film next focuses on the elderly Tannehill, who offers the young inmate's opposite. He suggests that there are three things that Angola will do: "bring you to a crossroads," "harden you," and then "kill you." Tannehill's retrospective prophecy provides a point from which to look backward, a historical point of view from which he sees all and foretells the rest. Crawford sifts through personal family photos, but in the Tannehill sequence the camera's gaze shifts to the broader history of Angola: a shot of black-and-white photos of dogs chasing escapees cuts to footage of dogs in kennels today. The editing implies the particular, and particularly racial, significance of pursuing dogs (like those of both *Light in August* and *Go Down, Moses*) on a Southern plantation turned prison. The black-and-white stills function as the same gesture to historical anteriority and actuality as the mug shots, as the documentary footage Jewison employs repeatedly in *The Hurricane*, as the flashbacks of memory in *American History X*. In all three films, black and white means past, the past means history, and history is real.

The next sequence introduces Witherspoon, the model inmate who acknowledges that he has "done everything in prison that [he] should have done as a community leader in society." Garbus describes him as "Mr. Rehabilitated" after twenty-five years[14]—one-third of his sentence—though his parole remains withheld. There is a painful irony prefacing Witherspoon's depiction in the film. In 1982 he published a poem titled "The Lifer" in *The Angolite,* while the same issue features a cartoon wherein a warden tells a prisoner, "Your rehabilitation went so well, we've decided to keep you as a model for others."[15] Witherspoon also acts as a proxy for Rideau, the codirector of the film, who also is known as "Mr. Rehabilitated" and whose requests for a pardon were stalled until 2005.[16] After Witherspoon, there is Thierot, dying of lung cancer in the prison hospital, whose account of prison life is a litany of affirmations: prison "is not as terrible a place as you would think"; "you can still have a life inside, you can help other inmates"; "you can help other people—that's not always self you have to look to." Things get a bit surreal after that, as the camera follows Crawford, amid other black inmates, to work in the fields of the prison's farms for pennies a day, overseen by armed guards on horseback, a sequence scored with a spiritual; the camera then cuts to the warden driving a truck.

The warden, Burl Cain, admits, "It's like a big plantation from days gone by. We hate to call it that in a way, but it kind of is because it's inmates, it's a prison. This was a plantation." His words recall that the Thirteenth Amendment forbids slavery except in the context of imprisonment, "except as a punishment for crime." The subsequent sequence in the film emphasizes the estrangement of the place—the prison's existence as a whole other world—as the camera takes a walk through the city that is Angola: aerial shots of the eighteen thousand

**Figure 8**
**"It's like a big plantation."** Warden Burl Cain's description of Angola Prison's working farm strikes a resonant chord with the overrepresentation of black men in prison and Louisiana's legacy of slavery.

acres of fields and buildings, on-site housing for staff, a baseball field for staffers' children, the DJ at the prison radio station playing gospel and wishing the "brothers up on death row a beautiful day." The montage seems to suggest the ambiguities of prison life, that it is at once an America viewers might immediately recognize and one completely foreign, where children play baseball and men in the J Block are in solitary confinement twenty-three hours a day. One of the men on death row is Brown, fruitlessly awaiting an appeal to his execution. After John Brown—whose own name, though unremarked, has its own historical resonances with race and racial violence in the Old South—the subsequent narrative sequence introduces the sixth of the film's characters, Simmons. He has served two decades of a century-long sentence, and twenty years after receiving a sixth-grade education and defending himself because he lacked the money for legal counsel, he has become a self-trained writ lawyer, appealing his case and protesting his innocence to the parole board.

Almost every reviewer of *The Farm* comments on the scene of Simmons's parole hearing, and the filmmakers acknowledge that it gets a "big response" from audiences.[17] Because the documentary begins in the prison itself, it cannot film any of the actual court hearings that previously sentenced the inmates and thereby named their criminality, initiating their identity as prisoners. Simmons's hearing and the consequent denial of his parole are therefore the reinscription of his criminal status, his identity of prisoner. He introduces what he describes as "exculpatory evidence," which includes a statement from one of the victims, who claimed that she could not identify her assailant because "all niggers look alike." Simmons's blackness, then, identifies him as criminal, an "any *one* will do" to parallel Carter's story, the anonymous "negro crime" of *Light in August,* the guilt of blackness facing Dale Pierre in *The Executioner's Song.*

During her own testimony to the parole board, recorded on camera, the victim acknowledges the racial consequence of her rape in a dialogue that includes a member of the parole board, a black man.

> VICTIM: I have a problem with black people. [ . . . ] I'm scared of 'em.
> BOARD MEMBER: You're not scared of me this morning, are you?
> VICTIM: No. [ . . . ] but I wouldn't be alone in a room with you.
> BOARD MEMBER: That goes both ways.

It seems unlikely that, had her assailant been a white man, the victim would have developed a racial fear of white men. The white fantasy of supermenial black men sexually assaulting white women broadens violent personal trauma into a social pathology of race-based fear familiar to both, who recognize the other: "You're black" / "You're white." A scene of the white Canadians tracking down a witness in *The Hurricane* includes this dialogue, but the Hegelian recognition of one's self in the other's acknowledgment of the self is addressed and passed over in favor of polite discussion over tea and cookies. Here the mutual recognition of "That goes both ways" means that the black parole-board member participates in a pathology of racisms, the victim's fear of his black masculinity and its social and historical context of consequences (the judicial lynching of Simmons, for example) precipitates his own response to her white femininity. For the documentary, it is as if the previous century and a half never happened, the past not history or even past but right now—the New South is just like the Old South, and Simmons's hundred-year sentence is just like a noose round a neck from a century before.

**Figure 9**
**The parole hearing.** Vincent Simmons appears before his parole board with what he claims to be "exculpatory evidence"; after approximately 40 seconds of deliberation, the board rejects his appeal.

However, like the red, white, and blue pen, like the prison guard boasting of her job security, and, most pertinent, like the warden admitting the likeness between plantation and prison, slave and inmate, the acknowledgment here does not precipitate any self-critical reflection on the part of the arbiters of justice. In what appears to be about forty seconds of unbroken footage—it is difficult to tell, as the editing of this sequence is particularly skillful—the parole board dismisses Simmons and conducts not discussion but half-spoken platitudes in ratifying their foregone conclusion of guilt before sending for Simmons: "He did it. He just didn't . . . You know, I have a . . . ." "Of course he did it. Of course." The scene is disorienting because the board knows it is being filmed, yet its members do not seem to care that their desultory judgment becomes part of the historical record, not only in the denial of parole they sign but also in the far more public manner of what became a Sundance Award–winning documentary.[18]

Certainly *The Farm* introduces Simmons's case in a sympathetic manner and does not, with any rigor, subject his claims of innocence to any evaluation. Nor does it make any comment on the likelihood that an appeal rather than parole hearing would address exculpatory evidence. The parole board focuses on events between the guilty verdict and the parole hearing, and the board does suggest that Simmons appeal, which he does, though the U.S. Supreme Court subsequently rejects that appeal. His innocence or guilt is less at stake than the board's failure even to pretend to listen. However, just as the record of the decision may shock audiences, they have seen it before. *The Shawshank Redemption* features longtime convict Red (Freeman) claiming not his innocence but his repentance and rehabilitation, only to have his petition for parole denied. It is not until a later scene of a subsequent parole hearing, when he renounces any meaning of rehabilitation, when he coldly acknowledges that he does not care if he is free or not, that his form is stamped "approved." The capriciousness of the judicial system, particularly in the predominantly white administration of black prisoners, is what prison films anticipate as their audiences' expectation.

Tannehill presents another case of redemption without release, though his conversion is not legal but spiritual. He has become an ordained minister in his almost four decades at Angola, and the film includes one of his sermons, which begins, "There is a way to escape and be born again and live a holy life, a victorious life. So what about being behind bars, Bishop? God still exists behind prison bars. Thank you, Jesus. He sanctifies and he qualifies and he specialize[s] the individual that take[s] knowledge of him and repent[s]." Tannehill is minister and sinner, speaker and audience, voicing both halves of the call and response. The sermon melds into a mythologized autobiography in which Bishop walks the Damascus road. "As a young man, twenty-four years old, thank you, Jesus. Met a man, innocent man, a good man, on a railroad track one morning [ . . . ]. I took that man's life. Went on down the railroad track. Got into rock and roll [ . . . ]. They picked me up and they rescued me and put me in jail." The sermon is completely insane, and brilliant, an apoplectic confession in rap rhyme, akin to Reverend Hightower's mad exposition of his grandfather's Civil War exploits in his Sunday exhortations to Jefferson in *Light in August,* a fusion of myth and memory in a hail to salvation. The Angola minister receives a better response than Hightower, and the closing applause beats the clapping hands that first bring Tannehill to the microphone. Time served and service such as this have placed a recommendation for Tannehill's pardon on the desk of Louisiana's governor, but in the course of his tenure the governor

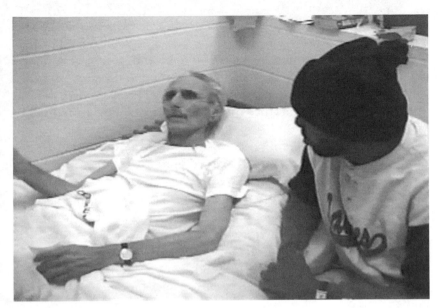

**Figure 10**
**An inmate's last days.** Logan "Bones" Theriot decides not be buried outside of prison grounds as his family wishes, opting instead to remain, "Where my friends are."

has never signed such a pardon, and has not done so by the film's end either.

All six focal characters are similarly cast in terms of transformation; irrespective of their guilt, they are saved by religion, good works, or critical self-reflection, made into better men in prison. Like Malcolm X, Tannehill is "Saved"—though by Southern Baptist Christianity rather than by the politicized Black Muslim faith the American Correctional Association tried and failed to bar from prisons in the early 1960s. Crawford, even though just admitted, acknowledges that though he is innocent of the murder that commits him, his prior crimes have caught up with him. Witherspoon admits his guilt for his crime but points out that the man he is today "is a totally different person"—like Cleaver, the prisoner of now is not the same man sentenced years before—and the film supports that view, chronicling his community work as a trustee on behalf of the prison administration. He and the warden speak very nearly the identical line of not giving up hope even during a life sentence, though (like Simmons, like Red) Witherspoon's parole bid fails, according to the rolling text that closes the film. In terms that coincidentally quote almost directly from Gary Gilmore, the death row prisoner Brown admits that he is further from Christ than he would like, but that he now has "more concern about [himself] and others." His affect, coupled with the awareness that he has not gone far enough in the time before his execution, nearly reproduces Theriot's feeling that he "wanted more time," and that one can turn to others in the diminishing time one has.

Theriot's final scene in the film hints at some of the challenges facing documentary film in the effort to testify, to tell the truth about imprisonment and its ends. Theriot's friends come to visit him in the hospital after he has ceased eating and has admitted that he only waits to die, and his friends think him lucky to expect to be buried outside of Angola. He surprises them, telling them that rather than being buried outside prison grounds at a family plot, he has chosen to be buried here, "where [his] friends are." Some of his black and white companions cry when they hear, and hands are held, his frail body embraced—"We love you. We love you." The scene appears far different from the romantic shot closing *The Shawshank Redemption,* though both feature black and white men transformed in the mutual love fostered in prison. There is no soft focus, no rising shot and orchestral cue, just a still camera, a cheap white room, a plate of leftover food, foil-wrapped and left on the floor, not to be eaten by a man who is not acting and will die and be buried at Angola during the course of the film.

Real life is never as glossy and slick as Hollywood productions, even those with claims to the real in their biographical narratives or the "heightened realism" of their style. Nevertheless, there is the sense that the foreclosure of life imprisonment has created the space for physical affection between men and across race. I am not suggesting that the love among Theriot and his friends is not felt, that love might not be experienced within confinement, that prisons' gendered populations and enforced time together do not ever foster valuable interracial relationships among men, expressed through bodies and language in a manner beyond what is generally sanctioned by mainstream U.S. culture. However, I am suggesting that films such as *Cool Hand Luke* and, to a far-greater extent, *The Shawshank Redemption* made that phenomenon part of the cultural imagination, a definitive aspect of what U.S. audiences expect from prison films, documentary or otherwise. The masculine homosociality of *Cool Hand Luke* occurs strictly among white men, while *The Shawshank Redemption* initiates the shift to cross-racial identification. As in Cleaver's *Soul on Ice* and Deleuze and Guattari's *Anti-Oedipus,* the shared identity of inmate trumps racial difference, though there is the significant lack of the revolutionary imperative to social change in Darabont's adaptation of Stephen King's novella. The character of Red (Freeman) originally was written as a white man, which contributes to the unremarked nature of racial difference in the film.

To understand the historical record of documentary film as unconsciously shaped to reify dominant cultural norms is, then, to understand historical records themselves as shaped by prior imaginings, a matter underscored in a strange sequence after Theriot's final scene, which takes place at Christmas. A radio-station DJ announces that the prison is on flood watch, and the film then cuts to an aerial shot of the river near the prison and the narration, "That spring, the Mississippi River rose to its highest level in a century."[19] To this point in its narrative, *The Farm* has not been concerned terribly with telling time, and the cut here seems informed by the desire to broaden from a personal to a public trauma, and to shift from death in winter to a spring that is both renewing and threatening land and inmates. The inmates work together through the night to stack the sandbags and build the levees to save the prison from a flooding Mississippi in a scene weirdly reminiscent of "The Old Man" section of Faulkner's *If I Forget Thee, Jerusalem,* originally published as *The Wild Palms* (1939),[20] where the "tall convict" also battles a Mississippi flood and afterward returns to prison.

The same historical and cultural forces that shaped Faulkner's writing shaped the South and its river, built Angola: its land, its racial identities, and its history. They also contributed to the strategies and the language of narration used to tell that history. Thus, *The Farm* sounds like Faulkner sometimes, as when the warden comments on signs that the flood might be a grave matter: "When they move the horses, you know it's serious." Floods are part of the South and its history, part of the novels that tell that history and, in circular fashion, then become a part of it. Rising rivers are imagined in novels and films, and are recorded in documentary, as in the pair of films both titled *The River* (1938, 1984). The 1938 film is a Depression-era documentary on the Mississippi floods released at the same time that Faulkner began his own (largely uncredited) film writing in Hollywood, and also the time he began writing *If I Forget Thee, Jerusalem.* The 1984 fictional feature film, also set in the South, received five

Academy Award nominations and similarly shows a battle against the rising waters that—like the battles of the novel and both documentaries—makes a natural disaster the objective correlative to some human conflict.

Certainly the near flooding of Angola during the two-year filming of *The Farm* took place, and it earns two mentions in a presentation given by Angola's Warden Cain (and Cathy Fontenot, Angola's director of classification) at the 2001 ACA meeting.[21] However, just as there are five thousand other inmates besides the six whose stories Garbus, Rideau, and Stack show in their narrative, there is much besides the rise of the Mississippi that happened at the Louisiana State Prison from 1996 to 1998. I am suggesting that, like the bonds among men and across racial lines formed inside prison walls, like uniformly violent crimes that lead to confinement, like the seemingly unjust imprisonment of black men, and like the inmates' redemption, the description of the flood of near-biblical proportion comprises the narrative in a manner that capitulates to the layers of prior representation that have become the cultural imagination, in all of its dubious facticity and less-determinate meaning.

The stock pieces of prison films are in place, from administration to visitation to shot/reverse shot sequences across prison bars. There is the casual cruelty of the admitting guard who equates new inmates with job security, the prison warden who delays evacuating the prison during the flood—though it is not mentioned in the film, the warden did eventually relocate three thousand inmates.[22] Crawford experiences a poignant visit from his mother, just as Vinyard sees his own mother, and Carter meets his wife. Crawford's mother exclaims, "This is no dream or nothing made up, this is for real"—and viewers know it is real because we have seen the scene before. Bruce Crowther's *Captured on Film* details the shared characteristics of prison films, first as offshoots of the 1920s and 1930s gangster films and then through the 1980s. Crowther identifies the generic features such as the main character's innocence, visits from the inmate's mother and her unremitting belief in her son, and cruel wardens and guards, types easily read in the documentary.

It is important to distinguish between prison as a setting and the prison film as a seemingly coherent genre, because prison is a setting with strings attached that shapes but does not wholly determine the sort of stories told in films set there. *The Farm* does not entirely capitulate to the expectations of prison as a setting cast in the cultural imagination. In *The Hurricane,* like so many courtroom scenes of films before, the full authority and power of the judicial system are embodied in magisterially robed justices, marble edifices, and eloquent arguments that in the last instance result in clearly righteous decisions. In *The Farm,* however, Simmons's hearing takes place in what appears to be a too-small trailer with shoddy fake paneling, and Brown's appeal of his execution includes competing arguments offered amid the bad suits and folding chairs populating what might be a junior high school cafeteria. Lacking the imagined trappings, justice looks like a cheap and ad hoc process. Still, the directors focus on the characters that they found most compelling, or that they felt audiences would find most compelling. Directors, after all, aim the camera and thereby the field of view, the characters and stories that can be seen on-screen. One reason that those characters and those stories may be most convincing is that those stories and those characters are most recognizable. At the end of the film, for instance, both white characters have died. The remaining four are black men. Crawford, Simmons, Tannehill, and Witherspoon are in prison, and none are represented as belonging there.

The fundamental problem with the logic of the redemption narratives of these films is that they largely endorse the use value of the same judicial system they at least in part describe as unjust. These films largely posit prison as man-making, as a setting for personal transformation, irrespective of an inmate's responsibility for crime. Simmons may or may not have committed the rapes of which he is accused—though *The Farm* implies he did not—but in his conviction he is named a criminal and is incarcerated, thereby becoming a better man, schooling himself beyond his sixth-grade education so as to contest his innocence in legal discourse. And while Tannehill and Witherspoon acknowledge their guilt for violent crime, they have become self-described changed men in the course of their decades-long sentences (thirty-eight and twenty-five years, respectively), who now participate in the functioning of the prison system that contains them. Crawford protests his innocence of the murder that sentences him, but acknowledges his guilt for other crimes.

Similarly, in *American History X,* Lamont admits to stealing a television, but he thereafter participates in the racial reeducation of a white supremacist murderer whose crime is greater but whose sentence is far shorter than his own. "The Hurricane" trades his flurries of physical violence for reasoned argument made in court, asking that the judge "embrace that higher principle": justice is not fought for; it is calm, compassionate, and rational. All of these black men are described in the context of their respective films as having been unjustly incarcerated but thereby improved. In the sedimentary layers of representation that constitute the cultural imagination, doing what comes naturally means understanding incarceration in terms of a pair of contradictions regarding black men behind bars: all black men are violent criminals, and black prisoners are innocent but made better through imprisonment.

Two claims clarify this enigma, the first from one of the films, the second from the discourse surrounding them. In *The Hurricane,* Lesra becomes increasingly aware of his own race in light of Carter's blackness and incarceration, juxtaposed with the whiteness of Lesra's guardians, which precipitates a brief, heated exchange between Lesra and them. Lisa offers that "not all white people are racists," to which Lesra replies that "not all black people are murderers." *The Film Journal*'s review of *The Farm* points out, "The filmmakers obviously set out to prove the existence of racism and other forms of prejudice in the judicial system that placed these men in Angola, and that continues to discriminate against them in parole hearings and appeals. However, *a prejudicial justice system isn't news*" (emphasis added).[23]

We can sort the causes and consequences of this contradiction of blackness equated with criminality, repudiated or not, and the acknowledged injustice of justice by referencing a heuristic of Slavoj Žižek, one built around the story of "The Emperor's New Clothes." In *For They Know Not What They Do: Enjoyment as a Political Factor* (1991),[24] Žižek offers an analysis of the apparent contradiction of willing participation in the false consciousness of an ideological symbolic order as immutable reality.[25] His is a critique of the phenomenon of members of a social order upholding the "naturalness" of cultural practices known to be arbitrary—in Lacanian terms, the simultaneous acknowledgment and disavowal of a gap between the symbolic and the real. Žižek describes the three most common responses of the crowd observing that the emperor's new clothes are in fact not there at all: conformity, cynicism, and perversion. The first recognizes that the Emperor has no clothes, but does nothing, so as not to disturb the social order. The second identifies the lack of completeness in the social reality but, rather than call attention to it, pretends to believe in order to profit from those who do not know. The third view is a capitulation to the need for completeness, the position that recognizes the gap but situates itself so as to fulfill the perceived completeness of the social order—the emperor wears only the clothes we give him.[26]

In terms of black men overrepresented in prison, these respective positions can be understood as follows. The conformist acknowledges that the system of justice is racist, but for the sake of social peace says nothing. The cynic knows that the system of justice is racist, but says, "Because I am white I say nothing, as I benefit from that system"; or, "Because I am black but not myself in prison, I say nothing." The third response admits that the system of social justice is racist, but in watching a film depicting that prejudicial order, sees justice done in the film—concluding that then there is in fact social justice. Representing racist injustice therefore runs risks related to those raised in familiar arguments regarding how representations of violence in film attempting to critique that violence nevertheless capitulate to the desire to see it, inadvertently glorifying that which they seek to condemn.[27] *American History X* occupies the second and third of these positions. There is an aspect of cynicism in Derek Vinyard's racist, murderous violence and, consequently, in his imprisonment, which is treated as the fulfillment of a prejudice originating in the oedipal family rather than one constituted in broader social history. Hence imprisonment is not prejudiced, because it happens to white people too. The way that the film treats race as a free-floating signifier seems cynical, but it is actually perverse. The identification of "you the nigger" makes the equation of blackness and prisoner complete and therefore justifies a prejudiced social system: if a white man is a "nigger" in prison, then there is no racial prejudice in the judicial system.

*The Hurricane* presents a more ambiguous case. On one hand, throughout the film the mise-en-scène, character, and dialogue repeatedly call out that the emperor is not wearing any clothes: the all-white jury of Carter's peers, the racist face of injustice in the white detective, Washington's "Any two will do?" On the other hand, the film radically condenses any harsh portrayal of Carter's imprisonment to the initiatory scene of solitary confinement, which ends with the appearance of the conciliatory prison guard, Jimmy (Barnes), who aids Carter's fight against an identity as inmate. Extranarratively, that characterization redeems Barnes's prior role as the criminally savage prison guard in *The Shawshank Redemption*. Within the narrative the closing shot of Carter's stance outside the prison on the steps of the federal courthouse endorses the ability of the justice system to make amends for itself, to correct its mistakes, an affirmation reinforced by the subsequent rolling text describing the events surrounding Carter after his release. In the end, *The Hurricane*'s flirtations with politics and history fade to its generic classification as a "triumph of the human spirit" film. Justice is slow but certain, and almost two decades in prison readily collapse to a couple of scenes of glossy production and powerful acting framed by testaments to its story being *really* real. Both *The Hurricane* and *American History X,* in repeatedly attesting to their own reality, further capitulate to Žižek's third position of perversity in suggesting that these are not fictions, that there really is social justice in prison practice, justice made manifest in narratives of redemption.

That aspect of salvation makes *The Farm* similarly problematic. All of the prisoners, both white and black, are described in sympathetic terms, sympathy largely predicated upon their self-reflection regarding their criminality and its attendant incarceration, and their transformation in response to that imprisonment. The perverse viewer can claim that Simmons may not be guilty, but at least his twenty years in prison have provided him with an education. A similar observation is that Theriot, instead of resisting his inmate identity, adopts his prisoner status, even choosing to be buried on prison grounds. Presumably there are plenty of inmates at Angola who are far more recalcitrant, who do not seem to have learned so much in their time, embraced the salvation of prison, or adopted it as home. Many Angola inmates might claim that prison has made them worse rather than better, but they are not included in a film as limited by cultural expectation as by budget and administrative access—which is not to say that the film functions in a perverse capacity. One of the aspects of lifetime incarceration as fantasized in the cultural imagination is the institutionalization of the long-term inmate, wherein the prisoner so fully adopts the identity of inmate as to be unable to function outside prison walls. This view is offered most fully in *The Shawshank Redemption,* where one released long-termer commits suicide, and Red (Morgan) contemplates violating his parole so as to return to prison.

In contrast, *The Farm* includes, at its end, lifers describing how much they desire to be free. Tannehill says, "It would be so much overfloatin' of joy that it would be hard for me to express myself";

Simmons says he has had "dreams of freedom for years." When performing community-service duties outside of Angola, class A trustees such as Witherspoon describe counting every blade of grass. Furthermore, the film does not end with the triumphant fulfillment of unprejudiced justice for black men in prison. Tannehill's pardon remains unsigned, Simmons's appeal is rejected, as is Witherspoon's, and Crawford's family is trying to raise three thousand dollars for trial transcripts so as to pursue an appeal. All of this information is provided in rolling text that attests to a far less optimistic reality than that which closes *The Hurricane*. Instead of concluding with the orchestral violins, there is the irony of the spiritual "Praise the Lord, I'm Free" and Theriot's burial on prison grounds, which fades to an aerial shot of Angola, where so many are not free and where the odds are not beaten. In the final analysis, the film suggests that justice is not blind and that the emperor is naked—and in telling the difference, it has produced at least one historical effect, as Simmons now has legal representation as a result of the film.[28] *The Farm* thereby functions as a writ of habeas corpus in the court of popular opinion, reintroducing to the cultural imagination the representation of actual prisoners speaking for themselves to actual consequence. That right to speak is foremost among the many contributions made by this extraordinary documentary.

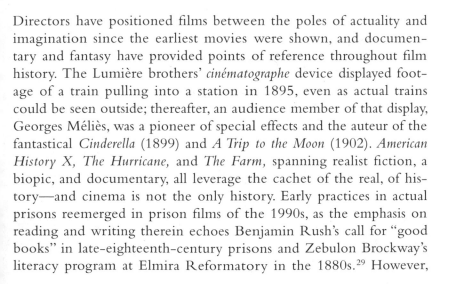

Directors have positioned films between the poles of actuality and imagination since the earliest movies were shown, and documentary and fantasy have provided points of reference throughout film history. The Lumière brothers' *cinématographe* device displayed footage of a train pulling into a station in 1895, even as actual trains could be seen outside; thereafter, an audience member of that display, Georges Méliès, was a pioneer of special effects and the auteur of the fantastical *Cinderella* (1899) and *A Trip to the Moon* (1902). *American History X, The Hurricane,* and *The Farm,* spanning realist fiction, a biopic, and documentary, all leverage the cachet of the real, of history—and cinema is not the only history. Early practices in actual prisons reemerged in prison films of the 1990s, as the emphasis on reading and writing therein echoes Benjamin Rush's call for "good books" in late-eighteenth-century prisons and Zebulon Brockway's literacy program at Elmira Reformatory in the 1880s.[29] However, history is not the only force that shapes imagination, either in the aesthetic axiom "Art imitates life," or in even historicist imperatives of reading a correspondence between actual events and imaginative fiction in a documentary record. The reiterative imaginations of the real have shaped the history these films offer. To read the relationship between history and imagination in one direction, the realistic fiction of *American History X* features Norton touting statistics he culled from the California governor's office, and *The Hurricane*'s dialogue regularly quotes from Carter's prison writing and from actual court testimony. To read the relationship in reverse, a documentary shaped by the fantasies of imprisonment projects actual prison walls as redemptive spaces of male bonding.

Of course, anyone—director, film editor, screenwriter, casual audience member, cultural critic—can show or say anything for any reason. However, there are consequences, and some of those consequences are the assembly of the shape and size of a shared reality. Going to the movies, one finds that going to prison is a philosophical experience, wherein one learns to better situate oneself in the world. Going to the movies, one learns that history as public memory is a puzzle, pieced together retroactively. However, puzzles have a predetermined shape, and the cultural imagination demarcates the shape of inmate experience such that even prison documentaries perpetuate types and narratives deployed in popular mainstream fiction.

These films, in claiming the real, produce history. History is made in these films less in the resemblances and differences among them for which prison experience is more accurate, but more in the struggle of competing interpretations. It is made in the representations and conversations surrounding cultural artifacts such as these films, the discourse that sanctifies, qualifies, and specializes in them, discourse that would do well to draw together their disparate audiences. Popular audiences, critics, and theorists too often dismiss as irrelevant the viewing experience of those whose investments seem different from their own. Part of the distance between popular and critical audiences develops from the latter's overemphasis on criticism as censure rather than as analysis. Film critics, especially academics, often emphasize the pejorative sense of the job description, not seeming to like very much the films they have watched the numerous times that detailed accounts require. This apparent absence of any pleasure in viewing distances them from the viewers who see films for enjoyment, education, and distraction. Indeed, the separation among critics, audiences, and theorists is tremendous.

For example, the theoretically invested critic of these prison films might attempt to sort them in Lacanian terms, delineating between their status as phi (φ) or *objet petit a*—that is, whether they represent the imagination or the symbolization of the unattainable real.[30] It is possible that uncritical viewing treats them as the former, critical viewing the latter, and that criticism never affirming the completeness of the order of representation thereby fulfills Žižek's fourth position—the naysayer who suggests that telling history is a matter of sorting among the flurry of competing scripts, a sustained revision, telling the difference over and over again. That constant skepticism is more in line with Deleuze and Guattari, for whom sorting between the fields of the imaginary and the symbolic is a red herring, as the production of the real is the crux. Crucial to these films are the social investments in the racism that equates blackness and criminality, contrasted with the blocked desires of inmates such as Crawford, Simmons, Tannehill, and Witherspoon—a desire for life such as that spoken in the latter's life-affirming sentence, "I want real freedom." Furthermore, *The Farm* functions within the field of what Deleuze and Guattari describe as "minor literature," given Rideau's position as prisoner and codirector and coeditor of the collection *Life Sentences,* and the film's enunciation of the collective social identity of prisoners for audiences not themselves imprisoned.[31] In de Certeau's terms, the films take viewers for a walk in the prisons that are their real and imagined settings, representing the bars, cells, crimes, and visiting rooms that define enclosure. Prisoners' bodies are thereby written within contained space. In a fusion of Foucault and Lacan, de Certeau describes the relationship of law and subject in terms of imprisonment: "Because the law is already applied with and on bodies, 'incarcerated' in physical practices, it can make people believe that it speaks in the name of the 'real.'"[32] Incarceration as an effect of law therefore inscribes not only actuality but also righteousness: all prisoners are guilty of violent crime because they are in prison.[33]

What is most important in this theoretical glossing is the degree to which it foregrounds the simultaneous desire for and unavailability of the real, which is precisely the crux of the films, according to their popular and critical reviews. Various audiences of theorists, critics, reviewers, historians, and popular viewers can be joined because most—and likely all—viewers do not exclusively inhabit one identity or another. I have hoped to demonstrate such crossover in working among these various discourses of theory, review, and criticism within a selection of 1998 and 1999 films set in prisons and united by claims to the real. The analysis of *American History X* and *The Hurricane* demonstrates the pervasiveness of imprisonment in the cultural imagination and the difficulty of drawing connections between that visibility of imagined imprisonment and the accompanying invisibility of its actual corollary. *The Farm* presents a more difficult case, wherein a documentary film that is de facto part of the historical record fulfills expectations shaped in popular imaginings. What is at stake is telling the difference.

Telling the difference, testifying in a present that is itself constantly becoming the past, casts history in terms of performance, participation in a "now" whose textualization is a record, but never can be the stuff of the real itself. These films, in attesting to their actuality, are part of the flurry of documents narrating the history of now, but "now" is fluid and dynamic, and, like de Certeau's walk in the city, resists textualization. *The Hurricane*'s documentary footage showing 1974 protests of Carter's incarceration features the soundtrack of Gil Scott-Heron's song released that same year, "The Revolution Will Not Be Televised."[34] The lyrics begin, "You will not be able to stay home, brother"—because the revolution will not be mediated—and close with, "It will be live." Crawford's mother says, in her visit with her son, who is imprisoned for life at Angola, "This is no dream or nothing made up, this is for real." As the next chapter will demonstrate, the best efforts of representing prisoners will be live and "for real," and will include prisoners' testifying, performing themselves in the history of now.

# 8

## Staging Prisons and the Performance of History

INTERVIEWER: Then you think it is possible to reconcile politics and literature? To use the theatre or one's fiction to achieve political ends?
BULLINS: Oh, yes, if that is what you wish to do.
    —An interview with Ed Bullins in the *Negro American Literature Forum*[1]

We don't expect to find anything the same even one minute later because
one minute later is history.
                        —Huey Newton, Black Panther Party cofounder[2]

**B**OOKS SUCH as those by Faulkner, Cleaver, and Mailer circulate
among audiences, leaving scarce traces of the actual experience
of their reading, and while sales figures, book clubs, awards, reviews,
syllabi, and subsequent critical attention provide types of records, the
act of the reading itself remains largely closed from analysis. Films
too are often viewed in more-private spaces, and even conventional
theatrical screenings pose challenges to gauging a sense of any particular audience's responses and investments. Two live performances
from the fall of 1999 directly concerning imprisonment provide the
basis for the analysis of this final chapter, first because their overlapping activist agendas invite audiences on the grounds of a preexisting
social commitment, and second because those audiences are materially
present, providing a sense of their immediate reactions. "Live from

Death Row" is a series of death penalty protests staged with some conventions of theater, while *Jury Duty* is a drama based on a true story, performed once in the context of a fundraiser for a social work program.[3]

The first is a social and political ritual understood in theatrical terms, while the second is a more traditional dramatic enterprise explicitly staged in one instance as a social work production. The field of performance studies provides the tactics by which to pair these different though related sorts of cultural events.[4] In this chapter, we will see how both the protest and the play demonstrate the degree to which race and class inform criminalization and its attendant imprisonment. The former maintains the emphasis on the degree to which black masculinity has become commensurate with criminality, while the latter, with a focal character who is a white woman, expands in an important manner the sense of who is imprisoned. This matter is given greater urgency by the fact that women, particularly women of color, are the fastest-growing group of prisoners in the United States, according to the Department of Justice.[5] In a manner distinct from the greater ambiguity of most of the works surveyed in the prior chapters, both of these performances clearly protest aspects of imprisonment and the death penalty. However, like *The Farm, The Executioner's Song, Soul on Ice,* and *Go Down, Moses,* "Live from Death Row" and *Jury Duty* are less concerned with attesting to the innocence of particular individuals than they are with inviting their audiences to view criminality and incarceration as matters of social responsibility.

Making use of the strategies and the descriptive terms of the theater is not limited only to performance studies; activism concerning imprisonment and its appraisal has done so before as well. In *Barred: Women, Writing, and Political Detention* (1992), Barbara Harlow refers to the 1990 indictment of the U.S. Government for violating the rights of political prisoners such as Mumia Abu-Jamal, an activist and writer whose death sentence has garnered much public and academic attention. Harlow writes, "The *staging* of the tribunal followed months of preparation . . . [and involved] a set of temporary *role* reversals (*casting* defending attorneys as prosecutors and prisoners as plaintiffs)."[6] Harlow points the way toward challenging the distinction between prisoners and their others; the tribunal, held at the New York City Hunter College Playhouse, represents a social as well as linguistic reversal, a staged deconstruction of the judicial process. According to

Harlow, such performances offer an important social function.[7] To show injustice, while not an end in itself, is an act of signification and significance, giving public voice and representative body to the subaltern in ways that make inequity visible.

In the case of Abu-Jamal, that tribunal sat at the midpoint of two decades of activist involvement that has seen his death sentence commuted to life imprisonment, though an international struggle continues for a judicial reexamination of his conviction. The degree to which staged events such as the one Harlow describes contribute directly to subsequent legal action is a matter beyond the scope of this analysis. Still, this chapter does describe some of the processes by which staged activism operates, and doing so may well contribute to analyses of how engaging audiences as social bodies can contribute to historical change. Nevertheless, my primary purpose is to describe how two performances situate themselves with regard to specific actualities of criminality and incarceration, how they hail their audiences, and how they thereby provide a model of plural identity upon which social action likely depends. Like the other works surveyed in this book, both performances emphasize their implication in their contemporary history and in its practices of imprisonment.

Both "Live from Death Row" and *Jury Duty* demonstrate the production of a social body, and each illustrates a different sort of activism and performance implicated in the ethics of incarceration and execution, with stakes in social justice and claims to the real. "Live from Death Row" is staged activism, social protest that employs tactics of performance, sometimes to mixed results, while *Jury Duty* is activist performance, more conventional stage drama deliberately located within a particular political project. In that terminological distinction between these two performances is their difference and the difference the difference makes; in their similarity one can find a model of agency that competes with bleaker Althusserean versions of human subjectivity. The audiences that such performances address are not a priori monoliths; their unity is invoked, hailed into becoming. Social protests such as these either deliberately or inadvertently draw on the conventions of theater to produce the shared convictions of *communitas* in addressing their audiences via their political investments, treating such spectators as a social body joined in affect. The method and purpose of these performances is to call into being an audience unified through a shared social commitment, an alliance that may or may not be directed toward specific political action, be it renewed dedication to one's cultural work, protest, voting practices, letter-writing campaigns, or other forms of activism. "Live from Death Row" and *Jury Duty* hail audiences in their staging of personal and social history, and both provide a model of spectatorship that is at least potentially participatory.

# "Live from Death Row" and *Jury Duty*

The social protest "Live from Death Row" has since 1998 conducted an ongoing series of protests and is sponsored by the Campaign to End the Death Penalty. The organization held its September 23, 1999, forum at the University Teaching Center on the campus of the University of Texas at Austin, in conjunction with Mumia Awareness Week. "Live from Death Row" takes its name from Abu-Jamal's 1995 volume of prison writings, a collection of essays drawing from personal observation, court records, and other research, almost always pairing the experience of the individual with a broader cultural history. It is a rhetorical approach that has its clearest precedent in Cleaver's *Soul on Ice* and Rideau's award-winning *Angolite* essays of the 1970s and 1980s, many of which are collected in *Life Sentences*. The series of community-held forums circulate flyers, blanket e-mails, and employ other grassroots methods to invite an audience to hear prisoners on death row tell their stories, offering an opportunity for dialogue between those in and out of prison. The implication is that to communicate "live" with death row inmates is more fully to conceive of them as alive and thus to take a stand against their executions. That particular September evening drew an audience of almost one hundred spectators, mostly white students from the university. Two administrators—both white men—of the local chapters of the activist organizations sponsoring the event began the forum, before giving way to an African-American woman, Rosa Thigpen, mother of inmate Kenny Collins. Thereafter, the prisoners Jody Lee Miles, John Booth, and Collins phoned in from prison first to give speeches and then to answer questions.

The other performance, *Jury Duty*, was written and directed by Ken Webster and is based on his experience as a member of a criminal trial jury in Travis County, Texas, which rendered a guilty verdict—convicting Rebecca Walton in the shooting of Luis Flores—and a subsequent sixty-year prison sentence. The play recounts, in a series of retrospective monologues, the story of a white female drug addict and prostitute who murdered her pimp. It includes her trial and the deliberations about her culpability both by the accused and by several of the jurors during her sentencing. The playwright acknowledges that he "wrote the play as a protest of a broken justice system, and as a release for [himself] after the unpleasant experience of being a participant in the broken process."[8] Indeed, correspondence with friends in which Webster describes the painful experience of serving on the jury inadvertently served as an early draft of the play. The performance was offered as a fund-raiser for the Diversity Institute at the University of Texas at Austin's School of Social Work and was held in the social work auditorium. Institute staff members prefaced the performance with a discussion of the program, mentioning the play only with regard to its role as a "perfect fund-raiser," because of both its content and its cachet in being "based on a true story."

"Live from Death Row" features local activists, families of condemned inmates, and, via speakerphone, inmates themselves. For the September meeting, the staff has taped a photo of Abu-Jamal behind the lectern to one side, and a large sign hangs in the middle: "Stop Executions!" it reads in big letters, subtitled with the forum's sponsor, "Campaign to End the Death Penalty." The panelists and their table are at the center of the stage; a speakerphone and a microphone to one side complete the mise-en-scène. The audience is reminded that the inmates will call after seven, and then the first panelist, Jim Harrington of the Texas Civil Rights Project, speaks. The audience is silent, except for the scribbling of pens and the occasional murmur of agreement or disgusted half laugh of acknowledgment when Harrington cites that those on death row are mostly minorities, poor, mentally disabled—grist for what he describes three times as the "machinery of death." When he finishes, the audience applauds, and the organizer, Quentin Reese, again reminds us that the convicts will call a little after seven—the repetition suggesting that their call is what we are really here for. Until then, Thigpen, mother of one of the death row inmates, will speak.

Thigpen, an African-American woman in her forties, says, "Good evening," and we reply in unison, "Good evening!"—a call-response oratory that continues, contrasting with the uninterrupted monologue of the previous, white speaker. She provides a brief narrative of her son's trial and the incompetence of his court-appointed lawyer. Collins has maintained his innocence, and Thigpen shows a photograph of her son, one of her last, as the Supermax prison in Baltimore, Maryland, will not allow photos of inmates to be taken. Unlike Harrington, Thigpen frequently elicits our verbal response and invokes a "we" of which the audience is a part. She says, for example, "The lawyer and the judge are in cahoots together, as we well know," and there are murmurs of agreement from the audience.

There are two important implications here, the first regarding class and the legal system, the second regarding cross-racial identification. The alliance arrayed against the defendant is one that Gilmore in *The Executioner's Song* gestures toward as well, when he points out that the state psychiatrist judging him competent to stand trial is "paid by the same people who pay [Gilmore's] lawyers." The doctor, Gilmore's defense, opposing counsel, and the judge all represent the "State of Utah. [Gilmore] can't win for losing."[9] Similarly, *The Hurricane* calls attention to an all-white jury finding a black man guilty, a group described by the judge as a "jury of your peers." Such recognitions are not new; in a story published in *Esquire* in 1944, Chester Himes writes, "The only lawyers I know are the ones who defended me. They were appointed by the state, and to tell the truth, they must have been working for it."[10] Judge, jury, and the lawyers for both defense and prosecution become part of the same machine of the state arrayed against the accused. The convention of court-appointed defense does play into the paranoia fostered in such trial narratives organized around the defendant as the focal character, narratives that become part of the cultural imagination. However, also part of that imagination are matters of the historical record, and lapses on the part of court-appointed defense counselors are legion, and a matter of regional and national media attention.[11]

Thigpen's assertion of complicity between judge and lawyers is one that "we well know." She invokes a "we," joining audience and speaker in a community with already well-formed, shared knowledge, even if she does provide us with more; for example, she points out that there are no educational courses for her son in Supermax, as there were in the previous penitentiaries where he had served. She implores those in the audience to help—almost all of us are students at the university housing the event—as she addresses us as a "we" composed largely of young, white, middle-class men and women. She asks us to speak out later in life when we are the leaders of our communities, to help "these people," assuming that these people are not us, and that her audience will have the power to speak that she lacks. Her claim belies the circumstances, given that she stands at the lectern and we are her audience. Nevertheless, her performance is an incredibly sophisticated one, bridging the gaps between herself, her audience, and prisoners in a demonstration of the ways race and affluence mediate voice.

Thigpen makes rhetorical moves that both breach cultural difference and reinscribe it. She identifies the audience of mostly white college students as those who can change what she cannot. Her appeals to a shared humanity assume that "we" know the inequities of the legal system and are prepared to help "these people," including her son. Indeed, "Live from Death Row" largely shapes its audience's sense of itself by distinguishing "us" from "these people" in prison. We are there to protest the death penalty, but we are also there to be reminded that "we" are not "these people." She identifies the audience as those who can speak, and thus change what she cannot, whether because of our youth, our education, our class position, or the color of our skin. Thigpen appeals to an essential, shared, and simple humanity, assumed in our presence as that protesting audience, a "we" who know the inequities of the legal system, who can help "these people." "Live from Death Row" produced the shared identity of its audience in part by distinguishing them from those in prison, and it offered the means to renew its unity in advertising the next protest against the death penalty. We were there to be reminded of ourselves.

After the closing applause for Thigpen, Reese reminds us of the next protest date. He asks us to take a stand when then Governor George W. Bush or another politician speaks in support of the death penalty. Then the phone rings and Reese cocks the microphone closer to the speakerphone. It is Jeannette, our link to inmate Jody Lee Miles. When prison officials discovered "Live from Death Row," they barred the prisoners from calling directly to the performance. The prisoners are allowed phone calls only to friends and family. Jeannette is a friend and our link. We cannot speak directly to the inmates, and audience members instead direct questions for the inmates to Reese. He repeats those questions over the phone to Jeannette, who repeats them to the inmates on a second phone, and then relays the prisoners' responses by holding the phone receiver she uses to speak to the inmates next to the phone with which she speaks to Reese. When Reese explains these Byzantine barriers to us, we laugh, a surprising sound in this room. The whole procedure is absurd, a farce—but it does reveal the circuitry of power at work, a Foucauldian system of concealment, control, and disidentification, whereby extrinsic and repressive forces block the flow of the communication and self-representation so formative of identity.

We could turn to Foucault's description of the degree to which statements constitute the subject, which he makes in *The Archaeology of Knowledge* (1972)[12] and elsewhere, but we are better served in turning to Mumia Abu-Jamal, the man whose book, *Live from Death Row*, gives the protest its inspiration and name. Abu-Jamal forcefully proclaims precisely this communicative relationship, the strategy of self-making dependent on an audience. He describes his gratitude to readers in the preface to the paperback edition: "You have made my repressive isolation more than worthwhile. In those darkest of days, under a death warrant, with a date to die, your simple act of reading this book fed my soul." His thanks comes in the face of the isolation consequent to writing the book, as he alleges that time spent in solitary confinement was suffered as punishment for publishing.[13] Such solitary confinement recently has been linked to increased rates of inmate suicide,[14] meaning that Abu-Jamal's position, like so many inmates on death row and in other areas of maximum security, is doubly fraught, and the stay to his death sentence in 1995 did not protect him from that dangerous isolation. Nevertheless, given the life-sustaining nature of meaningful human communication, Abu-Jamal and Jody Miles decided it was worth the risk.

Some of what Miles has to say disappears in the static of his enforced dislocation, but we get the general picture as he reads his statement. He has lived on Maryland's death row for two years, and spent a year in prison prior to his move to Supermax; he "know[s] how the system works." What that system might be becomes clear only after Miles speaks of the enforcement of the death penalty, even while insisting, "It's transparent that there is no clear consensus among legislators and citizens concerning [it]." Miles reiterates race as a primary determinant in its implementation. He argues that a white person accused of killing a white person may receive the death penalty, and a black person accused of killing a white person likely will, but he claims that a white defendant in the murder of a black person has at most received a sentence of eleven years—a claim with more rhetorical force than historical accuracy, though indicative of general trends. Miles repeatedly asserts his innocence, pointing out evidence used against him in his trial obtained through an illegal wiretap, evidence not objected to by his court-appointed lawyer. In Miles's polemic, the system works as a closed circuit of race and class, of enforced difference between white and black, of victims of the judicial process—and as a stark contrast between those who can afford attorneys and those who cannot.

Miles's voice grows indistinct when the phone transmission fades, as it often does. During these lags, the audience silently faces the speakerphone. A few look down at their tables in embarrassment or frustration, or strain to hear. After Miles finishes, we clap only for a moment before realizing that Miles cannot hear our response. The technological mediation grows more crippling to discourse when Thigpen's son, Collins, begins speaking, and the transmission is virtually nil. Adjusting the microphone and the telephone and tinkering with the amplifier do not help. A few remarks are clear, though: "thirteen years," "Supermax," "I basically don't know what lies ahead," "subjected to being placed in a situation such as myself," and "no matter what color you are." Collins's speech is far less distinct than Gilmore's voice, recorded by his lawyers with smuggled tape recorders to be transcribed by Schiller's typists, so that even after death, "Gilmore's voice coming in over the earphones" is clear.[15] Still, even if his voice is garbled, Collins speaks at length and in detail about the challenges he has faced in the appeals process.

Ironically, the constraints imposed by the institution make his meaning clearer: we in the audience may not be able to hear, but our understanding of imprisonment increases precisely because we are not able to understand what Collins is saying. Playwrights, theorists, and critics have grappled with the tension of theater and the representation of pain at least since Antonin Artaud.[16] Critics of Artaud have suggested that the French visionary "wanted spoken words delivered, to some extent, for the sake of their sonority, explosiveness, sensuous and associative properties"—for their connotative rather than denotative qualities—to communicate not language but experience.[17] This is exactly the unintended result for Collins, whose speech in its very unintelligibility best conveys his circumstances. The audience cannot understand all of Collins's words, but thereby better understands his position, and thus "hears" him better. If this account offers too easy a gloss of his contested subjectivity, it certainly illustrates the technological mediation by which institutional power accomplishes its object: the constructed silence and invisibility of prisoners, the difficulty of communicating from the inside to the outside. The voices of the condemned speaking in an unintelligible broadcast is a version of Bel-Imperia's prison letter written in her own blood to Hieronoimo, in Thomas Kidd's Jacobean drama, *The Spanish Tragedy*—the meaning invested in the condition of writing or speaking overwrites the words themselves.

There are several key similarities between "Live from Death Row" and *Jury Duty*. Though the inmates of the former are men in prison and those of the latter are actors playing roles, both are concealed in one way or another. Collins and the others appear only in voice, while the actual circumstances upon which *Jury Duty* is based are overwritten by the ironic disclaimer in its program, "Any similarities to any person, living or dead, is purely coincidental"—even though the play is introduced as being "based on a true story." Both performances stage dialogue between those in and out of prison, and both make extensive use of biographical and autobiographical monologues, as do *Soul on Ice, The Executioner's Song, The Hurricane,* and *The Farm.*

The reliance on biography and on telling one's own story is not surprising. According to Ioan Davies, who surveys the writing practices of prisoners in *Writers in Prison,* the performance of the narrative of self matches the actual writing that takes place in prison: "Most prison writing is autobiographical, and yet, like all autobiographies, it is inserted into other situations."[18] When one's subjectivity is contested—which Foucault and Melossi and Pavarini argue is the primary function of imprisonment—speaking or writing the self offers an affirmation of selfhood in face of forces arrayed against it. In *Soul on Ice,* Cleaver claims, "I started to write. To save myself." And the prisoner needs to save himself, because as Cleaver notes, prison can cause an inmate "to lose his sense of self."[19] The self-declarations of prisoners, then, are inserted into "other situations," in Gilmore's letters reframed in Mailer's *The Executioner's Song,* in passages of Carter's *The Sixteenth Round* incorporated verbatim in Jewison's *The Hurricane,* and in the spoken autobiographical vignettes of prisoners in Angola included in *The Farm.* For *Jury Duty,* itself the work of a dramatist and jury member reconstructing the situation of a prisoner testifying on her own behalf, one of those "other situations" is a fund-raiser for a social work program celebrating human diversity and cultural difference.

*Jury Duty*'s performance on October 9, 1999, was a special, one-night performance, a benefit/fund-raiser sponsored by the University of Texas at Austin's School of Social Work, for one of its programs,

the Diversity Institute, described in the theater program as "a collaborative, multidisciplinary project of faculty, staff, students and community members [ . . . ] dedicated to advancing better understanding
and more effective working relationships among the unique cultures
of our society." Two staff members of the School of Social Work
introduce what they repeatedly describe as a "perfect fund-raiser,"
perhaps because of its representation of cultural difference and the
inequities of the legal system, its local setting, or its blending of
humor, social realism, and empathy in the portrayal of drug addicts,
economic and social poverty, and the violence to which such lack
contributes.

The two Diversity Institute representatives do not mention the
play, though, as they discuss their program and invite DI participants
in the audience to stand and be recognized; some do, and there is
applause. Carol Lewis, associate director for the institute, is introduced
as having an "other life" as an actor and dancer, but she speaks instead
of the institute. Introducing these people, as well as staging the performance in the auditorium of the School of Social Work, frames
the drama less as a play than as social work. This particular audience
does not seem unsettled in any way by this. Rather, with those at the
proscenium asking institute staff in the audience to stand and receive
acknowledgment—a reversal of the typical audience applause for
those onstage—we seem to be other than a typical theater crowd.

Let me illustrate the distinction even while acknowledging the
problems of such terms as *typical* and *we*. I attended primarily because
it was an activist performance. My friend Jane, now a theater-history
professor, received notice of the fund-raiser through her work as
director for a student-services program. We arrived at the School
of Social Work early, so before the show began we walked to the
University of Texas at Austin Theater Building, where both Bertolt
Brecht's *Threepenny Opera* and Tennessee Williams's *Vieux Carré* were
playing that evening. We spoke with some acquaintances and then
returned to join the audience for *Jury Duty.* Back in the auditorium,
each of us noticed a change between this audience and the theatergo-
ers we had just seen; it is difficult to pin down the exact difference.
At *Jury Duty,* Jane and I were both a part of and apart from others in the auditorium. We, like everyone else, were there to see an
activist performance, but our clothes, our conversation, and our lack
of familiarity with others in the audience tagged us as "other." An
informal survey after the show suggested that almost all of those in the

audience knew one another from the School of Social Work. They discussed current classes and local services, while Jane and I talked of critical distance and dramatic convention. There was a community-is-here feeling that did not include us.

Concerning the play itself: the blocking is simple, with the twelve jury members sitting in two rows facing the audience. Ten of the jury remain seated and silent throughout the drama. A chair set stage right is for the defendant, who never sits but stands between chair and jury when she speaks, directly addressing the audience. Her monologues are interspersed with those of other characters who also rise to stand between the chair and the jury when they speak. The various characters abandon the speaking position with a voiced need to go to the bathroom, the repeated dramatic device for stage exit. Other conventions established within the play are employed less regularly. For example, though Bruce, the jury spokesperson, claims that his monologue is "all in my head," his commentary does elicit some nonverbal response from the other jurors, and when one, Maggie, later speaks, she is very much aware of Bruce's earlier monologues. The jury members never speak while they sit, maintaining an unbroken gaze on the various speakers to their right, reproducing the audience's communal spectatorship and focusing our gaze on the primary speakers. These include the defendant, Becky Wallace (played by Mary Furse), accused of murdering her pimp, Chico; Michael (played by Judson L. Jones), an accessory to the murder; and jurors Bruce and Maggie (played by Corey Gagne and Margaret Ann Hoard, respectively).

Becky describes a community of mostly absent characters, of other drug users, pimps, and prostitutes. She talks about Michael and Chico before they arrive onstage. The appearance of the dead pimp, Chico (played by Titos Menchaca), at the close, exchanging his violence in life for complacency and knowledge in death, ends an escalating conflict between the defendant and Bruce through mediation. The conflict between the two speaking jurors gives way to tension between Becky and her primary defender, between Bruce's "self-righteous" defense of Becky on humanistic grounds and the failure of that argument to significantly reduce her sentence. Other than a brief but telling interaction between Becky and Michael when she accuses him of telling her story and he replies, "It's my story too," the dialogue at the close is the first time that characters onstage have spoken to one another. Bruce tells some of Becky's story as well, "a grim tale of the worst possible childhood you can imagine," though she narrates most of her own personal history. She speaks of needing drugs so badly that she prostituted herself, and amplifies the magnitude of that need by acknowledging that though she is a lesbian, she had sex with men. Becky addresses the audience directly, asking the heterosexual men, "Can you imagine sucking dick?" and, similarly, the heterosexual women, "Or eating pussy? How bad do you want it?" Forced heterosexuality, against the grain of desire, becomes the high price Becky was forced to pay, the harsh terms and description an effort to force the audience to engage the pain these terms represent.[20]

Furse performs Becky Wallace in the Brechtian manner of epic acting that Harry Elam notes as common to social-protest performance. In this tradition, the actor "function[s] not only as the character but as a commentator on the actions of the character [ . . . and] compel[s] the audience to evaluate the social, political, and economic circumstances that created the character."[21] Playwright and director Webster constructs Becky's lived history to have positioned her in the denouement of violent murder, even as he presents the juror Maggie to challenge the inevitability of the violence emerging from that history. Whereas Bruce sees her act as unavoidable given her circumstances, Maggie assumes Becky's culpability. The two offer a convenient binary of mercy and justice. It is also the divide of historical determinism versus individual autonomy and agency, subject-*to* and subject-*of*, akin to the tensions raised in Faulkner's novels and between Cleaver's and Mailer's sense of human possibility. In terms of spectator identification, the social work students and professionals in the audience are not likely to see their present selves represented in the stories told by characters such as the self-described "crack whore," Becky, and drug user, Michael, both imprisoned for murder; or by Chico as he is invoked early in the play, a purveyor of sex, drugs, and violence, and dead to boot. In a move akin to Jewison's ironic cut to Carter's all-white jury in *The Hurricane,* Becky describes her own as a "jury of my peers, as they say [PAUSE]"—implying that they in fact are not.

The jury members may not see themselves in Becky any more than she sees herself in her jury; however, the jury does mirror the audience. In terms of staging, they are largely silent watchers, their gaze, like the gazes of the audience members, fixed on whoever speaks. The jury performs the reflection of the spectators, an expansion of what Vsevolod Meyerhold and Tom Stoppard sought to accomplish in scenery by framing the stage with large mirrors or suggesting a huge mirror as a backdrop.[22] The unpublished script of *Jury Duty* underscores this role in its description of the jury: "Ten of them are either audience members or special guest actors." Actual spectators are intended to perform the jury's reflection of the audience. Within the context of the performance, the jury collectively bears witness and sometimes individually offers responses to Becky's history and crime. Bruce points out the institutional and personal causes for Becky's current situation, addresses drug addiction as a disease, claims that the state's social welfare and legal systems let her down, and repeatedly maintains that she was "forced to have sex to keep a roof over her head." On the other hand, Maggie opts for justice rather than mercy, asking what sort of "message" a soft ruling for murder would send. A prison *sentence* becomes exactly that, a linguistic act, communicating what is thought and believed to be true of crime and punishment.

Both representative jurors perform the compromises necessary for the unanimity required of juries by the law. After determining guilt or innocence, the jury must next, if delivering a verdict of guilty, determine the sentence. The jury can deliberate as long as it needs—so long as its final judgments are singular. Like the collective population of Jefferson brought together by Stevens to witness the return of Butch Beauchamp at the close of *Go Down, Moses,* the jury is an assembly defined by its riven differences; unlike those citizens, though, the jurors must not only witness history but also decide it. Jurors Bruce and Maggie occupy dramatically opposed positions concerning what constitutes guilt, agency, and just punishment. Each also makes clear that the other jurors differ from them, particularly in terms of Becky's reproductive rights, as both recognize that one group of jurors subscribing to eugenics was primarily concerned that Becky remain in prison past her childbearing years. So various allegiances form and lines of disagreement are drawn among the disparate jurors. This is not the jury of the central trial of *The Hurricane,* a jury whose only characteristics are a shared whiteness and a verdict of guilty. The jury of *Jury Duty* is a perfect illustration of an institutional social body, the state's jury selection process "hailing" it into being. The individuals summoned were not a jury until selected; once selected, their membership constituted a particular and localized sociality, which subsequently becomes, for the audience, a model of the plural subject. The social body of the jury in the theater mirrors the social worker audience—an "I" that comprises and is compromised by its various and contradictory "we's."

However, in performance *Jury Duty* departs from its plural and conflicted jury, a "we" forced by a legal apparatus to speak in one voice, when the play leaves behind its "true story" to swing sharply to the imaginary, as the character of the murder victim, Chico, appears and offers Becky forgiveness. Like Gilmore's ghost in *The Executioner's Song* visiting Pete Galovan to explain, forgive, and acknowledge,[23] Chico appears to redeem Becky. Considering that the redemption comes from the murder victim himself, his authority is unequivocal. Chico is less a deus ex machina than machina ex deus, a machine of love and grace sprung from death to resolve the core conflict of the drama, transforming crisis into reconciliation. Brechtian alienation gives way to conventional catharsis. Chico offers a character who reflexively acknowledges his own past by both recuperating it and maintaining critical distance from it. He identifies with violence, even the ultimate degradation of his own murder, while still manifesting empathy. His cruel history and mysterious knowledge give him absolute authority in mediation; he is the social worker par excellence. The auditorium audience sees itself physically mirrored in the rows of seated jurors—a collective audience—who have offered, until this point, an excellent model of social agency, the various tensions that a person must resolve in taking a stand. The arrival of Chico undermines that complexity, smoothing out the difficulties of human experience. Audience members are invited to see themselves reflected in the transformed Chico, now so knowing and forgiving.

The magical resolution means that the jury, the audience's mirror, no longer needs to debate the agency of human action working through the tension between circumstance and autonomy. The symbolic order of the rule of law, where a social body is called upon, after internal debate, to speak univocally, is erased in favor of an imaginary unity, a specter of forgiveness. For the audience of social workers, *Jury Duty* at this moment dodges the complex social subjectivity it has heretofore modeled. The tension played out in the jury's debate with itself is evacuated by the fantasy of absolute knowledge. In effect, the ghost of Chico lets the jury, and by extension the audience, off the hook—at least until the final lines of the play. Becky asks Chico what death is like, and Chico, in the tradition of the ghost of Hamlet's father, replies, "I can't tell you." Becky asks, "Is it better than bein' alive?" Chico can only shrug, and exit; light fades on the jury and lingers only a little longer on Becky. For this particular theater audience of social workers, the close of the play is a demand to renew their commitment so that those with whom they work can harbor more hope. Like the audience of "Live from Death Row," their personal commitments are addressed and affirmed. Here the commitment is professional as well, and the box office proceeds to which they have contributed are donated to the social work organization in which many of them participate. They are reminded of themselves.

## Audiences as Social Bodies and "one minute later is history"

"Live from Death Row" and *Jury Duty* reflect both halves of what Richard Schechner describes as the "double-mirror" of performance: the theatrical reading of cultural moments and the cultural account of theatrical representation.[24] That "double-mirror," which has proven foundational for performance studies, offers a means to read *activism* and *performance* forward and backward, as staged activism and activist performance. By activist performance, I mean a production explicitly acknowledging itself as theater and framed by a dramatic convention that associates itself with a particular social project. While such a performance may or may not utilize Brechtian or other forms of narrative disruption and audience estrangement, the subject matter of activist performance makes its alliances explicit. Staged activism, on the other hand, even if it employs theatrical strategies of representation, asserts that what the audience experiences is *really* real.

Just as in the films surveyed in chapters 5, 6, and 7, there is a crucial difference between Collins phoning in from Supermax prison and an actor performing a character on trial. Indeed, like the case of John Artis appearing at a human rights symposium screening *The Hurricane,* one of the fundamental goals of staged activism is *telling the difference* between the real and the performed, providing the space for people to describe their positions in their own words, communicating as fully as possible their circumstances. Elaine Scarry argues that the collective effort to challenge inequity "depends centrally on its ability to communicate the reality of physical pain to those who are not themselves in pain," and that therefore "the human voice must aspire to become a precise reflection of material reality."[25] The garbled transmission of Collins in "Live from Death Row" and the character Becky's haunting final lines in *Jury Duty* both represent powerful examples of such aspirations of human voice—though there is the substantial difference of the actuality of the former and the fantasy of the latter. While much of the play may be based on a true story, that final dialogue is the playwright's effort to stage a sense of despair rather than to communicate exact circumstances. However, there are two actual people whose experience shapes those words: the defendant upon whom Webster based the character of Becky, Rebecca Walton, and Webster himself, the director's own pain regarding his participation in a "broken process."

Though an activist performance, *Jury Duty* is extremely conventional in that the interaction between actors onstage and seated audience members remains sharply regulated; they speak and move, while we sit and offer only laughter, silence, and applause. Similarly, "Live from Death Row" employs conventions that dictate how the principals and the audience interact. The performance attempts to revise those conventions by facilitating direct communication between the audience and the inmates. However, the mechanical difficulties that so precisely described the condition of those imprisoned also reinscribed the gulf between those in and out of prison, inhibiting the dialogue the program tried to establish. The technical problems reference the cultural and material differences between those in and out of prison, such as in *Jury Duty,* which invites the audience to see itself reflected in the dynamic of its jury, but not in the defendant.

Both the play and the protest "Live from Death Row" presume a social difference between their audiences and prisoners. As Thigpen made clear, the agency she imagined of her audience was based on the difference between the free and the incarcerated, a difference suggested in the circumstances of that particular performance as one between white and black. The audience may have more clearly understood Collins's precarious position because they could not see him or hear him distinctly. However, the audience did not necessarily hear themselves *in* the prisoner, a matter of identification. This unbridged gap between those in and out of prison poses a strategic challenge to staged activism and activist performances that are positioned against imprisonment practices.

The performances discussed in this chapter differ greatly from prison theater programs that stage shows within prison walls for and by prisoners.[26] Activist performance and staged activism both resemble some aspects of the "social protest performances" Elam describes, particularly in terms of their representation of specific social groups and opposition to what those groups conceive of as unjust conditions. However, activist performance and staged activism differ from such social-protest performances in the ways they communicate to their audiences. Elam claims that the social-protest performances modeled resistance, "direct[ed] the audience to take action," and "affirmed cultural unity,"; they are, in all of the instances he describes, contingent upon shared race and class markers and direct interaction between actors and audience.[27] Performances such as those of El Teatro Campesino and the Black Revolutionary Theater Movement treat the theater's fourth wall as a two-way mirror that both reflects and can be seen through, a means by which spectators not only recognize themselves and their struggles on stage, but also verbally or physically engage those representations during the production. They are less apart from the play than a part of the work.

Activist performance and staged activism, on the other hand, neither require the active participation of the audience nor reflect the identity of that audience. *Jury Duty* and "Live from Death Row" are staged for audiences not themselves in prison. Each of them reinscribes the differences between prisoners and audience members, and maintains theatrical conventions of largely passive audiences. Consequently, they do not provide a clear directive for what their audiences should do with regard to their shared social projects of protesting the death penalty and addressing imprisonment as a racial, class-based practice. At one level, they only remind their audiences of their shared belief, without providing clear means to transform that belief to action.

Given the lack of identification between audience members and prisoners in the activist performance of *Jury Duty* and the staged activism of "Live from Death Row," and the lack of a clear strategy for what their audiences should do after the performances, I seem to be painting a bleak picture of their efficacy. However, what these performances do accomplish is of vital importance. These performances invite their audiences to share social and professional commitments: opposition to the death penalty in "Live from Death Row" and the social work of *Jury Duty*. Furthermore, these two performances conduct a rich model of social subjectivity, particularly the latter, in its representation of the collective jury, its competing viewpoints, and its final sentence. Not least, acknowledging the very gulf drawn between those in and out of prison, reinscribed in these events, is a recognition of difference that allows that gulf to be seen anew, a re-vision.

The social subjectivity modeled in these two performances is one of interpellated communal spectatorship. Of course, "interpellate" immediately invokes Althusser, whose widely regarded—though not unchallenged—claim of subjects as hailed into being has been read by Janelle Reinelt and others as "anesthetizing," in that it "seem[s] to dematerialize agency and opposition."[28] However, the manner in which *Jury Duty* and "Live from Death Row" address their audiences makes available a recuperation of interpellation, a recovery that strips the term of its repressive connotations. Althusser's example of the policeman's call hailing the subject involves both the threat and the guilt presumed in such a call.[29] The example of the policeman assumes a wholly asymmetrical relation of authority, but that implication elides the more complex situation that the term *interpellation* carries with it, one of "a question put by a member of a legislative assembly to a minister or member of the government."[30] This richer conceptualization of interpellation grants greater authority and shifts identity from the isolated singular to the participatory plural. The subject is a participant, a member of a larger assembly.

In *Jury Duty,* the titular jury whose duty it is to consider its own conflicting positions before finally speaking in one voice best models such a social subjectivity, a union of singular and plural. The "I/we" of that social body, like activism and performance read in the double-mirror, reads two ways. Such a body becomes at once the multiple and contradictory investments of an individual, and the unity of a group hailed by common allegiance.[31] Staged performance thus becomes the crucible that fuses social body and individual body, united in affect. Similarly, Scarry associates agency with a collective subject, the need for social action best predicated upon a larger understanding of self, a self beyond one's own skin. The social body operates as a metaphor to mobilize social action: if "I" extend beyond my skin, "I" am more likely to extend the boundaries of what will cause me to act on my own behalf.

Scarry's implication of enlarging one's self speaks to Foucault's point that concludes chapter 4: "The soul is the effect and instrument of a political anatomy: the soul is the prison of the body."[32] That is, the rigid rhetoric of the autonomous individual sharply limits agency; destabilizing that subject enables social and contingent (rather than individual and autonomous) agency. The I/we of the social body as audience of staged activism and activist performance is at once singular and plural, composed of individuals hailed by allegiance to the activist project at hand. Such a sense of a hailed audience may counter some aspects of Althusser's sense of singular interpellation, but it accords with his claim specifically of theater (and Brechtian theater at that), which can offer "the production of a new spectator, an actor who starts where the performance ends."[33]

I do not mean to reduce the value of these two performances to the theoretical model of identity as a social body drawn from them. Performances in their production and reception may benefit from terms to describe them more richly, but they are more than that vocabulary. This is especially true for staged activism and activist performance, whose effect always has strings attached to a particular social project. While staged activism and activist performance differ in the degree to which they imbue their representation with truth-value and maintain dramatic conventions in their performance, both cast their audiences as communities, summon them through and unify them by the common identity established by the social project in which these performances situate themselves. In the case of "Live from Death Row," that commonality is the opposition to the death penalty held by those attending the protest; in *Jury Duty,* the audience attends the fund-raiser in support of a social work program. What works such as these two do most successfully is remind their audiences that they are a "we"—plural in number and singular in commitment. Those audiences are reminded of their position and the fact that others share it, and in being so reminded, maintain it.

The value of such a gathered audience cannot be determined solely on the basis of what immediate historical changes it brings about. For example, no prisoners are released, any more than the 1990 tribunal saw the immediate commutation of Abu-Jamal's death sentence; resistance is a process of transformation pitted against tremendous social and historical forces. The racial and class-based prison populations contested by "Live from Death Row" and *Jury Duty* are only recent examples of inequity. Nevertheless, the opacity and silence of the prison system is challenged by these kinds of public performances. By definition, prisons conceal their practices of erasure; the manner in which they do it is rendered audible by inmates such as Miles and Collins. To be enacted, social change must first be voiced, and *Jury Duty* and "Live from Death Row" both give voice to otherwise silenced populations, drawing attention to the actuality of incarceration at a time when many representations of imprisonment fill a shape determined in a cultural imagination that is in tension with historical actuality. These two performances hail their respective audiences in a manner that reminds them of their opposition to a racial and class-based prison system. However, both performances also reinforce the difference between "we" and "these people," a distinction that limits just how far the borders of the social body might be breached.

Still, embedded within these performances are at least two distinct strategies by which those limits might be tested. First, there is the role Webster plays as writer and director of *Jury Duty*. In drawing from his own experience as jury member, he demonstrates that the mechanisms of the U.S. legal system implicate its citizens in the set of claims and counterclaims that determine criminality and its attendant imprisonment. Second, while my analysis of "Live from Death Row" addresses it as a performance, it remains a historical event understood only here as staged, employing theatrical convention. As such, that reading might seem to run the risk of aestheticizing politics, which Walter Benjamin has famously associated with fascism.[34] However, there is a difference between deploying politics as art and interpreting political acts within a framework of analysis sensitive to both history and the mechanisms by which audiences may identify themselves vis-à-vis their moment. The culturally and historically nuanced interpretive practices pervasive in the past two decades of academic humanities study provide a powerful set of tools for the analysis of not only books and films, but also performances—even, and perhaps especially, when what is performed is history itself.

Such an understanding is a literalization of history, its textualization, and the analysis as to how its fleetingly available experience operates rhetorically. Of course, it is not unexpected to explore what some event *means;* at stake is what some confluence of actualities *does.* The juror Maggie is concerned about what sort of "message" mercy might send, and while she is a fictional character, her words echo not only the playwright Webster's fellow jury member upon whom her character is based, but also the words of "tough on crime" politicians and their electorates, whether noted by ACA officials or criminologists. Such a sense of a verdict and its accompanying prison sentence sending a message understands historical events as functioning rhetorically, and performance is the closest opportunity to "read" the real of history, not what it means, but how it works. Such an account is the reverse of the theatricality described in *The Executioner's Song.* Mailer portrays events in theatrical terms. He likens Gilmore's presentation in court to stage and film acting, writes that the prison officials rehearse his execution, and depicts the execution itself as a play of stage and spectators.[35] As staged and acted, the events seem unreal. This is the sense of theater critiqued by Deleuze and Guattari, who would replace theater with history.[36]

However, just as the purposes and methods of literary studies change after a historical turn, and just as the phrases "the personal is political" and "always historicize" are axiomatic to the point of being clichés, reading history as performance need not aestheticize and thus anesthetize it. Instead, such an understanding draws attention to the ephemeral quality of the real of history and the necessity to provide as full a record, as thick a description, as possible, even while recognizing the impossibility of doing so completely. Just as the ephemeral quality of performances means that no two are the same, history as performance leaves available the possibility of change as suggested by Huey Newton. No more than he can we "expect to find anything the same even one minute later because one minute later is history."[37] At stake is what sort of historical change and what new possibilities prove emergent at the expense of others.

# Conclusion

THE PREVIOUS chapters of this book chronicle how a postbellum Southern racist imagination cast black men as criminals, a trend recorded in the early National Prison Association transcripts and in historiography chronicling the jim crow era, as well as in Faulkner's fiction. That dangerous equation broadened nationally to be represented and critiqued in the writing not only of Cleaver (and, to a limited extent, Mailer), but also of American Correctional Association officials. In addition, it is pervasive in films and performances at the end of the twentieth century. Those chapters also document the diminishing possibilities for how various types of criminality might be defined and addressed, from the individuation of prisoners in the 1930s to the revolutionary possibilities of 1968 and then their foreclosure thereafter in the 1970s, with the nearly unilateral practice of incarceration for an increasing array of offenses through the 1980s, the enforcement of which specifically targeted inner-city communities in a manner capitulating to cultural expectation. Challenging the imagination, and thereby contributing to the transformation of history, demands writing its genealogy, naming the past and tracing the ways it has produced both the dramatic inequities and the imaginations of the present—testifying in order to imagine a different future.

It is one thing to imprison those who have committed violent crimes in order to incapacitate them, to deprive of freedom the people convicted of committing felonies that pose threats to the liberties, lives, pursuits, and properties of others. When prisons are imagined to contain only such violent, often-murderous offenders, it is extremely difficult for those not in prison to recognize themselves in prisoners.[1] However, the two performances, like the previous texts surveyed in this book, call attention to the racial and class-based enterprise of punishment. Chapter 1 lays the basis for prison history to be best understood as national history, and also demonstrates how it has been a racial practice, a matter best illustrated by a Southern prison administrator in 1888 claiming that prisons exist in order to house freed slaves.[2] Chapter 2 points out how Faulkner's fictional Jefferson desires Joanna Burden's murder to be a "negro crime," just as a nameless Southerner tells a visitor in 1908 that "we feel like killing a nigger," irrespective of guilt or even any offense at all.[3] The narrative arc of *Go Down, Moses* follows Lucas Beauchamp's father to Lucas's grandson, the first pages opening with an escaped slave, progressing through the threats and persecutions of jim crow, and on to a Northern prison's execution of Butch. That native son returns to a Jefferson no longer imagined of one mind, but divided by lines of identity painstakingly united for a moment and assembled to witness his return.

Chapters 3 and 4 track the potential for progressive change and its loss, as discussions in 1968 of crime as historically and socially situated and punishment as racial transform to crime being addressed as a raceless, random, and all-pervasive phenomenon that can be met only with incarceration. These transformations are especially visible between the Cleaver (and Mailer) of 1968 and the Mailer (and Cleaver) of 1979, but the changes are just as visible in the presentations of prison wardens, governors, and members of the ACA during that period. Chapters 5, 6, and 7 describe films set in prison in the late 1990s, prisons almost uniformly depicted as places of personal salvation, where even the black men unfairly imprisoned benefit from the experience. At the same time, the U.S. prison system surpassed every comparable country in terms of both rates of incarceration and the overall population of prisoners, and black men are radically overrepresented in those numbers.

In chapter 8, the "Live from Death Row" speaker and prisoner Miles, a white man, critiques at length the racial implementation of the death penalty, a critical matter as well in Abu-Jamal's book from which the series of protests takes its name.[4] The ghost of Chico in *Jury Duty* tells the sympathetic juror, Becky, and the audience that the "death penalty is for killin' cops or pretty white girls." The pairing of "pretty white girls" and police officers implies both the cultural myth instigating lynching as cited in chapter 2 and the regularly igniting tension between police forces and black and ethnic communities, tension that is the background to the texts of chapters 3 and 6.[5] The character of Becky (and the real person upon whom she is based) will not be executed, but her criminality remains a foregone conclusion for the jury of her "peers, as they say." Chico acknowledges, "Those people had made up their minds. They didn't see no person. They saw a junkie whore." The jury has already decided her fate because they recognize her not as a human being but as an addict and a prostitute, terms that recall the variations of "dope-fiend whore" so often repeated in Faulkner's *Requiem for a Nun*. Crime in these terms is a personal failure determined by identity difference, in which juries who would not see themselves as peers of the accused, who do not recognize themselves in the criminal, see in those such as Becky what Gavin Stevens first sees in Butch: a "seed not only violent but dangerous and bad."

Reimagining prisoners in other ways demands greater attention both to the broad cultural trends of race and class divisions just described, and to the historical actualities of imprisonment chronicled throughout the previous chapters. Imprisonment thereby is divorced from an imagined correlation to a violent or murderous offense, linked instead to unemployment, poverty, drug use, and the racism of profiling, targeted arrests, and inequitable sentencing. The 1993 president of the ACA cites an example of four black youths in Michigan all sentenced to life for simple robberies, just one case of many where the correlating indicators of sentencing are not the severity of the crime, but race, age, and gender.[6] Certainly many people in prison have committed serious crimes that endanger others, crimes that demand their separation. However, the conception that all prisoners are guilty of such offenses fails to take into account the enormous expansion of incarceration as the sine qua non of punishment taking place in the United States since the mid-1970s. According to the U.S. Department of Justice, property crime has declined steadily since 1973, and violent offenses since 1993, yet the prison population doubled in the 1980s and again in the 1990s.[7] Broadening the criminality of drug use, aggressively targeting black and poor populations, and dismantling treatment programs all contributed to an increase in the proportion of substance-abuse offenders and to the overrepresentation of black men in prisons and jails. Drug arrests among adults quadrupled between 1970 and 2002, from 322,300 to more than 1.3 million.[8] Prisons have filled not with murderers and rapists but with drug users, most often poor, and black or Hispanic.

There is thus a sharp divide in the quite-basic matter between the crimes prisoners are imagined to commit and their actual offenses. For example, the prisoners—real and imagined—surveyed in the books, films, and performances that this book addresses are all convicted of murder, assault, and rape, and these sorts of representations create in the cultural imagination a sense that prisons unilaterally warehouse dangerous, even murderous offenders. The gulf between actuality and imagination in this regard helps foster the apathy and even more pernicious hard-line positions of politicians and voters, a reactionary perspective insidiously made easier when criminals, and thus prisoners, are presumed to be black. However, that very rhetoric of "tough on crime" can be turned against itself, for which crimes—and committed by whom—are targeted? Participation in sex for money and in drug use brands the Becky of *Jury Duty* a "junkie whore" (just as Nancy Mannigoe is a "nigger dope-fiend whore" in *Requiem for a Nun*) and thus predetermines her criminalization in the view of the jury.

However, the back-page advertisements of many large-city weekly periodicals routinely feature advertisements for marijuana, as well as Xanax, Valium, Vicodin, and other prescription pharmaceuticals used recreationally, all for sale via online pharmacies promising discretion; other ads solicit customers for escorts and invite young women to work for such services. It is not the general crimes of illegal drug use and prostitution that police and courts must strictly enforce and prisons punish. Instead, laws differentiate the manner in which particular populations commit transgressions from how more-privileged groups (such as middle and upper classes) do so.

The clearest expression of how offenses are distinguished is brought into focus in the huge disparities in minimum sentencing for possession of cocaine between its crack and powder forms. The former is cheaper and more frequently used by low-income, inner-city populations. The Anti-Drug Abuse Act of 1986 equated the possession of five grams of crack cocaine with five hundred grams of powdered cocaine, an equation of personal use of the former with large-scale trafficking of the latter. For example, given White House estimates, those quantities represent street values of five hundred to a thousand dollars of crack versus upwards of twenty-five to fifty thousand dollars of cocaine.[9] Several high-profile cases have further tagged crack as a "black" drug, though a federal commission determined in 1995 that only one-third of crack cocaine users were black. However, nearly 85 percent of those convicted for possession were black, a factor at least suggesting targeted arrest patterns.[10] A 1989 National Institute of Drug Use survey, during the height of the purported crack epidemic among African-Americans, determined that only 12 percent of drug users were black men and women, but that 44 percent of those arrested for possession were black.[11] Norval Morris, who for more than two decades has been the most prominent historian of the U.S. prison system, points out the identical rates of drug use among racial groups. However, while rates of arrest for drug crimes were the same among white and black offenders in 1968, they had increased fivefold in arrests of black men and women by 1990.[12] Racially targeted arrests, therefore, have overrepresented black men and women in prison.

That problem is compounded by the mandatory minimum sentences initiated by the Sentence Reform Act of 1984 and the far-harsher penalties for crack cocaine instituted in the Anti-Drug Act of 1986. Those arrested were more likely to serve longer sentences, given incarceration's increased frequency, duration, and mandatory minimums. Drug arrests in the 1980s and 1990s targeted inner-city populations, particularly black and Hispanic users.[13] The tremendous discrepancies in sentencing for crack offenders are described by U.S. Supreme Court Justice John Paul Stevens, in a dissenting opinion, as "three to eight times longer" than those meted out for possession of cocaine in its powdered form.[14] Derrick Bell criticizes these discrepancies in 2004[15]—and the ACA raised these concerns a decade before that.

A senior circuit judge makes this point at the 1993 ACA meeting in a paper on the failures of mandatory sentencing titled "Revise the Guidelines Now."[16] Another paper at the same conference, given by the chair of the U.S. Sentencing Commission, identifies related problems and makes recommendations to address them. The chair suggests that the "most logical resolution" to mandatory sentencing would be to eliminate it and to institute guidelines, but recognizes that "such a prospect is not politically feasible."[17] A Pennsylvania Department of Corrections commissioner similarly indicates "that elected officials are reluctant to say or do anything that appears to be soft on crime."[18] Rather than effectiveness, fairness, or logic, political weakness and a fear of public perception and imagination have been the important causes for sentencing practices that have continued to incarcerate too many for too little. In 1995 the ACA itself shifted from the declared principles by which it had defined criminality since 1870 to a more "dynamic and flexible" vision statement advocating greater community involvement and legislative address of the causes of crime.[19] However, such vision has been merely optative, and public policy remains far more myopic.

Like the "probable felon" list developed in Florida for the 2000 national election, arrest and sentencing patterns in the 1980s and 1990s suggest that these punishments are not designed to eliminate crimes so much as incorporate them in a larger strategy of subjugation. Whether or not incarcerating a racial and class-based population of prisoners has been the intent of law enforcement, the judicial system, and prison administrations is immaterial. As with the Voter Rights Act, it is the effect of disenfranchisement that is the key. That effect began with the Rockefeller drug laws spreading nationally in the 1970s; continued in the Sentencing Reform Act of 1984, which virtually eliminated discretionary sentencing at the federal level; hugely escalated with the Reagan administration's Anti-Drug Act in 1986; and was cemented by that act's expansion two years later. The climate did not change in subsequent presidencies. William J. Bennett, the highly conservative critic of education, morality, and politics, served as both President Reagan's and President George H. W. Bush's drug czar, and Bennett's deputy, John P. Walters, became the White House director of national drug-control policy for the subsequent President Bush's administration in 2001.

The Clinton administration offered little in terms of difference in this regard. In his final year, President Bill Clinton granted clemency for five individuals serving extensive sentences for minimal participation in the drug trade,[20] but he resisted broader, more systemic changes, siding with Congress in rejecting the U.S. Sentencing Commission's recommendations to address the racial disparities brought about by the inequitable minimum sentences initiated under Reagan. A willingness to view black and low-income populations as criminals, a hard-line conservative stance casting drug use in general as a moral failure and certain forms of drugs in particular as beyond the pale, and the political fear of being perceived as soft on crime all combine to make predetermined criminality at once the cause and effect of jurisprudential conviction. Many prisoners—like the character and self-described "crack whore" Becky Wallace of *Jury Duty*, like Rosa Thigpen's son, Kenny Collins, in "Live from Death Row"— are thereby differentiated less by their crimes than by their poverty, race, or other cultural differences.

The prior analyses of "Live from Death Row" and *Jury Duty* suggest that mounting a challenge to incarceration demands an identification with prisoners by those not themselves imprisoned, but those two performances also highlight the difficulties of doing so. The sense of "feeling imprisoned" criticized in chapter 1 seems a poor strategy to foster such recognition, and the solipsistic excess of prison as a metaphor does little to critique inequity. Instead, what needs to be challenged is the relationship between crime and criminalization and the equation of criminality and prisoner, the attribution and distribution of offenses. The thirty-year experiment in wholesale imprisonment for virtually all crimes has proven inordinately expensive, both fiscally and socially. The mandatory minimum sentences for many crimes, and the lengthy imprisonment for millions of people that these mandatory minimums lead to, is not a constant in U.S. imprisonment, but a historically recent approach without a clear effect on crime rates.[21] Only in the past three decades has prison been the primary answer to questions of crime.

Furthermore, the enduring first principle of the ACA declares that it is not the commission of crime but the conviction in court that names one a criminal. From slavery, through jim crow, to anxiety over black militancy, to the history of now, whiteness in the United States has regularly feared and desired blackness to equate with criminality. That inequity has also contributed to a racial economic divide and, consequently, to that divide's relationship to crime, conviction, and punishment. As cited in chapter 1, research suggests that rather than incarceration rates matching crime rates, unemployment provides the clearest correlation to imprisonment patterns.[22] These are not new observations. Former U.S. president Rutherford B. Hayes, first president of the NPA, recognized the relationship between unemployment and imprisonment as early as 1888, an equation that was reiterated throughout the next century and beyond in meetings for that particular social body. Instead of basing identification across prison walls on everyone's feeling like a captive or prisoner sometimes, it is necessary to point out that many, perhaps most, people commit the crimes that are part of the texture of everyday life, but racial and class-based populations are far more likely to be targeted as criminals.

At stake is the problematic nature of social and cultural identity, long a mainstay of academic discussion and a key feature of the "culture wars" of the 1980s and 1990s. Incarceration as a division of identity underscores how it at once constitutes and is defined by individuals and social groups, including those in and out of prisons. If incarceration, like other cultural indices, can be understood as a category of difference, then, like those categories, its hinge between the individual and the social, between the *I* and the *we,* is identity. The Civil Rights Act of 1964, along with its expansion in writs of habeas corpus, provided the basis for much of the prison reform of the 1960s. The act makes this same point in its particular language, which prohibits discrimination based on race, sex, nationality, or religion: "The term *'person' includes one or more individuals,* governments, governmental agencies, political subdivisions" (emphasis added).[23] Singular and plural conflate in cultural markers of difference.

That approach applies well to strategies of reading that locate textual production and reception in particular cultural contexts. For example, Faulkner's narration of criminal consciousness in *Sanctuary* and *Light in August* is coincident both with competing psychoanalytic models of individual development and with the employment of those models in actual prisons, as demonstrated in the transcripts of the American Prison Association. However, Faulkner's willingness in *Go Down, Moses* to emphasize racial injustice and to broaden social agency follows Wright's more polemical take in *Native Son,* and would not be spoken by prison officials themselves until decades later. From the mid-1960s to the late 1970s, Cleaver, Mailer, and Deleuze and Guattari were all variously theorizing what they describe repeatedly as national or cultural "schizophrenia," which they all specifically relate to race. *Soul on Ice* and *The Executioner's Song* undertake analytical and narrative methods with a level of cultural and historical engagement that U.S. literary criticism did not broadly engage until the 1980s. Cleaver's (and Deleuze and Guattari's thereafter) attention to the revolutionary possibilities of black and inmate identities was at first shared and then largely dismissed by some of the officials writing prison policy and practice from 1968 to 1979, according to the American Correctional Association transcripts—and the beginning of a sharp increase in incarceration concluded that period.

As those trends intensified at the close of the twentieth century, race became the dominant sign in the equation of criminality (and its attendant incarceration) with black masculinity. The films of 1998 and 1999 that are surveyed here, as well as the performance "Live from Death Row," variously challenge and capitulate to the misrecognition of blackness and criminality—the fears and desires circulating around black men in prison. *Jury Duty* departs in this regard from the prior texts, broadening who might be considered a criminal and thus a prisoner. However, though the drama does not reinforce the misrecognition of black masculinity with criminality, it does, like many of these texts, simultaneously draw attention to the unjust practices of incarceration and thwart identification with the prisoner. Facilitating such identification is likely a crucial step for creating meaningful investments between those outside of prison and those within.

Such historical awareness and cultural recognition shifts identification between those not imprisoned and those who are from the glib cynicism of "it is not a crime if you don't get caught," to the less openly sustainable cynicism of racism, as well as to alienation and subjugation based on economic disparity. Again, the first principle of the most prominent association of prison administrators since 1870 has remained that not crime but conviction in court names one a criminal. However, determinations of criminality, conviction, and consequences have historically targeted disenfranchised populations in the United States. Ever since the Boston Selectmen's 1723 proclamation that a gathering of "more than two Indians, Negroes or Mulatto servants or slaves" was a punishable offense,[24] and the overrepresentation of black men and women began in the nation's first prison, there has been a demonstrated willingness to name black and poor people as criminals.

These eighteenth-century cases are only precedents for late-twentieth-century arrest patterns, sentencing inconsistencies, and prison populations, which are all part of the historical record. That history has been imagined, represented, and contested in the books, films, and performances described throughout this book. Documenting that history and its imagination demands that rather than adopting the positions Žižek describes as conformity, cynicism, or perverse capitulation to racial and class-based imprisonment practices, we embrace skepticism as necessary to challenge incarceration. Again, undoubtedly it is true that many prisoners have committed crimes that threaten public safety. However, criminalization, arrests, convictions, and sentencing in the past three decades have drawn on existing racist imaginations of black masculinity in determining crime and punishment.

Certainly, the boundaries of cultural difference can be difficult to breach in order to establish identification. However, incorporating incarceration as a division less of guilty and innocent or immoral and moral, and instead as a category of cultural identity in its own right, provides a means to foster such recognition. The multiple indices by which selfhood is located at once divide and unite human experience. Such determinations of subjectivity do not take place in the singularity of an idealized, pure, and simple humanity or in an imagined autonomous individuality. Instead, strategies of selfhood are negotiated through the multiple lines of approach to gender, race, class, ethnicity, nationality, sexuality, and imprisonment, among others. Those separated in their identities as inmates from those not imprisoned are nevertheless joined in terms of other shared identities, other hinges of *I* and *we*. Performances such as *Jury Duty* and "Live from Death Row" offer models of materially present audiences, demonstrating the social bodies in which the negotiation of identity takes place, recognizing the "I" not in the other but in the "we." They also emphasize the social responsibility of imprisonment. Understanding the demonstration of "Live from Death Row" as a performance also provides a sense of how historical events themselves are subject to analysis that is sensitive to how they operate and what they produce.

Such implications of identity, performance, politics, and history in texts both literary and otherwise echo the prescient claims of Richard Poirier in 1971, the title of whose book *Performing Self* resonates with more recent theories of selfhood as performed. Chapter 1 cites his description of Mailer's "engagements with language as political."[25] As the chapters of this book individually and in sum demonstrate, that claim holds true of all the cultural works surveyed, not only because the producers of the books, films, and performances engage the political, but also because literary studies in the past quarter century has emphasized the historical and cultural implications of production and reception.

Those transformations in humanities study make Ed Bullins's response in a 1973 interview, which opens chapter 8, seem a little quaint in its historical distance. His claim—that one's cultural work might have political goals "if that is what you wish to do"—comes before what has since become the larger sense that books, films, and performances already operate politically. This matter certainly held true for Bullins, who found himself embroiled in a bitter dispute with Cleaver regarding the role of radical black theater with respect to politics, and with the Black Panther Party as a whole in the matter of black nationalists versus the practical edge of cross-racial alliances. These conflicts led to Bullins's departure from the party being maneuvered by Cleaver, though it was Cleaver himself who had appointed the playwright as minister of culture.[26] That particular internecine battle, one of many within a particular social body rife with such struggles, demonstrates the value for those initiating social change to recognize the necessity of broad-based alliances. As an American Prison Association participant observes in 1929, "The trouble with good people is that they waste so much effort fighting one another."[27] Those whose work is situated in literary, historical, and political studies must work together and account for other forms of cultural work—or the divisions among them will provide the means for defeat in detail, the division, isolation, and destruction that have been the very practice of actual imprisonment. A provocative example of "good people" working together occurred in 2004, when NAACP leadership proposed an alliance with the American Correctional Association to address the challenges of race and imprisonment.[28]

A "we" of scholars, teachers, historians, critics, activists, and citizens may not agree on the best tactics for challenging the social inequities most starkly represented within the U.S. prison system. However, we can agree that expanded criminalization, extended sentencing, and arrest patterns through the 1980s and 1990s targeting particular populations are practices that have produced a prison population overrepresenting minorities. Accompanying these matters of the historical record is the saturation of imprisonment in a cultural imagination that equates blackness with criminality. This saturation took place even though practices of incarceration have largely concealed the actual experience of more than two million people in prison or jail, with an additional 4.7 million people under another form of judicial control, whether parole or probation. The effort of this book has been to participate in the attempt to bring a series of problematic dualities to the forefront of literary and cultural studies: racism's pervasiveness and invisibility, the huge numbers and concealment of prison populations, the dynamic between imprisonment's actuality and imagination, and an insufficient corresponding critique of all of these crucial matters.

The texts surveyed in this book not only make visible what is largely a concealed practice, but also offer a variety of strategic positions by which to imagine and thereby produce the social transformations necessary to alter the ways prison history has shaped national history. For example, Webster, the writer and director of *Jury Duty*, draws attention to how the jury operates as a particular form of public sphere emblematic of the broader sociality it represents. As the play is staged, jury and *Jury* reflect both the audience and what the playwright describes as a "broken process"; for the particular audience of social workers present for one performance, the play demands that they fix this broken process. Similarly, there are the participants in "Live from Death Row," not only Collins and Miles but also Harrington, Reese, Jeannette, and Thigpen, those not in prison who serve as intermediaries between those who are and those who are not, facilitating communication, and thereby identification, across prison walls.

Earlier chapters include a litany of such intermediary roles, both imagined and real. There is Faulkner's character of the attorney Gavin Stevens, whose initial racist (mis)recognition gives way to his efforts and expenditures at the unmade request of a black woman he barely knows. In the final pages of the novel, he spends his time and money to assemble, if just for a moment, a community that is differentiated along lines of race and class but nevertheless brought together to witness the return of its native son, initiated into history, recorded in the daily paper. Then there is Cleaver's depiction of his white female lawyer, Beverly Axelrod, who works on his behalf, as well as Cleaver's self-representation of himself as part of the nation and history in and through which he writes himself. There is Mailer, his efforts on behalf of Cleaver's release and his chronicle, however brief, of the attorney Gil Athay and his work to free Dale Pierre, just a fragment in a larger whole describing the forces involved in history and story, imprisonment and execution. There are Rideau, Garbus, and Stack, the prisoner as journalist and director working alongside two documentary filmmakers to incorporate into the historical record and cultural imagination the lives of prisoners typically hidden from view. These books, films, and performances all increase prisoners' visibility and thereby provide an opportunity to revise national history, literary and otherwise, to incorporate more fully a sense of the lived experience of millions in the United States.

Making prison history central to the study of national history begins to account for the degree to which the former has shaped the latter. Reading the writing of prisoners and their depictions by others is part of that project, incorporating narratives of imprisonment into a story of nation. There is much more of this story to tell, including looking back further historically and in greater detail. We can more closely examine the early discussions of prisons—which involved Benjamin Rush and others—the expansion of the prison system through the nation in the early and mid-nineteenth century, and prison reform at the end of that century, informed in part by the ideals of a liberal humanities education, even as a rhetoric of imperialism proved as pervasive in the NPA as elsewhere. There are many, many more works whose representations of imprisonment demand a richer account, whether these representations are unremarked in familiar texts, or are in books and films that have thus far escaped attention. Expanding the theorization and analysis of inmate identities will foster more-nuanced senses of how various matters of cultural difference shape and are shaped by the experience of imprisonment as it has been endured through more than two centuries.

Such a body of study and the accompanying framework are necessary in order to bring a richer discussion of prisons and prisoners to the forefront of both the academic and, more important, the general public consciousness. Scholarship in this vein works in concert with classrooms, which play their own roles by organizing knowledge, identifying lines of inquiry, and serving as places of staged readings, where materially present audiences engage literary, historical, and scholarly texts.[29] Performed analysis in the social sphere of the classroom is only one of the many spaces in which incarceration needs to be addressed in order to recognize both its centrality to national experience and the necessity of a more informed critical conversation. That discourse is necessary to challenge a clear threat to the promise of the United States—a threat that curtails liberties, limits pursuits, and ends lives behind prison walls in racial and class-based populations that have been targeted for arrest and warehoused with little recourse. Challenging these practices will bring closer to fulfillment the impossible but necessary "becoming" of a full democracy, never to be realized, but nevertheless to be attempted. The *Angolite* poem quoted in chapter 1 reads: "Go ahead / Lock us up / Lock us all up / Lock away the ones you see / In the mirror." However, we who incarcerate have locked up millions of people precisely because we do *not* recognize ourselves among them, and that is among the greatest failures in U.S. history.

# Notes

## Preface

1. The National Prison Association formed in 1870 in response to an examination of existing imprisonment practices that demonstrated their inhumane conditions. Members met to discuss and propose prison reform in a manner similar to many such movements of the late nineteenth century. That same period also saw the move to the professionalization and consolidation of a variety of fields and disciplines, which in part was accomplished by the formation of institutional organizations such as the NPA, the American Historical Association in 1884, and the Modern Language Association in 1886. The organization meets twice each year, though until 1989 they published only the summer conference proceedings. Since then, the papers from both summer and winter meetings have appeared in the annual volumes.

2. Hamilton Mabie, "The Press and Crime," *Proceedings of the Annual Congress,* 1886 (Chicago: R. R. Donnelley & Sons, 1887), 146–47. On Mabie, see Edwin W. Morse, *The Life and Letters of Hamilton W. Mabie* (New York: Dodd, Mead and Company, 1920). George C. Erksine, "President's Address," *Proceedings of the 59th Annual Congress of the American Prison Association* (Toronto, Canada, 1929), 2.

3. Reginald A. Wilkinson, "Best Practices: Tools for Correctional Excellence," American Correctional Association, *The State of Corrections: Proceedings American Correctional Association Annual Conferences, 1998* (Upper Marlboro, MD: Graphic Communications, 1999), 85.

4. Angela Davis, "A World unto Itself: Multiple Invisibilities of Imprisonment," Michael Jacobson-Hardy, ed., *Behind the Razorwire: Portrait of a Contemporary American Prison System* (New York: New York UP, 1999), x.

5. Dana E. Mastro and Amanda L. Robinson, "Cops and Crooks: Images of Minorities on Primetime Television," *Journal of Criminal Justice* 28.5 (Sept./Oct. 2000), 394. In a related vein, sensational television news depictions of crime regularly skew public fears of crime and perceptions of minorities. See Julian V. Roberts and Loretta J. Stalans, "Crime, Criminal Justice, and Public Opinion," *The Handbook of Crime and Punishment,* Michael Tonry, ed.; Ronald Weitzer and Charis E. Kubrin, "Breaking News: How Local TV News and Real-World Conditions Affect Fear of Crime," *Justice Quarterly* 21.3 (2004); Mary Bosworth and Jean Flavin, eds., *Race, Gender, and Punishment: From Colonialism to the War on Terror* (New Brunswick, NJ: Rutgers UP, 2007); Carol Stabile, *White Victims, Black Villains: Gender, Race, and Crime News in US Culture* (New York: Routledge, 2006). Sharon Willis briefly mentions racial disparities in actual and fictional criminal justice systems in *High Contrast: Race and Gender in Contemporary Hollywood Film* (Durham and London: Duke UP, 1997), 5.

6. *The Shawshank Redemption* (Frank Darabont, dir., Castle Rock Entertainment/Columbia Pictures, 1994).

7. Martin Luther King III, "State of Our Nation Today in Relationship to the Criminal Justice System," The American Correctional Association, *The State of Corrections: Proceedings ACA Annual Conferences, 2001* (Alexandria, VA: Magnet Print Brokers, 2002), 2.

8. "Live from Death Row" (Campaign to End the Death Penalty, University of Texas at Austin, 23 September 1999).

9. Jim Craddock's *VideoHound's Golden Movie Retriever 2003* (Detroit: Thomson/Gale, 2002). As of July 2007, the Internet Movie Database (online: http://www.imdb.com) lists 1,707 matches for the key term *prison,* but their list includes television episodes, international films, metaphoric imprisonment, and works scheduled for future release.

10. Henry A. Giroux, *Fugitive Cultures: Race, Violence, and Youth* (New York: Routledge, 1996) and *Breaking in to the Movies* (Malden, MA: Blackwell, 2002); Ed Guerrero, *Framing Blackness: The African American Image in Film* (Philadelphia: Temple UP, 1993); bell hooks, *Reel to Real: Race, Sex, and Class at the Movies* (New York: Routledge, 1996).

11. Suncoast [advertisement], *Premiere* (April 2002), 25.

12. Quoted in Norval Morris, "The Contemporary Prison: 1965–Present," Norval Morris and David J. Rothman, eds., *The Oxford History of the Prison: The Practice of Punishment in Western Society* (New York: Oxford UP, 1998), 203. Critique such as Guitierrez's is common in prison writing. In Robert Kelsey's story "Suicide!" anthologized in Bell Gale Chevigny's collection, *Doing Time: 25 Years of Prison Writing* (New York: Arcade Publishing, 1999), inmates are watching *Penitentiary III,* commenting on its lack of realism in terms suggestive of Stanley Kubrick's *A Clockwork Orange:* "Later on in the movie, he would be chained up in the penitentiary basement and made to watch violent movies while smoking crack" (89).

13. William Faulkner, *Sanctuary* (New York: Vintage, 1993), *Light in August* (New York: Vintage, 1990), *Go Down, Moses* (New York: Vintage, 1990); Eldridge Cleaver, *Soul on Ice;* Norman Mailer, *The Executioner's Song* (New York: Vintage, 1998), *American History X* (Tony Kaye, dir., New Line Cinema, 1998); *The Hurricane* (Norman Jewison, dir., Universal, 1999); *The Farm: Life inside Angola Prison* (Jonathan Stack, Liz Garbus, Wilbert Rideau, dirs., Gabriel Films/A&E Home Video, 1998); Ken Webster, *Jury Duty* (unpublished manuscript, performed by The Subterranean Theatre Company in Austin, Texas, 9 September 1999).

14. Joseph D. Lehman, "Solving the Crowding Problem: Linking Resources to Corrections Policy," American Correctional Association, *The State of Corrections: Proceedings American Correctional Association Annual Conferences, 1993* (Springfield, VA: Goodway Graphics, 1994), 76.

15. Allen J. Beck and Thomas P. Bonczar, "Prevalence of Incarceration in the United States," American Correctional Association, *The State of Corrections: Proceedings ACA Annual Conferences, 2004* (Upper Marlboro, MD: Graphic Communications Inc., 2005), 29. The comparative statistics are based on the U.S. Department of Justice's records of the number of black and Hispanic male inmates per one hundred thousand black and Hispanic men compared to white male inmates per one hundred thousand white men in the United States. And while men still vastly outnumber women in state and federal penitentiaries by almost nine to one, the number of women in prison, particularly women of color, is increasing. U.S. Department of Justice, "Incarceration Rates 1980–2002," Bureau of Justice Statistics (online: http://www.ojp.usdoj.gov/bjs/glance/tables/incrttab.htm).

16. Lionel Trilling, *The Liberal Imagination: Essays on Literature and Society* (Garden City, NY: Doubleday, 1950).

17. Antonio Gramsci, *Selections from the Prison Notebooks,* ed. and trans. Quintin Hoare and Geoffrey Nowell Smith (New York: International Publishers, 1971), 126.

18. Ja Rule, *Blood in My Eye* (Def Jam, 2003); George Jackson, *Blood in My Eye* (Baltimore: Black Classic Press, 1990). Unfortunately, Ja Rule fails to uphold the insight of the earlier text, and the album largely plays as a continuation of Rule's feud with fellow rap star 50 Cent.

19. Ice Cube stars in *Boyz n the Hood* (1991); Snoop Dogg appears in *Baby Boy* (2001); DMX and Nas star in *Belly* (1998); Shakur stars in *Juice* (1992) and *Poetic Justice* (1993).

20. Public Enemy, *It Takes a Nation of Millions to Hold Us Back* (Def Jam, 1988); NWA, *Straight Outta Compton* (Priority Records, 1988).

21. Public Enemy, *There's a Poison Goin' On* (Atomic Pop, 1999).

22. Rage Against the Machine, "Calm Like a Bomb," *The Battle of Los Angeles* (Sony, 1999).

23. Mos Def, *Black on Both Sides* (Priority Records, 1999).

24. System of a Down, *Toxicity* (Sony, 2001).

25. Such arguments are present but peripheral in the works of Derrick Bell: *Faces at the Bottom of the Well: The Permanence of Racism* (New York: Basic Books,

1992), *Ethical Ambition: Living a Life of Meaning and Worth* (New York: Bloomsbury, 2002), *Silent Covenants:* Brown v. Board of Education *and the Unfulfilled Hopes for Racial Reform* (New York: Oxford UP, 2004). Incarceration is central in Chevigny, *Doing Time;* David Cole, *No Equal Justice: Race and Class in the American Criminal Justice System* (New York: New Press, 1999); Angela Davis, *Are Prisons Obsolete?* (New York: Seven Stories, 2003); Steven Donziger, *The Real War on Crime: The Report of the National Criminal Justice Commission* (New York: HarperPerennial, 1996); H. Bruce Franklin, "The Literature of the American Prison," *Massachusetts Review* 18 (Spring 1977), *Prison Literature in America: The Victim as Criminal and Artist* (New York: Oxford UP, 1989), *Prison Writing in 20th-Century America* (New York: Penguin, 1998); Ruth Wilson Gilmore, "Globalisation and US Prison Growth: From Military Keynesianism to Post-Keynesian Militarism," *Race and Class* 40.2–3 (1998), and *Golden Gulag: Prisons, Surplus, Crisis, and Opposition in Globalizing California* (Berkeley: U California P, 2007); Tara Herivel and Paul Wright, eds., *Prison Nation: The Warehousing of America's Poor* (New York: Routledge, 2003); and Marc Mauer and the Sentencing Project, *Race to Incarcerate* (New York: New Press/Norton, 1999). Ali Ek's *Race and Masculinity in Contemporary American Prison Narratives* (New York: Routledge, 2005) offers a critique of prisoner subjectivity and analyses of *Soul on Ice* and *The Farm.*

26. Franklin, "The American Prison in the Culture Wars," "The Imprisonment of American Culture" panel at the Modern Language Association Convention (Washington, DC, December, 2000 [online: http://andromeda.rutgers.edu/~hbf/priscult.html]). He repeated aspects of that argument and the telling claim of imprisonment as a necessary context for twentieth-century literary production at the 2006 MLA panel "Detention in/as American Literature." See also Mary Helen Washington, "Disturbing the Peace: What Happens to American Studies If You Put African-American Studies at the Center?," *American Quarterly* 50.1 (1998): 1–23.

# Chapter 1

1. Faulkner, *Intruder in the Dust, Faulkner: Novels 1942–1954* (New York: Library of America, 1994), 320.

2. Since the watershed studies of Norval Morris and David J. Rothman—*The Future of Imprisonment* (Chicago: U Chicago P, 1974) and *Conscience and Convenience: The Asylum and Its Alternatives in Progressive America* (Boston: Little, Brown, 1980), respectively—U.S. prison historiography has grown considerably. Thomas G. Blomberg and Karol Lucken's *American Penology: A History of Control* (New York: Aldine De Gruyter, 2000) follows the thesis of Michel Foucault's *Discipline and Punish: The Birth of the Prison,* trans. Alan Sheridan (New York: Vintage, 1979), but with a more rigorous historiographic method, and concludes that tactics of imprisonment are indeed broadening to a larger strategy of general social control. Scott Christianson's *With Liberty for Some: 500 Years of Imprisonment in America* (Boston: Northeastern UP, 1998) provides too broad a

view to be especially specific, but it does draw close relationships between slavery and imprisonment in U.S. history, pointing out how race and class have been implicated in social control and punishment since pre-Revolutionary America. Thomas L. Dumm's *Democracy and Punishment: Disciplinary Origins of the United States* (Madison: U Wisconsin P, 1987) offers another Foucauldian history, arguing that producing and incarcerating criminality occurs in an opposition that helps define the idea of freedom as conducted in liberal democratic discourse. Adam Jay Hirsch's *The Rise of the Penitentiary: Prisons and Punishment in Early America* (New Haven: Yale UP, 1992) anticipates many of Christianson's points regarding the relationship of slavery and imprisonment. Paul W. Keve's *Prisons and the American Conscience: A History of U.S. Federal Corrections* (Carbondale: Southern Illinois UP, 1991) serves as an administrative history, an official view from the inside and from the top, as he served as the commissioner of corrections in Minnesota. Marc Mauer in *Race to Incarcerate* demonstrates that black men are in prison out of proportion not only with their overall population but also with the number of crimes committed. Morris and Rothman's *The Oxford History of the Prison: The Practice of Punishment in Western Society* (New York: Oxford UP, 1998) is an edited collection that includes essays offering a broad overview of U.S. and international imprisonment practices. David M. Oshinsky's *"Worse Than Slavery": Parchman Farm and the Ordeal of Jim Crow Justice* (New York: Free Press Paperbacks, 1997) is the most rigorously documented account organized around the Mississippi prison, and it demonstrates how imprisonment in the jim crow South perpetuated practices of slavery. William L. Selke's *Prisons in Crisis* (Bloomington and Indianapolis: Indiana UP, 1993) conducts a sociological study in determining that the U.S. prison system fails to accomplish its intent because its purposes (punishment, incapacitation, and rehabilitation) are misguided or unreasonable and often contradictory; imprisonment practices often exacerbate rather than alleviate the problems the system seeks to solve. John M. Sloop's *The Cultural Prison: Discourse, Prisoners, and Punishment* (Tuscaloosa: U Alabama P, 1996) surveys popular news periodicals from 1950 to 1993 to demonstrate how the representation of prisoners has several distinct types at different periods, particularly with regard to raced and gendered criminality. Michael Tonry has held a longtime commitment to the study of imprisonment as a vital component of criminology, and his edited collection *The Handbook of Crime and Punishment* (New York: Oxford UP, 1998) is an invaluable survey of correctional policies and practices.

3. That understanding of historicism traces back to Jameson's *The Political Unconscious* (Ithaca, NY: Cornell UP, 1981) and its synthesis of largely French theory, rewriting Lacan, Deleuze and Guattari, Althusser, and Foucault in sorting the tensions between history and the subject, between causality and narrativity, and among real, imaginary, and symbolic. It is worth noting that Lacan's own work contesting and revising Freudian psychoanalysis already lays the basis less for a subject without history than for a subject composed in history (see chapter 1, n36)—and even the Freudian superego, however undertheorized, leaves room for such cultural and historical contingencies.

4. Sloop, 17.

5. Such a cultural imagination has been theorized in a variety of related ways with regard to public spheres, collective identity, and popular culture. Martha Nussbaum uses the term "civic imagination" in *Cultivating Humanity: A Classical Defense of Reform in Liberal Education* (Cambridge, MA: Harvard UP, 1997). Benedict Anderson's *Imagined Communities: Reflections on the Origin and Spread of Nationalism* (London: Verso, 1991) has proven a watershed text in describing fantasies of nationality, which Timothy Powell uses in describing how nineteenth-century texts constructed a "national imaginary" in *Ruthless Democracy: A Multi-Cultural Interpretation of the American Renaissance* (Princeton, NJ: Princeton UP, 2000).

6. Rage Against the Machine, "Testify," *The Battle of Los Angeles*.

7. Deleuze and Guattari, *Anti-Oedipus: Capitalism and Schizophrenia,* trans. Robert Hurley, Mark Seem, and Helen R. Lane (Minneapolis: U Minnesota P, 1983), 2. This description of language, space, and subjectivity is extended by de Certeau in the chapter "A Walk in the City" of *The Practice of Everyday Life:* "The act of walking is to the urban system what the speech act is to language or to the statements uttered" (97).

8. William Wells Brown, *Clotel: Or, The President's Daughter* (New York: Carol Publishing, 1989).

9. Faulkner, *Intruder in the Dust,* 296, 299, 327.

10. Faulkner, *Go Down, Moses,* 33–34, 68.

11. Norton W. Brooker, "[Address]," *Proceedings of the Annual Congress, 1888* (Chicago: Knight & Leonard, 1888), 70.

12. R. H. Dawson, "[Address]," *Proceedings of the Annual Congress, 1888* (Chicago: Knight & Leonard, 1888), 84.

13. Rush offered his model for the penitentiary in "An Enquiry into the Effects of Public Punishments upon Criminals and upon Society," *A Plan for the Punishment of Crime,* ed. Negley K. Teeters (Philadelphia: Pennsylvania Prison Society, 1954), 10–12. Robert R. Sullivan locates Rush as the progenitor of U.S. prisons in "The Birth of the Prison: The Case of Benjamin Rush," *Eighteenth-Century Studies* 31.3 (1998): 333–44. Cesare Beccaria offers a similar model of reform in 1764 in *On Crimes and Punishments,* trans. David Young (Indianapolis, IN: Hackett, 1986), which saw extensive circulation in France and some comment in North America in the 1760s and 1770s, according to Wai-chee Dimock, *Residues of Justice: Law, Literature, Philosophy* (Berkeley: U California P, 1996), 14–15.

14. Leslie Patrick-Stamp, "Numbers That Are Not New: African Americans in the Country's First Prison, 1790–1835," *Pennsylvania Magazine of History and Biography* 119.1–2 (1995): 95–128.

15. See Hirsch; Keve; Dario Melossi and Massimo Pavarini, *The Prison and the Factory: Origins of the Penitentiary System,* trans. Glynis Cousin (London: Macmillan, 1981); and Rothman, "Perfecting the Prison: United States, 1789–1865," in Morris and Rothman, *The Oxford History of the Prison.*

16. Alexis de Tocqueville, *Tocqueville's America, the Great Quotations,* ed. Frederick Kershner Jr. (Athens: Ohio UP, 1983).

17. Edgardo Rotman, "The Failure of Reform: United States, 1865–1965," in Morris and Rothman, *The Oxford History of the Prison*, 151–77; Rothman, "Perfecting the Prison."

18. Rutherford B. Hayes, "President's Annual Address," *Proceedings of the Annual Congress, 1888* (Chicago: Knight & Leonard, 1888), 14–24. In 1977 Pennsylvania Pardon Board member Laurel L. Rans suggests the same argument as Hayes: "When inflation and unemployment increase, so do prison and mental health institution populations" ("Developing Positive Correctional Policy," The American Correctional Association, *Proceedings of the One Hundred and Seventh Annual Congress of Correction of the American Correctional Association, 1977* [College Park, MD, 1977], 58). Unemployment remains the clearest corollary to incarceration rates, according to Eric D. Gould, Bruce A. Weinberg, and David B. Mustard, "Crime Rates and Local Labor Market Opportunities in the United States: 1977–1997," *The Review of Economics and Statistics* 84.1 (2002).

19. Myron W. Reed, "Remarks," *Proceedings of the Annual Congress, 1888* (Chicago: Knight & Leonard, 1888), 27.

20. A civil suit was brought against the Louisiana State Prison at Angola in 1975 regarding how conditions there violated prisoners' constitutional rights and led to numerous reforms (Rideau and Wikberg, eds., *Life Sentences: Rage and Survival behind Bars* [New York: Times Books, 1992], 41). A similar case in Arkansas was the basis for the film *Brubaker* (1980).

21. Derrick Bell describes the 1960s as a "second Reconstruction" in *Silent Covenants*, 195. He also claims, "Litigation and legislation intended to ensure fair trials, fair sentences, and human prison facilities has achieved little to none of the above" (*Ethical Ambition: Living a Life of Meaning and Worth* [New York: Bloomsbury, 2002], 166). Bell is at the forefront of a tradition of legal and historical critique that emerged in the 1970s in the wake of the failures of civil rights gains. Bell and others guard against overstating gains in racial equality, at times arguing that perceived advancements conceal greater injustices in criminal justice, education, and law. In the 1970s, Bell and Alan Freeman largely initiated the critique later known as critical race theory; other scholars working within this field include Richard Delgado and Jean Stefancic. See *The Derrick Bell Reader*, Delgado and Stefancic, eds. (New York: New York UP, 2005); Delgado and Stefancic, *Critical Race Theory: An Introduction* (New York: New York UP, 2001); Delgado and Stefancic, eds., *Critical Race Theory: The Cutting Edge* (Philadelphia: Temple UP, 1995); Crenshaw, Neil Gotanda, Garry Peller, and Kendall Thomas, eds., *Critical Race Theory: The Key Writings That Formed the Movement* (New York: New Press/Norton, 1995).

22. W. E. B. DuBois, *The Souls of Black Folk*, 22nd ed. (Chicago: A. C. McClury & Co., 1938), 1.

23. King III, 7.

24. Henry Louis Gates Jr., *Thirteen Ways of Looking at a Black Man* (New York: Random House, 1997), xxii.

25. Faulkner, *Light in August*, 288.

26. Mailer, *The Executioner's Song*, 872.

27. The American Prison Association, *Proceedings of the Sixtieth Annual Congress of the American Prison Association, 1930* (Cheshire, CT: Printing Department, CT Penitentiary, 1930), 249.

28. Anthony Travisono reiterates the original goals in his 1990 plenary address, his farewell after serving as the American Correctional Association Executive Director since 1975 ("ACA's Future," *The State of Corrections: Proceedings ACA Annual Conferences, 1990* [Washington, DC: St. Mary's Press, 1990], 95–96).

29. See U.S. Commission on Civil Rights, *Voting Irregularities in Florida during the 2000 Presidential Election* (online: http://www.usccr.gov/pubs/vote2000/report/main.htm, 2002) and Christopher Uggen and Jeff Manza, "Democratic Contraction? Political Consequences of Felon Disenfranchisement in the United States," *American Sociological Review* 67 (December 2002): 777–803. The *Washington Post* featured an investigative series on the story in 2001; see *Washington Post*, "Botched Name Purge Denied Some the Right to Vote" (31 May 2001, online: http://www.washingtonpost.com/ac2/wp-dyn/A99749-2001May30), and "Rights Commission's Report on Florida Election" (5 June 2001, online: http://www.washingtonpost.com/wpsrv/onpolitics/transcripts/ccrdraft060401.htm). The controversy continued in a 2003 debate between *Harper's* and *The National Review* as to the racial intent of voter disenfranchisement.

30. Foucault, *Discipline*, 272.

31. U.S. Commission on Civil Rights, *Voting Irregularities in Florida during the 2000 Presidential Election* (2002, online: http://www.usccr.gov/pubs/vote2000/report/main.htm).

32. The American Correctional Association, "Resolution on the Restoration of Voting Rights," *The State of Corrections: Proceedings ACA Annual Conferences, 2001* (Alexandria, VA: Magnet Print Brokers, 2002), 97.

33. Slavoj Žižek suggests instead in *The Sublime Object of Ideology* (New York: Verso, 1989) that Michel Pêcheux "has given us the most elaborated version of the theory of interpellation" (3). Others trace the term back to Lacan—see Neil Nehring, *Flowers in the Dustbin: Culture, Anarchy, and Postwar England* (Ann Arbor: U Michigan P, 1993), 139.

34. Louis Althusser, *Lenin and Philosophy and Other Essays,* trans. Ben Brewster (New York: Monthly Review, 1972), 169–74. Althusserean interpellation is largely addressed as a single authority hailing a single subject. The model of the judicial body in the APA declaration matches the sense of interpellation not as a singular call but as the interruption or summons offered in legislative assembly to one of its members. As we shall see in chapter 8, this plural and participatory sense of interpellation opens more possibilities than that those left available by Althusser.

35. Frantz Fanon, *Black Skin, White Masks,* trans. Charles Lam Markmann (New York: Grove, 1967), 109, 111, 112; Judith Butler, *Bodies That Matter: On the Discursive Limits of "Sex"* (New York: Routledge, 1993), 232.

36. There are latent historicist aspects to Lacanian psychoanalytic theory. A passage from among Lacan's earliest work provides a sense of the subject in history offered in a manner that, coincidentally, speaks directly to imprisonment.

In a brief and highly elusive image of the trope of the prison as a model of subjectivity offered in "The Mirror Stage as Formative of the Function of the I," likely the most fundamentally important essay with regard to the application of psychoanalytic approaches to cultural study, Lacan suggests that "the historical effort of a society to refuse to recognize that it has any function other than the utilitarian" produces a false liberty of imagined autonomy. Such individualism denotes "a freedom that is never more authentic than when it is within the walls of a prison" (*Écrits: A Selection,* trans. Alan Sheridan [New York: Norton, 1977], 6). Lacan rejects that naïve existentialist model to acknowledge the constructive force of history, which is only the first suggestion of the degree to which he regards psychoanalysis and history as paired disciplines, "both sciences of the particular" (51). He continues, "What we teach the subject to realize as his unconscious is his history—that is to say, we help him to perfect the present historization of the facts that have already determined a certain number of the historical 'turning-points' in his existence" (52). The equation of unconscious and history, the "historicization of the facts," and the focus on formative "turning-points" recognized after the fact make this analysis of the subject something of a blueprint for historicist approaches developed and refined more than a quarter-century later.

37. Prominent examples of such work after Fanon and at least in part situated in U.S. cultural study include Elizabeth Abel, Barbara Christian, and Helene Moglen, eds., *Female Subjects in Black and White: Race, Psychoanalysis, Feminism* (Berkeley: U California P, 1997); Christopher Lane, ed., *The Psychoanalysis of Race* (New York: Columbia UP, 1998); a special issue of *Black Renaissance/Renaissance Noire,* "The American Dilemma Revisited: Psychoanalysis, Social Policy, and the Socio-Cultural Meaning of Race" (2003); and Peter Coviello's "Intimacy and Affliction: DuBois, Race, and Psychoanalysis," *Modern Language Quarterly* 64.1 (2003).

38. Joan Copjec argues in *Read My Desire: Lacan against the Historicists* (Cambridge, MA: MIT UP, 1994) that historicism in the vein of Foucault makes marginal or lacks entirely the power of desire that psychoanalytic approaches make central. Lane's work is divided between arguing for the relevance of psychoanalytic criticism in the study of works across historical periods and polemicizing against historicism.

39. Carolyn Porter, "Are We Being Historical Yet?," *South Atlantic Quarterly* 87 (1988).

40. See M. Nandi, "Re/constructing Black Masculinity in Prison," *The Journal of Men's Studies* 11.1 (2002); William F. Pinar, *The Gender of Racial Politics and Violence in America: Lynching, Prison Rape, and the Crisis of Masculinity* (New York: Peter Lang, 2001); Donald F. Sabo, Terry A. Kupers, and Willie London, eds., *Prison Masculinities* (Philadelphia, PA: Temple UP, 2001).

41. Paul Lauter, ed., *The Heath Anthology of American Literature 2,* 2nd ed. (Lexington, MA: D. C. Heath, 1994), xxxii–xxxiii.

42. Richard Yarborough, "The Problem of Violence and Black Masculinity in Recent U.S. Historical Cinema: A Look at *Amistad, Rosewood,* and *Hurricane*"

(University of Texas at Austin, 1 May 2003, and the University of Maryland, 7 November 2003).

43. Žižek offers an interpretation of Lacan's pun, *Unbewusste—une bévue*, that casts such an oversight as at once symptomatic and constitutive of an unconscious participation in the real: "The unconscious is not a kind of transcendent, unattainable thing of which we are unable to take cognizance, it is rather [ . . . ] an overlooking: we overlook the way our act is already part of the state of things we are looking at, the way our error is part of the Truth itself" (*The Sublime Object,* 59). Yarborough's analysis of black men in these historical films *overlooks* the pattern of racial control (slavery, jim crow, incarceration) that is not above or transparent in that history, but so visible as to not be seen.

44. Bruce Crowther, *Captured on Film: The Prison Film* (London: BT Batsford, 1989).

45. Nicole Rafter, *Shots in the Mirror: Crime Films and Society* (New York: Oxford UP, 2000).

46. Imprisonment is central to Jack Henry Abbot, *In the Belly of the Beast* (New York: Random House, 1981); Cleaver, *Soul on Ice;* Truman Capote, *In Cold Blood* (New York: Vintage, 1994); George Jackson, *Soledad Brother;* Richard Wright, *Native Son* (New York: Harper & Row, 1989); Malcolm X, *The Autobiography of Malcolm X* (New York: Grove Press, 1966); Joseph Bruchac and William Witherup, eds., *Words from the House of the Dead: Prison Writings from Soledad* (Trumansburg, NY: Crossing, 1974). Prisons also appear at the periphery of William Wells Brown, *Clotel;* Don DeLillo, *Underworld* (New York: Scribner, 1997); Theodore Dreiser, *An American Tragedy* (New York: Signet Classic, 2000); Faulkner, *Sanctuary, Light in August,* and *Go Down, Moses;* Nathaniel Hawthorne, *House of Seven Gables* (New York: Bantam Classics, 1981) and *Blithedale Romance* (New York: Penguin Books, 1986); Harriet Jacobs, *Incidents in the Life of a Slave Girl* (Cambridge, MA: Harvard UP, 1987); Henry James, *The Princess Casamassima* (New York: Penguin Classics, 1987).

47. Auli Ek, *Race and Masculinity in Contemporary American Prison Narratives* (New York: Routledge, 2005), 20.

48. Ibid., 15.

49. See Sanford Levinson and Steven Mailloux, *Interpreting Law and Literature* (Evanston, IL: Northwestern UP, 1988); Richard Posner, *Law and Literature* (Cambridge, MA: Harvard UP, 1998); Ann Algeo, *The Courtroom as Forum: Homicide Trials by Dreiser, Wright, Capote, and Mailer* (New York: P. Lang, 1996); Wai-chee Dimock, *Residues of Justice;* William E. Moddelmog, *Reconstituting Authority: American Fiction in the Province of Law* (Iowa City: U Iowa P, 2000); Brook Thomas, *American Literary Realism and the Failed Promise of Contract* (Berkeley: U California P, 1997); and Jay Watson, *Forensic Fiction: The Lawyer Figure in Faulkner* (Athens: U Georgia P, 1993).

50. David Guest, *Sentenced to Death: The American Novel and Capital Punishment* (Jackson: UP of Mississippi, 1997).

51. Morris and Rothman, *The Oxford History of the Prison,* viii. Such criticism

is legion—see especially Melossi and Pavarini, who catalog much of the early debate in that regard in *The Prison and the Factory.*

52. Foucault, *Discipline*, 31.

53. Richard Hebdige, *Subculture: The Meaning of Style* (London: Methuen, 1979).

54. Many critics' Foucauldian analysis leads them to treat representations of imprisonment, criminality, and law enforcement as symptomatic of more generalized mechanisms of social control. See John B. Bender, *Imagining the Penitentiary: Fiction and the Architecture of the Mind in Eighteenth-Century England* (Chicago: U Chicago P, 1987); D. A. Miller, *The Novel and the Police* (Berkeley: U California P, 1988); and Mark Seltzer, "The *Princess Casamassina*: Realism and the Fantasy of Surveillance," *Nineteenth-Century Fiction* 35 (1980–81).

55. Fredric Jameson, *The Prison-House of Language* (Princeton: Princeton UP, 1972).

56. Martha G. Duncan, *Romantic Outlaws, Beloved Prisons: The Unconscious Meanings of Crime and Punishment* (New York: New York UP, 1996).

57. Frederick Douglass, *Narrative of the Life of Frederick Douglass, An American Slave: Written by Himself* (New Haven, CT: Yale UP, 2001), 60; DuBois, *The Souls of Black Folk,* 3; Wright, 334; James Baldwin, *Collected Essays* (New York: Library of America, 1998), 16. Malcolm X, "After the Bombing," *Malcolm X Speaks: Selected Speeches and Statements,* George Breitman, ed. (New York: Grove Press, 1965), 69. Walter B. Rideout, in his foreword to Mercer Cook and Stephen E. Henderson's *The Militant Black Writer in Africa and the United States* (Madison: U Wisconsin P, 1969), is slightly more circumspect, describing open discrimination as "the jailing of black leaders or the socioeconomic imprisonment of black people in ghettos" (vii).

58. Ioan Davies, *Writers in Prison* (Toronto: Between the Lines, 1990), 40, 189. Chevigny guards against that *misprision* when she acknowledges, "Though from a certain vantage point we all sit on death row, some of us know this better than others" (*Doing Time,* 301).

59. Such is the title of the first chapter of Franklin, *Prison Literature in America.*

60. Franklin, *Prison Writing in 20th-Century America,* xiii; Chevigny, *Doing Time,* 4.

61. Robert Ellis Gordon and the inmates of the Washington Corrections System, *The Funhouse Mirror: Reflections on Prison* (Pullman: Washington State UP, 2000); Kathleen O'Shea, *Women on the Row: Revelations from Both Sides of the Bars* (Ithaca, NY: Firebrand Books, 2000). John Edgar Wideman uses the same discursive tactic, writing back and forth through bars with his imprisoned brother in *Brothers and Keepers* (New York: Holt, Rinehart and Winston, 1984).

62. The poem, submitted by Allen Carter Jr., prisoner #87750, is attributed to Judy Deputy, *The Angolite* (March/April 1985), 101.

63. Chevigny, *Doing Time,* xviii; Tom Wicker, "Foreword," Franklin, *Prison Writing in 20th-Century America,* xii, emphasis added.

64. Richard Poirier, *The Performing Self: Compositions and Decompositions in the Languages of Contemporary Life,* (New York: Oxford UP, 1971), 5.

65. Sacvan Bercovitch is the critic of U.S. literature most associated with such dissent in *The American Jeremiad* (Madison: U Wisconsin P, 1978), "America as Canon and Context: Literary History in a Time of Dissensus," *American Literature* 58.1 (1986), and *The Rites of Assent: Transformations in the Symbolic Construction of America* (New York: Routledge, 1993). David Howard-Pitney in *The Afro-American Jeremiads* (Philadelphia: Temple UP, 1990) points out the degree to which such dissent is insufficiently associated with African-American discourse, arguing that black literature in the United States has consistently maintained that edge of critique and prophecy. Eric J. Sundquist demonstrates that some African-American literature therefore results as a "strange combination of fiction and cultural analysis" (*The Hammers of Creation: Folk Culture in Modern African-American Fiction* [Athens: U Georgia P, 1992], 6). This description resonates with Cleaver's *Soul on Ice* and "The Flashlight" (*Playboy* [December 1969]).

66. Rubin Carter, *The Sixteenth Round: From Number 1 Contender to #45472* (Toronto: Macmillan, 1974), 4.

67. Mailer, "The White Negro," *Advertisements for Myself.*

68. Chevigny, *Doing Time;* Franklin, *Prison Writing in 20th-Century America;* Harlow, *Barred: Women, Writing, and Political Detention* (Hanover, NH: Wesleyan UP, 1992).

69. Sigmund Freud, *Civilization and Its Discontents,* trans. James Strachey (New York: Norton, 1961), chapter V.

# Chapter 2

1. Faulkner, *Go Down, Moses,* 68.

2. Oshinsky, 232.

3. Faulkner described his fictional county in those terms in a 1955 interview (James B. Meriwether, ed., *Lion in the Garden: Interviews with William Faulkner, 1926–1962* [New York: Random House, 1968], 255). The description exactly parallels the description seven years earlier, in *Intruder in the Dust* and Lucas's ownership of "the house and the ten acres of land it sat in—an oblong of earth set forever in the middle of the two-thousand-acre plantation like a postage stamp in the center of an envelope" (289). The likeness between Faulkner's right to ownership and that of Lucas is suggestive in its cross-racial identification. There are many ways to describe the proprietorship of some small thing that is at once the sum of and the field for all one's labor, after all, and Faulkner chooses the same for himself and Lucas, a black man and one of the writer's most powerfully rendered characters.

4. The first edition of *Absalom, Absalom!* (New York: Vintage, 1986) opens with Faulkner's hand-drawn map of his fictional county, a map that identifies the topography and the population: "Whites, 6298; Negroes, 9313." Robert W. Kirk identifies twelve hundred characters in nineteen novels, as well as ninety-four shorter works, and one hundred seventy-five of these characters appear in multiple texts (*Faulkner's People: A Complete Guide and Index to Characters in*

*the Fiction of William Faulkner* [Berkeley: U California P, 1963], vii). Thomas E. Dasher offers a more detailed index that does not substantively alter prior accounts in *William Faulkner's Characters: An Index to the Published and Unpublished Fiction* (New York: Garland, 1981).

5. In 1963 Cleanth Brooks could write of Faulkner's "masterpieces" and "greatest works" as bracketed in this period (*William Faulkner: The Yoknapatawpha Country* [New Haven and London: Yale UP, 1963], viii, ix). The books stay the same even while the descriptions and criteria change, as the New Criticism that Brooks played a part in inventing through reading Faulkner gave way to emphases on history and subjectivity. Twenty years after Brooks, Eric Sundquist argues, "Faulkner's best work reflects a turbulent search for fictional forms" to address historical racial conflict (*Faulkner: The House Divided* [Baltimore: Johns Hopkins UP, 1983], ix–x). A decade later, Philip M. Weinstein contends that Faulkner's best work is fulfilled in conflicts of subjectivity, and "Faulkner's supreme novels are those in which the project of subjective coherence is under maximal stress" (*Faulkner's Subject: A Cosmos No One Owns* [Cambridge: Cambridge UP, 1992], 2). This chapter takes up both matters of history and subjectivity, though with regard to aesthetic value, I am less certain than these critics that later work, particularly *Requiem for a Nun* (*Faulkner: Novels 1942–1954* [New York: Library of America, 1994]), does not figure among Faulkner's finest.

6. Stewart E. Tolnay and E. M. Beck, *Festival of Violence: An Analysis of Southern Lynchings, 1882–1930* (Chicago: U Illinois P, 1995), 202; Oshinksy, 209–13.

7. Arthur F. Raper, *The Tragedy of Lynching* (New York: Arno, 1969), 36.

8. Between 1930 and 1942, 1,002 of those executed were white: 959 for murder, 20 for rape, and 23 for other offenses. One thousand thirty-four of the executed were black: 852 for murder, 165 for rape, and 34 for other offenses (U.S. Department of Justice, *Sourcebook of Criminal Justice Statistics 2003* [State University of New York at Albany, online: http://www.albany.edu/sourcebook/pdf/t686.pdf]).

9. Noel Polk, "'I Have Taken an Oath of Office Too': Faulkner and the Law," *Fifty Years of Yoknapatawpha: Faulker and Yoknapatawpha, 1979,* eds. Doreen Fowler and Ann J. Abadie (Jackson: UP of Mississippi, 1980), 159.

10. The American Prison Association, "Declaration of Principles of 1870 as Revised and Reaffirmed at the Sixtieth Annual Congress of the American Prison Association Held in Louisville, Kentucky," *Proceedings of the Sixtieth Annual Congress of the American Prison Association, 1930* (Cheshire, CT: Printing Department, CT Penitentiary, 1930), 249.

11. William Banks Taylor, *Down on Parchman Farm: The Great Prison in the Mississippi Delta* (Columbus: The Ohio State UP, 1999), 9.

12. Faulkner, *Light in August,* 416.

13. Neil R. McMillen and Noel Polk, "Faulkner on Lynching," *The Faulkner Journal* 8.1 (1992): 6.

14. Oshinsky, 6.

15. Ibid., 211.

16. Joel R. Moore, "The Future of Probation in the United States," *Proceedings of the Sixtieth Annual Congress of the American Prison Association, 1930,* 69.

17. *Go Down, Moses,* 33–34, 68.

18. *Sanctuary,* 225, 229, 231, 236.

19. Lacan, 1–7.

20. *Sanctuary,* 302–9.

21. A. G. Fraser, "The Value of Case Records," *Proceedings of the 59th Annual Congress of the American Prison Association, 1929,* 79; Walter N. Thayer, "A Doctor Surveys the Criminal Problem," *Proceedings of the Sixtieth Annual Congress of the American Prison Association, 1930,* 202.

22. Faulkner, *Sanctuary* (New York: The Modern Library, 1932), vi. That introduction, one of the few Faulkner wrote, was included with the Modern Library edition of *Sanctuary* in 1932, though he thereafter recommended against its use. The 1993 Vintage edition describes that introduction as "misleading, but often quoted" to preface its reprinting (321). Some criticism takes issue with Faulkner's seemingly low opinion of the work and place the novel among the writer's finest; see André Bleikasten's *The Ink of Melancholy* (Bloomington and Indianapolis: Indiana UP, 1990) and Philip Cohen's "'A Cheap Idea . . . Deliberately Conceived to Make Money': The Biographical Context of William Faulkner's Introduction to *Sanctuary,*" *Faulkner Journal* 3.2 (1988). Faulkner's introduction suggests that he anticipated popular beliefs and "current trends," which echoes eight years later in Wright's description of his process of writing *Native Son.* Wright offers that he used "terms known and acceptable to a common body of readers, terms which would, in the course of the story, manipulate the deepest held notions and convictions of their lives. That came easy" (xxvii).

23. Erksine, 2.

24. Ibid., 8, 9.

25. American Prison Association (1930), 222.

26. *Oxford English Dictionary* (online: http://www.oed.com).

27. Alfred Adler, *The Case of Miss R: The Interpretation of a Life Story,* trans. Eleanore Jensen and Friedrich Jensen (London: George Allen & Unwin, 1929).

28. *Light in August,* 119.

29. Ibid., 122.

30. Ibid., 156.

31. Ibid., 206–7.

32. Ibid., 323.

33. Ibid., 337.

34. Ibid., 119, 219.

35. Ibid., 448.

36. Ibid., 448.

37. Taylor, 86.

38. Edwin J. Cooley, "The Genesis of the Criminal," *Proceedings of the 59th Annual Congress of the American Prison Association, 1929,* 21–28; Moore, 73–74; Thayer, 202–3.

39. Bennet Mead, "[Address]," *Proceedings of the 59th Annual Congress of the American Prison Association, 1929,* 168–75.

40. Faulkner, *Light in August,* 98.

41. Oshinsky, 100.

42. Faulkner, *Light in August,* 288.

43. Faulkner, *Light in August,* 464. The seeming inevitability of Popeye's and Christmas's ends see a parallel in Chester Himes's account of his coming of age in prison, where "it must have seemed to others that I was bent on self-destruction" (Himes, *The Quality of Hurt: The Autobiography of Chester Himes, vol. 1* [Garden City, NY: Doubleday & Company, 1972], 60). In order to prepare for another prison story that would become *Cast the First Stone* (New York: Norton, 1998) in 1952, Himes read *Light in August* (104).

44. Faulkner, *Light in August,* 339, 448.

45. Ibid., 339.

46. Faulkner, *Light in August,* 465.

47. Guest, 135.

48. Faulkner, *Go Down, Moses,* 351–52.

49. Guest, 135.

50. Faulkner, *Go Down, Moses,* 352.

51. Ibid., 355.

52. Mary B. Harris, "Personality in Prison," *Proceedings of the 59th Annual Congress of the American Prison Association, 1929,* 293; Austin H. MacCormick, "Education and the Library in the Prison," *Proceedings of the Sixtieth Annual Congress of the American Prison Association, 1930,* 41. Such individuation is largely the function of prisons in Foucault's argument in *Discipline and Punish* as well, although he focuses on eighteenth- and early-nineteenth-century practices.

53. American Prison Association, *Proceedings of the Sixty-Second Annual Congress of the American Prison Association, 1932,* Indianapolis, IN (Baltimore, MD: Printing Department, MD Penitentiary, 1932), 440.

54. Maud Ballington Booth, "Individualization in Prison," *Proceedings of the Sixty-Second Annual Congress of the American Prison Association, 1932,* Indianapolis, IN, 189.

55. James V. Bennett, "Military Service for Prisoners and Former Prisoners," *Proceedings of the Seventy-Second Annual Congress of the American Prison Association, 1942* (Asheville, NC, 1942), 50.

56. Foucault, 272.

57. Referenced by Robert Bright, "The Self-Proclaimed Political Prisoner," *Proceedings of the One Hundred and Second Annual Congress of Correction of the American Correctional Association, 1972* (College Park, MD, 1972), 109.

58. Some theorists identify individuation as a primary purpose of imprisonment. In an argument parallel to that of Foucault's *Discipline and Punish,* Melossi and Pavarini describe the prison as a factory for the manufacture of a particular person, the transformation of the criminal "real subject" into a prisoner, an "ideal subject" disciplined to the designs of the state (144–45). Such a manufacture is viewed negatively here, though it is less a by-product of a

critique of punishment practices than of an analysis of the political economy of capitalism.

59. Faulkner, *Light in August,* 444.

60. Faulkner, *Go Down, Moses,* 353.

61. Faulkner, *Absalom, Absalom!,* 224.

62. Watson, 93.

63. Faulkner, *Light in August,* 448.

64. Faulkner, *Go Down, Moses,* 360. More than either a Freudian or Lacanian subject, Gavin Stevens at the end resembles Deleuze and Guattari's model in *Anti-Oedipus* of socially constituted selfhood, wherein a "schizophrenic out for a walk is a better model than a neurotic lying on the analyst's couch" (2). A related account is offered by de Certeau in "A Walk in the City," 97–110.

65. Faulkner sometimes spells the grandmother's name as "Molly," other times as "Mollie."

66. Faulkner, *Go Down, Moses,* 360.

67. Ibid., 364.

68. Faulkner, *Light in August,* 393.

69. Ibid., 47.

70. Faulkner, *Go Down, Moses,* 360.

71. Ibid., 364.

72. Ibid., 365.

73. Ibid., 364.

74. Erik Dussere, "Accounting for Slavery: Economic Narratives in Morrison and Faulkner," *Modern Fiction Studies* 47.2 (Summer 2001).

75. Weinstein, 63–64.

76. Sundquist, *Faulkner: The House Divided,* 159.

77. Thadious M. Davis, *Games of Property: Law, Race, Gender, and Faulkner's* Go Down, Moses (Durham, NC: Duke UP, 2003).

78. Faulkner, *Sanctuary,* 316.

79. Ibid., 316, 317.

80. Faulkner, *Go Down, Moses,* 352, 365.

81. Ibid., 50.

82. Toni Morrison, "Faulkner and Women," *Faulkner and Women,* Doreen Fowler and Ann J. Abadie, eds. (Jackson: UP of Mississippi, 1986), 296.

83. Michael Grimwood, *Heart in Conflict: Faulkner's Struggle with Vocation* (Athens: U Georgia P, 1987), 267. The story of Butch Beauchamp is told in the titular episode of the novel that was first published in *Collier's* (January 25, 1941).

84. Faulkner, *Intruder in the Dust,* 320; Faulkner, *Requiem for a Nun,* 616.

85. Faulkner, *Intruder in the Dust,* 296, 299, 327; Faulkner, *Requiem for a Nun,* 511, 513, 515, 518, 520, 553, 554, 557, 579, 612.

## Chapter 3

1. Cleaver, *Soul on Ice,* 98.

2. In the first seventy years of the association's history, two presidents

represented the South; between WWII and 1979, there were eight. In *Dixie Rising: How the South Is Shaping American Values, Politics, and Culture* (New York: Time Books/Random House, 1996), Peter Applebome describes the expansion of Southern policies and practice, particularly how divides over civil rights split the Democratic party, sending many conservative Democrats to the right and making Southern states largely Republican. Of course, Malcolm X in his April 3, 1964 speech, "The Ballot or the Bullet," reprinted in *Malcolm X Speaks: Selected Speeches and Statements,* George Breitman, ed. (New York: Pathfinder, 1989), predicted that very split for those exact reasons, even foretelling the expansion of violent riots that summer (23–44).

3. The 1964 Civil Rights Act proved a turning point in the federal government's "hands-off" policy for the oversight of state prisons. The Arkansas ruling in *Holt v. Sarver* (1970) was the broadest of several states' similar findings. Earlier rulings focused particularly on the First Amendment rights of black prisoners. U.S. prisons tried to bar the religious practices of Black Muslims in the early 1960s, but the federal courts upheld the latter's religious freedom in *Pierce v. LaVallee* (1962, 1963) and *Sewell v. Pegelow* (1962).

4. Kathleen Rout, *Eldridge Cleaver* (Boston: G. K. Hall, 1991), vii.

5. Cleaver's *Soul on Fire* (Waco, TX: World Books, 1978) chronicles his turn to Christianity, and by 1980 he was supporting Ronald Reagan for president, a stark contrast to his heated conflict with the then-governor in 1968. Kathleen Rout titles this section of Cleaver's biography "Advertisements for Himself," a gesture to Mailer's *Advertisements for Myself* (Cambridge, MA: Harvard UP, 1992), first published in 1959.

6. These include the legitimacy of writ lawyers in *Johnson v. Avery* (1969), communication with the press in *Nolan v. Fitzpatrick* (1971)—although *Pell v. Procunier* (1974) would limit that right—and prisoners' rights to receive both mail and visitors in *Procunier v. Martinez* (1974).

7. The most dismissive read Cleaver's description, "Rape was an insurrectionary act," as a rationalization and seem to stop there, never getting as far as his admission that he was wrong, sick, and evil—see 3, 34–35. George Jackson in *Soledad Brother* similarly situates his own crime of robbery as revolution: "When the peasant revolts, the student demonstrates, the slum dweller riots, the robber robs, he is reacting" (179). Unlike Cleaver, he does not admit the larger wrongdoing of his act. However, that lack of apology is likely a consequence of the disparity between his crime of stealing $70 and the sentence he received, one year to life.

8. According to Franklin's "The Literature of the American Prison," prison practices in the United States so disproportionately have contained black men that the African-American literature written on the margins of dominant culture paradoxically has proven the dominant discourse within prison literature (51–52). Deleuze and Guattari's definition of a minor literature offered in *Kafka: Toward a Minor Literature* (Minneapolis: U Minnesota P, 1986) illuminates the rhetorical position of prison writers such as Cleaver—and in a more mediated fashion, the prisoners who represent themselves in *The Farm* and "Live from Death Row" in chapters 7 and 8. Deleuze and Guattari identify three characteristics of minor

literature: the articulations of the oppressed in the language of the oppressor, which they relate specifically to "blacks in America today"; the political nature of writing and its implication in social conflicts and asymmetrical power relations; and the collective value and political expression of writing, as "*literature is the people's concern*" (16–17). These are precisely the terms M. Karenga uses to define African-American cultural expression in "Black Art: Mute Matter Given Force and Function," in *The Norton Anthology of African American Literature,* Henry Louis Gates Jr. and N. Y. McKay, eds. (New York: Norton, 1997), 1973–77. In *The Political Unconscious,* Jameson similarly privileges resistant discourse, which he also explicitly associates with "black language," one of the "still vital sources of language production," prior to its assimilation by dominant language use (87).

9. Himes, "The Meanest Cop in the World" and "On Dreams and Reality," *The Collected Stories of Chester Himes* (New York: Thunder's Mouth Press, 1991), 209–13, 214–26. In contrast, Malcolm X notes in his autobiography, "I can't remember any of my prison numbers. That seems surprising, even after the dozen years since I have been out of prison. Because your number in prison became part of you. You never heard your name, only your number. On all of your clothing, every item, was your number, stenciled. It grew stenciled on your brain" (152).

10. D. Quentin Miller makes a related point regarding "minority prison narratives" in "'On the Outside Looking In': White Readers of Nonwhite Prison Narratives," *Prose and Cons: Essays on Prison Literature in the United States* (Jefferson, NC: McFarland, 2005). Of James Baldwin, Wideman, and Leonard Peltier, Miller writes that "the ethnic prison narrative cannot follow a conventional narrative order," instead opting to "disrupt chronology" and incorporate "letters, poems, and vignettes" to reorient the context of crime and punishment for white readers (16).

11. Cleaver, *Soul on Ice,* 21.

12. Parker L. Hancock, "Presidential Address," *Proceedings of the Ninety-Eighth Annual Congress of Correction, 1968* (ACA: Washington, DC, 1968), 13.

13. Ibid., 15, 19.

14. Ibid., 23.

15. Vincent O'Leary, "Current Issues in Community Based Correction," *Proceedings of the One Hundredth Annual Congress of Correction of the American Correctional Association, 1970* (College Park, MD, 1970), 131. The next few years would see the same points raised in nearly identical terms. The 1971 ACA President Louie L. Wainwright notes that "society is experiencing a period of cultural and social revolution" ("Presidential Address," *Proceedings of the One Hundred and First Annual Congress of the American Correctional Association, 1971* [College Park, MD, 1971], 3).

16. Others' views were more extreme. In 1969, Warden R. W. Meier describes university riots not as symptomatic of social change but as a pernicious direct cause of unrest in prison ("Administration and Problems in Correctional Institutions," *Proceedings of the Ninety-Ninth Annual Congress of Correction of the American Correctional Association, 1969* [Washington, DC, 1969], 62). He offers a

list of troublemakers: "resistors, draft dodgers, professional agitators, communists, hippies and revolutionaries [ . . . and] former prisoners, militants, far-out liberals, subversives, and even a few clergymen, educators and social workers," whose "delight in fomenting unrest" he parallels with "drunken Mexicans" rioting in prison (62–63). Presidential addresses remain significantly less reactionary and racist through this twelve-year period.

17. Sloop, 16, 63, 91.

18. Leon J. Quinn, "Militant Black: A Correctional Problem," *Proceedings of the Ninety-Ninth Annual Congress of the American Correctional Association, 1969,* 222–24.

19. Ibid., 224, 227–28.

20. James W. L. Park, "The Politics of Predators," *Proceedings of the One Hundred and Second Annual Congress of Correction of the American Correctional Association, 1972* (College Park, MD, 1972), 112–13.

21. Scott Fleming, "Lockdown at Angola: The Case of the Angola 3," Kathleen Cleaver and George Katsiaficas, eds., *Liberation, Imagination, and the Black Panther Party Liberation: A New Look at the Panthers and Their Legacy* (New York: Routledge, 2001), 230. Fleming chronicles the three decades of imprisonment at the Louisiana State Prison endured by Herman Wallace, Robert King Wilkerson, and Albert Woodfox, whose incarceration he describes as a part of the longstanding persecution of the Black Panther Party. Regarding the associate warden's comment regarding communism, it is at odds with Cleaver's observations that black revolutionary radicalism conflicted with the Communist Party—a charge disputed in U.S. Senate hearings as described in G. Louis Heath, ed., *The Black Panther Leaders Speak* (Metuchen, NJ: Scarecrow Press, 1976), 79–80. See also Charles E. Jones, ed., *The Black Panther Party Reconsidered* (Baltimore: Black Classic Press, 1998), 1.

22. Joseph M. Dell'Olio, "The Public, Crime, and Corrections—Acceptance or Rejection," *Proceedings of the Ninety-Ninth Annual Congress of Correction of the American Correctional Association, 1969,* 85–86.

23. A. Leon Higginbotham, "Is Yesterday's Racism Relevant Today in Corrections?," *Proceedings of the One Hundredth Annual Congress of Correction of the American Correctional Association, 1970,* 19–35.

24. The Goldman Panel supervised the prisons directly after the riot. The McKay Commission held public hearings in April 1972 in a broader examination of the state's practices and concluded by criticizing the violent response and Rockefeller's failure to visit the prison in person. The "Rights of People" session at the 1972 ACA conference focuses largely on the rights of corrections officers and administrators (American Correctional Association, 1972, 136–51). The shift between the 1968 meeting in San Francisco and four years later in Pittsburgh is significant, and the violence of Attica likely set the tone for the 1972 opening address. The Governor of Pennsylvania, Milton J. Shapp, rather than begin with the customary congratulatory remarks saluting the ACA, begins with a vignette of a furloughed youth raping and murdering a young girl ("Governor's Address," *Proceedings of the One Hundred and Second Annual Congress*

*of Correction of the American Correctional Association, 1972* [College Park, MD, 1972], 1).

25. Benjamin J. Malcolm, "The Self-Proclaimed 'Political Prisoner,'" *Proceedings of the One Hundred and Second Annual Congress of Correction of the American Correctional Association, 1972* (College Park, MD, 1972), 108.

26. Robert Bright, "The Self-Proclaimed Political Prisoner," *Proceedings of the One Hundred and Second Annual Congress of Correction of the American Correctional Association, 1972* (College Park, MD, 1972), 110.

27. James P. Collins, "Attica: Anatomy of the New Revolutionary," *Proceedings of the One Hundred and Second Annual Congress of Correction of the American Correctional Association, 1972* (College Park, MD, 1972), 193–95.

28. Vernon Fox, "Racial Issues in Corrections: Cultural Awareness—How to Achieve It!," *Proceedings of the One Hundred and Second Annual Congress of Correction of the American Correctional Association, 1972* (College Park, MD, 1972), 175–78.

29. Ibid., 181–82.

30. David R. Struckhoff, "A Sociological Perspective on Classification, Discretionary Judgment, and Racism," *Proceedings of the One Hundred and Second Annual Congress of Correction of the American Correctional Association, 1972* (College Park, MD, 1972), 185–87.

31. E. Eugene Miller, "Necessary Preconditions to Achieving Cultural Awareness," *Proceedings of the One Hundred and Second Annual Congress of Correction of the American Correctional Association, 1972* (College Park, MD, 1972), 171–74.

32. C. B. Farrar, "Criteria of Responsibility," *Proceedings of the 59th Annual Congress of the American Prison Association, 1929,* 349.

33. Robert Sheer describes these in his introduction to Cleaver's *Eldridge Cleaver: Post-Prison Writings and Speeches* (New York: Ramparts/Random House, 1969), ix.

34. One lengthy presentation in 1974, by far the longest of that year's conference, by West Virginia Warden Donald E. Bordenkircher, titled "Prisons and the Revolutionary," manages to at one moment decry McCarthyism and then lay the blame for grassroots and inmate-led prison reform movements at the feet of the Communist Party (*Proceedings of the One Hundred and Fourth Annual Congress of Correction of the American Correctional Association, 1974* (College Park, MD, 1974), 109–17, 132. The next year, Robert H. Fosen dismisses the term "political prisoner" in an aside as a wholly pejorative bogeyman, designating a black man who is "loud and demanding, half articulate, aware of his rights and blind to the rights of others" ("Accreditation: A New Challenge to the Old Dilemma," *Proceedings of the One Hundred and Fifth Annual Congress of Correction of the American Correctional Association, 1975* [College Park, MD, 1975], 31).

35. The legislation of that model takes place in Senate Bills 1437 and 2699, among others introduced there and in the House between 1976 and 1984, which provided for standardized rather than indeterminate sentencing and deemphasized parole. These efforts culminated in the Sentencing Reform Act of 1984. Those "just desserts" reforms were the consequence of, on the one hand, liberals

who were critical of what they perceived as harsher sentences for minority criminals and, on the other hand, conservatives adopting a "tough on crime" posture—see Roy D. King, "Prisons," Michael Tonry, ed., 592–93.

36. Cleaver, *Soul on Ice*, 98–100.

37. In *Écrits: A Selection,* Alan Sheridan translates Lacan's *manque* as "lack"—with the exception of "the expression, created by Lacan, *manque-à-être,* for which Lacan himself proposed the English neologism 'want-to-be'" (xi). Bruce Fink similarly clarifies "want in being or want to be" as distinct from "lack of being" (*The Lacanian Subject: Between Language and Jouissance* [Princeton: Princeton UP, 1995], 103). Without the dashes, the phrase emphasizes lack more than the impossible desire to fill the lack; with the dashes, then, *manque-à-être* emphasizes the *desire* rather than the *absence* in Lacanian subject formation.

38. Deleuze and Guattari, *Anti-Oedipus,* 14, 21.

39. Ibid., 23.

40. Ibid., 381.

41. Cleaver, *Soul on Ice,* 35.

42. Ibid., 36.

43. As determined in *Coffin v. Reichard* (1944), "A prisoner retains all the rights of an ordinary citizen except those expressly, or by necessary implication, taken from him by law." However, that affirmation of rights must be read in conjunction with *Price v. Johnston* (1948): "Lawful incarceration brings about the necessary withdrawal or limitation of many privileges and rights, a retraction justified by the considerations underlying our penal system." Prisoners' rights as citizens are both retained and withdrawn.

44. Deleuze and Guattari, *Anti-Oedipus,* 136–37, 389n64. Wideman similarly describes his goal in *Brothers and Keepers* as the "attempt to break out, to knock down the walls" (18).

45. Cleaver, *Soul on Ice,* 36.

46. Cleaver, *Soul on Ice,* 38, 79, 110. Cleaver, *Post-Prison Writing,* 165. Similarly, Rubin Carter in his biography quotes at length from a statement John Brown made the morning of his execution (233).

47. Deleuze and Guattari, *Anti-Oedipus,* 270.

48. Cleaver, *Soul on Ice,* 21, 29.

49. Ibid., 30.

50. Ibid., 30–31.

51. Deleuze and Guattari, *Anti-Oedipus,* 23, 105.

52. Cleaver, *Soul on Ice,* 49, 51.

53. Rout, 10.

54. Cleaver, "Flashlight," 120.

55. Ibid., 124.

56. Ibid., 302.

57. *Playboy* (December 1969), 288.

58. Ibid., 288.

59. Cleaver, *Soul on Ice,* 183–220.

60. Ibid., 191.

61. Ibid., 219. The analysis has a clear debt to Fanon. Cleaver refers to Fanon's *The Wretched of the Earth* as the "Black Bible," and the relationship between black men and white men in Cleaver's model here demonstrates how "historical and economic realities come into the picture" when Fanon adds race to Lacanian identification in *Black Skin, White Masks* (161). According to Fanon, the anxiety of white masculinity produces its own fulfillment: "Projecting his own desires onto the Negro, the white man behaves 'as if' the Negro really had them" (165).

62. Cleaver's paean to black women in the final chapter reads as something of an apology both to racist misogyny in general and to Cleaver's own involvement with Beverly Axelrod, his white lawyer. His painfully derisive descriptions of homosexuality are numerous and have received comment elsewhere, as in Amy Abugo Ongiri's "We Are Family: Miscegenation, Black Nationalism, Black Masculinity, and Black Gay Cultural Imagination," in *Race-ing Representation: Voice, History, and Sexuality*, Kostas Myrsiades and Linda Myrsiades, eds. (Lanham, MD: Rowman & Littlefield, 1998), and Shelton Waldrep's "'Being Bridges': Cleaver/ Baldwin/Lorde and African-American Sexism and Sexuality," *Critical Essays: Gay and Lesbian Writers of Color*, Emmanuel S. Nelson, ed. (New York: Haworth, 1993). What has not received much attention is how the predatory homosexuality endemic among men in prison might shape Cleaver's perceptions.

63. Robert Felgar, "*Soul on Ice* and *Native Son*," *Negro American Literature* 8 (1974): 235.

64. Cleaver, *Soul on Ice*, 217.

65. Ibid., 217.

66. CNN, "'He was a Symbol': Eldridge Cleaver Dies at 62," U.S. News Story Page (1 May 1998, online: http://www.cnn.com/US/9805/01/cleaver. late.obit).

67. John P. Conrad, "Looking toward the Year 2000: The Role of Correctional Research," *Proceedings of the One Hundredth Annual Congress of Correction of the American Correctional Association, 1970*, 335.

68. Ibid., 337.

69. Park, 112.

70. Fox, 180; Struckhoff, 188.

71. Cleaver, *Soul on Ice*, 185, 229. The bodily convulsions brought on by the tension of history also have a parallel in *The Executioner's Song*. Larry Schiller debates whether or not to agree to sell his firsthand exclusive account of the execution for $125,000, and his deliberations focus on "true history" versus "journalistic crap," a tension that he internalizes. He finally rejects the monetary reward, quite literally rejecting such "crap" in a wild episode of diarrhea before he turns down the deal (857–59).

72. Cleaver, *Soul on Ice*, 220.

73. Jackson, *Soledad Brother*, 187, 298.

74. Ibid., 283, 136, 283, 27.

75. Cleaver, *Soul on Ice*, 242.

76. Ibid., 3.

77. Jackson, *Soledad Brother*, 300.

78. Cleaver, *Soul on Ice,* 26.

79. Cleaver's analysis of racial struggle in the 1960s leads him to an extended quote from Frederick Douglass's Fourth of July speech juxtaposed with a gloss of *Uncle Tom's Cabin.* That turn to Stowe anticipates her critical reevaluation in the 1970s and 1980s, although his reading of the popular response to *Uncle Tom's Cabin* remains flat-out inaccurate: the "most alienated view of America was preached by the Abolitionists, and by Harriet Beecher Stowe in her *Uncle Tom's Cabin.* But such a view of America was too distasteful to receive wide attention" (76). Upon its publication, Stowe's novel received very wide attention in terms of both sales and popular comment.

80. Cleaver, *Soul on Ice,* 222–35.

81. Ibid., 117.

82. Ibid., 137.

83. Intercollegiate Studies Institute, "The Fifty Worst Books of the Century" (online: http://www.isi.org/publications/ir/50worst.html).

# Chapter 4

1. Mailer, *The Armies of the Night,* 188.

2. That Vintage International imprint, also borne on recent editions of Faulkner novels, effectively serves as Random House's latest incarnation of the Modern Library series, which became a contributing force in consolidating mid-twentieth-century U.S. literature, as I suggest in *"Go Down, Moses* [*and Other Stories*]: Bibliography as a Novel Approach to a Question of Genre," *The Papers of the Bibliographical Society of America* 96:4 (2002).

3. Mailer's *The Armies of the Night* offers similar challenges of genre. Its own categorization is "History/Writing," and its jacket praise includes that of the *New York Times Book Review:* "Only a born novelist could have written a piece of history so intelligent, mischievous, penetrating, and alive." *Time* offers that the book is "worthy to be judged as literature."

4. In 1972, *Furman v. Georgia* reversed the death sentences of two men convicted in Georgia, one for murder and one for rape, and of another man in Texas convicted of rape. Such sentences for black men convicted of rape echo the similar circumstances of the United States during the 1930s addressed in chapter 2. The 5–4 decision was contested bitterly, resulting in nine separate opinions.

5. Mailer, "The Man Who Studied Yoga," 157; Mailer, *Miami and the Siege of Chicago* (Cleveland: World, 1968), 42, 140, 174; Mailer, *The Armies of the Night,* 141, 161, 188, 189, 197, 270. In *An American Dreamer: A Psychoanalytic Study of the Fiction of Norman Mailer* (London/Toronto: Associated University Presses, 1980), Andrew Gordon touches on Mailer's loose use of "schizophrenia," and he associates it with the tension between author and nation, between liberty and despotism (187). However, in the absence of a Deleuzo-Guattarian sense of the term, the cultural and historical ramifications remain hazy.

6. Mailer, *Miami,* 140; Mailer, *Armies,* 197.

7. Mailer, *Armies,* 51, 190. Mailer clarifies his response as "a miserable recognition, and on many a count, for if he felt even a hint this way, then what immeasurable tides of rage must be loose in America itself?" (51). He reiterates the point later even as he defends its basis: "Of course that was why he was getting tired of hearing of Negro rights and Black Power—every Black riot was washing him loose with the rest, pushing him to that point where he would have to throw his vote in with revolution—what a tedious perspective of prisons and law courts and worse; or stand by and watch as the best Americans white and Black would be picked off, expended, busted, burned and finally lost" (187). Mailer wants to cover his bases, to defend even a borderline-racist refusal to identify himself with blackness in terms of hesitant sympathy for revolution: "And all the Left-wing Blacks would be his polemical associates—the Lord protect him!" (214). Cleaver proved more unified in his cross-racial political allegiances, as his presidential campaign with the Peace and Freedom Party demonstrated an alliance between its mostly white membership and the Black Panthers.

8. Mailer, *The Armies of the Night,* 3–4.

9. Mailer, *The Executioner's Song,* 983, 984. In his own prison story, *Adams v. Texas* (New York: St. Martin's P, 1991), Randall Adams offers his description of Gilmore's last words and prisoners' responses to his execution (46). Errol Morris's documentary *The Thin Blue Line* (Third Floor Productions/Miramax, 1988) contributed to renewed attention to Adams's case, which subsequently led to Adams's release in 1989.

10. Robert Merrill, "Mailer's Sad Comedy: *The Executioner's Song,*" *Texas Studies in Literature and Language* 34.1 (1992): 141.

11. Mailer, *The Executioner's Song,* 798.

12. Mary V. Dearborn, *Mailer: A Biography* (New York: Houghton Mifflin, 1999), 348.

13. Ibid., 1024–25.

14. Jonathan Dee, "The Reanimators: On the Art of Literary Graverobbing," *Harper's* (June 1999): 80.

15. Dee, 84. Gregg Easterbrook makes the same point in the exact same terms in "It's Unreal: How Phony Realism in Film and Literature Is Corrupting and Confusing the American Mind," *Washington Monthly* (October 1996). Easterbrook castigates another "true story" account of multiple murder in terms he might apply to Mailer as well, suggesting that *In Cold Blood* muddies "the lines of realism and the invented not so much in the pursuit of an otherwise unobtainable truth (as Truman Capote initially claimed about *In Cold Blood*) but in pursuit of an improved story that would call attention to the writer (as Capote later admitted was his real goal)" (42).

16. Mailer's use of news excerpts works slightly differently from that of John Dos Passos in *U.S.A.* (New York: Random House, 1937). The accounts in that novel provide a texture of the historical real, commenting on coincident events as a gesture between history and fiction and a testament to the "truth" of the latter. *The Executioner's Song,* with its emphasis on the narrativization of history, attests

not only to the narrative equivalency between the novel's events and the news excerpts, but also to mutual causality. By including more-complete excerpts and the process of narrativization, Mailer's gambit is that of realer-than-thou, which, in a different context, Phil Barrish suggests is a transhistorical phenomenon in U.S. letters, in *American Literary Realism, Critical Theory, and Intellectual Prestige, 1880–1995* (New York: Cambridge UP, 2001).

17. Wright, xxviii.

18. Mailer, *The Executioner's Song,* 511.

19. Ibid., 1051–52.

20. Ibid., 1051.

21. Ibid., 1053.

22. Merrill, 129.

23. Mailer, *The Executioner's Song,* 793, 831.

24. Mark Edmundson views the bond between writer and written as that of "Romantic Self-Creations: Mailer and Gilmore in *The Executioner's Song,*" *Contemporary Literature* 31.4 (1990)—an account Merrill also suggests. David Guest goes the furthest in reading author and object alike as in the romantic outlaw's double-bind of resistance. If Gilmore disavows his own self-determination and agency, he might receive a life sentence; if he declares himself the sum of his actions, he pits himself against the state in a contest that at once asserts his importance (*he is so dangerous* that the state must kill him) and condemns him (he is so dangerous that *the state must kill him*). Guest in his critique conflates character and author: "The more Gilmore and Mailer advertise their outlaw status, the more they participate in the work of the police" (168). However, it hardly seems necessary to read author and subject in the same double-bind, particularly as it is Gilmore who actually is killed by the authorities.

25. Mailer, *Conversations with Norman Mailer,* J. Michael Lennon, ed. (Jackson: UP of Mississippi, 1988), 263.

26. Ibid., 348.

27. Mailer, *The Executioner's Song,* 715, 734, 736, 799, 802, 833, 850–51.

28. Ibid., 834.

29. Ibid., 851, 496.

30. Ibid., 1049, 1050, 1051–56.

31. Ibid., 106, 235, 305. Later, Gilmore again describes his soul as more "evil" than most, that he is "further from God" and "would like to come closer" (833). The description resonates with the words of a prisoner from the documentary *The Farm* examined in chapter 7; inmate John Brown admits that he would like to live like Christ, but he does not know "if I got that far yet."

32. Ibid., 600.

33. Ibid., 714.

34. Ibid., 719, 857, 859.

35. Jennifer Roscher also suggests: "Perhaps the novel is more of an autobiography with Lawrence Schiller [ . . . ], standing in for Mailer, representing the (im)possibility of narrating a life," in "The Ambivalence of *The Executioner's Song:* Postmodern Captivity from Death Row," D. Quentin Miller, ed., *Prose and Cons,* 221.

36. Lawrence Schiller, *Master Spy: The Robert Hanssen Story* (Twentieth Century Fox, 2002); Richard Lacayo, "Books by the Buddy System," *Time* (6 May 2002): 8

37. Lawrence Schiller and James Willwerth, *American Tragedy: The Uncensored Story of the Simpson Defense* (New York: Random House, 1996); Mailer, *Oswald's Tale: An American Mystery* (New York: Random House, 1995); Schiller and L. M. Kit Carson, *The American Dreamer* (Corda Productions/Kabak, 1971); Mailer, *An American Dream* (New York: The Dial Press, 1965); Mailer, *Conversations with Norman Mailer,* 239.

38. Richard Poirier, "The Ups and Downs of Mailer," *The New Republic* 164.4 (January 23, 1971): 23–26. Rpt. in *Norman Mailer: A Collection of Critical Essays,* Leo Braudy, ed. (Englewood Cliffs, NJ: Prentice-Hall, 1972), 167. Andrew Gordon makes that confluence of personal and collective unconscious the starting point of *An American Dreamer: A Psychoanalytic Study of the Fiction of Norman Mailer* (London/Toronto: Associated University Presses, 1980), 15.

39. Steve Shoemaker, "Norman Mailer's 'White Negro': Historical Myth or Mythical History?," *Twentieth-Century Literature* 37.3 (Fall 1991): 343, 349, 353.

40. Mailer, *The Executioner's Song,* 359, 797.

41. When the policeman Nielsen questions Gary as to why he shot the two men, Gary can never offer any satisfying answer as to why them, why there: "I don't know. I don't have a reason"; "I don't know"; "It was there" (ibid., 288).

42. Ibid., 715, 799.

43. Ibid., 602.

44. Ibid., 603.

45. Ibid., 627.

46. Ibid., 651.

47. Ibid., 711–12.

48. Franklin, *Prison Literature,* xii.

49. Mailer, *The Executioner's Song,* 627, 669.

50. Ibid., 831.

51. Ibid., 703.

52. Lacan, 6.

53. Mailer, *The Executioner's Song,* 841.

54. Ibid., 773.

55. Ibid., 639.

56. Ibid., 784.

57. David Baldus and George Woodworth, "Racial Discrimination and the Death Penalty in the Post-Furman Era: An Empirical and Legal Overview, With Recent Findings from Philadelphia," *Cornell Law Review* 83 (1998): 1638.

58. Ibid., 872.

59. Ibid., 873.

60. Mailer, *Miami and the Siege of Chicago,* 190.

61. Mailer, *The Executioner's Song,* 860.

62. Ibid., 983.

63. According to the online magazine *Crime,* Gilmore's case set a precedent

for voluntary executions, which accounted for approximately one-eighth of executions in the late 1990s (Robert Anthony Phillips, "Volunteering for Death: The Fast Track to the Death House," *Crime* magazine [online: http://crimemagazine.com/deathrowvolunteers.htm]). Then–death row prisoner Mumia Abu-Jamal addresses this topic but challenges the prevalence of the phenomena in the essay "The Demand for Death" in *Live from Death Row* (Reading, MA: Addison-Wesley, 1995), 103–5. Wilbert Rideau offers a rich analysis of the social poverty of life imprisonment in "Conversations with the Dead," an essay that closes with an exchange between two prisoners serving life sentences at Angola: "'You know,' Billy said, 'I'm convinced that Gary Gilmore was trying to tell us something.'" Rideau responds with a simple, "Yep" (*Life Sentences,* 71). The 1978 *Angolite* article in which Rideau's account first appeared won the American Bar Association's Silver Gavel Award, given to the "communications media that have been exemplary in helping to foster the American public's understanding of the law and the legal system" (American Bar Association, "Awards and Contests" [online: http://www.abanet.org/publiced/gavel/home.html]). This was the first time a prisoner had ever received the award.

64. Mailer, *The Executioner's Song,* 736–38.

65. Cleaver, "The Flashlight," 120, 122, 289.

66. Foucault, *Discipline and Punish,* 30. The image also appears in a poem by Angola prisoner James E. Sutton Jr., #96250: "There's a prison inside my body, / That has a cell with no key" (*The Angolite* [Nov./Dec. 1983]: 116).

67. Richard H. Warfel, "A Report of Drug Treatment Programs in America's State Prison Systems," *Proceedings of the One Hundred and Second Annual Congress of Correction of the American Correctional Association, 1972* (College Park, MD, 1972), 50. Robert Martinson, "The Effectiveness of Correctional Treatment: A Survey of Treatment Evaluation Studies," *Proceedings of the One Hundred and Fifth Annual Congress of Correction of the American Correctional Association, 1975* (College Park, MD, 1975), 106, 107.

68. Ibid., 108–9; King, 591. Martinson sought to redress those misconceptions, and his research is among the most frequently cited in ACA presentations of the late 1970s. Nevertheless, the damage had been done; a 2000 *Newsweek* cover article points to Martinson's research as providing the "intellectual rationale" for shifting from a treatment model to more frequent and longer prison sentences (Ellis Cose, "The Prison Paradox," *Newsweek* [13 November 2000]: 48).

69. Mailer, *The Executioner's Song,* 814.

70. Anthony Travisono, "Prison Crisis—Over 280,000 Men and Women in Our Nations Prisons," *The American Journal of Correction* (May–June 1977).

# Chapter 5

1. According to Daniel Frampton, founding editor of the online journal *Film-Philosophy,* "The quote is actually transcribed from Ian Christie's British television program called *The Last Machine*" (http://www.driftline.org/cgi-bin/

archive/archive_msg.cgi?file=spoon-archives%2Ffilm-theory.archive%2Ffilm-theory_1998%2Ffilm-theory.9809&msgnum=11&start=328). Bergson made the similar point that film "could suggest new things to a philosopher. It might be able to assist in the synthesis of memory, or even of the thinking process. [ . . . ] [M]emory is, like the cinema, composed of a series of images." Qtd. in Richard Abel, "Before the Canon," *French Film Theory and Criticism: A History/Anthology, 1907–1939, Volume 1: 1907–1929,* Richard Abel, ed. (Princeton, NJ: Princeton UP, 1988), 22.

2. Schiller, *The Executioner's Song* (Film Communications, 1982); Mikal Gilmore, *Shot in the Heart* (New York: Doubleday, 1994); Agnieszka Holland, dir., *Shot in the Heart* (HBO, 2001). In addition, 2005 and 2006 saw the release of the prime-time series *Prison Break* (Fox) and *InJustice* (ABC).

3. Norman A. Carlson, "Presidential Address," *Proceedings of the One Hundred and Tenth Annual Congress of Correction of the American Correctional Association, 1980,* 21.

4. U.S. Department of Justice, "Violent Crime Rates Have Declined Since 1994, Reaching the Lowest Level Ever Recorded in 2002," Bureau of Justice Statistics (online: http://www.ojp.usdoj.gov/bjs/glance/viort.htm); U.S. Department of Justice, "Property Crime Rates Continue to Decline," Bureau of Justice (online: http://www.ojp.usdoj.gov/bjs/glance/house2.htm).

5. The number of people in state prisons by year and type of crime are:

| | Violent | Property | Drug | Public Order |
|---|---|---|---|---|
| **1980** | 173,300 | 89,300 | 19,000 | 12,400 |
| **1999** | 570,000 | 245,000 | 251,200 | 120,600 |

(U.S. Department of Justice, "Number of Persons in Custody of State Correctional Authorities by Most Serious Offense, 1980–2001," Bureau of Justice Statistics [online: http://www.ojp.usdoj.gov/bjs/glance/tables/corrtyptab.htm]; U.S. Department of Justice, "Prisoners in 1999," Bureau of Justice Bulletin [August 2000, online: http://www.ojp.usdoj.gov/bjs/pub/pdf/p99.pdf]). The overall population of the United States increased by almost 25 percent over those two decades, and I have adjusted the proportional increases in the categories to account for that population growth.

6. Eric Schlosser, "The Prison-Industrial Complex," *Atlantic Monthly* (December 1998): 54.

7. U.S. Department of Justice, "Incarceration Rates 1980–2002," Bureau of Justice Statistics (online: http://www.ojp.usdoj.gov/bjs/glance/tables/incrttab.htm).

8. U.S. Department of Justice, "Prisoners in 1999," 9.

9. U.S. Department of Justice, "Lifetime Likelihood of Going to State or Federal Prison," Bureau of Justice Statistics Special Report (March 1997, online: http://www.ojp.usdoj.gov/bjs/pub/pdf/llgsfp.pdf).

10. Schlosser, 54; Morris, "The Contemporary Prison," 215–16; Sloop, 174; Tonry, *Handbook,* 19–20.

11. Bruce Western and Becky Pettit, "Incarceration and Racial Inequality in Men's Employment," *Industrial and Labor Relations Review* 54.1 (2000).

12. Quoted in Schlosser, 52.

13. Then–U.S. Attorney, former U.S. Associate Attorney General, and later New York Mayor Rudolph W. Giuliani's opening remarks at the height of the Reagan era prove a rare exception, as he points to the increasing prison population as the cause for decreasing crime. He describes criminality as a matter of the "soul" and of individuals rather than social groups ("Keynote Address," *Proceedings of the One Hundred and Fifteenth Annual Congress of Correction of the American Correctional Association, 1985*, 1–4). The only general addresses that maintain such a conservative tone during this time are those of federal government officials appointed by the Reagan and Bush administrations.

14. Lee P. Brown, "Violence in America: A Challenge for the '80s," *Proceedings of the One Hundred and Twelfth Annual Congress of Correction of the American Correctional Association, 1982*, 11.

15. David C. Evans, "Managing Overcrowding with Limited Resources," *Proceedings of the One Hundred and Twelfth Annual Congress of Correction of the American Correctional Association, 1982*, 175.

16. George H. Cox, "Building Our Way Out of the Prison Crisis," *The State of Corrections: Proceedings ACA Annual Conferences, 1988* (U.S., 1989), 104; Ann W. Richards, "Invest in People, Not Institutions," *The State of Corrections: Proceedings ACA Annual Conferences, 1989* (Washington, DC: St. Mary's Press, 1990), 8, 12; Kurt L. Schmoke, "Alleviating Our Prison Crisis: National Policy Changes Are Needed," 1990, 108; M. Wayne Huggins, "Changing Public Perception," *The State of Corrections: Proceedings ACA Annual Conferences, 1992* (Arlington, VA: Kirby Lithographic, 1993), 5.

17. Cox, 108.

18. Perry M. Johnson, "Corrections Should Take the Lead in Changing Sentencing Practices," American Correctional Association, *The State of Corrections: Proceedings American Correctional Association Annual Conferences, 1993* (Springfield, VA: Goodway Graphics, 1994), 3–4; Joseph D. Lehman, "Solving the Crowding Problem: Linking Resources to Corrections Policy," *The State of Corrections, 1994*, 77.

19. William W. Wilkins Jr., "The Practicality of Structured Sentencing," American Correctional Association, *The State of Corrections, 1994*, 107; Gerald W. Heaney, "Revise the Guidelines Now," American Correctional Association, *The State of Corrections, 1994*, 112.

20. "Debunking the Demonology of Crime," American Correctional Association, *The State of Corrections: Proceedings ACA Annual Conference, 1994* (Laurel, MD: American Correctional Association, 1995), 95.

21. Ibid., 96, 97.

22. Robert C. Scott, "Keynote Address," American Correctional Association, *The State of Corrections: Proceedings American Correctional Association Annual Conferences, 1996* (Fredericksburg, VA: BookCrafters, 1997), 1–6; Elizabeth Alexander, "A Time for Courage," American Correctional Association, *The State of Corrections, 1996:* 19–22; Flora Brooks Boyd, "Responsible versus Responsive Justice," American Correctional Association, *The State of Corrections, 1996:* 111–12.

23. Mike DeWine, "126th Congress Keynote Address," American Correctional Association, *The State of Corrections, 1996,* 101–3.

24. Reginald A. Wilkinson, "Best Practices: Programs We Can Live With," American Correctional Association, *The State of Corrections: Proceedings American Correctional Association Annual Conferences, 1997* (Sterling, VA: Technigraphix, 1998), 85–91.

25. Ibid., 92. He returns to this point in his keynote address the subsequent year, when he offers an anecdote of two women, one released from jail and the other leaving gang life. Each responds to mentorship and joins a larger community, a "we." Wilkinson claims that we "recognize ourselves in these stories," though the identification is with the mentoring organization, not the women themselves (Wilkinson, "Tools," 11). This differs from the more radical suggestion to identify with prisoners, which he makes in his speech the previous year, itself an echo of the call for prison administration and staff to identify with prisoners offered in 1929 and 1972 conference presentations (Farrar, 349; E. Eugene Miller, 171–74).

26. Wilkinson, "Tools," 85.

27. Rafter, 137.

28. Stuart Hall, in "What Is This 'Black' in Black Popular Culture?" (*Stuart Hall: Critical Dialogues in Cultural Studies,* D. Morley and K. H. Chen, eds. [London: Routledge, 1996, 465–75]), summarizes dominant strands of Birmingham School cultural studies approaches to social identification when he describes popular culture, specifically film, as "where we go to discover who we are" (474).

29. Such corporate integration and the formation of media conglomerates can lend itself to conspiracy theory regarding the culture industry in the vein of Horkheimer and Adorno. Certainly, the mergers have a clear economic downside in terms of inflated CEO salaries coupled with the layoffs that occur in corporate mergers. The degree to which vertical and horizontal monopolies limit artistic freedom is a far more complex matter. For example, Liz Garbus offers accolades of the Time Warner cable company HBO in interview: "HBO is a very special place. They really support the filmmaker's vision. They give you the support you need, and if your film wants a longer schedule because it's gonna be a better film with a longer schedule, they'll give that to you. They'll give you another year. And their notes are always so helpful and great. It was like heaven making a film with them" (qtd. in Liz Stubbs, *Documentary Filmmakers Speak* [New York: Allworth Press, 2002], 122). On the other hand, it would be difficult to argue that Rupert Murdoch's Fox News has not tilted television news to conservative punditry.

30. Loren Hemsley, personal e-mail to author (16 December 2000).

31. Abu-Jamal, 65.

32. Dave McNary, "Kaye's Lawsuit Is 'History,'" *Variety* (1 May 2000): 16.

33. Reviews in *Time,* the *Chicago Sun-Times,* and *Arena* magazine draw attention to the film's racial ambiguities or offer an outright negative response. See Richard Corliss, "Thug Chic: Motion Picture *American History X* Draws Controversy," *Time* (2 November 1998): 100; Roger Ebert, "*American History X* [Review]," *Chicago Sun-Times* (online: http://www.suntimes.com/ebert/ebert_reviews/1998/10/103004.html); Pete Lentini, "A Standard American History,"

*Arena* magazine (October 1999): 52. Lentini proposes that the film features a retrograde American history of racism, although some other reviewers offer acclaim.

34. Lentini cites a *Beat* magazine review as describing the Amnesty International plans (52). An online forum of predominantly young adult film viewers mentions that the film both has been and should be screened in high schools as an educational tool. The discussion among seven members began when one post raised the question of whether or not the film is based on a true story (For the Ravers, "*American History X* [Messages]" [online: http://www.fortheravers. com/forum/viewtopic.php?TopicID=1712]). Sean O'Sullivan points out that *American History X* is "widely used as a basis for discussion across a variety of courses in American universities and in other educational settings ("Representations of Prison in Nineties Hollywood Cinema: From *Con Air* to *The Shawshank Redemption*," *Howard Journal of Criminal Justice* 40.4 [2001]: 322).

35. O'Sullivan offers a related argument regarding *American History X,* although his account of the film is both brief and highly derivative of one of his sources, an online review of the film posted to www.prisonflicks.com.

36. Andrew O'Hehir, "Review [*American History X*]," *Sight and Sound* (May 1999, online: http://www.bfi.org.uk/sightandsound/reviews/details.php?id=92); Todd McCarthy, "*American History X* [Movie Reviews]," *Variety* (26 October 1998): 41, 42.

37. de Certeau, 102.

38. Brooks has fulfilled this role before, as he played Uncle Tom in the television adaptation of Harriet Beecher Stowe's novel in 1987.

39. The MPAA claims that representations of sex and violence merit similar treatment in their ratings decisions, but casual viewing suggests otherwise, as does a 2002 study by Ron Leone of two hundred ten sequences from thirteen films ("Contemplating Ratings: An Examination of What the MPAA Considers 'Too Far for R' and Why," *Journal of Communication* 52.4 [2002]).

40. John Irwin, *Prisons in Turmoil* (Boston: Little, Brown, 1980), 230–40; Sloop, 132–41; Larry E. Sullivan, *The Prison Reform Movement: Forlorn Hope* (Boston: Twayne, 1990), 211.

41. The Internet Movie Database top two hundred fifty is compiled from ratings based on a minimum of 1,250 votes by regularly contributing users. The ranking is based on a "Bayesian estimate" that includes factors of the movie's mean rating, the number of votes, the minimum number of votes, and the mean vote among all films on the Internet Movie Database's "Top 250 Films as Voted By Our Users" (online: http://www.imdb.com/top_250_films).

42. John Simon, "Film: Songbirds & Skinheads [Review]," *The National Review* (December 31, 1998): 50; McCarthy, 41, 42.

# Chapter 6

1. Carter, 77.

2. Phillip Kerr, "Token Credit," *The New Statesman* (15 April 2002): 43–44.

3. Lewis M. Steel, "Rubin Carter: The Movie," *The Nation* (3 January 2000): 8; O'Hehir, Salon Review: *The Hurricane* (20 January 2000, online: http://dir.salon.com/ent/movies/review/2000/01/07/hurricane/index. html?CP=SAL&DN=11); Ebert, "*The Hurricane* [Review]," *Chicago Sun-Times* (online: http://www.suntimes.com/ebert/ebert_reviews/2000/01/010705. html).

4. Quoted in "In the Eye of *The Hurricane:* Off screen, Denzel Washington is grounded. As boxer Rubin Carter, he's a force of nature," *Newsweek* (10 January 2000): 60.

5. Charles Whitaker, "The Hurricane of Denzel Washington," *Ebony* (April 2000): 154–62; "Denzel Washington Stars as Rubin 'Hurricane' Carter in Movie, *The Hurricane,*" *Jet* (10 January 2000): 56–60.

6. "John Artis to Deliver Keynote Address at Annual UT Heman Sweatt Symposium on Civil Rights," *On Campus* (13 April 2001): 1.

7. James S. Hirsch, *Hurricane: The Miraculous Journey of Rubin Carter* (New York: Houghton Mifflin, 2000), 35–36.

8. Mailer, *The Executioner's Song,* 835.

9. Mark Golub takes issue with the historical reconstruction in *Glory* in "History Died for Our Sins: Guilt and Responsibility in Hollywood Redemption Histories," *Journal of American Culture* 21.3 (Fall 1998). In "Legitimation Crisis and Containment: The 'Anti-Racist-White-Hero' Film," *Critical Studies in Mass Communication* 16.4 (1999), Kelly J. Madison points out how white protagonists combating racism such as Kevin Kline's portrayal of Donald Woods in *Cry Freedom* supersede black men and women, thereby whitewashing racial conflict.

10. The journal *History and Theory* for much of the 1990s grappled with how to "tell" history responsibly after the challenges to narration, history, and authoring posed by critical theory in a postmodern vein of the 1970s and 1980s. In a special issue devoted specifically to film, Marita Sturken argues in "Reenactment, Fantasy, and the Paranoia of History: Oliver Stone's Docudramas," *History and Theory* 36.4 (1997), that Oliver Stone's docudramas do not tell the difference between imagination and reality. In an interview, documentary filmmaker Jill Godmilow sides with Paula Rabinowitiz, that the "real" of documentary often follows the conventions of fictional narrative film ("How Real Is the Reality in Documentary Film? Jill Godmilow, in Conversation with Ann-Louise Shapiro," *History and Theory* 36.4 [1997]: 80–81). Even Liz Stubbs, when championing documentary, describes their truth-value in terms quite similar to Rabinowitz's, xi.

11. Hayden White, "The Modernist Event," *The Persistence of History: Cinema, Television, and the Modern Event,* ed. Vivian Sobchack (New York: Routledge, 1996), 19.

12. In the critique of the Courtroom Television Newtwork, "TV or Not TV—That Is the Question," *Journal of Criminal Law & Criminology* 86.3 (Spring 1996), Christo Lassiter argues that news cameras in the courtroom undermine the judicial process, overly politicizing it.

13. Sam Chaiton and Terry Swinton, *Lazarus and the Hurricane: The Freeing of Rubin "Hurricane" Carter* (New York: St. Martin's Griffin, 1999).

14. Faulkner, *Light in August,* 288.

15. All of Jewison's comments on the film are from director's commentary available on the DVD release of *The Hurricane.* Such special features are a valuable tool for film criticism, although they are far from serving as any authoritative last word. That is, accounting for them presents no return to auteur theory, and it would be a mistake to read them as a record of directorial intent; such voiceovers are, after all, recorded after the film is complete and included for the most part to boost DVD sales.

16. Steel, 8; Ebert, "*The Hurricane* [Review]."

17. "In the Eye of *The Hurricane,* 60.

18. James S. Hirsch, 124.

19. In sorting those various actualities, I draw from Hirsch's biography of Carter, especially chapters 13 and 14, "Final Judgment" and "The Eagle Rises," as well as Jewison's directorial comment on the DVD release of the film.

20. Carter, 338.

21. Carter's argument is more in line with Deleuze and Guattari's claim in *Anti-Oedipus* that lack is not an a priori condition but is instead "created, planned, and organized in and through social production. [ . . . ] It is never primary," 29. In effect, Carter's self-sustaining strategy relies on an antioedipal formulation of desire to maintain his oedipal autonomy, which short-circuits itself. His reintroduction to history occurs with his reintegration to social participation outside the prison through freeing the blocks to the circulation of desire, which Deleuze and Guattari characterize as the first order of schizoanalysis.

22. The cast and crew first tried shooting the second episode with two Washingtons in the cell, like the first, but the director felt that it did not work. Instead, Jewison himself stood off-camera in the cell and read the other Carter's lines, and Washington responded to them. The other Hurricane's dialogue was looped later in postproduction. Whether historical accident or an unconscious endorsement of consciousness made manifest in the social rather than singular, Jewison so participating in Washington's performance of Carter's mind seems far more Deleuzo-Guattarian than Lacanian.

23. Carter, 310.

24. American Psychiatric Association, *Diagnostic and Statistical Manual of Mental Disorders,* 4th ed. (Washington, DC: American Psychiatric Press, 1994).

25. From 1962 to 1999, three actors have won Academy Awards in Jewison's films: Rod Steiger for *In the Heat of the Night* (1967), and Cher and Olympia Dukakis for *Moonstruck* (1987). However, for Washington's portrayal in this "most original and powerful" of scenes, Jewison then ascribes its excellence to the camera and the editing.

26. In another connection, Spike Lee, who directed *Malcolm X,* directed Norton in *25th Hour* (40 Acres & a Mule/Touchstone, 2002), chronicling his character's last twenty-four hours before going to prison—a tight parallel of Norton's character in *American History X* and its chronicle of his character's first twenty-four hours *after* prison.

27. Presumably, these are the sorts of depictions the American Correctional

Association seeks to challenge. The organization's mission statement as of 2002 includes eight goals, the sixth of which is to "enhance positive public perception of the corrections field" (ACA, "Vision Statement" [online: http://www.aca.org/images/doc_vision statement2.pdf]).

28. Understanding the film in these terms challenges O'Sullivan's claim of a subversive subtext inhabiting the rehabilitation narrative of *The Shawshank Redemption* (326–27).

29. The closing shot of the New York Supreme Court motto is a recapitulation of the opening shot of Sidney Lumet's *12 Angry Men* (Orion-Nova/UA, 1957), where Henry Fonda leads the jury from an 11–1 straw vote to convict to a 12–0 verdict of innocence. Where Lumet's film opens with the quote and reproduces in nearly real time the jury's deliberations, Jewison closes with it and has the film drastically telescope almost two decades of imprisonment.

30. Not all stories of prisoners are consolidated so completely. The material of Gary Gilmore's story is divided among three of the largest media conglomerates. Mailer's novel is published by Random House, and Doubleday, a division of Random House, offers Mikal Gilmore's account. However, the German media giant Bertelsmann is the parent company of Random House. HBO, a division of Time Warner, produced and distributed the television movie adaptation of *Shot in the Heart,* while the television movie version of *The Executioner's Song* is an NBC Universal (General Electric) property. With Viacom, Disney, Sony, and News Corp. (Fox), the seven companies control the vast majority of media communications in the United States and internationally: their collective holdings include film, television, music, and book publishing—both the intellectual properties and the means of distribution, from theaters, to video rentals, to the video stores, to cable networks, to the cable itself. However, as Liz Garbus points out of HBO's production of *The Farm,* such ownership does not necessarily limit artistic freedom.

# Chapter 7

1. Rideau, then serving a life sentence for murder at the Louisiana State Prison, rose to national prominence as the editor of the highly acclaimed prison magazine *The Angolite.* His journalism there merited him several awards, including the American Bar Association's Silver Gavel Award, and he coauthors with fellow Angolite editor Wikberg *Life Sentences.* That prominence possibly extended his time in prison. His fame may have delayed his release, as several boards recommended his pardon, but no governor signed it. According to former Louisiana Governor Edwin Edwards, "In my judgment, I think he has effectively forever barred any possibility for clemency because of his self-generated press. That's unfortunate, because that should not be a consideration" (*The Angolite* [July/August 1990]: 34). A new trial led to his 2005 release as it reduced his earlier conviction to manslaughter, the maximum penalty for which he had already served in his forty-four years at Angola.

2. U.S. Department of Justice, "Prison and Jail Inmates at Midyear 1999," Bureau of Justice Statistics Bulletin (April 2000), 1.

3. It received the Grand Jury Prize at the Sundance Film Festival and two Emmy Awards, and it was named Best Documentary by The National Society of Film Critics, The New York Film Critics Circle, and The Los Angeles Film Critics Association.

4. Glen Lovell, "*The Farm:Angola, USA* [Review]," *Variety* (2 February 1998, online: http://www.findarticles.com/cf_dls/m1312/n12_v369/ 20520805/p1/ article.jhtml).

5. Anne S. Lewis, "Life and Nothing But," *Austin Chronicle* (online: http:// www.austinchronicle.com/issues/v0118/issue10/screens.doctour.html).

6. Godmilow, 80–81.

7. Ibid., 84.

8. Nancy F. Partner, "Historicity in an Age of Reality-Fictions," *New Philosophy of History,* Frank Ankersmit and Hans Kellner, eds. (Chicago: U Chicago P, 1995).

9. Rabinowitz, "Wreckage upon Wreckage: History, Documentary, and the Ruins of Memory," *History and Theory* 32.2 (1993): 119.

10. Stubbs, 110, 111.

11. Ibid., 120.

12. Lewis (online).

13. Godmilow, 96.

14. Lewis (online).

15. *The Angolite* (Sept./Oct. 1982), 72.

16. *The Angolite* (July/Aug. 1990), 34.

17. Lovell's review in the industry trade *Variety* claims that the scene "will have viewers shaking their fists at the screen" (online). *The Film Journal* describes the scene as "startling" (Maria Garcia, "*The Farm* [Review]," *The Film Journal Review* [online: http://www.filmjournal.com/PublSystem/objects/MovieCommon/ _detail.cfm/StructID/10212050]). Lewis addresses it at length in her introductory comment preceding an interview with Garbus (online).

18. Rideau offers a description of a far more knowledgeable and professional parole board at Angola in *Life Sentences,* 124–28.

19. The tone here and elsewhere in the narration is reminiscent of Rideau's writing in *The Angolite* and Wikberg's in *Life Sentences,* where each several times recalls earlier floods in the history of Angola, in 1912, 1922, 1973, and 1982 (Nov./Dec. 1982): 17, 63.

20. Faulkner, *If I Forget Thee, Jerusalem* (New York: Vintage, 1995).

21. Burl Cain and Cathy Fontenot, "Managing Angola's Long-term Inmates," The American Correctional Association, *The State of Corrections: Proceedings ACA Annual Conferences, 2001* (Alexandria, VA: Magnet Print Brokers, 2002), 23, 25.

22. Ibid., 25.

23. Garcia (online).

24. Slavoj Žižek, *For They Know Not What They Do: Enjoyment as a Political Factor* (London, New York: Verso, 1991).

25. Ibid., 249–53.

26. Ibid., 253.

27. Oliver Stone's films, particularly *Natural Born Killers* (1994), are a lightning rod for such criticism, as are war films such as *Saving Private Ryan* (1998).

28. Lewis (online).

29. Brockway was the president of the National Prison Association in 1898 and frequently cited in its annual conferences through the twentieth century as one of its most important early leaders.

30. Žižek cites Jacques-Alain Miller's then-unpublished seminar differentiating between imaginary and symbolic identification (*Sublime*, 105; *Looking*, 135). See also Jacques-Alain Miller, "Extimacy," *Lacanian Theory of Discourse: Subject, Structure, and Society*, Mark Bracher et al., eds. (New York: New York UP, 1994), 75.

31. Garbus says of her and Stack's directorial intentions in the film that it was an effort "to get a view from the inside—which of course we never can, because we're not locked up" (qtd. in Anthony Kaufman, "An Interview with Jonathon Stack and Liz Garbus of the *The Farm*," Indiewire.com [online: http://www.indiewire.com/people/int_Farm_The_980126.html]). Rideau was then a life prisoner at Angola, and the extent to which the direction is his therefore locates the film as prisoner discourse. However, he was far less a part of the editing, and this was a film Garbus acknowledges as "made in the editing room" (Stubbs, 120). That split in its production leaves ambiguous the film's position in and out of prison writing.

32. de Certeau, 148.

33. This litany of theorized interpretations runs a double risk, on the one hand that of specious appropriation, and on the other a pretense of mastery over a broad array of challenging discourses. Their incorporation here is focused in the confluence of imagined and actual prisons and the deployment of an inmate identity. I leave the reader to judge the use here less on the breadth of reach than the merit in application.

34. Gill Scott-Heron, "The Revolution Will Not Be Televised," *The Revolution Will Not Be Televised* (Flying Dutchman, 1974).

# Chapter 8

1. John O'Brien, "Interview with Ed Bullins," *Negro American Literature Forum* (Autumn 1973): 108.

2. Qtd. in Michael L. Clemons and Charles E. Jones, "Global Solidarity: The Black Panther Party in the International Arena," *Liberation, Imagination, and the Black Panther Party: A New Look at the Panthers and Their Legacy*, Kathleen Cleaver and George Katsiaficas, eds. (New York: Routledge, 2001), 30.

3. The October 9, 1999, performance benefited the Diversity Institute, a division of the School of Social Work at the University of Texas at Austin. It

was offered more conventionally in September 1999 and then again in January 2004.

4. The field of performance studies emerged in the 1980s as a combination of strategies from theater studies and cultural anthropology to describe both social events in terms of dramatic convention and drama in terms of cultural work. The conventional origin narrative of the field traces performance studies to Victor Turner's *From Ritual to Theatre: The Human Seriousness of Play* (New York: Performing Arts Journal Publications, 1982) and Richard Schechner's *Between Theater and Anthropology* (Philadelphia: U Pennsylvania P, 1985). That project radically expanded in the late 1980s and 1990s with the work of Judith Butler, Jill Dolan, Peggy Phelan, Joseph Roach, and others at the intersections of critical theory, drama, and gender and cultural studies.

5. U.S. Department of Justice, "Additional Corrections Facts at a Glance," Bureau of Justice Statistics (online: http://www.ojp.usdoj.gov/bjs/gcorpop.htm).

6. Harlow, *Barred*, 181–82; emphasis added.

7. Ibid., 184.

8. Ken Webster, e-mail to author (30 September 2003).

9. Mailer, *The Executioner's Song*, 370.

10. Himes, *The Collected Stories*, 195. In *Adams v. Texas*, young white prisoner Randall Adams describes a similar situation where his jury differs from him in terms of age and class: "Most of them were well past middle age and lived in the more affluent Dallas suburbs. In theory, they were my peers" (70).

11. *The New Abolitionist*, a newsletter sponsored by the same organization that sponsors "Live from Death Row," was among the first to chronicle failures of public defenders in the 1990s, including a court-appointed lawyer repeatedly falling asleep while defending a man facing a murder charge (Alex Roth, "The Politics of Execution: Interview with Stephen Bright, Part 2," *The New Abolitionist* 2.5 [1998, online: http://www.nodeathpenalty.org/newab009/brightPt2.html]).

12. Michel Foucault, *The Archaeology of Knowledge*, trans. A. M. Sheridan Smith (New York: Pantheon, 1972), 102.

13. Abu-Jamal, xxi.

14. Kevin Johnson, "Inmate Suicides Linked to Solitary," *USA Today* (27 December 2006), A1.

15. Mailer, *The Executioner's Song*, 1001.

16. Antonin Artaud, *The Theatre and Its Double*, trans. Mary Caroline Richards (New York: Grove Press, Inc., 1958). Artaud's conception of a "Theatre of Cruelty" sought to unite audience and stage in a communion initiated by trauma, where the depiction of cruelty—and the tactics of that representation—preclude disassociative spectatorship.

17. Albert Bermel, *Artaud's Theatre of Cruelty* (New York: Taplinger, 1977), 106.

18. Davies, 120.

19. Cleaver, *Soul on Ice*, 34, 35.

20. Descriptions of forced sex are a regular means of conducting a sort of

theater of cruelty to confront an audience with pain. Rideau's chronicle of rape in men's prisons in "The Sexual Jungle," originally printed in *The Angolite* and reprinted in *Life Sentences,* includes the most graphic horror of the collection. *American History X* draws on the social cachet of representing such violence in Derek's prison rape scene.

21. Harry J. Elam Jr., *Taking It to the Streets: The Social Protest Theater of Luis Valdez and Amiri Baraka* (Ann Arbor: U Michigan P, 1998), 110.

22. Susan Bennett, *Theatre Audiences: A Theory of Production and Reception* (London: Routledge, 1990), 6; Tom Stoppard, "The Real Inspector Hound," *The Norton Anthology of English Literature,* vol. 2, 5th ed., ed. M. H. Abrams et al. (New York: Norton, 1986), 2432.

23. Mailer, *The Executioner's Song,* 997.

24. Schechner, 296.

25. Elaine Scarry, *The Body In Pain: The Making and Unmaking of the World* (New York: Oxford, 1985), 9.

26. See James Thompson, *Prison Theatre: Perspectives and Practices* (London: Jessica Kingsley, 1998); Julie Taylor, "Desdemona's Lament," *TDR* 45.4 (2001); Lorraine Moller, "A Day in the Life of a Prison Theatre Program," *TDR* 47.1 (2003).

27. Elam, 12, 14, 128.

28. Janelle Reinelt, *Crucibles of Crisis: Performing Social Change* (Ann Arbor: U Michigan P, 1996), 4.

29. Althusser, *Lenin and Philosophy and Other Essays,* 171–74.

30. *Oxford English Dictionary* (online: http://www.oed.com).

31. Such an account is in accord with Habermas's theorization of public spheres as enabling rather than precluding social action, in *The Structural Transformation of the Public Sphere,* trans. Thomas Burger and Frederick Lawrence (Cambridge, MA: MIT UP, 1993). He points out that such spheres are constructed: "Today occasions for identification have to be created—the public sphere has to be 'made,' it is not 'there' any more" (201). One might contest "any more," the possibility that at some earlier point in history such homogenous publics could be engaged in medias res. In a related context—and in yet another example of the metaphorical prison overwriting actuality—potential public spheres are framed in terms of the prison visiting room: written with power, simultaneously bringing together and keeping apart the inside and out. In "On Negt and Kluge," Jameson describes the boundaries that distinguish each within that space: visitors from outside, prisoners from inside are constrained within a system of rules regulating contact ("On Negt and Kluge," *The Phantom Public Sphere,* ed. Bruce Robbins [Minneapolis: U Minnesota P, 1993], 72). "Live from Death Row" in its actuality evacuates the rhetorical force of such a metaphorical prison.

32. Foucault, *Discipline,* 30.

33. Althusser, *For Marx,* trans. Ben Brewster (New York: Vintage, 1969), 51.

34. Benjamin, "The Work of Art in an Age of Mechanical Reproduction" in *Illuminations,* trans. Harry Zohn (New York: Schocken Books, 1978), 242.

35. Mailer, *The Executioner's Song,* 675, 677; 916; 974, 979, 980, 981. *The Farm*

features prison officials rehearsing John Brown's lethal injection, joking among themselves as they do so.

36. Deleuze and Guattari, *Anti-Oedipus,* 381.

37. Clemons and Jones, 30.

# Conclusion

1. However, it is not impossible for such recognition to take place. Cleaver's rhetorical flourishes and ingenuous loops and dips in prose, as well as his invitations to cross-racial identification, invite nonprisoners to recognize themselves in *Soul on Ice.* *The Farm*'s sympathetic portrayal of inmates encourages viewers not only to look to them, but, in the cases of Tannehill and Witherspoon, look *up* to them.

2. Brooker, 70.

3. Oshinsky, 100.

4. Abu-Jamal, 12, 29–33, 77.

5. The violent police suppression of civil rights activists in particular and black neighborhoods in general in the early 1960s merits Rubin Carter's widely publicized comments—taken out of context—regarding killing policemen offered in Carter's autobiography, *The Sixteenth Round,* 226; the scene also appears in the film *The Hurricane.* The violence he imagines for rhetorical effect became actual shoot-outs between some of the Black Panthers and the Oakland police from 1967 to 1973, the responsibility for which remains bitterly contested, but which contributed to the fear of black militancy exhibited in the American Correctional Association transcripts in the early 1970s. The social tensions producing such violence as a recurrent phenomenon see their reiteration in the similarly contested shooting that led to Abu-Jamal's imprisonment.

6. Johnson, "Corrections," 3.

7. While the Department of Justice acknowledges these declines as cited in chapter 5, they nevertheless attribute increasing prison and jail populations to violent crime: "Over half of the increase in State prison population since 1995 is due to an increase in the prisoners convicted of violent offenses" ("Over Half of the Increase in State Prison Population Since 1995 is Due to an Increase in the Prisoners Convicted of Violent Offenses," Bureau of Justice Statistics [online: http://www.ojp.usdoj.gov/bjs/glance/corrtyp.htm]). However, elsewhere, that increase is described in more specific terms that clarify the alleged increase. According to the U.S. Department of Justice, "At the end of 2000, 49% of State prisoners were serving time for violent offenses, up from 47% in 1995" ("Prisons in 2002," Bureau of Justice Statistics [online: http://www.ojp.usdoj.gov/bjs/abstract/p02.htm]). Furthermore, other Department of Justice figures demonstrate that the rate of offenses has declined steadily, reaching its lowest level ever in 2002 ("Violent Crime" [online]). In addition, by shifting the focus strictly to state prisoners rather than a combination of federal prisoners, these particular figures ignore the fact that more than 40 percent of people

accused of a federal crime are charged with a drug offense, according to federal officials (John P. Walters, Executive Office of the President, Office of National Drug Control Policy, "Cocaine" [online: http://www.whitehousedrugpolicy.gov/publications/pdf/ncj198582.pdf], 3). Other federal accounts place this proportion at 60 percent, according to the U.S. Sentencing Commission, *Special Report to the Congress Cocaine and Federal Sentencing Policy* (U.S, 1995, online: http://www.ussc.gov/crack/exec.htm., chapter 3). Some anecdotal evidence suggests that the harsher federal penalties for drug offenses encourage zealous or politically aspiring prosecutors to shift trials to the federal courts.

8. U.S. Department of Justice, "Estimated Arrests for Drug Abuse Violations by Age Group, 1970–2002" (online: http://www.ojp.usdoj.gov/bjs/glance/tables/drugtab.htm).

9. Walters, 3.

10. U.S. Sentencing Commission, chapters 7 and 8, appendices B and C.

11. Margaret A. Moore, "Race, Gender, and the Criminal Justice System," American Correctional Association, *The State of Corrections: Proceedings ACA Annual Conferences, 1992* (Arlington, VA: Kirby Lithographic, 1993), 197.

12. Morris, "The Contemporary Prison," 214–15.

13. Tonry, *Handbook*, 19–20; U.S. Sentencing Commission, chapter 8.

14. *U.S. v. Christopher Lee Armstrong* (1996).

15. Bell, *Silent Covenants*, 45–46.

16. Heaney, 114.

17. Wilkins, 111.

18. Lehman, 77.

19. American Correctional Association, "Mission Statement, Core Values and Guiding Principles, Vision Statement," *The State of Corrections: Proceedings American Correctional Association Annual Conferences, 1995* (Laurel, MD: American Correctional Association, 1996), 347–48.

20. Nell Bernstein, "Swept Away: Thousands of women, often guilty of little more than lousy judgment, are serving long prison sentences as drug 'conspirators,'" Salon.com (20 July 2000, online: http://dir.salon.com/mwt/feature/2000/07/20/conspirators/index.html); Ernest Dumas, "Chasing Amy's Freedom: It took the devoted intervention of a former U.S. senator and a presidential pardon, but an Arkansas woman finally tasted freedom last week after nine years in prison," *The Arkansas Times* (14 July 2000, online: http://www.arktimes.com/000714coverstory.html).

21. Property crime has declined steadily since the expansion of imprisonment. No correlation has been demonstrated authoritatively between rates of imprisonment and the commission of crimes of theft or violence. Ruth Wilson Gilmore traces the expansion of California's prison system, identifying the economic factors and cultural costs of the twenty-two prisons the state built at roughly $300 million apiece in the 1980s and 1990s (1998, 171–72). Abu-Jamal and Morris in the 1990s both point out that the U.S. imprisons its citizens at a rate far higher than comparable nations. There is not only the matter of rates of

incarceration and length of sentences, but also the issue of the variable definitions of crime itself. In 1973, the ACA president posed the questions, "Are there some kinds of behavior defined as illegal which the community is now willing to tolerate? On the other hand, are there some kinds of behavior which were formerly tolerable but are no longer?" (Wheeler, "Presidential Address," *Proceedings of the One Hundred and Third Annual Congress of Correction of the American Correctional Association, 1973* [College Park, MD, 1973], 3–4). While the term *socially constructed* has become passé, the president's view suggests the degree to which prison leadership itself realizes crime to be a set of acts historically fluctuating in their definition. Looking backward through the over three decades since her questions, what has become no longer tolerable is wholesale and long-term imprisonment demarcating lines of race and class.

22. In addition to Western and Petit's observations regarding imprisoned black men and unemployment trends, Gould, Weinberg, and Mustard conclude that rather than incarceration rates matching crime rates, unemployment provides the clearest correlation to imprisonment patterns.

23. U.S. Code, Civil Rights Act, v. 42 section 2000e (1964, online: http://caselaw.lp.findlaw.com/casecode/uscodes/42/chapters/21/subchapters/vi/sections/section_2000e.html).

24. Bright, 109.

25. Poirier, *The Performing Self,* 5.

26. Mike Sell, "The Black Arts Movement: Performance, Neo-Orality, and the Destruction of the 'White Thing,'" *African American Performance and Theatre History: A Critical Reader,* Harry J. Elam Jr. and David Krasner, eds. (New York: Oxford UP, 2001), 61–62, 77–78n37. Bullins's life and work provide something of a crucible for some of the historical tensions of the late 1960s and 1970s, as well as matters of identity and identification raised in chapters 3 and 4. Richard G. Scharine opens a 1979 essay in which he argues for the autobiographical qualities of much of the playwright's work with a description of Bullins as an "ex-Philadelphia street-gang member, ex-Navy boxing champ, ex-L.A. college student, ex-San Francisco Black Panther Minister of Information" ("Ed Bullins Was Steve Benson (But Who Is He Now?)," *Black American Literature Forum* 13.3 [1979]: 103. The description reads as an amalgam of Eldridge Cleaver and Rubin Carter as well, although Scharine mistakenly lists Bullins as minister of information rather than of culture. Cleaver was actually minister of information. Scharine further describes the main character of *The Reluctant Rapist* as "Bullins' best metaphor yet for the revolutionary artist" (108). Bullins replies to Scharine's observations in terms that echo the focus on schizophrenia in chapters 3 and 4: "I believe my characters sometimes have multiple identities, as parts of a whole, an ever-changing, interchangeable universe, as the points in a vision which expands—dreamlike" (Bullins, "Who He Is Now: Ed Bullins Replies," *Black American Literature Forum* 13.3 [1979]: 109).

27. Harris, 295–96.

28. Vanessa St. Gerard, "Mfume Urges a Partnership between ACA and the

NAACP," American Correctional Association, *The State of Corrections: Proceedings ACA Annual Conferences, 2004* (Upper Marlboro, MD: Graphic Communications, 2005), 1–2.

29. I had the opportunity to teach such courses in the English Department at The University of Texas at Austin in 2001 and 2002 and in criminal justice at the University of South Carolina Upstate in 2006.

# Works Cited

*12 Angry Men*. Sidney Lumet, dir., Orion-Nova/UA, 1957.

*25th Hour*. Spike Lee, dir., 40 Acres & a Mule/Touchstone, 2002.

Abbot, Jack Henry. *In the Belly of the Beast: Letters from Prison*. New York: Random House, 1981.

Abel, Elizabeth, Barbara Christian, Helene Moglen, eds. *Female Subjects in Black and White: Race, Psychoanalysis, Feminism*. Berkeley, CA: Berkeley UP, 1997.

Abu-Jamal, Mumia. *Live from Death Row*. Reading, MA: Addison-Wesley, 1995.

Adams, Randall, with William Hoffer and Marilyn Mona Hoffer. *Adams v. Texas*. New York: St. Martin's, 1991.

Adler, Alfred. *The Case of Miss R: The Interpretation of a Life Story*, trans. Eleanore and Friedrich Jensen. London: George Allen & Unwin, 1929.

Alexander, Elizabeth. "A Time for Courage." American Correctional Association, *The State of Corrections, 1996*: 19–24.

Algeo, Ann M. *The Courtroom as Forum: Homicide Trials by Dreiser, Wright, Capote, and Mailer*. New York: P. Lang, 1996.

Althusser, Louis. *For Marx*, trans. Ben Brewster. New York: Vintage, 1969.

———. *Lenin and Philosophy and Other Essays*, trans. Ben Brewster. New York: Monthly Review, 1972.

American Bar Association. "Awards and Contests." Online. Accessed 20 May 2004. http://www.abanet.org/publiced/gavel/home.html.

American Correctional Association. *Proceedings of the Ninety-Eighth Annual Congress of Correction, 1968*. American Correctional Association: Washington, DC, 1968.

————. *Proceedings of the Ninety-Ninth Annual Congress of Correction of the American Correctional Association, 1969*. Washington, DC, 1969.

————. *Proceedings of the One Hundredth Annual Congress of Correction of the American Correctional Association, 1970*. College Park, MD, 1970.

————. *Proceedings of the One Hundred and First Annual Congress of Correction of the American Correctional Association, 1971*. College Park, MD, 1971.

————. *Proceedings of the One Hundred and Second Annual Congress of Correction of the American Correctional Association, 1972*. College Park, MD, 1972.

————. *Proceedings of the One Hundred and Third Annual Congress of Correction of the American Correctional Association, 1973*. College Park, MD, 1973.

————. *Proceedings of the One Hundred and Fourth Annual Congress of Correction of the American Correctional Association, 1974*. College Park, MD, 1974.

————. *Proceedings of the One Hundred and Fifth Annual Congress of Correction of the American Correctional Association, 1975*. College Park, MD, 1975.

————. *Proceedings of the One Hundred and Sixth Annual Congress of Correction of the American Correctional Association, 1976*. College Park, MD, 1976.

————. *Proceedings of the One Hundred and Seventh Annual Congress of Correction of the American Correctional Association, 1977*. College Park, MD, 1977.

————. *Proceedings of the One Hundred and Eighth Annual Congress of Correction of the American Correctional Association, 1978*. College Park, MD, 1978.

————. *Proceedings of the One Hundred and Ninth Annual Congress of Correction of the American Correctional Association, 1979*. College Park, MD, 1979.

————. *Proceedings of the One Hundred and Tenth Annual Congress of Correction of the American Correctional Association, 1980*.

————. *Proceedings of the One Hundred and Eleventh Annual Congress of Correction of the American Correctional Association, 1981*.

————. *Proceedings of the One Hundred and Twelfth Annual Congress of Correction of the American Correctional Association, 1982*.

————. *Proceedings of the One Hundred and Thirteenth Annual Congress of Correction of the American Correctional Association, 1983*.

————. *Proceedings of the One Hundred and Fourteenth Annual Congress of Correction of the American Correctional Association, 1984*.

————. *Proceedings of the One Hundred and Fifteenth Annual Congress of Correction of the American Correctional Association, 1985*.

————. *Proceedings of the One Hundred and Sixteenth Annual Congress of Correction of the American Correctional Association, 1986*.

————. *Proceedings of the One Hundred and Seventeenth Annual Congress of Correction of the American Correctional Association, 1987*.

————. *The State of Corrections: Proceedings ACA Annual Conferences, 1988*.

————. *The State of Corrections: Proceedings ACA Annual Conferences, 1989*. Washington, DC: St. Mary's Press, 1990.

————. *The State of Corrections: Proceedings ACA Annual Conferences, 1990*. Washington, DC: St. Mary's Press, 1990.

————. *The State of Corrections: Proceedings ACA Annual Conferences, 1991*. Springfield, VA: Goodway Graphics, 1992.

———. *The State of Corrections: Proceedings ACA Annual Conferences, 1992.* Arlington, VA: Kirby Lithographic, 1993.

———. *The State of Corrections: Proceedings American Correctional Association Annual Conferences, 1993.* Springfield, VA: Goodway Graphics, 1994.

———. *The State of Corrections: Proceedings ACA Annual Conferences, 1994.* Laurel, MD: American Correctional Association, 1995.

———. *The State of Corrections: Proceedings American Correctional Association Annual Conferences, 1995.* Laurel, MD: American Correctional Association, 1996.

———. "Mission Statement, Core Values and Guiding Principles, Vision Statement." *The State of Corrections, 1995:* 347–48.

———. *The State of Corrections: Proceedings American Correctional Association Annual Conferences, 1996.* Fredericksburg, VA: BookCrafters, 1997.

———. *The State of Corrections: Proceedings American Correctional Association Annual Conferences, 1997.* Sterling, VA: Technigraphix, 1998.

———. *The State of Corrections: Proceedings American Correctional Association Annual Conferences, 1998.* Upper Marlboro, MD: Graphic Communications, 1999.

———. *The State of Corrections: Proceedings American Correctional Association Annual Conferences, 1999.* Upper Marlboro, MD: Graphic Communications, 2000.

———. *The State of Corrections: Proceedings ACA Annual Conferences, 2000.* Baltimore: VictorGraphics, 2001.

———. *The State of Corrections: Proceedings ACA Annual Conferences, 2001.* Alexandria, VA: Magnet Print Brokers, 2002.

———. "Resolution on the Restoration of Voting Rights." *The State of Corrections: Proceedings ACA Annual Conferences, 2001:* 97.

———. *The State of Corrections: Proceedings ACA Annual Conferences, 2002.* Upper Marlboro, MD: Graphic Communications, 2003.

———. *The State of Corrections: Proceedings ACA Annual Conferences, 2003.* Upper Marlboro, MD: Graphic Communications, 2004.

———. *The State of Corrections: Proceedings ACA Annual Conferences, 2004.* Upper Marlboro, MD: Graphic Communications, 2005.

———. "Vision Statement." Online. http://www.aca.org/images/doc_vision statement2.pdf

*American History X.* Tony Kaye, dir., New Line Cinema, 1998.

The American Prison Association. *Proceedings of the 59th Annual Congress of the American Prison Association,* 1929. Toronto, Canada, 1929.

———. *Proceedings of the Sixtieth Annual Congress of the American Prison Association, 1930.* Louisville, Kentucky. Cheshire, CT: Printing Department, CT Penitentiary, 1930.

———. "Declaration of Principles of 1870 as Revised and Reaffirmed at the Sixtieth Annual Congress of the American Prison Association Held in Louisville, Kentucky." *Proceedings of the Sixtieth Annual Congress of the American Prison Association:* 249–56.

———. *Proceedings of the Sixty-First Annual Congress of the American Prison Association, 1931.* Baltimore, MD. Baltimore, MD: Printing Department, MD Penitentiary, 1931.

―――. *Proceedings of the Sixty-Second Annual Congress of the American Prison Association, 1932.* Indianapolis, IN. Baltimore, MD: Printing Department, MD Penitentiary, 1932.

―――. *Proceedings of the Seventy-Second Annual Congress of the American Prison Association, 1942.* Asheville, NC.

American Psychiatric Association. *Diagnostic and Statistical Manual of Mental Disorders,* 4th ed. Washington, DC: American Psychiatric Press, 1994.

Anderson, Benedict. *Imagined Communities: Reflections on the Origin and Spread of Nationalism.* London: Verso, 1991.

*The Angolite.* September/October 1982.

―――. November/December 1982.

―――. November/December 1983.

―――. March/April 1985.

―――. July/August 1990.

Applebome, Peter. *Dixie Rising: How the South Is Shaping American Values, Politics, and Culture.* New York: Time Books/Random House, 1996.

Artaud, Antonin. *The Theatre and Its Double,* trans. Mary Caroline Richards. New York: Grove Press, Inc., 1958.

*Baby Boy.* John Singleton, dir., New Deal/Columbia, 2001.

Baldus, David and George Woodworth. "Racial Discrimination and the Death Penalty in the Post-Furman Era: An Empirical and Legal Overview, With Recent Findings from Philadelphia." *Cornell Law Review* 83 (1998).

Baldwin, James. *Collected Essays.* New York: Library of America, 1998.

Barrish, Phil. *American Literary Realism, Critical Theory, and Intellectual Prestige, 1880–1995.* New York: Cambridge UP, 2001.

Becarria, Cesare. *On Crimes and Punishments,* trans. David Young. Indianapolis, IN: Hackett, 1986.

Beck, Allen J. and Thomas P. Bonczar. "Prevalence of Incarceration in the United States." American Correctional Association, *The State of Corrections: Proceedings ACA Annual Conferences, 2004:* 29–41.

Bell, Derrick. *The Derrick Bell Reader, ed.* Richard Delgado and Jean Stefancic. New York: New York UP, 2005.

―――. *Ethical Ambition: Living a Life of Meaning and Worth.* New York: Bloomsbury, 2002.

―――. *Faces at the Bottom of the Well: The Permanence of Racism.* New York: Basic Books, 1992.

―――. *Silent Covenants:* Brown v. Board *of Education and the Unfulfilled Hopes for Racial Reform.* New York: Oxford UP, 2004.

Bender, John B. *Imagining the Penitentiary: Fiction and the Architecture of the Mind in Eighteenth-Century England.* Chicago: U Chicago P, 1987.

Benjamin, Walter. *Illuminations,* trans. Harry Zohn. New York: Schocken Books, 1978.

Bennett, James V. "Military Service for Prisoners and Former Prisoners." *Proceedings of the Seventy-Second Annual Congress of the American Prison Association, 1942:* 45–51.

Bennett, Susan. *Theatre Audiences: A Theory of Production and Reception*. London: Routledge, 1990.

Bercovitch, Sacvan. "America as Canon and Context: Literary History in a Time of Dissensus." *American Literature* 58.1 (1986): 99–107.

———. *The American Jeremiad*. Madison: U Wisconsin P, 1978.

———. *The Rites of Assent: Transformations in the Symbolic Construction of America*. New York: Routledge, 1993.

Bermel, Albert. *Artaud's Theatre of Cruelty*. New York: Taplinger, 1977.

Bernstein, Nell. "Swept Away: Thousands of women, often guilty of little more than lousy judgment, are serving long prison sentences as drug 'conspirators.'" Salon.com., 20 July 2000. Online. Accessed 16 June 2004. http://dir.salon.com/mwt/feature/2000/07/20/conspirators/index.html.

*Black Renaissance/Renaissance Noire* 8.1 (2003). "The American Dilemma Revisited: Psychoanalysis, Social Policy, and the Socio-Cultural Meaning of Race."

Bleikasten, André. *The Ink of Melancholy*. Bloomington and Indianapolis: Indiana UP, 1990.

Blomberg, Thomas G. and Karol Lucken. *American Penology: A History of Control*. New York: Aldine De Gruyter, 2000.

Booth, Maud Ballington. "Individualization in Prison." *Proceedings of the Sixty-Second Annual Congress of the American Prison Association, 1932:* 187–95.

Bordenkircher, Donald E. "Prisons and the Revolutionary." *Proceedings of the One Hundred and Fourth Annual Congress of Correction of the American Correctional Association, 1974:* 102–35.

Bosworth, Mary and Jean Flavin, eds. *Race, Gender, and Punishment: From Colonialism to the War on Terror*. New Brunswick, NJ: Rutgers UP, 2007.

Boyd, Flora Brooks. "Responsible versus Responsive Justice." American Correctional Association, *The State of Corrections, 1996:* 111–18.

Bright, Robert. "The Self-Proclaimed Political Prisoner." *Proceedings of the One Hundred and Second Annual Congress of Correction of the American Correctional Association, 1972:* 109–11.

Brooker, Norton W. [Address]. *Proceedings of the Annual Congress,* 1888. Chicago: Knight & Leonard, 1888: 67–71.

Brooks, Cleanth. *William Faulkner: The Yoknapatawpha Country*. New Haven and London: Yale UP, 1963.

Brown, Lee P. "Violence in America: A Challenge for the '80s." *Proceedings of the One Hundred and Twelfth Annual Congress of Correction of the American Correctional Association, 1982:* 5–11.

Brown, William Wells. *Clotel: Or, The President's Daughter*. New York: Carol Publishing, 1989.

Bruchac, Joseph and William Witherup, eds. *Words from the House of the Dead: Prison Writings from Soledad*. Trumansburg, NY: Crossing Press, 1974.

Bullins, Ed. "Who He Is Now: Ed Bullins Replies." *Black American Literature Forum* 13.3 (1979): 109.

Butler, Judith. *Bodies That Matter: On the Discursive Limits of "Sex."* New York: Routledge, 1993.

Cain, Burl and Cathy Fontenot. "Managing Angola's Long-term Inmates." The American Correctional Association, *The State of Corrections: Proceedings ACA Annual Conferences 2001.* Alexandria, VA: Magnet Print Brokers, 2002: 21–26.

Campaign to End the Death Penalty. "Live From Death Row." Austin, Texas, 23 September 1999.

Capote, Truman. *In Cold Blood.* New York: Vintage, 1994.

Carlson, Norman A. "Presidential Address." *Proceedings of the One Hundred and Tenth Annual Congress of Correction of the American Correctional Association, 1980:* 17–22.

Carter, Rubin. *The Sixteenth Round: From Number 1 Contender to #45472.* Toronto: Macmillan, 1974.

Caster, Peter. "*Go Down, Moses [and Other Stories]:* Bibliography as a Novel Approach to a Question of Genre." *The Papers of the Bibliographical Society of America* 96:4 (2002): 509–19.

de Certeau, Michel. *The Practice of Everyday Life.* Berkeley: U California P, 1984.

Chaiton, Sam and Terry Swinton. *Lazarus and the Hurricane: The Freeing of Rubin "Hurricane" Carter.* New York: St. Martin's Griffin, 1999.

Chevigny, Bell Gale. *Doing Time: 25 Years of Prison Writing.* New York: Arcade Publishing, 1999.

Christianson, Scott. *With Liberty for Some: 500 Years of Imprisonment in America.* Boston: Northeastern UP, 1998.

Cleaver, Eldridge. *Eldridge Cleaver: Post-Prison Writings and Speeches.* New York: Ramparts/Random House, 1969.

———. "The Flashlight." *Playboy* (December 1969): 120ff.

———. *Soul on Fire.* Waco, TX: World Books, 1978.

———. *Soul on Ice.* New York: Delta/Random House, 1992.

Cleaver, Kathleen and George Katsiaficas, eds. *Liberation, Imagination, and the Black Panther Party: A New Look at the Panthers and Their Legacy.* New York: Routledge, 2001.

Clemons, Michael L. and Charles E. Jones. "Global Solidarity: The Black Panther Party in the International Arena," ed. Kathleen Cleaver and George Katsiaficas. 20–39.

CNN. "'He was a Symbol': Eldridge Cleaver Dies at 62." U.S. News Story Page, 1 May 1998. Online. 10 November 2001. http://www.cnn.com/US/9805/01/cleaver.late.obit/

*Coffin v. Reichard.* 143 F.2d 443, 445 (6th Cir.), 1944; cert. denied, 325 U.S. 887, 65 S. Ct. 1568, 89 L. Ed. 2001, 1945.

Cohen, Philip. "'A Cheap Idea . . . Deliberately Conceived to Make Money': The Biographical Context of William Faulkner's Introduction to *Sanctuary.*" *Faulkner Journal* 3.2 (1988): 54–66.

Cole, David. *No Equal Justice: Race and Class in the American Criminal Justice System.* New York: New Press, 1999.

Collins, James P. "Attica: Anatomy of the New Revolutionary." *Proceedings of the*

*One Hundred and Second Annual Congress of Correction of the American Correctional Association, 1972:* 190–96.

Conrad, John P. "Looking toward the Year 2000: The Role of Correctional Research." *Proceedings of the One Hundredth Annual Congress of Correction of the American Correctional Association, 1970:* 326–39.

Cook, Mercer and Stephen E. Henderson. *The Militant Black Writer in Africa and the United States.* Madison: U Wisconsin P, 1969.

Cooley, Edwin J. "The Genesis of the Criminal." *Proceedings of the 59th Annual Congress of the American Prison Association, 1929:* 13–28.

*Cool Hand Luke.* Stuart Rosenberg, dir. Warner Bros., 1967.

Copjec, Joan. *Read My Desire: Lacan against the Historicists.* Cambridge, MA: MIT UP, 1994.

Corliss, Richard. "Thug Chic: Motion Picture *American History X* Draws Controversy." *Time* (2 November 1998): 100.

Cose, Ellis. "The Prison Paradox." *Newsweek* (13 November 2000): 41–49.

Coviello, Peter. "Intimacy and Affliction: DuBois, Race, and Psychoanalysis." *Modern Language Quarterly* 64.1 (2003): 1–32.

Cox, George H. "Building Our Way Out of the Prison Crisis." *The State of Corrections: Proceedings ACA Annual Conferences, 1988:* 104–9.

Craddock, Jim, ed. *VideoHound's Golden Movie Retriever 2003.* Detroit: Thomson/Gale, 2002.

Crenshaw, Kimberle, Neil Gotanda, Garry Peller, and Kendall Thomas, eds. *Critical Race Theory: The Key Writings That Formed the Movement.* New York: New Press/Norton, 1995.

Crowther, Bruce. *Captured on Film: The Prison Film.* London: BT Batsford, 1989.

Dasher, Thomas E. *William Faulkner's Characters: An Index to the Published and Unpublished Fiction.* New York: Garland, 1981.

Davies, Ioan. *Writers in Prison.* Toronto: Between the Lines, 1990.

Davis, Angela. *Are Prisons Obsolete?* New York: Seven Stories, 2003.

———. "A World unto Itself: Multiple Invisibilities of Imprisonment." *Behind the Razorwire: Portrait of a Contemporary American Prison System,* ed. Michael Jacobson-Hardy. New York: New York UP, 1999. ix–xviii.

Davis, Thadious M. *Games of Property: Law, Race, Gender, and Faulkner's Go Down, Moses.* Durham, NC: Duke UP, 2003.

Dawson, R. H. [Address]. *Proceedings of the Annual Congress, 1888.* Chicago: Knight & Leonard, 1888: 82–84.

Dearborn, Mary V. *Mailer: A Biography.* New York: Houghton Mifflin, 1999.

Dee, Jonathan. "The Reanimators: On the Art of Literary Graverobbing." *Harper's* (June 1999): 80ff.

Deleuze, Gilles and Félix Guattari. *Anti-Oedipus: Capitalism and Schizophrenia,* trans. Robert Hurley, Mark Seem, and Helen R. Lane. Minneapolis: U Minnesota P, 1983.

———. *Kafka: Toward a Minor Literature,* trans. Dana Polan. Minneapolis: U Minnesota P, 1986.

Delgado, Richard and Jean Stefancic, eds. *Critical Race Theory: The Cutting Edge.* Philadelphia: Temple UP, 1995.

———. *Critical Race Theory: An Introduction.* New York: New York UP, 2001.

DeLillo, Don. *Underworld.* New York: Scribner's, 1997.

Dell'Olio, Joseph M. "The Public, Crime, and Corrections—Acceptance or Rejection." *Proceedings of the Ninety-Ninth Annual Congress of Correction of the American Correctional Association, 1969:* 84–87.

"Denzel Washington Stars as Rubin 'Hurricane' Carter in Movie, *The Hurricane.*" *Jet* (10 January 2000): 56–60.

DeWine, Mike. "126th Congress Keynote Address." American Correctional Association, *The State of Corrections, 1996:* 101–5.

Dimock, Wai-chee. *Residues of Justice: Law, Literature, Philosophy.* Berkeley: U California P, 1996.

The Diversity Institute. *Jury Duty* [program]. The Diversity Institute: School of Social Work, University of Texas at Austin, 1999.

Donziger, Steven. *The Real War on Crime: The Report of the National Criminal Justice Commission.* New York: HarperPerennial, 1996.

Dos Passos, John. *U.S.A.* New York: Random House, 1937.

Douglass, Frederick. *Narrative of the Life of Frederick Douglass, An American Slave: Written by Himself.* New Haven, CT: Yale UP, 2001.

Dreiser, Theodore. *An American Tragedy.* New York: Signet Classic, 2000.

DuBois, W. E. B. *The Souls of Black Folk,* 22nd ed. Chicago: A. C. McClury & Co., 1938.

Dumas, Ernest. "Chasing Amy's Freedom: It took the devoted intervention of a former U.S. senator and a presidential pardon, but an Arkansas woman finally tasted freedom last week after nine years in prison." *The Arkansas Times,* 14 July 2000. Online, 16 June 2004. http://www.arktimes.com/000714coverstory.html.

Dumm, Thomas L. *Democracy and Punishment: Disciplinary Origins of the United States.* Madison: U Wisconsin P, 1987.

Duncan, Martha G. *Romantic Outlaws, Beloved Prisons: The Unconscious Meanings of Crime and Punishment.* New York: New York UP, 1996.

Dussere, Erik. "Accounting for Slavery: Economic Narratives in Morrison and Faulkner." *Modern Fiction Studies* 47.2 (Summer 2001): 329–55.

Easterbrook, Gregg. "It's Unreal: How Phony Realism in Film and Literature Is Corrupting and Confusing the American Mind." *Washington Monthly* (October 1996): 41–43.

Ebert, Roger. "*American History X* [Review]." *Chicago Sun-Times.* Online, 10 November 2003. http://www.suntimes.com/ebert/ebert_reviews/1998/10/103004.html

———. "*The Hurricane* [Review]." *Chicago Sun-Times.* Online, 10 November 2003. http://www.suntimes.com/ebert/ebert_reviews/2000/01/010705.html.

Edmundson, Mark. "Romantic Self-Creations: Mailer and Gilmore in *The Executioner's Song.*" *Contemporary Literature* 31.4 (1990): 434–47.

Ek, Auli. *Race and Masculinity in Contemporary American Prison Narratives.* New York: Routledge, 2005.

Elam, Harry J. Jr. *Taking It to the Streets: The Social Protest Theater of Luis Valdez and Amiri Baraka*. Ann Arbor: U Michigan P, 1998.

Erksine, George C. "President's Address," *Proceedings of the 59th Annual Congress of the American Prison Association, 1929*. Toronto, Canada: 2–8.

Evans, David C. "Managing Overcrowding with Limited Resources." *Proceedings of the One Hundred and Twelfth Annual Congress of Correction of the American Correctional Association, 1982*: 173–78.

Fanon, Frantz. *Black Skin, White Masks*, trans. Charles Lam Markmann. New York: Grove, 1967.

———. *The Wretched of the Earth*, trans. Constance Farrington. New York: Grove Press, 1963.

*The Farm: Life inside Angola Prison*. Jonathan Stack, Liz Garbus, and Wilbert Rideau, dirs., Gabriel Films/A&E Home Video, 1998.

Farrar, C. B. "Criteria of Responsibility." *Proceedings of the 59th Annual Congress of the American Prison Association, 1929*: 343 49.

Faulkner, William. *Absalom, Absalom!* New York: Vintage, 1986.

———. "Go Down, Moses." *Collier's* (25 January 1941): 19–20, 45–46.

———. *Go Down, Moses*. New York: Vintage, 1990.

———. *If I Forget Thee, Jerusalem*. New York: Vintage, 1995.

———. *Intruder in the Dust. Faulkner: Novels 1942–1954*. New York: Library of America, 1994.

———. *Light in August*. New York: Vintage, 1990.

———. *Requiem for a Nun. Faulkner: Novels 1942–1954*. New York: Library of America, 1994.

———. *Sanctuary*. New York: The Modern Library, 1932.

———. *Sanctuary*. New York: Vintage, 1993.

———. *The Sound and the Fury*. New York: Vintage, 1991.

Felgar, Robert. "*Soul on Ice* and *Native Son*." *Negro American Literature* 8 (1974): 235.

Fink, Bruce. *The Lacanian Subject: Between Language and Jouissance*. Princeton, NJ: Princeton UP, 1995.

Fleming, Scott. "Lockdown at Angola: The Case of the Angola 3," ed. Kathleen Cleaver and George Katsiaficas. 229–36.

For the Ravers. "*American History X* [Messages]." Online, 24 December 2003. http://www.fortheravers.com/forum/viewtopic.php?TopicID=1712.

Fosen, Robert H. "Accreditation: A New Challenge to the Old Dilemma." *Proceedings of the One Hundred and Fifth Annual Congress of Correction of the American Correctional Association, 1975*: 31–34.

Foucault, Michel. *The Archaeology of Knowledge*, trans. A. M. Sheridan Smith. New York: Pantheon, 1972.

———. *Discipline and Punish: The Birth of the Prison*, trans. Alan Sheridan. New York: Vintage, 1979.

Fox, Vernon. "Racial Issues in Corrections: Cultural Awareness—How to Achieve It!" *Proceedings of the One Hundred and Second Annual Congress of Correction of the American Correctional Association, 1972*: 175–83.

Frampton, Daniel. listserv posting, 7 September 1998 (http://www.driftline.

org/cgi-bin/archive/archive_msg.cgi?file=spoon-archives%2Ffilm-theory.archive%2Ffilm-theory_1998%2Ffilm-theory.9809&msgnum=11&start=328).

Franklin, H. Bruce. "The American Prison in the Culture Wars." "The Imprisonment of American Culture" panel at the Modern Language Association Convention, Washington, DC, December 2000. Online, 15 March 2001. http://andromeda.rutgers.edu/~hbf/priscult.html.

————. "The Literature of the American Prison." *Massachusetts Review* 18 (Spring 1977): 51–78.

————. *Prison Literature in America: The Victim as Criminal and Artist.* New York: Oxford UP, 1989.

————. *Prison Writing in 20th-Century America.* New York: Penguin, 1998.

Fraser, A. G. "The Value of Case Records." *Proceedings of the 59th Annual Congress of the American Prison Association, 1929:* 75–82.

Freud, Sigmund. *Civilization and Its Discontents,* trans. James Strachey. New York: Norton, 1961.

*Furman v. Georgia.* 408 U.S. 238; 92 S. Ct. 2726; 33 L. Ed. 2d 346, 1972.

Garcia, Maria. "*The Farm* [Review]." *The Film Journal Review.* Online, 10 December 2003. http://www.filmjournal.com/PublSystem/objects/MovieCommon/_detail.cfm/StructID/10212050.

Gates, Henry Louis, Jr. *Thirteen Ways of Looking at a Black Man.* New York: Random House, 1997.

Gilmore, Mikal. *Shot in the Heart.* New York: Doubleday, 1994.

Gilmore, Ruth Wilson. "Globalisation and US Prison Growth: From Military Keynesianism to Post-Keynesian Militarism. *Race and Class* 40.2–3 (1998): 171–88.

————. *Golden Gulag: Prisons, Surplus, Crisis, and Opposition in Globalizing California.* Berkeley, CA: U California P, 2007.

Giroux, Henry A. *Breaking in to the Movies.* Malden, MA: Blackwell, 2002.

————. *Fugitive Cultures: Race, Violence, and Youth.* New York: Routledge, 1996.

Giuliani, Rudolph W. "Keynote Address." *Proceedings of the One Hundred and Fifteenth Annual Congress of Correction of the American Correctional Association, 1985:* 1–4.

Godmilow, Jill. "How Real Is the Reality in Documentary Film? Jill Godmilow, in Conversation with Ann-Louise Shapiro." *History and Theory* 36.4 (1997): 80–101.

Golub, Mark. "History Died for Our Sins: Guilt and Responsibility in Hollywood Redemption Histories." *Journal of American Culture* 21.3 (Fall 1998): 23–46.

Gordon, Andrew. *An American Dreamer: A Psychoanalytic Study of the Fiction of Norman Mailer.* London/Toronto: Associated University Presses, 1980.

Gordon, Robert Ellis and the inmates of the Washington Corrections System. *The Funhouse Mirror: Reflections on Prison.* Pullman: Washington State UP, 2000.

Gould, Eric D., Bruce A. Weinberg, and David B. Mustard. "Crime Rates and Local Labor Market Opportunities in the United States: 1977–1997." *The Review of Economics and Statistics* 84.1 (2002): 45–61.

Gramsci, Antonio. *Selections from the Prison Notebooks*, ed. and trans. Quintin Hoare and Geoffrey Nowell Smith. New York: International Publishers, 1971.

*The Green Mile.* Frank Darabont, dir., Castle Rock/Warner, 1999.

Grimwood, Michael. *Heart in Conflict: Faulkner's Struggle with Vocation.* Athens: U Georgia P, 1987.

Guerrero, Ed. *Framing Blackness: The African American Image in Film.* Philadelphia: Temple UP, 1993.

Guest, David. *Sentenced to Death: The American Novel and Capital Punishment.* Jackson: UP of Mississippi, 1997.

Habermas, Jurgen. *The Structural Transformation of the Public Sphere,* trans. Thomas Burger and Frederick Lawrence. Cambridge: MIT UP, 1993.

Hall, Stuart. "What Is This 'Black' in Black Popular Culture?" *Stuart Hall: Critical Dialogues in Cultural Studies,* ed. D. Morley and K. H. Chen. London: Routledge, 1996. 465–75.

Hancock, Parker L. "Presidential Address." *Proceedings of the Ninety-Eighth Annual Congress of Correction, 1968:* 13–25.

Harlow, Barbara. *Barred: Women, Writing, and Political Detention.* Hanover, NH: Wesleyan UP, 1992.

Harris, Mary B. "Personality in Prison." *Proceedings of the 59th Annual Congress of the American Prison Association, 1929:* 292–300.

Hawthorne, Nathaniel. *The Blithedale Romance.* New York: Penguin Books, 1986.

———. *The House of Seven Gables.* New York: Bantam Classics, 1981.

———. *The Scarlet Letter.* Boston: Bedford Books of St. Martin's Press, 1991.

Hayes, Rutherford B. "President's Annual Address." *Proceedings of the Annual Congress, 1888.* Chicago: Knight & Leonard, 1888: 14–24.

Heaney, Gerald W. "Revise the Guidelines Now." American Correctional Association, *The State of Corrections: Proceedings ACA Annual Conferences, 1994:* 112–18.

Heath, G. Louis, ed. *The Black Panther Leaders Speak.* Metuchen, NJ: Scarecrow Press, 1976.

Hebdige, Richard. *Subculture: The Meaning of Style.* London: Methuen, 1979.

Hemsley, Loren. Personal e-mail to author. 16 December 2000.

Herivel, Tara and Paul Wright, eds. *Prison Nation: The Warehousing of America's Poor.* New York: Routledge, 2003.

Higginbotham, A. Leon. "Is Yesterday's Racism Relevant Today in Corrections?" *Proceedings of the One Hundredth Annual Congress of Correction of the American Correctional Association, 1970:* 19–35.

Himes, Chester B. *Cast the First Stone.* New York: Norton, 1998.

———. *The Collected Stories of Chester Himes.* New York: Thunder's Mouth Press, 1991.

———. *The Quality of Hurt: The Autobiography of Chester Himes, vol. 1.* Garden City, NY: Doubleday & Company, 1972.

Hirsch, Adam Jay. *The Rise of the Penitentiary: Prisons and Punishment in Early America.* New Haven: Yale UP, 1992.

Hirsch, James S. *Hurricane: The Miraculous Journey of Rubin Carter.* New York: Houghton Mifflin, 2000.

hooks, bell. *Reel to Real: Race, Sex, and Class at the Movies.* New York: Routledge, 1996.

Howard-Pitney, David. *The Afro-American Jeremiads: Appeals for Justice in America.* Philadelphia: Temple UP, 1990.

Huggins, M. Wayne. "Changing Public Perception." *The State of Corrections: Proceedings ACA Annual Conferences, 1992:* 1–6.

*The Hurricane.* Norman Jewison, dir., Universal, 1999.

"In the Eye of *The Hurricane:* Off screen, Denzel Washington is grounded. As boxer Rubin Carter, he's a force of nature." *Newsweek* (10 January 2000): 60.

Intercollegiate Studies Institute. "The Fifty Worst Books of the Century." http://www.isi.org/journals/ir/50best_worst/50worst.html.

Internet Movie Database. "Top 250 Films as Voted By Our Users." Online. http://www.imdb.com/top_250_films.

Irwin, John. *Prisons in Turmoil.* Boston: Little, Brown, 1980.

Jackson, George. *Soledad Brother.* New York: Coward-McCann, 1970.

———. *Blood in My Eye.* Baltimore: Black Classic Press, 1990.

Jacobs, Harriet. *Incidents in the Life of a Slave Girl: Written By Herself.* Cambridge, MA: Harvard UP, 1987.

James, Henry. *The Princess Casamassima.* New York: Penguin Classics, 1987.

Jameson, Fredric. "On Negt and Kluge." *The Phantom Public Sphere,* ed. Bruce Robbins. Minneapolis: U Minnesota P, 1993. 42–74.

———. *The Political Unconscious.* Ithaca, NY: Cornell UP, 1981.

———. *The Prison-House of Language.* Princeton: Princeton UP, 1972.

Ja Rule. *Blood in My Eye.* Def Jam, 2003.

"John Artis to Deliver Keynote Address at Annual UT Heman Sweatt Symposium on Civil Rights." *On Campus* (13 April 2001): 1.

*Johnson v. Avery,* Commissioner of Correction, et al. No. 40 U.S. 393 U.S. 483; 89 S. Ct. 747; 21 L. Ed. 2d 718. 1969.

Johnson, Kevin. "Inmate Suicides Linked to Solitary." *USA Today* (27 December 2006), A6.

Johnson, Perry M. "Corrections Should Take the Lead in Changing Sentencing Practices." American Correctional Association, *The State of Corrections: Proceedings American Correctional Association Annual Conferences, 1993:* 1–8.

———. "Debunking the Demonology of Crime." American Correctional Association, *The State of Corrections: Proceedings ACA Annual Conferences, 1994:* 91–97.

Jones, Charles E., ed. *The Black Panther Party Reconsidered.* Baltimore: Black Classic Press, 1998.

Karenga, M. "Black Art: Mute Matter Given Force and Function." *The Norton Anthology of African American Literature,* ed. Henry Louis Gates Jr. and N.Y. McKay. New York: Norton, 1997.

Kaufman, Anthony. "An Interview with Jonathon Stack and Liz Garbus of the *The Farm.*" Indiewire.com. Online, 10 December 2003. http://www. indiewire.com/people/int_Farm_The_980126.html.

Kelsey, Robert. "Suicide!," ed. Bell Gale Chevigny. 86–96.

Kerr, Phillip. "Token Credit." *The New Statesman* (15 April 2002).

Keve, Paul W. *Prisons and the American Conscience: A History of U.S. Federal Corrections.* Carbondale: Southern Illinois UP, 1991.

King, Martin Luther III. "State of Our Nation Today in Relationship to the Criminal Justice System." The American Correctional Association, *The State of Corrections: Proceedings ACA Annual Conferences, 2001.* Alexandria, VA: Magnet Print Brokers, 2002.

King, Roy D. "Prisons." *The Handbook of Crime and Punishment,* ed. Michael Tonry. 589–625.

Kirk, Robert W. *Faulkner's People: A Complete Guide and Index to Characters in the Fiction of William Faulkner,* Berkeley: U California P, 1963.

Lacan, Jacques. *Écrits: A Selection,* trans. Alan Sheridan. New York: Norton, 1977.

Lacayo, Richard. "Books by the Buddy System." *Time* (6 May 2002): 8.

Lane, Christopher, ed. *The Psychoanalysis of Race.* New York: Columbia UP, 1998.

Lassiter, Christo. "TV or Not TV—That Is the Question." *Journal of Criminal Law & Criminology* 86.3 (Spring 1996): 928–35.

Lauter, Paul, ed. *The Heath Anthology of American Literature 2,* 2nd ed. Lexington, MA: D. C. Heath, 1994.

Lehman, Joseph D. "Solving the Crowding Problem: Linking Resources to Corrections Policy." American Correctional Association, *The State of Corrections: Proceedings American Correctional Association Annual Conferences, 1993.* Springfield, VA: Goodway Graphics, 1994: 76–80.

Lentini, Pete. "A Standard American History." *Arena* magazine (October 1999): 52.

Leone, Ron. "Contemplating Ratings: An Examination of What the MPAA Considers 'Too Far for 'R' and Why." *Journal of Communication* 52.4 (2002): 938–55.

Levinson, Sanford and Steven Mailloux, eds. *Interpreting Law and Literature: A Hermeneutic Reader.* Evanston, IL: Northwestern UP, 1988.

Lewis, Anne S. "Life and Nothing But." *Austin Chronicle.* Online, 10 December 2003. http://www.austinchronicle.com/issues/v0118/issue10/screens. doctour.html

"Live from Death Row." Campaign to End the Death Penalty. University of Texas at Austin, 23 September 1999.

Lovell, Glenn. "*The Farm: Angola, USA* [Review]." *Variety.* 2 February 1998. Online. http://www.findarticles.com/cf_dls/m1312/n12_v369/ 20520805/p1/article.jhtml.

Mabie, Hamilton. "The Press and Crime." *Proceedings of the National Prison Congress, 1886.* Chicago: R. R. Donnelley & Sons, The Lakeside Press, 1887: 145–51.

MacCormick, Austin H. "Education and the Library in the Prison." *Proceedings of the Sixtieth Annual Congress of the American Prison Association, 1930:* 35–49.

Madison, Kelly J. "Legitimation Crisis and Containment: The 'Anti-Racist-White-Hero' Film." *Critical Studies in Mass Communication* 16.4 (1999): 399–417.

Mailer, Norman. *Advertisements for Myself.* Cambridge, MA: Harvard UP, 1992.

———. *An American Dream.* New York: The Dial Press, 1965.

———. *The Armies of the Night.* New York: Penguin, 1994.

———. *Conversations with Norman Mailer,* ed. J. Michael Lennon. Jackson: UP of Mississippi, 1988.

———. *The Executioner's Song.* New York: Vintage, 1998.

———. *Miami and the Siege of Chicago.* Cleveland: World, 1968.

———. *Oswald's Tale: An American Mystery.* New York: Random House, 1995.

Malcolm, Benjamin J. "The Self-Proclaimed 'Political Prisoner.'" *Proceedings of the One Hundred and Second Annual Congress of Correction of the American Correctional Association, 1972:* 104–9.

Martinson, Robert. "The Effectiveness of Correctional Treatment: A Survey of Treatment Evaluation Studies." *Proceedings of the One Hundred and Fifth Annual Congress of Correction of the American Correctional Association, 1975.* College Park, MD: 105–11.

Massey, Dennis. *Doing Time in American Prisons: A Study of Modern Novels.* New York: Greenwood P, 1989.

Mastro, Dana E. and Amanda L. Robinson. "Cops and Crooks: Images of Minorities on Primetime Television." *Journal of Criminal Justice* 28.5 (Sept./Oct. 2000): 385–96.

Mauer, Marc and the Sentencing Project. *Race to Incarcerate.* New York: New Press/Norton, 1999.

McCarthy, Todd. "*American History X* [Movie Reviews]." *Variety* (26 October 1998): 41–42.

McMillen, Neil R. and Noel Polk. "Faulkner on Lynching." *The Faulkner Journal* 8.1 (1992): 3–14.

McNary, Dave. "Kaye's Lawsuit Is 'History.'" *Variety* (1 May 2000): 16.

Mead, Bennet. "[Address]." *Proceedings of the 59th Annual Congress of the American Prison Association, 1929:* 168–75.

Meier, R. W. "Administration and Problems in Correctional Institutions." *Proceedings of the Ninety-Ninth Annual Congress of Correction of the American Correctional Association, 1969:* 61–65.

Melossi, Dario and Massimo Pavarini. *The Prison and the Factory: Origins of the Penitentiary System,* trans. Glynis Cousin. London: Macmillan, 1981.

Meriwether, James B., ed. *Lion in the Garden: Interviews with William Faulkner, 1926–1962.* New York: Random House, 1968.

Merrill, Robert. "Mailer's Sad Comedy: *The Executioner's Song.*" *Texas Studies in Literature and Language* 34.1 (1992): 129–48.

Miller, D. A. *The Novel and the Police.* Berkeley: U California P, 1988.

Miller, D. Quentin. "'On the Outside Looking In': White Readers of Nonwhite Prison Narratives." *Prose and Cons,* ed. D. Quentin Miller. 15–32.

———, ed. *Prose and Cons: Essays on Prison Literature in the United States.* Jefferson, NC: McFarland, 2005.

Miller, E. Eugene. "Necessary Preconditions to Achieving Cultural Awareness." *Proceedings of the One Hundred and Second Annual Congress of Correction of the American Correctional Association, 1972:* 170–74.

Miller, Jacques-Alain. "Extimacy." *Lacanian Theory of Discourse: Subject, Structure, and Society,* ed. Mark Bracher et al. New York: New York UP, 1994.

Moddelmog, William E. *Reconstituting Authority: American Fiction in the Province of Law.* Iowa City: U Iowa P, 2000.

Moller, Lorraine. "A Day in the Life of a Prison Theatre Program." *TDR* 47.1 (2003): 49–73.

Moore, Joel M. "The Future of Probation in the United States." *Proceedings of the Sixtieth Annual Congress of the American Prison Association, 1936.* Cheshire, CT: Printing Department, CT Penitentiary: 66–75.

Moore, Margaret A. "Race, Gender, and the Criminal Justice System." American Correctional Association, *The State of Corrections: Proceedings ACA Annual Conferences, 1992.* Arlington, VA: Kirby Lithographic, 1993: 195–200.

Morse, Edwin W. *The Life and Letters of Hamilton W. Mabie.* New York: Dodd, Mead and Company, 1920.

Morris, Norval. "The Contemporary Prison: 1965–Present." *The Oxford History of the Prison: The Practice of Punishment in Western Society,* ed. Norval Morris and David Rothman. New York: Oxford UP, 1998. 202–31.

———. *The Future of Imprisonment.* Chicago: Chicago UP, 1974.

——— and David J. Rothman, eds. *The Oxford History of the Prison: The Practice of Punishment in Western Society.* New York: Oxford UP, 1998.

Morrison, Toni. "Faulkner and Women." *Faulkner and Women,* ed. Doreen Fowler and Ann J. Abadie. Jackson: UP of Mississippi, 1986. 295–302.

Mos Def. *Black on Both Sides.* Priority Records, 1999.

Nandi, M. "Re/constructing Black Masculinity in Prison." *The Journal of Men's Studies* 11.1 (2002): 91–108.

National Prison Association. *Proceedings of the Annual Congress, 1886.* Chicago: R. R. Donnelley & Sons, 1887.

———. *Proceedings of the Annual Congress, 1888.* Chicago: Knight & Leonard, 1888.

Nehring, Neil. *Flowers in the Dustbin: Culture, Anarchy, and Postwar England.* Ann Arbor: U Michigan P, 1993.

Nussbaum, Martha. *Cultivating Humanity: A Classical Defense of Reform in Liberal Education.* Cambridge, MA: Harvard UP, 1997.

NWA. *Straight Outta Compton.* Priority Records, 1988.

O'Brien, John. "Interview with Ed Bullins." *Negro American Literature Forum* 7.3 (1973): 108–12.

O'Hehir, Andrew. "Review [*American History X*]." *Sight and Sound* (May 1999). Online, 5 November 2003. http://www.bfi.org.uk/sightandsound/reviews/details.php?id=92

———. Salon Review: *The Hurricane.* Online, 20 January 2000. http://dir.salon.com/ent/movies/review/2000/01/07/hurricane/index.html?CP=SAL&DN=110

O'Leary, Vincent. "Current Issues in Community Based Correction." *Proceedings of the One Hundredth Annual Congress of Correction of the American Correctional Association, 1970:* 131–38.

Ongiri, Amy Abugo. "We Are Family: Miscegenation, Black Nationalism, Black Masculinity, and Black Gay Cultural Imagination." *Race-ing Representation: Voice, History, and Sexuality,* ed. Kostas Myrsiades and Linda Myrsiades. Lanham, MD: Rowman & Littlefield, 1998. 231–46.

O'Shea, Kathleen. *Women on the Row: Revelations from Both Sides of the Bars.* Ithaca, NY: Firebrand Books, 2000.

Oshinsky, David M. *"Worse Than Slavery": Parchman Farm and the Ordeal of Jim Crow Justice.* New York: Free Press Paperbacks, 1997.

O'Sullivan, Sean. "Representations of Prison in Nineties Hollywood Cinema: From *Con Air* to *The Shawshank Redemption." Howard Journal of Criminal Justice* 40.4 (2001): 317–34.

*Oxford English Dictionary.* Online. http://www.oed.com.

Park, James W. L. "The Politics of Predators." *Proceedings of the One Hundred and Second Annual Congress of Correction of the American Correctional Association, 1972:* 111–13.

Partner, Nancy F. "Historicity in an Age of Reality-Fictions." *New Philosophy of History,* ed. Frank Ankersmit and Hans Kellner. Chicago: Chicago UP, 1995. 21–39.

Patrick-Stamp, Leslie. "Numbers That Are Not New: African Americans in the Country's First Prison, 1790–1835. *Pennsylvania Magazine of History and Biography* 119.1–2 (1995): 95–128.

Phillips, Robert Anthony. "Volunteering for Death: The Fast Track to the Death House." *Crime* magazine. Online. http://crimemagazine.com/deathrowvolunteers.htm.

Pinar, William F. *The Gender of Racial Politics and Violence in America: Lynching, Prison Rape, and the Crisis of Masculinity.* New York: Peter Lang, 2001.

Poirier, Richard. *The Performing Self: Compositions and Decompositions in the Languages of Contemporary Life.* New York: Oxford UP, 1971.

———. "The Ups and Downs of Mailer." *The New Republic* 164.4 (23 January 1971): 23–26. Rpt. *Norman Mailer: A Collection of Critical Essays,* ed. Leo Braudy. Englewood Cliffs, NJ: Prentice-Hall, 1972. 167–74.

Polk, Noel. "'I Have Taken an Oath of Office Too': Faulkner and the Law." *Fifty Years of Yoknapatawpha: Faulker and Yoknapatawpha, 1979,* ed. Doreen Fowler and Ann J. Abadie. Jackson: U Mississippi P, 1980. 159–78.

Porter, Carolyn Porter, "Are We Being Historical Yet?" *South Atlantic Quarterly* 87 (1988): 743–86.

Posner, Richard A. *Law and Literature.* Cambridge, MA: Harvard UP, 1998.

Powell, Timothy. *Ruthless Democracy: A Multi-Cultural Interpretation of the American Renaissance.* Princeton: Princeton UP, 2000.

*Price v. Johnston.* 334 U.S. 266, 285, 68 S. Ct. 1049, 1060, 92 L. Ed. 1356, 1948.

Public Enemy. *It Takes a Nation of Millions to Hold Us Back.* Def Jam, 1988.

———. *There's a Poison Goin' On.* Atomic Pop, 1999.

Quinn, Leon J. "Militant Black: A Correctional Problem." *Proceedings of the Ninety-Ninth Annual Congress of Correction of the American Correctional Association, 1969:* 222–28.

Rabinowitz, Paula. "Wreckage upon Wreckage: History, Documentary, and the Ruins of Memory." *History and Theory* 32.2 (1993): 119–37.

Rafter, Nicole. *Shots in the Mirror: Crime Films and Society.* New York: Oxford UP, 2000.

Rage Against the Machine. *The Battle of Los Angeles.* Sony, 1999.

Raper, Arthur F. *The Tragedy of Lynching.* New York: Dover, 1970.

Reed, Myron W. "Remarks." *Proceedings of the Annual Congress, 1888.* Chicago: Knight & Leonard: 26–28.

Reinelt, Janelle. *Crucibles of Crisis: Performing Social Change.* Ann Arbor: U Michigan P, 1996.

Richards, Ann W. "Invest in People, Not Institutions." *The State of Corrections: Proceedings ACA Annual Conferences, 1989:* 8–12.

Rideau, Wilbert and Ron Wikberg, eds. *Life Sentences: Rage and Survival behind Bars.* New York: Time Books, 1992.

Rideout, Walter B. "Foreword." *The Militant Black Writer in Africa and the United States,* Mercer Cook and Stephen E. Henderson, v–x.

Roberts, Julian V. and Loretta J. Stalans. "Crime, Criminal Justice, and Public Opinion." *The Handbook of Crime and Punishment,* ed. Michael Tonry. 31–57.

Roscher, Jennifer. "The Ambivalence of *The Executioner's Song:* Postmodern Captivity from Death Row." *Prose and Cons,* ed. D. Quentin Miller. 217–32.

Roth, Alex. "The Politics of Execution: Interview with Stephen Bright, Part 2." *The New Abolitionist* 2.5 (1998). Online. http://www.nodeathpenalty.org/newab009/brightPt2.html.

Rothman, David J. *Conscience and Convenience: The Asylum and Its Alternatives in Progressive America.* Boston: Little, Brown, 1980.

———. "Perfecting the Prison: United States, 1789–1865." *The Oxford History of the Prison: The Practice of Punishment in Western Society,* ed. Norval Morris and David Rothman. New York: Oxford UP, 1998. 100–116.

Rotman, Edgardo. "The Failure of Reform: United States, 1865–1965." Morris and Rothman, eds. 151–77.

Rout, Kathleen. *Eldridge Cleaver.* Boston: G. K. Hall, 1991.

Rush, Benjamin. "An Enquiry into the Effects of Public Punishments upon Criminals and upon Society." *A Plan for the Punishment of Crime,* ed. Negley K. Teeters. Philadelphia: Pennsylvania Prison Society, 1954.

Sabo, Donald F., Terry A. Kupers, and Willie London, eds. *Prison Masculinities.* Philadelphia: Temple UP, 2001.

Scarry, Elaine. *The Body in Pain: The Making and Unmaking of the World.* New York: Oxford UP, 1985.

Scharine, Richard G. "Ed Bullins Was Steve Benson (But Who Is He Now?)" *Black American Literature Forum* 13.3 (1979): 103–9.

Schiller, Lawrence. *The Executioner's Song.* Film Communications, 1982.

————. *Master Spy: The Robert Hanssen Story.* Twentieth Century Fox, 2002.

———— and L. M. Kit Carson. *The American Dreamer.* Corda Productions/Kabak, 1971.

———— and James Willwerth. *American Tragedy: The Uncensored Story of the Simpson Defense.* New York: Random House, 1996.

Schechner, Richard. *Between Theater and Anthropology.* Philadelphia: U Pennsylvania P, 1985.

Schlosser, Eric. "The Prison-Industrial Complex." *Atlantic Monthly* (December 1998): 51–77.

Schmoke, Kurt L. "Alleviating Our Prison Crisis: National Policy Changes Are Needed." *The State of Corrections: Proceedings ACA Annual Conferences, 1990:* 107–8.

Scott, Robert C. "Keynote Address." American Correctional Association, *The State of Corrections, 1996:* 1–8.

Scott-Heron, Gill. "The Revolution Will Not Be Televised." *The Revolution Will Not Be Televised.* Flying Dutchman, 1974.

Selke, William L. *Prisons in Crisis.* Bloomington and Indianapolis: Indiana UP, 1993.

Sell, Mike. "The Black Arts Movement: Performance, Neo-Orality, and the Destruction of the 'White Thing.'" *African American Performance and Theatre History: A Critical Reader,* ed. Harry J. Elam Jr. and David Krasner. New York: Oxford UP, 2001. 56–80.

Seltzer, Mark. "*The Princess Casamassima:* Realism and the Fantasy of Surveillance." *Nineteenth-Century Fiction* 35 (1980–81): 506–34.

Shapp, Milton J. "Governor's Address." *Proceedings of the One Hundred and Second Annual Congress of Correction of the American Correctional Association, 1972:* 1–6.

*The Shawshank Redemption.* Frank Darabont, dir., Castle Rock Entertainment/Columbia Pictures, 1994.

Sheer, Robert. "Introduction." *Eldridge Cleaver: Post-Prison Writings and Speeches,* Eldridge Cleaver, vii–xxxiii.

Sheridan, Alan. "Translator's Note." *Écrits: A Selection,* Jacques Lacan, vii–xii.

Shoemaker, Steve. "Norman Mailer's 'White Negro': Historical Myth or Mythical History?" *Twentieth-Century Literature* 37:3 (Fall 1991): 343–60.

*Shot in the Heart.* Agnieszka Hollan, dir., HBO, 2001.

Simon, John. "Film: Songbirds & Skinheads [Review]." *The National Review* (31 December 1998): 50.

Sloop, John M. *The Cultural Prison: Discourse, Prisoners, and Punishment.* Tuscaloosa: U Alabama P, 1996.

Stabile, Carol. *White Victims, Black Villains: Gender, Race, and Crime News in US Culture.* New York: Routledge, 2006.

St. Gerard, Vanessa. "Mfume Urges a Partnership between ACA and the NAACP." American Correctional Association, *The State of Corrections: Proceedings ACA Annual Conferences, 2004:* 1–2.

Steel, Lewis M. "Rubin Carter: The Movie." *The Nation* (3 January 2000): 8.

Stoppard, Tom. "The Real Inspector Hound." *The Norton Anthology of English Literature*, vol. 2, 5th ed., ed. M. H. Abrams et al. New York: Norton, 1986. 2432–62.

Struckhoff, David R. "A Sociological Perspective on Classification, Discretionary Judgment, and Racism." *Proceedings of the One Hundred and Second Annual Congress of Correction of the American Correctional Association, 1972*: 183–89.

Stubbs, Liz. *Documentary Filmmakers Speak*. New York: Allworth Press, 2002.

Sturken, Marita. "Reenactment, Fantasy, and the Paranoia of History: Oliver Stone's Docudramas." *History and Theory* 36.4 (1997): 64–79.

Sullivan, Larry E. *The Prison Reform Movement: Forlorn Hope*. Boston: Twayne, 1990.

Sullivan, Robert R. "The Birth of the Prison: The Case of Benjamin Rush." *Eighteenth-Century Studies* 31.3 (1998): 333–44.

Suncoast [advertisement]. *Premiere* (April 2002): 25.

Sundquist, Eric J. *Faulkner: The House Divided*. Baltimore: Johns Hopkins UP, 1983.

———. *The Hammers of Creation: Folk Culture in Modern African-American Fiction*. Athens: U Georgia P, 1992.

System of a Down. *Toxicity*. Sony, 2001.

Taylor, Julie. "Desdemona's Lament." *TDR* 45.4 (2001): 106–24.

Taylor, William Banks. *Down on Parchman Farm: The Great Prison in the Mississippi Delta*. Columbus: The Ohio State UP, 1999.

Thayer, Walter N. "A Doctor Surveys the Criminal Problem." *Proceedings of the Sixtieth Annual Congress of the American Prison Association, 1930*: 196–207.

Thomas, Brook. *American Literary Realism and the Failed Promise of Contract*. Berkeley: U California P, 1997.

Thompson, James. *Prison Theatre: Perspectives and Practices*. London: Jessica Kingsley, 1998.

de Tocqueville, Alexis. *Tocqueville's America, the Great Quotations*. Ed. Frederick Kershner Jr. Athens: Ohio UP, 1983.

Tolnay, Stewart E. and E. M. Beck. *Festival of Violence: An Analysis of Southern Lynchings, 1882–1930,* Chicago: U Illinois P, 1995.

Tonry, Michael, ed. *The Handbook of Crime and Punishment*. New York: Oxford UP, 1998.

——— and Bruce Fein. "The Great Debate." American Correctional Institute, 1993. 95–106.

Travisono, Anthony. "Prison Crisis—Over 280,000 Men and Women in Our Nations Prisons." *The American Journal of Correction* (May–June 1977): 14–15, 44.

———. "ACA's Future." *The State of Corrections: Proceedings ACA Annual Conferences 1990* (Washington, DC: St. Mary's Press, 1990): 93–97.

Trilling, Lionel. *The Liberal Imagination: Essays on Literature and Society*. Garden City, NY: Doubleday, 1950.

Turner, Victor. *From Ritual to Theatre: The Human Seriousness of Play*. New York: Performing Arts Journal Publications, 1982.

Uggen, Christopher and Jeff Manza. "Democratic Contraction? Political Consequences of Felon Disenfranchisement in the United States. *American Sociological Review* 67 (December 2002): 777–803.

U.S. Code. Civil Rights Act, v. 42 section 2000e, 1964. Online. http://caselaw. lp.findlaw.com/casecode/uscodes/42/chapters/21/subchapters/vi/sections/ section_2000e.html.

U.S. Commission on Civil Rights. *Voting Irregularities in Florida during the 2000 Presidential Election* (2002). Online. http://www.usccr.gov/pubs/vote2000/ report/main.htm.

U.S. Department of Justice. "Additional Corrections Facts at a Glance." Bureau of Justice Statistics. Online. http://www.ojp.usdoj.gov/bjs/gcorpop.htm.

———. "Estimated Arrests for Drug Abuse Violations by Age Group, 1970–2002." Online. http://www.ojp.usdoj.gov/bjs/glance/tables/drugtab.htm.

———. "Incarceration Rates 1980–2002." Bureau of Justice Statistics. Online. http://www.ojp.usdoj.gov/bjs/glance/tables/incrttab.htm.

———. "Lifetime Likelihood of Going to State or Federal Prison." Bureau of Justice Statistics Special Report (March 1997). Online. http://www.ojp.usdoj. gov/bjs/pub/pdf/llgsfp.pdf.

———. "Number of Persons in Custody of State Correctional Authorities by Most Serious Offense, 1980–2001." Bureau of Justice Statistics. Online. http://www.ojp.usdoj.gov/bjs/glance/tables/corrtyptab.htm.

———. "Over Half of the Increase in State Prison Population Since 1995 Is Due to an Increase in the Prisoners Convicted of Violent Offenses." Bureau of Justice Statistics. Online. http://www.ojp.usdoj.gov/bjs/glance/corrtyp. htm.

———. "Prison and Jail Inmates at Midyear 1999." Bureau of Justice Statistics Bulletin (April 2000). Online. http://www.ojp.usdoj.gov/bjs/pub/pdf/ pjim99.pdf.

———. "Prisons in 2002." Bureau of Justice Statistics. Online. http://www.ojp. usdoj.gov/bjs/abstract/p02.htm.

———. "Prisoners in 1999." Bureau of Justice Statistics Bulletin (August 2000). Online, 20 January 2004. http://www.ojp.usdoj.gov/bjs/pub/pdf/p99.pdf.

———. "Probation and Parole." Bureau of Justice Statistics. Online. http://www. ojp.usdoj.gov/bjs/pandp.htm.

———. "Property Crime Rates Continue to Decline." Online. http://www.ojp. usdoj.gov/bjs/glance/house2.htm.

———. "Serious Violent Crime Levels Declined Since 1993." Online. http:// www.ojp.usdoj.gov/bjs/glance/cv2.htm.

———. *Sourcebook of Criminal Justice Statistics 2003*. Online. State University of New York at Albany. http://www.albany.edu/sourcebook/pdf/t686.pdf.

———. "Violent Crime Rates Have Declined Since 1994, Reaching the Lowest Level Ever Recorded in 2002." Bureau of Justice Statistics. Online. http:// www.ojp.usdoj.gov/bjs/glance/viort.htm.

U.S. Sentencing Commission. *Special Report to the Congress Cocaine and Federal Sentencing Policy*. U.S: 1995. Online. http://www.ussc.gov/crack/exec.htm.

Wainwright, Louie L. "Presidential Address." *Proceedings of the One Hundred and First Annual Congress of the American Correctional Association, 1971:* 3–9.

Waldrep, Shelton. "'Being Bridges': Cleaver/Baldwin/Lorde and African-American Sexism and Sexuality." *Critical Essays: Gay and Lesbian Writers of Color,* ed. Emmanuel S. Nelson. New York: Haworth, 1993. 167–80.

Walters, John P. Executive Office of the President, Office of National Drug Control Policy. "Cocaine." Online. http://www.whitehousedrugpolicy.gov/publications/pdf/ncj198582.pdf.

Warfel, Richard H. "A Report of Drug Treatment Programs in America's State Prison Systems," *Proceedings of the One Hundred and Second Annual Congress of Correction of the American Correctional Association, 1972.* College Park, MD: 42–57.

Washington, Mary Helen. "Disturbing the Peace: What Happens to American Studies If You Put African-American Studies at the Center?" *American Quarterly* 50.1 (1998): 1–23.

*Washington Post.* "Botched Name Purge Denied Some the Right to Vote" (31 May 2001). Online. http://www.washingtonpost.com/ac2/wp-dyn/A99749-2001May30.

———. "Rights Commission's Report on Florida Election." 5 June 2001. Online. http://www.washingtonpost.com/wpsrv/onpolitics/transcripts/ccrdraft060401.htm.

Watson, Jay. *Forensic Fiction: The Lawyer Figure in Faulkner.* Athens: U Georgia P, 1993.

Webster, Ken. *Jury Duty* (unpublished manuscript). Performed by The Subterranean Theatre Company in Austin, Texas, 9 September 1999.

———. E-mail to Peter Caster. 30 September 2003.

Weinstein, Philip M. *Faulkner's Subject: A Cosmos No One Owns,* Cambridge: Cambridge UP, 1992.

Weitzer, Ronald and Charis E. Kubrin. "Breaking News: How Local TV News and Real-World Conditions Affect Fear of Crime." *Justice Quarterly* 21.3 (2004): 497–520.

Western, Bruce and Becky Pettit. "Incarceration and Racial Inequality in Men's Employment." *Industrial and Labor Relations Review* 54.1 (2000): 3–16.

Wheeler, Barbara. "Presidential Address." *Proceedings of the One Hundred and Third Annual Congress of Correction of the American Correctional Association, 1973:* 1–13.

Whitaker, Charles. "The Hurricane of Denzel Washington." *Ebony* (April 2000): 154–62.

White, Hayden. "The Modernist Event." *The Persistence of History: Cinema, Television, and the Modern Event,* ed. Vivian Sobchack. New York: Routledge, 1996. 17–38.

Wicker, Tom. "Foreword." *Prison Writing in 20th-Century America,* H. Bruce Franklin, xi–xv.

Wideman, John Edgar. *Brothers and Keepers.* New York: Holt, Rinehart and Winston, 1984.

Wilkins, William W., Jr. "The Practicality of Structured Sentencing." American Correctional Association, *The State of Corrections: Proceedings ACA Annual Conferences, 1994:* 107–11.

Wilkinson, Reginald A. "Best Practices: Programs We Can Live With." American Correctional Association, *The State of Corrections, 1997:* 85–92.

———. "Best Practices: Tools for Correctional Excellence." American Correctional Association, *The State of Corrections: Proceedings American Correctional Association Annual Conferences, 1998.* Upper Marlboro, MD: Graphic Communications, 1999: 85.

Willis, Sharon. *High Contrast: Race and Gender in Contemporary Hollywood Film.* Durham and London: Duke UP, 1997.

Wright, Richard. *Native Son.* New York: Harper & Row, 1989.

X, Malcolm. "After the Bombing." *Malcolm X Speaks: Selected Speeches and Statements,* ed. George Breitman. New York: Grove Press, 1965. 157–77.

———. *The Autobiography of Malcolm X.* New York: Grove Press, 1966.

———. "The Ballot or the Bullet." *Malcolm X Speaks: Selected Speeches and Statements,* ed. George Breitman. New York: Pathfinder, 1989. 23–44.

Yarborough, Richard. "The Problem of Violence and Black Masculinity in Recent U.S. Historical Cinema: A Look at *Amistad, Rosewood,* and *Hurricane.*" University of Texas at Austin (1 May 2003).

Žižek, Slavoj. *The Sublime Object of Ideology.* New York: Verso, 1989.

———. *For They Know Not What They Do: Enjoyment as a Political Factor.* London, New York: Verso, 1991.

———. *Looking Awry: An Introduction to Jacques Lacan through Popular Culture.* Cambridge, MA: MIT UP, 1991.

# Index

## Black Performance and Cultural Criticism
Valerie Lee and E. Patrick Johnson, Series Editors

The Black Performance and Cultural Criticism series includes mono-
graphs that draw on interdisciplinary methods to analyze, critique, and
theorize black cultural production. Books in the series take as their
object of intellectual inquiry the performances produced on the stage
and on the page, stretching the boundaries of both black performance
and literary criticism.

*Mutha' Is Half a Word: Intersections of Folklore, Vernacular, Myth, and
Queerness in Black Female Culture*
L. H. Stallings